C000081538

THE DIVINE RENAISSANCE

PITY COMPASSION LOVE

The Order of the Cross

SELF-ABANDONMENT SELF-SACRIFICE SELF-DENIAL

REDEMPTION REGENERATION ILLUMINATION

AIMS AND IDEALS

THE Order is an informal Brotherhood and Fellowship, having for its service in life the cultivation of the Spirit of Love towards all Souls: Helping the weak and defending the defenceless and oppressed; Abstaining from hurting the creatures, eschewing bloodshed and flesh eating, and living upon the pure foods so abundantly provided by nature; Walking in the Mystic Way of Life, whose Path leads to the realization of the Christhood; And sending forth the Mystic Teachings unto all who may be able to receive them — those sacred interpretations of the Soul, the Christhood, and the Divine Love and Wisdom, for which the Order of the Cross stands.

SERVICE DEVOTION PURITY

The DIVINE RENAISSANCE

By J. TODD FERRIER

VOL. TWO

FIRST PUBLISHED 1929

SECOND EDITION 1947

THIRD EDITION 1963

Made and Printed in Great Britain by

PERCY LUND, HUMPHRIES & CO. LTD

LONDON AND BRADFORD

CONTENTS

PART I

THE ASCENT OF THE SOUL

PAGE

PAGE

PART III

THE RENASCENT PATH

List of Publications at end of Volume.

THE VISION OF THE LORD

I saw the LORD.
HE was enthroned on High,
And HIS Glory filled the Temple.
Around the Throne stood the Seraphim:
Each of them had six Wings:
With twain each covered his Face;
With twain he covered his Feet;
And with twain he did fly.

And each unto the other thus spake in song,
Holy, Holy, Holy is the Lord of Hosts;
The Heavens are full of His Glory,
And the fulness of the Earth manifests His Glory.

Then the Veils dividing the Thresholds moved,
For the Voice of HIM from within the Sanctuary spake;
And the Temple was filled with HIS Radiance.

Because of the Glory of the Vision,
I was as one who is overwhelmed;
For I felt as if my praise of HIM
Were uttered by unclean lips,
And that I dwelt amongst a people
Whose ways were as of the unclean;
For I had looked upon the King,
The LORD of the heavenly Hosts.

Then flew unto me one of the Seraphim:
In His hand he bore the Sacred Flame,
Which in appearance was as a Glowing Stone;
From out the Fire upon the Altar had he taken it.
With it he touched my Lips, and spake,
Behold! The Mystery of His Love!
It is thine to know it,
For it hath touched thee and made thee whole.

Then spake the LORD within the Sanctuary,
And HIS Voice was as when many waters meet;
And HE said unto the Hosts of the Heavens,
Who will go down for us? Whom shall we send?
And my Being was uplifted unto HIM,
And I spake, saying, *Send me!*
And HE said, *Go then to the People*
As the Servant of the Lord.

THE MESSAGE UNTO ISRAEL

Comfort ye! Comfort ye! My People!
Thus saith your LORD:
Speak ye My Word unto Ierusalem,
That her warfare is being accomplished
That her mistake is being healed,
That when she issues from her wrong states,
Again shall she receive the double portion
As inheritance from the Lord's hand.

* * * *

The voice of the Messenger of the LORD
Amid the Wilderness crieth—
Prepare ye the way for the coming of the Lord;
Build ye across the Desert the Highway of God!
Thus every Valley shall be exalted,
The Hills and the Mountains made clear;
The crooked ways straightened out,
The rough places made smooth;
Then the Glory of the Lord shall be revealed
And all Souls shall behold its Radiance.
The Word of the Lord hath declared this!

* * * *

In the strength of thy LORD lift up thy voice
And proclaim unto Ierusalem, the Glad Tidings,
That the LORD cometh in the greatness of HIS Power,
To make manifest HIS Kingdom unto HIS People
How HE doth bear rule over them;
And unto all those who look for HIS coming,
To wait upon HIM and serve HIM,
Shall be great recompense; for, in HIS coming,
HE doth give the Glory of HIS Presence:
It is HIS Inheritance restored unto them.

HE shall nourish them through HIS Word
Even as the Shepherd feedeth his flock:
For HE is the Shepherd of them all.
HE shall gently lead those who be still young
Bearing them up and carrying them in HIS Arms;
For in HIS Bosom dwelleth the Lamb of GOD.

* * * *

It is the LORD Who holdeth the Waters of Life;
In HIS Hand is contained their full measure:
HE meteth them out unto the Heavens,
HIS span doth encompass them all:
HE giveth comprehension unto Souls upon the Earth,
That they may have Understanding, whereby
They may know the measure of HIS Tierce:
HE giveth Balance unto those ascending HIS Hills,
And Power to all who scale the great Mountains;
HE giveth the motion of HIS Spirit unto all,
And His direction unto those who seek HIS Counsel;
HE giveth unto such HIS instruction
How to walk in the Paths of HIS Righteousness,
And doth shew unto their Understanding
The meaning of all HIS Judgments;
For HE doth fill these with knowledge of HIS Way.

* * * *

O Ya-ǎkob! Why sayest thou?
My way is hidden from the sight of God.
O Israel! Why speakest thou thus?
In His Judgment hath the Lord passed over me.
Unto whom do ye liken HIM?
Compare ye HIM in HIS ways towards you
With those who bear not HIS likeness?
Have ye not known HIM of old time

When HIS Voice spake unto you
Concerning the Word of HIS Message?

* * * *

Unto the Messenger HIS Voice spake, saying,
Cry the Message unto Ierusalem.
And the Servant made request of HIM
How shall I proclaim it?
And the Voice commanded him to cry—
All that is of the Flesh is as the Grass,
And even as the Flower of the Field;
For the Grass withereth, and the Flower fadeth away;
And thus do the People when the Breath of the Lord
Faileth to rest upon them and move through them:
Then surely they are as the Grass. But when
The Spirit of the Lord moveth within them,
They know Him as the Word, El Adonai,
Whose Presence maketh them endure for evermore.

* * * *

Behold, O Zion! It is the Word of thy LORD
Who standeth sure for evermore.
O Zion! Hearest thou the Glad Tidings?
Arise, then! And come unto HIS high mountain;
From thence shalt thou bear the Glad Tidings,
Even the Message of thy LORD,
To cry unto the cities of Judah, saying
Behold, your GOD!

* * * *

Thy LORD is the Everlasting GOD,
The Creator of the Heavens and the Earth.
From the beginning hath this been revealed to you,
Even before the foundations of this world.
HE fainteth not in the way of HIS going,
Nor groweth weary in HIS regnancy;

HE understandeth all HIS children's needs;
HE reigneth upon the Earth's encompassing circles,
And filleth them with the Glory of HIS Presence.
The Heavens move with the Motion of HIS Spirit,
HE doth curtain them in HIS Overshadowing;
HE maketh Tents within them for our dwelling.

* * * *

Hast thou not known this, O Ya-ǎkob?
Hast thou not heard of it, O Israel?
The Eternal ONE is still thy GOD, O Ya-ǎkob!
The LORD is refashioning the Earth, O Israel!

* * * *

To HIS faint children HE will give power
And all weakened in the way, increase of strength;
In HIM the young shall grow rich,
And those who seemed failing shall overcome;
HIS Might shall be unto all who wait upon HIM,
On the Wings of HIS Spirit shall they be upborne;
As they soar, they shall know no weariness;
And none shall faint nor fall who walk
In the Path of the LORD.

EXPLANATION OF SOME OF THE TERMS IN ABOVE POEMS.

ZION, a term expressing Christhood Estate. The children of Zion, were the Ancient Christhood Communities.

JUDAH. The Name of the Planet-Soul. The Land of Judah was her Planetary Sphere, whose Kingdom was rent.

IERUSALEM. The City of Peace, and the Spiritual Household of the Planet-Soul, whose former glory was such that the whole Communal Life was beautiful for situation.

ISRAEL, was one who had become a Prince of God, who was the inheritor, by attainment, of the Holy Spirit, the Radiant Presence, and the Indwelling One. The House of Israel comprized the Ancient Christhood, the Sons of God.

YA-ǍKOB (Jacob) was the name of one of the Planetary Angels whose administration had to do with Soul generation and evolution of the Planetary Children. The term has a Greek correspondence in IACCHOS.

ISAIAH, a Cryptic name, containing the roots of three Divine Names. The Name expresses the purpose of the Revelation.
The passages are renderings of Isaiah VI and XL.

PART I

THE ASCENT OF THE SOUL

UNTO THE GREAT SILENCE

SCIENCE AND RELIGION

THE INFINITE AND THE FINITE

THE ANGELIC REALMS

THE FESTIVAL OF CORPUS CHRISTI

THE SABBATH OF THE LORD

THE MYSTERY OF THE ASCENSION

UNTO
THE GREAT SILENCE

UNTO THE GREAT SILENCE

THE FLIGHT OF THE SPIRIT

How blessed an experience for the Soul who can take its flight from out the midst of the world's noises begotten of its most inharmonious conditions, and reach the Sanctuary of Being, and stand mid the Great Silence of the Presence Who fills that sacred House! How transcendent the experience of the Soul who has power to move from out the heart of the world's maelstrom with its life-destroying whirlpools resulting from the breaths of contrariety, and soar into those rarefied atmospheres represented by the Angelic and Divine Worlds, there to be the recipient of the blessing begotten of the magnetic motion of the Breaths wafted from out the Sanctuary of all Being!

Within the Sanctuary and amid the Great Silence, the Soul comes into the vision glorious, and stands before the high Altar where the Eternal Presence mediates. From out of the bosom of that hidden Mystery there flow unto such an one the living streams, magnetic, energizing, life-giving, and illumining; and the Soul knows that the overshadowing canopy above the Altar before which it bows and on which it sacrifices, is verily that Overshadowing and Encompassing which are expressive of the motion of the Eternities.

THE INNER SANCTUARY

That Sanctuary is rich indeed, in every part of it, with the testimonies of the glory of HIM Whose Presence fills it. The floor, which acts as a threshold of Divine approach, and expresses many degrees of estate in realization, is at first as burnished gold reflecting the *within* glory like a thousand specula radiant as stars; and as the Soul progresses in its inward procession towards the Altar which is the Divine Reredos, even the splendour of the threshold within its outer gates becomes changed into the Sea of Crystal, wherein everything finds exposition in glorious reflection, even to the highest formulation of the Eternal Mystery. The vaulting of the Sanctuary is supernal; its attribute-pillars amazing in the exquisite beauty of their grace, the majesty of their strength, and the excellency of their crowns. For even the Sanctuary of the Eternal in the innermost realms takes fashion to the Soul's vision. The House is full of Divine resplendence. The Soul learns how to bow and sacrifice before the Altars within its shrines. The entrant and high Initiate learns how to process in being through its aisles and its galleries, triforia and clerestories, guided by the Angels who are in high estate, glorious Beings who have touched the keystone of the Sacred Mystery, and are members of the Divine Arch. These interpret unto the Soul the sacred, manifold Mystery, unveiling to it more and more in its processional motion through the great Sanctuary of Being, even until it so knows the Mystery that henceforth it may process unto the most secret place and be even as the Angels of God who are in Arche-Presbuteros estate.

THE INHERITANCE AWAITING THE INITIATE

The entrant and high Initiate who can cross the thresholds represented by the three glorious Divine Altars, and pass through the three veils, enters in high consciousness into the magnetic stream which, within the atmospheres of the Earth and all worlds, gives life; but which, as it flows through all the Sanctuary of Being in the Divine World, so interfuses the Substance and Breath of the Soul, that the latter takes on the very glory of that One Who fills the Sanctuary with the Sacred Mystery expressed as The Great Silence.

It is into this World that the Message herein set forth would lead all who are equal to the following on to the knowing of the Lord in divine estate, as the Eternal Mystery at the heart of all creation; and also the most-sacred Mystery in the secret Sanctuary of every Soul's Being.

SCIENCE AND RELIGION

SCIENCE AND RELIGION

RELIGIOUS BELIEFS AND SCIENCE

Much is being written in these days upon the irreconcilability of the modern religious outlook with the scientific interpretation of the world. On this account I am moved to take you with me to the realm of true outlook and inlook; that realm where Truth is known in all its aspects; where mystery is unravelled; where everything receives its true value and becomes sacred; where there is nothing misunderstood nor misinterpreted, but where all things are known. I would show to you that Religion and Science are not irreconcilable; that they are one, when understood; that there is no contradiction between them; that they are two great aspects of the one testimony to the reality of the Divine Mystery and speak to us of GOD.

In the Divine World there could not be other than harmony.

Wheresoever the Divine World is truly expressed, the expression is interpretive of HIM Who is all harmony, because HE is the Perfect ONE. And this is true whether it be predicated of the Divine Centre of all things; or of the glorious systems ruled over by the Gods through the great Celestial Hierarchies; or of the Divine accommodation to a world even so small, and yet so great, as this Earth.

In the Divine World, harmony always obtains and prevails. The Law of GOD is perfect. Though it is infinite in its manifestations and accommodations, it is one in its nature; and though manifold in the degrees of its power, its motion and its service, it is one in purpose.

Contradictions arise through misunderstanding. The misunderstanding leads to misinterpretation, and the misinterpretation to misrepresentation.

To understand the Law of the LORD is to understand the manifestations of the Divine Mystery. It is true that it may happen, as in a world like this where the elements are out of order and, in a sense, disobedient to the Law of the LORD, that contradictions arise. They are contradictions relating to the Divine Nature and Purpose: these are misunderstood, consequently they are misinterpreted. As a result, even the Divine Creation effected by our FATHER-MOTHER, is misrepresented. So also is the Divine Purpose concerning man. Though in the Divine World all is harmony, yet here we are confronted with contradictions. And it must needs be realized that these arise from limitations, and from changes such as reveal fallen states, and through not understanding such fallen states and changes.

THE MANIFEST AND UNMANIFEST ARE ONE

Yet at the heart of the divine balance of things, there is no contradiction between Science and Religion. *The manifest in the Divine World is the perfect exposition of the Unmanifest.* And the like obtains through all the Celestial Realms. And, indeed, wheresoever embodiments of the Divine Purpose are unveiled and sent forth on their mission, and remain in the perfect state of balance, these declare the Glory of GOD. There is no contradiction between the embodiments of the various Spheres. In all of them, Science and Religion are one.

What does Science mean? The word is related to knowledge. Pure Science is knowledge. The word prescience, which we make use of to indicate to know beforehand, is pre-Science, or to have the power of vision which can penetrate all things so that you know without tabulation of the phenomena; you know that which lies behind the phenomena. The Soul has prescience; it has discernment; it understands. Therefore, Science is the inner knowledge of things.

Religion has relation to life. *It is Life.* It is the motion of life, the potency of life, the realization of life. Thus shall we see presently how comprehensively it affects us; for by both Science and Religion are we deeply touched and influenced, especially by the Religion which ultimates in becoming *the Science;* and there is no other.

All true Science is Divine. All true knowledge is of the Divine. Pure Science is knowledge. It is not, however, supposition. It is not the outworking from hypothetical premises, and the resultant of uncertain syllogisms. *Pure Science is to know.*

All the paths of material Science are paths which men pursue in the hope of knowing. Though they may know much through observation, and still more through the application of the knowledge gathered in observation, yet the secrets lying behind all the outer realms of knowledge are of the Mystery of GOD; and such secrets are never acquired by outer paths of investigation. They are of the Inner Realms.

The phenomenal world is a manifestation of manifold effects of secret causes, and these testify of potency within the elements. But what the elements are in themselves in the secret world, is a matter of Divine concern. What the elements are within the world of the Divine, can be unveiled only to the Soul as it ascends in state and consciousness into the realm of the Divine Science. That is the realm where earthly Science becomes illumined. The revelation is an illumination. It brings real knowledge.

TRUE SCIENCE IS ILLUMINED

True Science is Divine. It has relation to knowledge of the elements and their potencies. It should be able to interpret these. It should understand the purpose for which they are here. It should be able always to relate them to the Divine. True Science does so relate everything. For there is no illumination from without; it is from within. Men grope in the dark when their vision is circumscribed by the phenomenal world. Until they turn to seek from the within, and go onward to relate all things to their real source, and to seek to understand all the elements and their potencies in the light of the Divine Mystery, they do not truly know.

True Science brings illumination to the mind. It gives understanding to the heart. It is related not only to the elemental world, and to the understanding of that world; but it is also related to the whole earth, in all its planes, its constitution, and its motion. And it is related to man, to his constitution, and to the motion of the Divine potencies within him. True Science speaks of the elemental world in a language of the understanding of the elements; of the earth's planes, in the knowledge of their motion, in the constitution of the world-spiral, and in the fashion and motion of it unseen by the human eye.

True Science also understands Man. It comprehends his constitution as the microcosm of the macrocosm, as the miniature of the Divine Mystery. It sees Man to be in the very fashion of a Son of GOD. Material Science is not able to apprehend what the fashion of a Son of GOD is; for such a vision cannot be come at from without, but only from within. True Science understands man, why he is here, how he came here, the elements of which he is built up in his body, and in his mental and spiritual constitution; because true Science is both objective and subjective. It deals with the inner and outer realms, and unites the two.

A TRUE SCIENCE CANNOT BE IRRELIGIOUS

A true Science would understand not only the arterial system of the body, but also the arterial system of each of the vehicles through which Man makes himself manifest. For there is a correspondence from the innermost of Man's Being to the outermost of his manifest life. Even the fashion of his inner Temple named the Soul, has to be corresponded to a world like this, to enable him to function upon its planes as a Son of the Gods. True Science understands the creation, the generation, the fashioning, the unfolding, the growth, the evolution of a Soul. *For illumined Science is living knowledge.* It is knowledge begotten of sure and certain realization. It is the crown of enlightened empiricism, resulting from the inner motion of the Soul whose feet are planted on the Rock of the Eternal Ages, and who is conversant with the real Mystery, the immovable

Truth, the immutable Mystery of Divine Love and Wisdom.

True Science leads to and ultimates in the knowledge of GOD. It does not repudiate the Divine Idea. It could not, because GOD is at the heart of all things which are living expositions of Truth. It does not turn its back upon the radiance that streams from the Divine Orient. It could not; because all its illumination comes from that glorious Divine Centre.

True Science is not irreligious, though it may have to disturb the traditional religious mind by its unveilings, its interpretations, its affirming of things that are true. True Science is a knowledge that fills the whole Being with lowliness: it is essentially religious. The knowledge of one's self ultimates in the knowledge of GOD; and to truly know one's self, even in a limited degree, fills one with lowliness. For it is to know the greatness of life, the possibilities of life, the mystery of life in its motion, its emotion, its depths, its qualities, its capabilities, its power of comprehension as well as apprehension, and the heights into which it can soar. Thus, true Science is true knowledge; and true knowledge is divine knowledge; and that is a lowly thing within the Soul.

FALSE CLAIMS LEAD TO CONTRADICTIONS

Now the apparent contradictions between what is called physical Science and ecclesiastical Religion, arise from the mistaken claims of both, and consequently, a misunderstanding on the part of both. There is much confusion. In the claims of physical Science, there is the confounding of knowledge gathered through observation with the vital truth of which the observed phenomena are the testimony. The latter is that real inner knowledge which is the knowing that comes from realization. The knowledge gathered from observed phenomena is only concerned with the outer aspects, and it is knowledge *about* things. But everything has a subjective side; and real knowledge is subjective, and is the becoming of divine knowledge within the Being. And Religion, as you will know, is confounded with traditions and beliefs, rituals and symbols—all of which things may be helpful, and may be associated with the religious expression, but are, nevertheless, quite apart from true Religion. For people can hold traditions and beliefs, and observe their ritual and all that they would associate with religious credal expositions, without being religious in the true divine sense. And it is good that material Science through its pronouncements should disturb the professed religious communities, with their amazing pretensions to be the repositories of the Truth. But when, on the one hand, material Science claims to be the arbiter of knowledge and the final word in each department of knowledge gathered from without; and ecclesiastical Religion claims to be arbiter of human thought and outlook, belief and service, then they both enter into the realm of conflict, and are antagonistic to each other.

RELIGION AND SCIENCE ARE ONE

Yet in the true scientific world and the true religious world, there is no contradiction. Science and Religion are one. And where Science is divorced from Religion, and Religion from Science, they both tread a path which is of the night, with no ultimate, assured and abiding knowledge. There is no Rock of Ages, sure and steadfast, upon which a scientist's feet should ever be planted, if Science be divorced from true religious motion and vision. Where Religion is circumscribed by traditions and beliefs, ritual and symbol (all of which may be valuable in a limited manner, and in the degree of their exposition of anything that may be true and beautiful), there is no true knowledge of the Eternal, no understanding of the Divine Mysteries. Religion can exist, nay it can *be*, without any of these other adjuncts. They belong to the realm of existence; *Religion is of Being*. It can do without these, though it can be expressed through them. Religion is Life. It is the Divine Spirit-motion in us. Why should it not touch everything? Why should it pass by the realm of Science in relation to the outer world of manifestation? All true Science is Divine; all true Religion is scientific. Both understand the elements. They both have knowledge which is begotten of prescience.

Perfect Science understands the world. It knows how it first became; also how it became what it is to-day. It understands the Earth's interior motions as well as its outward motions. The dimension of the circle of its vision is far, far greater than the horizon described by the realm of observed phenomena. It extends into the beyond of the Beyond. Its vision penetrates into the heart of the Planet itself. It looks at the glory of its life as once it was. It beholds the motion of the Earth's unfallen elements, and the splendour of the ministries rendered from the Divine World through her. And it witnesses the Divine ministries unto the Earth to-day, to restore her to her ancient glory.

DIVINE SCIENCE IS REALIZATION

True Science also knows what Man is, and whence he came. Divine Science knows how the spiritual Man was generated, and not simply the generation of his body. Divine Science understands Man's substance, and the nature of the breath that interfuses his substance. Divine Science knows that Man is fashioned in the Divine likeness; that his real Life is a Spiral; and that he grows through the motion of his planes, as these move in obedience to Divine Law; and how the motion of these is from without to the within. Divine Science understands how he became a child of the Eternal Mystery, with divine potency in the Principle of his Life; and how he contains within himself, in miniature, the very secret of that Mystery. Divine Science thus knows Man, because the knowledge is from within. It is prescience. Therefore, it does not learn these mysteries from without. *Divine Science is realization.* All Souls grow through the inward motion. When they are attaining, they have their motion from without, inward; but it is through the motion of the Divine Principle in the innermost, that the outward motion is made harmonious. It is thus the Soul grows, and evolutes, and attains. It grows richer, stronger, and greater, and becomes illumined. And at last it enters the realms of realization, and ascends through those realms from degree to degree. The realization becomes more intensified. It becomes greater and more exalted, till it partakes of the very nature of the Eternities. In this way Divine Science understands Man. And although it is most evident that material Science, and the knowledge arrived at by means of it, is not to be despised; yet none of the Sciences, nor all of them put together—Physiography, Chemistry, Physics, Anatomy, Physiology, Geology and Astronomy, and the collateral Sciences—can give to Man a true understanding of himself, or the World of which he is a denizen, or the Universe of which this Earth is a small member. All these Sciences, however valued and honoured, touch only the outer aspects of Man, the World, and the Universe. They move along the circulus of the nucleus of the nucleole of the spiralled Being, seeing and knowing only the outer. *The real Man is untouched by them.*

THE SCIENCE OF THE SOUL

Even the Psychology of modern times, whilst contributory to the inspiration of the mind in relation to Thought concerning the spiritual qualities and quantities of Man, is nevertheless so interpreted that its followers can never get at the very innermost of the Man. The word itself is misinterpreted and misapplied. It means the Science of the Soul. It relates to the doctrine of the Son of God in Man. It predicates the union of Psyche and the Logos. It speaks of God in the Soul. Therefore, to understand the psychology of Man, is to understand the inner Being. And this is attained by no mere mental process. For no one can get there by occult means. It is the result of knowledge which is realization. A true psychology is true Religion. The truth of this will presently become obvious. Like true Science, it is God-begotten. It has to do with spiritual growth and evoluting, enriching and attaining, illumination and realization.

When the study of Science and Psychology is from this standpoint, how different it will be! When those who teach

Science and Psychology have this vision, how illumined will be their interpretations of things! The various Schools are not yet ready to hear much in this direction. But the day is coming, the light is breaking, and there is motion. Even the greatest Scientists are feeling after a Science that is other than limited to the manifest world. They are sensing much, and seeking for the meaning of many things physical Science of itself cannot explain. They are awakening to the fact that there is an unseen Universe whose secrets are not revealed to those who simply pursue the path of the earthly Sciences. They are even coming gradually to the understanding that all true Science is spiritual, and to apprehend that even this world may have a spiritual and inner history, as well as an outer, such as physical Science deals with. They are surely seeking for that realm where alone they can learn how the Soul grows, evolutes, attains, becomes enriched, ascends, attains illumination, and enters into the realm where it knows in realization; and how GOD gives to it, by the very process of its growth, Divine Prescience.

TRUE RELIGION IS DIVINE SCIENCE

And now we will look at Religion. *Religion has relation to the Spirit's motion.* Religion does not belong to the Schools, although the Schools lay special claim to it. It is not the heritage of any particular race, though some races have made special claims. All races have their own different religious beliefs and expressions. *All Religion is one*, whether it be of the east or the west, the north or the south. Those things that are called Religions, if they be not departments of revelation from the Divine World, are only the accretions which have grown up around the idea of Religion. Religion is Life. It is the Principle of Life which, when in motion, gives direction to Man. When Religion is realized, Life is crowned with that for which all Souls were created and fashioned, even the knowledge, through realization, of the sublime Mystery we name the FATHER-MOTHER. The real Life of Man is a thing quite apart from traditional belief, or outward ritual, or the use of age-long associations; though he himself, through the inner motion of his Being, may throw light upon these. In this latter case they may become expressions of the inner Life. *Religion is of the Spirit. It is related to the Soul. It is the Life of the Soul. It is Being. Being is Divine consciousness.* It therefore belongs to the realm of the Divine Mystery. That Mystery can be known; yet only through realization. Who shall ascend unto the Heavens to bring it down? No one can bring Being down. Being relates to the eternal consciousness which pervades all substance and spirit. And it is through that consciousness in the Being of man as an individuate life from God that man comes to know the Father-Mother. The consciousness of the Father-Mother is never attained as a knowledge acquired from without. Though Man may gather of the knowledge he finds coming to his hands through scientific research, knowledge of the elements, of the earth, of the worlds, in so far as physical Science can interpret these, yet the outer aspects fail to give that vision of God which comes through realization. No one can discover the secret at the heart of a flower, though one may know all about its form, its habit, or manner of growth, the time of its bloom, the fashion of its leaves, and the manner of the unfolding or unveiling of that which makes the mystery manifest in the bloom and the fragrance. The secret is hidden. The secret is always there, but it belongs to the Inner World. *It is the secret of the Spirit.* For even that glorious Mystery, through accommodated elements is also mediated unto the lovely created embodiments of the Divine Thought in the trees and the flowers. And if that be so in what is accounted Nature, how much more must it be so in relation to the Divine Mystery that Man has to realize about himself. He may learn about the manifestations, but he can understand the causation of the manifestations only through the motion of that holy Religious Spirit within himself. Each Soul has within it the elements, the potencies, the Spirit in motion, the perfect polarization of which ultimates in the Soul's high consciousness wherein it comes into the vision and realization of the Eternal ONE. *That is Religion*, the acme of attainment, Life in its perfectionment. That is Religion in the Divine Principle of Man's nature, in his constitution, in Life's manifestation, and in its realization.

RELIGION IS BEGOTTEN OF SPIRIT-MOTION

From this it will be understood how Religion has relation to Life and is related to the Principle of Life, and is nothing less than Divine Love within the Being. And it will be seen that its manifestation is in the Life of harmony, the harmonious conditions which spring forth from harmonious thought, desire, feeling, and purpose. For Religion is GOD in the Soul, as distinguished from all the things which have veiled Religion from men and women, and led them to attach importance to limited concepts of great doctrines wherein they have confused the things which have not been true with those great truths concerning the Eternal Mystery of the FATHER-MOTHER, the mystery of a man's constitution, his beginnings, his nature, his holy potencies, and his Sonship to the FATHER-MOTHER. Through the misconceptions of men and women regarding Religion, just as through the misconceptions relating to Science, great contradictions have arisen. And in both domains and between each other, warfare has raged.

Yet Religion is the Divine Science; and Divine Science is true Religion. It is Divine knowledge. Neither Religion nor Science is knowledge gathered from without, nor acquired in the Schools. It is the Divine knowledge acquired psychologically. The knowing comes through the Soul's expansion, deepening, and ascension. It is that experience in illumined consciousness of the Divine Mystery, acquired as the Being has arisen on the wings of the Spirit, and taken flight into those realms where all things are known. Religion is the only true, certain, and abiding Science; for it is the knowledge of GOD.

Merely to trim beliefs, like a ship having to trim its sail to contrary winds, to the affirmations and claims of Science, will not bring Religion into harmony. That is not the way to harmonize Religion and Science. Science has not dreamed in the way the Church has dreamed, and spoken of the dream in vague and uncertain terms; though Science has often affirmed many deductions which have been found uncertain, and has had to change its premises many times in every department. For material Science is the path of a growing knowledge upon voyages of discovery. There is no certainty because it deals with ever changing conditions. No sooner does a branch of the scientific world think it has found the ultimate of something, than bye and bye there is a shaking of trust in that ultimate; and then there comes a new pronouncement.

THE DAY OF RECONCILIATION IS AT HAND

And it has been thus in Religion. Religion according to the Schools, and as an outward interpretation of Man's spiritual motion, has had to trim its sails to meet the new spirit of inquiry. There was a time when it persecuted Science. There is no wonder that Science sometimes scoffs at Religion. Reverent Scientists do not do this; but there has been much scoffing where pride of mind has held sway. The Soul that seeks truly, is always reverent. It is lowly. There is no pride of mind or of heart where knowledge is purely sought, though the results be in limited degree. Indeed, where Souls are earnest in their pursuit and pure in their motives, though they may not have acquired correct knowledge, they are reverent and lowly. And it would be good for Religion, even through its traditions and its beliefs, to be lowly also. All the great doctrines that Religion in its outward manifestations has clung to, are true; but the interpretations of them have been most calamitous. The darkness upon and within the Church universal, not only throughout the Christian age, but in other ages also, has been appalling. It has been one of the outstanding resultants of the terrible darkness that overtook the world and all its children great ages ago. But we are coming to the day when there will be the perfect reconciliation between Religion and Science. Yet it will not be through Religion, or the avenues of Religion, merely trimming the sails to the contrary breaths. No, it will be in rightly interpreting Religion, and getting to the root foundations of Life. It must be through a true apprehension of how Religion has to do with Life and not with beliefs, with the true interpretation of Life and the living of it, and the giving in manifestation, embodied grace as a resultant of true living. It must be through showing that Religion is the Divine Principle within the Being, and the Mystery motion of the Spirit of the FATHER-MOTHER. For Religion is that motion which gives to the Soul its growth, its true evolutory acts of ascension, its increase of power through ingathering of the wealth of GOD'S Ætheria from the Divine World, and through the Angelic World—that Ætheria out of which all things have become, and taken their fashion for manifestation.

THE RELIGION OF BEING

Religion is this ingathering by the Soul of that glorious Stream unto the nourishing of the Being and the building of it up into the estate wherein, through attaining one degree after another, it becomes enlightened, and is henceforth one illumined from the LORD, so that it knows and has divine prescience. When, in such a state, the Soul sees anything, it looks through it, understanding that for which it stands, that of which it is the manifestation. It enters into the realization of the Angelic World, is conscious of the touch of the Angels, breathes the atmosphere full of the breaths of the Angels. It treads the path of the Angels, walks amid the flowers of the Angelic realms, inhales the fragrance of the flowers of the Angelic breaths. And still inward and upward it goes, through that glorious kingdom of exquisite beauty, to that yet higher Holy City of Zion, the citadel of glorious Christhood where the LORD Shaddai reigns.

That is the Science of Being. It is the Science of Being realized, wherein is the knowledge of the Divine Mystery of *Being*, in which the Soul contacts the realm of Being and knows its LORD; and from its LORD learns, *even until the illumination comes to give the Soul understanding of all things through the Divine Indwelling.*

THE SCIENCE OF BEING

Science and Religion are one. Science is of the realm of understanding and knowledge; Religion is of the realm of realization. Let those who are seeking through Religion, recognize that it is through their understanding that light may be thrown upon all the paths of life, until the interpretation of the innermost illumines the interpretation of the outermost, giving to all things their real meaning wherein they become one. *For in the Divine World of harmony, Religion and Science are of the same Temple.* Science is Divine Religion; it is a resultant of *the religare.* For Religion is the Life of the Spirit in Man. The Science or realization of Being is the knowledge with which the Divine Indwelling crowns a Man, so that he knows, in the light of that Presence, all things. He knows the FATHER-MOTHER. He understands divine creations, divine fashionings, divine manifestations. He apprehends the meaning of a manifest world like this, for he has Divine Prescience. He understands and can interpret a fallen world like this, for he has inner knowledge. He understands those departments which have become paths for the seeking of knowledge and the understanding of the elements. Through the Divine Gift he understands all things. He understands all things, not because he is omniscient, but because GOD's glorious Omnisciency or All-knowledge, fills him when he enters the Great Silence. There is but the one Omniscient Realm and the one glorious Omniscient Being: for GOD is Being. But the Soul is an individuation of Being; therefore Man can touch that Realm and function within it, even until he shares in the Omniscience of that Kingdom of which the Archangel, Zachariel, is the glorious Guardian.

Let the children of the FATHER-MOTHER love HIM adoringly; yes, love HIM, and trust HIM, and seek in their trust to understand HIM. Let them not be carried off their feet by extraneous things and false claims. Let them be assured that the real knowledge is with GOD. *The secrets of all things are with Him.* And HE unveileth these secrets unto HIS children, when they come lowlily, humbly, full of the graciousness of HIS Own tenderness, the beauty of HIS Own gentleness, and the resplendence of HIS Love. Let all learn to love HIM Who is all knowledge. And let that Love and the knowledge that comes through it, touch everything in your life, and through you the Life of everyone, the world in which you are, and the elements with which you have to deal, and through which you have to minister. *Thus make Life a perfect whole.* Let your Religion, the Principle of GOD in you which binds you to HIM, come through to touch everything. Let nothing be done that would be an ignoble act, but everything that becometh a son of GOD, thus making manifest all that is of true Sonship to the FATHER-MOTHER. For to do that, is surely to be like HIM.

Ever Blessed be HIS most glorious Name Who is our LORD, our FATHER and our MOTHER, the revealer and interpreter of all things!

THE INFINITE
AND
THE FINITE

THE INFINITE AND THE FINITE

THE DIVINE POSSIBILITIES OF MAN

As the term implies, we think of the infinite as boundless, and the finite as bounded; the illimitable and the limited. The finite, when expressed in relation to a Human Soul, seems small in comparison with the boundless Universe and the Mystery Whose glory interfuses and pervades it, and manifests itself in all embodiments. And yet the finite as expressed in a Human Soul seems infinite when contrasted with the other finite embodiments of the Eternal Mystery. Indeed there is a sense in which even the apparently greatly limited Human unit is capable of becoming infinite. If not boundless and illimitable, yet so great are man's potencies that he can transcend the bounded and the limited.

In such transcension he appears to reach even to the illimitable; and in such an outreaching it does seem as if his possibilities were boundless.

It is of the mystery of the constitution of man that, whilst he is finite and a little child in the boundless Universe of Being, a gem amidst the wealth of infinite riches, a solitary dewdrop amidst the million dew drops, all of which are but the finite expressions of the illimitable sea of Being; yet there is that which is of the infinite within him. Indeed, so true is this that the possibilities for man are those of a boundless wealth of Being, infinite estate of consciousness, illimitable progression through the ascension of Life into and through the Spheres which represent high degrees of consciousness as well as great systems. For, as it is in the above, so is it in the beneath. The microcosm is even as the macrocosm. It is of the Mystery of God in man that he has been endowed with infinite possibilities, and can reach, through the realization of the things that are possible, the realms of the Infinite.

Great is the mystery of Godliness! But Godliness reveals how great the Mystery of God is within the Soul. It means

Godlikeness. Great is the mystery of Godlikeness in the children of men, for HE has given to them those potencies which, when rightly and fully cultured, enable each Soul to know HIMSELF.

Now, there is a sense in which the finite cannot comprehend the Infinite. In the illimitable, all that is limited is gathered up. Yet there is within a Human Soul that which enables it to transcend all limitations.

HOW FINITE MAN REACHES UNTO THE INFINITE

In the motion of its potency, and acquisition through such motion, and the ascension of the Soul from realm to realm in its consciousness through manifold degrees of realized Being, the Infinite becomes known. At first there is simply a glimpsing of the Eternal. But that is a long way from the infinite vision. There are many glimpses on the way, increasing in their number and their intensity and glory as the Soul unfolds. But the vision of the Infinite is the gift of living in the consciousness of HIS glorious Presence. Then the Soul looks upon HIM Who is, as it were, a Jasper and a Sardius stone. The stones do not convey adequately what is meant. They are but glyphs to veil and yet reveal great truths. For the Sardius stone represents the transcendent glory, and the Jasper stone the veil that grades the Divine Vision. Latent in its very constitution, lies the gift of GOD by which the Soul is empowered to look upon the Divine Radiance, and know the Infinite.

It has been said most truly through the ages by many who have perceived these things, that to know one's self was the way to discover GOD. Only one who had known the great reality could have given such utterance, though it is attributed to one of the Greek philosophers. The Sons of GOD knew such a truth, for it was of the Mysteries which they taught. *The Above can be known only from the Beneath; and the Beneath can know the Above only through climbing to it.* You cannot bring down the Above; you must ascend to it. GOD is manifested everywhere where truth and beauty reign. But HE is known only through the ascension of the Being into high consciousness, and that means through following the whole path of the life by which a Soul can ascend and gain this consciousness.

THE ONE ROYAL ROAD TO GOD

There is only one royal road to GOD. It is HIS way. It is the way of the Truth. It is the path of the true growth and evolution of the Being.

Much is written and spoken concerning growth and evolution that has little to do with the real growth and evolution of the Human Being. The fallacy has arisen through the veiling to the human vision of the true nature of man, and the application of what is apparently outward history to the doctrine of growth and evolution. And thus the evolution and growth concerning mankind have come to be associated with the development of physical form and mental states; whereas these are but vehicles, which, at one time, were beautiful and adequate for the purpose, though capable of great expansion, not only in the stature, but also in refinement, the ascension of state, the dynamic elevation of the elements of the body, and the exaltation of the mind in its outlook, in its purpose, and through its ministries.

As it is in the Above, so is it in the Beneath. We can know the above through the Beneath; we can apprehend unto knowing the Infinite through the finite. The Human Soul is so constituted that the bounded in it contains the mystery which relates it to the Infinite, and which enables it to come at last into the consciousness of what has been termed the Illimitable and the Eternal. It can come into that state of consciousness and power wherein it can move through and amongst the Mysteries of the Eternities. For the Eternities have no relation whatsoever to time. Their periodicity is dependent upon the Divine Fiat. They move as they are commanded, and unto those who attract them. The ancient word for the Eternal, denoted quality and state. As the "Eternal Life," denotes the degree of Life, the quality of the Life, the vision appertaining to the Life; so the Eternities relate to the quality of Being. And in the Divine World their motion has relation to the Four

Living Ones described in the glorious vision set forth in the Apocalyptic Drama.

THE MYSTERY OF THE INFINITE WITHIN MAN

In a fragmentary way I would unveil to you something of GOD's Mystery in yourselves. And if you can apprehend my meaning, if you even glimpse the vision truly, the thought that you have infinite possibilities within yourselves, and that your potencies, when grown and expanded through the evolutory acts of your own Being, will bring you into contact with the Infinite Presence, will not make you to be proud and lifted up. Divine things never make a Soul vain. I would have you understand that anything that makes you feel vain, has something wrong with it; or your response to it has been wrong. You will not misunderstand me, even though I seem to emphasize it.

The greater a Soul grows, the more greatly increased its potencies become. The degrees into which it enters by evolutory acts, lift it up higher and still higher; for it has, in its illimitable pilgrimage, a tremendous way to go if it would apprehend in a large sense, the Infinite ONE. But the higher it goes, more and more it learns the nature of meekness and lowliness. Some people think that meekness and lowliness mean weakness. But that could not be so. The reverse is true. Pride and vanity mean weakness. Lowliness of mind and humbleness of heart are great qualities. They are full of Power. They are of GOD Who is the lowliest of all; for HE reveals HIMSELF in the humblest fashions. HE does not despise the creative act that gives the estate to the humblest flower. Even the blade of grass reveals HIM. HIS Mystery is in the blade of grass. It is full of spiritual nourishment for the creatures which have to live upon the grass. The flowers are full of beauty begotten of HIS glory, not only in their form, but in their exquisite breaths and their contribution to the economy of the world in its atmospheric conditions. HE does not deem it beneath the dignity of HIS sublime Majesty, to stoop to create even that which is unseen to the human eye. HE is revealed in the infinitesimally small.

There is an unseen Universe the exquisite beauty of whose forms and colours is unobserved by the human eye, because its lenses are not accommodated to such a realm. Yet when man increases by temporary aids the power of his vision, that world of exquisite beauty becomes unveiled and revealed.

The Wisdom of the FATHER-MOTHER is revealed in the lowliest things in creation, where these are pure and true and beautiful. And if that be so, how much more is HIS Wisdom revealed in the superstructure of a Human Soul, in its fashion, in its potencies, and in the wonderful purpose lying behind it. He has put an infinite world within you. And you can discern and know that world only through yourself. The unveiling within you of that world, is the unveiling of your divinity. The Presence is there Whose countenance is like a Jasper and a Sardius stone. HIS Presence is glorious to look upon, though it must needs be partially veiled. To look upon that Presence from the centre of the Being, is an accomplishment that comes gradually to the Soul. You can see HIM revealed in the exquisite outward fashion; but you come to behold HIM in the exquisite beauty of the fashion of the sanctuary of the Being. To see HIM embodied in such a world as our own Sun even, is to look upon the most transcendent glory. For the Sun is, in His own glorious Self as an embodiment, but a microcosmic embodiment of the macrocosm of the Universe. Thus the Sun is Infinite. We are finite in comparison, small units in his great system. Yet, as an embodiment of the Eternal Mystery, the Sun himself is only finite in relation to the great Illimitable. And yet in the glory of the Solar Body, the transcendency of the Presence is beyond description.

A TRANSCENDENT VISION OF THE PRESENCE

In the Divine Vision portrayed in the Apocalypse, the Presence appeared as a Jasper and a Sardius stone. The Sardius stone is a marvellous golden orange. And that is the true colour of our Sun. It is his glorious tincture. But the full glory has to be veiled. And none but one who can function within his realm can behold the Presence within. Elsewhere I have spoken of that Presence as expressed in the sum of Archangelic and Angelic ministries as these fill that most sacred abode and are poured forth in ministry to the various members of the system, and very specially, and in a specific way, to this world. That Presence is within each one who is there, and who is a representative of the glory of the Solar Body. The LORD is our Sun and our Shield. HE is the Radiance and the Veil. HE is the transcendent Light, and HE HIMSELF curtains the full resplendence. The LORD HIMSELF is our Luminary. We have no light apart from the LORD. All other light is communicated externally. All knowledge that is not born through the realization of HIS Indwelling, is knowledge acquired on the way. Such is not to be despised. All helpful knowledge should be cherished. The Soul thus grows. But those who have acquired great knowledge in other ages, and are able to bring forth that knowledge and transmute it into power in these days, unto them the LORD is to become as the Sun, the indwelling Luminary. HE is within you. The microcosm is glorious, even as the macrocosm. The finite is full of HIS resplendence, even as the Infinite; for the Eternal ONE is resident in the Principle of the Soul's Being.

It is said in an old scripture, that the LORD sits upon the circles of the Heavens. That is, HE holds the regnancy of all the Spheres. *His throne is upon the very apex of our Being; and when He reigns, He sits upon the circles, or planes of our Being.*

That which is of the Infinite in relation to the Solar Body, and indeed in relation to the Eternal World, is within you; even the Presence, the Throne, the Rainbow, the Sea that looked like crystal, the Four Living Creatures, the Seven Sacred Lamps whose flames are of the Seven Spirits of GOD, and the Four and Twenty Elders. When you think of the Hierarchies, you think of the Hierarchy of the Planet, or the Hierarchy of the System, the Hierarchy of the Solar Body, or the Divine Hierarchy of the Universe. But as is the Above, so is the Beneath. As is the great world, so is the little world. As is the Infinite, so is the finite. The world of GOD in the Eternities is microcosmically within you. Ye are of GOD. Ye are GOD's little worlds.

THE DIVINE DIGNITY OF OUR LIFE

Now, look at the dignity of it! In doing so you will understand how it comes to pass that the children of GOD who have realized the glory of HIS Overshadowing Presence, can neither think, nor say, nor do, those things which are beneath the dignity of such a Divine relationship. The Presence is within us; we must live in the consciousness of it. The Mystery is within us; we must act as those who are sharing in the Infinite. GOD reveals HIMSELF to us within. HE reveals the majesty of HIS outworking in the Universe through all we are able to look out upon, to apprehend and understand through the mind, through the understanding, through the reason, through relation and correlation in the outer manifest world. But HE very specially reveals HIMSELF within us. And this is in harmony with HIS Mystery in us; for we can understand GOD only through becoming like HIM. And in the measure in which we become like HIM, in that measure do we understand HIM; and the more we understand HIM, the more we call out in prayer to become like HIM. The essaying of the Being to realize, brings the realization. Through our Godward motion, our obedience to the Eternities, we become more and more like GOD. In our embodiment, we appear in the fashion of the Supreme Good, the Supreme Love. Thus do we the more fully liken HIM Who is our FATHER-MOTHER.

REMEMBRANCE OF THE PRESENCE ALL-POTENT

Remember HIS Presence within you. When you go in prayer in the hour of worship or need, or dire distress, should such sorrow have come to you, do not pray to HIM as if HE were far away, but remember that HE is all about you. If ye cannot do this, unhappy are ye. If HE be not near you in your consciousness, how sad your state! For HE is about you. It may be that there is something lying heavily upon your vision, hiding HIM; something more than a Jasper stone which is only a protecting veil; something that is obliterating the vision of HIMSELF. Let any such veil be put away. Remember this; all that is best in you is of HIMSELF. You cannot have any good without Him. You cannot love without HIS love. You cannot bless without HIS blessing. You cannot grow strong in those things which are truly beautiful in their vision and their manifestation apart from HIM. For all Truth, all Beauty, all Goodness, are from HIM. Hold this sublime truth sacred, that the Infinite is within your finite Being. The Illimitable is in the potencies of your apparently most limited Life. The Boundless is present. As you grow in Grace—which means, the Fashion of GOD—the world recedes. The world as understood by men and women, with its dominating Zeitgeist, passes away. It is still there to be ministered unto, but your vision is not circumscribed by its manifestation, nor held in the bondage of its claims. You grow beyond it. You transcend it. The things that once satisfied you in it, no longer satisfy. You are liberated from the bondage of the mortal estate, through ascending into the consciousness of the immortal estate. That new state does not mean that you fly away from your daily duties in the home, or in the world where you may be called to minister; but it does mean that you are not in bondage to any of these things, and that your ministries in the earth spheres are ministries touched by the glory of the consciousness of the Presence Who is within you. You cannot be conscious of HIS Presence without making the Divine influence touch everything you touch; it is not possible.

How glorious HE is! HE is even as the Sardius stone. How radiant HE is! HE is the Light of ineffable whiteness unto the Being. There is no bringing of those glorious mysteries down, in applying them to ourselves. They cannot be brought down, blessed be HIS glorious Name Who hath set them in the Firmament of HIS Dwelling! But they are oft-times brought down in expression and meaning in writings. They are brought down from their high estate and misdirected from their right uses, when they are only held as knowledges.

THE DIVINE REGNANCY WITHIN US

But when they become realities, then they are in their true realm. The Presence reigns. HIS Throne is within. HE holds regnancy. HIS is the dominion, the power, and the glory. The Presence is in the finite; but the Presence is Infinite. By this sacred mystery the Infinite is in you. The Illimitable is in you. The Boundless is in you. The realization of HIM enables you to transcend all the worlds of objective manifestations wherein there are limitations, and to get into the realm of the Eternal ONE, and feel and be one with the motion of the Eternities.

Who can measure the dignity of this great Truth, that within you is HIS Presence Who reigns in the Eternal World? The Eternal World, in and through His Presence, comes to you and is with you. You are thus connected with it. Magnetic streams proceed from it to you. Borne upon the motion of your Being, your prayers expressing your deepest desires reach unto the Eternal. For HIS Throne is within you. You recognize it from time to time.

How sublime is the dignity HE confers, that HE should reign within the unit as well as in the whole cosmic life; that HE should reign in the individual children of His creation, as well as in celestial embodiment! Men and women worship worldly things. They love principalities and powers on the outer planes. They eagerly grasp at man-created dignities, even though these oft-times elude them, or bring to them no great joy and blessing. And all the while they miss the dignities that are within. They see not the dignity of the Human Soul so endowed that it is capable of being like GOD—creating, fashioning, and expressing beauty in the true glory of Life and nobility of purpose.

Oh, how wonderful is this finite life, with its latent prophetic potencies of the Infinite! It makes the Soul one in and with the Infinite. And then, as if HE could not enrich the Soul sufficiently, GOD has given such a perfect expression of that macrocosmic vision within the constitution of our own Being that we have even the mystery of the Sea of Crystal. Crystal reflects, and it also refracts. The elements within us are not fixed but volatile. They are like crystal, but not crystallized and fixed. In the crystal the divine elements are fixed. Within us are the corresponding elements which are not fixed; they are volatile in their nature and state.

THE SEA OF DIVINE ÆTHERIA Now, around that Presence Who is at the very centre of your elements and potencies, and Who is the Regnant ONE in the mystery of your Being, Whom you will come to recognize there one day (and may that day be hastened unto you and for you!) and HIS Throne, is this glorious mystery of Divine Ætheria. It is in a state accommodated to the Soul's constitution, wherein the very Mysteries of the Divine World can be reflected. In the Apocalyptic vision the Sea took the fashion of a rainbow. It reflected the rainbow. That means that the spectrum of ELOHIM was revealed. And then it changed to become like an Emerald. And it did this just because it is the Sea of Divine Ætheria. For when the magnetic stream which proceeds from the Love-principle flows through that Sea, it becomes as an Emerald; it is full of the beauty of Divine compassion and pity. Compassion and Pity are the centrifugal and centripetal modes of Love in its ministry. But the Sea is always also as a Sea of crystal in its reflective and prismatic power. It can reveal the Divine Mystery. It can reflect the glory of the Light of that Presence. It can show forth the tinctures of ELOHIM, the Sacred Seven.

There is a reason for your love of colours. There is a reason why you love pure colours, and colours pure in their combination. There is a reason for the effect colours have upon you. The reason is within yourself. It is part of your constitution. It is not something acquired from outward training. Outward training is oft-times most useful; and, indeed, in the Soul's motion onward and upward, it is necessary. For the Soul passes through countless ages. Even in the Angelic Worlds it gets outward training. But all the outward expression has for its purpose an appeal to that which is within. You cannot respond to that which you have not. Your power of response is itself the testimony to that which is within you. If you could see yourself in the light of the wonderful mystery which is in your Being, if you could see yourself in the glory of your constitution, in the splendour of your fashion, in the resplendence of HIS glory around you, then ye would know that ye were created to be as Gods. And as minor Gods ye would henceforth embody HIM, reveal HIM, and interpret HIM in all the service of life. In language unspoken ye would speak for HIM. Every act would reveal the majesty of HIS Presence, testifying of HIM Who is with you, and of the dignity with which HE hath crowned you.

THE MYSTERY OF THE FOUR DIMENSIONS

Yes, this mystery is in the Kingdom within. And great is its motion as represented in "the Four Living Creatures." For the Four Living Creatures are also within. They represent the Fourfold Mystery of the Eternities in their motion. They also signify the Fourfold Mystery of the Elements in their primal estate.

The Four Living Creatures had each six wings. With twain they covered their face; with twain they covered their feet; and with twain they did fly. They were full of adoration. They were absolute in their service. Their motion was perfect. In their motion they revealed and veiled the mystery of the four great dimensions within the Being, the four atmospheres which correlate the Soul to the Eternities, the Power of the Divine motion through the four quarters, called the east and the west, the north and the south. They filled all these dimensions by their ministry. Within the Soul they move from the west, eastward, through the north and the south. For according to the constitution of the Soul, the motion of its growth and evolution is from the west or outer manifestation, gradually coming in through the sanctuary of Being into the mind's understanding or the north, and the heart's deep emotion or the south, and gradually passing on to endure that yet more intense degree of motion of the Eternities expressed as the Divine Orient.

FROM THE OCCIDENT TO THE ORIENT

These Four Living Ones are within you. They represent four kingdoms of your Being; in the true Human, which is the west of the outer activities; in the true Angelic, which is the south where the streams of Love flow and make manifest perpetually; through the Celestial, which is the north, the land of magnetic light wherein the Divine World gives transcendent revealings unto the divine mind in the Being; and then unto the east, the realm of the Orient, or the vision in its splendour, the vision wherein is realization, the vision that enraptures the Soul until it becomes one with and in the Divine.

The Four Living Creatures seen in the macrocosmic vision, were perfect in their motion, perfect in their adoration, perfect in their service, perfect in their ministry for the Divine unto HIS children. And herein we may behold the increasing dignities of the estate with which the FATHER-MOTHER hath endowed us. Oh, when one has to hear from another the belittling of some who should be cherished and have compassion given them, how conscious one is that it is beneath the dignity of anyone to belittle any child of the FATHER-MOTHER! All Souls are in different degrees of consciousness. All are in different states of acquisition and attainment. All, however, have the Mystery within them. The Divine realm of their Being is also crowned with the dignity of the Presence. HIS Throne and the Rainbow around about it are there in the sanctuary. The mysterious Sea of the Divine Elements is present. The Fourfold motion of the Eternities can be felt. And each one shares the Mystery expressed as the Twenty-four crowned Elders around the Throne. For everyone has the divine attributes, even though they be not yet crowned. The twenty-four Elders are the twelve attributes in their dual power and motion. When an attribute is perfectly crowned, it has perfectly attained. It has been cultured. It has grown up, and is able to stand before the

Throne, to serve in the consciousness of the Presence, and to endure HIS regnancy.

MAN'S ATTRIBUTES IN THEIR DUAL MINISTRIES

Some people can endure the Divine Regnancy in some attributes, but not in others. They can endure that the Divine Will be accomplished in some of their attributes, but refuse to have it done in others. But we have to be made complete and perfect. Every attribute is to be crowned. The whole of the twelve attributes of the Soul must needs be crowned. And it is well to observe that they have to be crowned, not only in their positive aspect, or, in contrast, in their negative aspect, or in their positive or negative mode; they have to be crowned in both. They make the twenty-four Elders or rulers. Every attribute is both positive and negative. It has its centrifugal force, and its centripetal force. It is creative; and it is also fashioning. It can serve positively; it can likewise serve negatively. But these express modes. Each attribute is magnetic, and it has its dual poles.

The Great Love has made us finite expressions of HIS Illimitable Being, and so we are to be perfect even as HE is perfect. But in the fashioning of us HE has given to our constitution such a combination of elements as enables us, when those elements are properly unified and polarized, to understand the Infinite, and to function in consciousness within the Illimitable Realms.

There are many things I would love to say to you here, but they may be broken only in a fragmentary way. Yet I would say this, that, when the Initiate understands those inner realms, he will understand Art and whence it comes; Music and whence it comes; even the mystery of creation and how it is accomplished; the way of Divine knowledge through the Indwelling Presence, which is of the realm of Omnisciency, and how that knowledge becomes; the Mystery of the Omnipotency of the FATHER-MOTHER; and the secret of the Sacred Fire which is expressed as sevenfold in the vision, lighting the seven Lamps of the Being.

THE DIVINE IS IN PERFECT ART AND MUSIC

Until all the Lamps are lit, and you have gone through the realms they represent in a state of illumined understanding, you cannot know. Yet that which is indicated is within you. The Infinite is here in you. The macrocosm is here in microcosmic expression. The Illimitable in its motion is within that which seems bounded and limited. The Eternal has HIS Dwelling even where the life seems but of the changing conditions of a world of time regulated by its triple motion. The Mystery of the FATHER-MOTHER is in you. HE is in your Art and your Music, in the measure in which they are perfect. HE is your vision and your motion in the perfect day. The Divine Motion in the realm of Art within you, is that of Oriphiel; and of Music, is that of Anael. And the other Divine qualities spoken of above, are of the yet more inward realms; and they are all in you. The Divine Art, Music, and Motion; the Wisdom, the Counsel, the Mystery of Omnisciency, even of Omnipotency, crowned with the sacred Fire; these are all within you, and are the royal gifts of a Royal LORD. They are the royal gifts of our Divine King. And with such gifts all other things worth having come. For in the realization of such gifts, all things become the Soul's possession.

Behold, then, the dignity of the finite exposition of the Infinite Mystery in the Human Soul. It is a world, not only of GOD'S creation, but for the Indwelling of GOD. The Soul becomes crowned with the consciousness of the Presence Who atmospheres it, Who overshadows it, Who embowers it in the Cloud of HIS Radiance, and Who sheds the glory of HIS Countenance within its Sanctuary.

When you go forth from the Sanctuary and the Silence, and pass into the world to bear your burdens in the earth-life, to contact and overcome conditions, to accomplish the ministries to which you have put your hands, to render service unto others, to receive service from others, to direct those who serve under you, to train those who have to learn from you how to serve, remember the dignity of your childhood to the FATHER-MOTHER. The consciousness will keep you lowly, and it will clothe you with beauty. The memory of your childhood to HIM will cause HIS radiance to shine forth from the midst of you, and the power of HIM will become expressed through you. Thus your service, even in the lowliest things, will partake of something (in the degree of the service and the vehicles of the service) of HIS own glory, HIS wonderful way of ministering. And even in your lowly estates of outer service, as those who have been crowned with such dignity, *ye shall be as Gods;* that is, *ye shall be revealers of God.*

THE REALMS
OF THE
ANGELS AND ARCHANGELS

THE ANGELIC REALMS

MEDIATION WITHIN THE ANGELIC REALMS

The Heavens are full of the glory of GOD. Wheresoever HIS glory breaks, there is HIS own sublime Radiance, and the Heavens become. For the Heavens in their state and manifestations, are just the expositions in manifold degrees of the FATHER-MOTHER'S sublime Presence.

That Presence is mediated unto all within the Heavens. The Angels who are in the estate of angelic childhood, are ministered unto by those who are older in their estate. Even the elders within one realm are mediated unto from another realm by those appointed to break the Sacred Mystery of the Divine Love and Wisdom as it obtains within such a realm. Those children of the FATHER-MOTHER who are crowned with high angelic Life, are mediated unto from the Divine Love and Wisdom through other children who are in yet higher estate, and who know more fully in their realization the Sacred Mystery of that Love and Wisdom. Even those children in the Heavens who attain through high Divine Initiation to be members of the Sacred Arch in one of the great aspects of the Divine manifestation within those Heavens, are mediated unto by those who stand yet nearer to the Divine Centre of all things. Even the Archangels belonging to the seventh sphere of the Divine World, counting from the within outward, are mediated unto by the FATHER-MOTHER through HIS ELOHIM, and these glorious members give Cherubic and Seraphic motion to the glorious Divine Ætheria, causing that most sacred mystery-stream to move unto and within all who are dwellers within those spheres.

The realms of the Angels and the Archangels are within the various Heavens; and the Divine Mystery reigns within all those realms through the Angels and Archangels, according to their various degrees of realization, embodiment, and ministry.

HOW THE SOUL ATTAINS WITHIN THOSE REALMS

Even whilst dwelling upon the earth-planes, we touch those realms; we enter them; we may pass through their spheres; we may behold their ministries; we may gather great understanding of the nature of the mediatorial service rendered within each realm; and we can, if we will, provided the estate within us permits of it, hold intimate communion with the glorious citizens of those Heavens.

The path of the Soul into the highest estates of consciousness and realization, is just the path the Angel-child must take to grow older, in the sense of realization, increase of potency, deepening of consciousness, enlargement through expansion of the vision, and the ascension of the whole Being in its estate. For though the mind naturally thinks of the Angelic realms as quite distinct from the realms of the earthly manifestation, yet, in the inner world of Being, the Soul who knows the Divine, contacts the realms between the earthly and the innermost. And in the hour wherein it essays to move unto the Altar of God in high estate, it passes through the spheres occupied by the Angel-child, the older Angel, even the realms occupied by the Archangel. For when a Soul ascends in consciousness to the Sanctuary of the glorious Presence to worship before the high Altar where His Overshadowing is in divinest estate, the whole Being of that one passes through all the realms between its earthly dwelling and its divine centre. And herein is the perfectionment of the Divine Love and Wisdom made manifest. For, on its way, the Soul acquires the breaths, the qualities, the elemental substances, even the essences, in the various degrees in which these obtain from realm to realm; and thus that Divine Initiate becomes like the realms he enters, taking on of the glory of the Father-Mother which obtains in the various degrees within each realm. And not one is passed by. Not one realm is missed as the Soul treads the divine highway unto the citadel within the Sanctuary where the crown jewels are preserved for it, even those sacred Mysteries of the Divine Regnancy within the Soul itself, even as within the Heavens.

Thus it will be understood how it comes to pass that a Soul grows until it becomes Divine; not only Divine in the Arche or Principle of its Life, which it ever is, but Divine in its estate. And herein also may be learnt something more of the Divine Love and Wisdom as expressed in the glorious mediations from the very Centre of all Being, through Cherubim and Seraphim, Archangel and high Angel, and Angel in lowlier degree, as the result of the ever energizing, illumining, transforming, transfiguring, and glorifying motion of the ELOHIM within the Soul.

THE SEVEN PORTALS OF THE ASCENSION

When a Soul essays to ascend into the Heavens of the Divine, it must needs pass through the sevenfold Gateway. It must take its initiations within each Archangelic sphere, and pay its tribute before the high Altar of those spheres. When a Soul would rise beyond the Love-embodiment and devotion expressed in the Angelic child, and enter the spheres of the yet intenser play of magnetic elements, it passes through the Gateway guarded by Oriphiel. That glorious Archangel of GOD represents the outer sphere of the Divine World. He is magnificent in embodiment; and the sphere of his guardianship and highly active ministries is far flung with the glory of the transcendent Presence. For the ministry of Oriphiel cannot be formulated in a human sense. Nor is he to be thought of after the human formulated idea of a Divine person. He represents the Eternal Mystery who is informulate, whilst at the same time He embodies ADONAI Who becomes formulate to the Soul when its vision is the outcome of a high state of realization.

Oriphiel is the guardian of the portals through which the Soul enters the Divine realms to stand upon the outer threshold. Unto the Soul he is *the speech of God*, for he is the interpreter upon the outer Divine sphere of the mystery of creation. And whilst the Soul can know that mystery only in a state of high realization, yet it is permitted to peer into the Crystal Sea wherein the Divine Mystery is reflected, and learn many things of value unto it. For in the ascension through the seventh sphere of the Divine realm, the Soul acquires knowledge and power—knowledge concerning the creative mystery, and power to enter into the great realization of it.

HOW ARCANA ARE UNVEILED In the mystery of creation there is so much to learn. The principle of Life is one, but the manifestations are manifold. The secret is one, and it belongs to the Eternal; but the revelation of the secret is partial, and is given in departments. What obtains on the earth in most imperfect degrees of manifestation, obtains in all the Heavens in perfect estate, and motion, and manifestation. Though the mystery of Life on the earth planes is one in principle, the degrees of its manifestations are various and manifold. Thus, the generation of a vehicle in lowly estate, whose entity is not of the abiding and permanent order, but only for passing uses and services in different realms, differs in nature, and in the degree and intensity of life, from the Life generated within the higher degrees of the human estate, where the vehicles are so fashioned that they can be used for the manifestation of Life of most exalted nature and order, such as we associate with a noble Human Soul.

Elsewhere I have indicated that there are not only Divine creations in the Angelic and Celestial Worlds, but there are Spiritual and Celestial generations. For, whilst the principle of Life is one, and the law of manifestation one, the processes by which embodiments become, are manifold. For there are not only divine creations such as we associate with the beautiful things to be found within this world and such high embodiments as noble men and women, but in the Angelic World there are Heavenly generations as well as creations, and these come forth into manifestation. For the law of evolution in its great ascending arcs, as well as in its intermediary processes of growth between the various arcs and degrees, is of the ETERNAL ONE, and it obtains right up to the realms of the Gods.

THE OFFICE OF ORIPHIEL

It is this great and glorious mystery that is reflected within the seventh sphere of the Divine World. That reflection is the Word of GOD revealed for the Soul's mind. The revelation is interpreted by Oriphiel. He is the most sacred messenger of interpretation upon the seventh Divine Sphere. Though in writing of him one has had to individualize him, yet he is more than a formulation of the Divine Mystery. *He is the vehicle of the Elohim for the distribution, within that sphere, of knowledge and power unto the Soul. And that sphere is the vehicle of the Elohim for all Divine-Angelic ministry unto the various realms of the Gods; though each Celestial realm has its corresponding sphere.*

Great is the Wisdom of the FATHER-MOTHER revealed in those transcendent ministries through which all the embodiments of HIS Sacred Mystery are unified, and become sharers in the revelation of that Mystery through embodiment and ministry. For the one law obtains within each embodiment, and reveals itself in the departmental ministry which obtains from the innermost sphere outward and downward, even unto the Angelic realm of such a world as this is.

It will thus be seen that Oriphiel represents such Divine administration as touches the whole creation, and makes of all the Celestial, as well as all the Divine embodiments, a glorious unified whole.

It was an unfortunate association that philosophy gave to Oriphiel when it confounded him with Satan, or the Maya influences which obtain where materialization has taken place and the realms of realities have been changed into those of illusion. For Oriphiel is no fallen Angel, nor mal-administrator, nor deflector of Soul magnetic streams, nor a potentate holding the realm of spiritual darkness. Only a deflected vision within any child of the FATHER-MOTHER could have led to such a misrepresentation of one so high and holy, so Divine and of the

Eternal, so Godlike and part of the Eternal Mystery and motion; for he occupies the place of the Arche-Presbuteros of the Heavens. He is the Angel of the Arch of the Divine Sevenfold Mystery. He is the Friend of all who worthily approach the Divine World; for unto such doth he mediate of the FATHER-MOTHER Mystery whereby the whole Being of the Initiate becomes enriched and empowered so that ascension may take place through the realm of Oriphiel. Thus, through his ministry, he becomes not only guardian of the portals, but also the shepherd for GOD, who mediates in opening the portals to the Being in the hour of the Soul's most transcendent realization, and, in this most real sense, leads that one through all his Sphere, to the threshold of one yet more inward.

* * * * * * *

THE PORTALS OF THE SIXTH SPHERE

When the Soul has accomplished its divine processional journey through the seventh sphere counting from the Divine Centre, and has offered itself sublimely in sacrifice upon the high Altar, into which all the motion and purpose and ministry of that sphere are upgathered, then the Soul approaches the gateway of Anael.

In entering this sphere, the Initiate passes through the portals to touch and be touched by those Divine Elements, which experience to the Being eventuates in the Soul's acquisition of the power of harmony, and brings the endowment through which the divine secret of that harmony becomes known. For, like the seventh sphere under the administration of Oriphiel, the sixth sphere is reigned over by Anael; and the sphere itself is the concrete expression of the ultimates of all intonation. It is, therefore, a sphere expressing the divine harmony as that obtains in the innermost. It is, therefore, the sphere upon which the magnetic streams of the Eternities meet and dispense power.

Within the Being of the Initiate there is the correspondence to this sphere. Therefore, when the Divine World would communicate in some specific way unto the Soul of its harmonics, the motion of the Eternities gives such intonation within the Initiate's sanctuary of Being as enables him to understand and interpret the Divine Will. For all true harmony is a resultant of the motion of the magnetic streams of the Eternities breaking upon the elements of the sixth sphere. It is thus that Anael becomes the sweet song of GOD, for such is the meaning of the name. It is a realm of divine harmonics, where the highest symphonic combinations are met with. All the spheres are full of music, but the intonations resulting from their motion are heard within the sphere of Anael. The divine artist who has to create in formulations and express divine ideas in concrete form, derives his inspiration from Oriphiel; but the divine musician feels the inspiring motion of Anael. For Anael is unto the musician, the exposition in rhythm, in motion of the breaths, and in sound or intonation, of the harmony which crowns the motion of the Eternities, as these move in obedience to the Will of the FATHER-MOTHER.

THE REALM OF DIVINE HARMONY The reader will thus recognize the transcendent nature of the experiences entered into within the kingdom of Anael. He will sense something of the sacred mystery of divine motion, the manifoldness of the rhythmic action, the sublime resultant of the breaths, and how it comes to pass that transcendent harmonies can be created and given forth.

All harmony resulting from the intonations produced from the perfect rhythmic motion of the spheres, proceeds from the realm of Anael, even though that harmony has to be expressed on the outer kingdoms. It is in this way that all true music is inspired, though the realm of its relationship and exposition may be mental, soulic, angelic, celestial, as well as divine. The quality is related to the realm of the manifestation, and is also dependent upon the receiver, which, in this case, is a Human Soul. In this way all true music is related to the seven spheres of the Innermost World; and wheresoever the sweet song of Anael is sung, it is perfect after the degree in which it can be expressed within that Soul and through the realm wherein the interpretation and exposition take place.

Herein it will be perceived that all music worthy of the name is related to the Divine; but the intonations through which it is expressed are related to the realm of the manifestation and interpretation. Thus it comes to pass that a perfect composition may have for its realm of manifestation and exposition, the lower mental, or the higher mental, or the lower spiritual, or the higher spiritual, or the angelic, or the celestial, or the divine. And these seven realms in the Human Soul can receive, according to the degree of their culture and the Soul's realization, and the purpose for which the harmony is to be expressed, the vibrations which play from the Inner Worlds as these are gathered up into and sent forth from the sphere of Anael. Thus the reader may perceive how the sweet song of GOD in perfect rhythmic motion and combination of intonation, may be sung, orally or instrumentally, upon each of the planes of the Soul's consciousness according as it is affected from the Inner Worlds.

Here we stand upon the threshold of the Great Mystery. And as the Soul ascends through the sphere of Anael, it acquires a wealth of interior knowledge concerning motion, its primary causation, and the sacred purpose hidden in it but made manifest in most glorious manifold resultants. And having passed through the most blessed experiences following upon its ascension through the seven degrees of the sphere of Anael, it is prepared, through the wealth of the divine riches within it, to enter the portals of which Salamiel is the guardian.

THE REALM AND OFFICE OF SALAMIEL

The fifth Divine Realm from the Innermost, outward, is that wherein the Initiate is brought face to face with the most sacred mystery which lies at the very heart of all motion and all manifestation. The portals which open to the Initiate, and, in a sense, close behind him, admit him to the realm of the spiral breath. Like the two preceding realms, it is full of the Mystery of God, unveiled to all who can dwell there, but veiled to the Initiate, and only revealed as he processes through the kingdom represented by that fifth sphere. Within this realm, motion is not only felt and heard, but it is cognized and seen. It is the realm corresponding to the realm in the Soul where the Divine breath moves through the spiral of Being. The sacred mystery of creation is learnt from Salamiel who here becomes God's vicegerent. He interprets the mystery of the Soul's fashion through unveiling to it the mystery of Divine Fashion, and how the most sacred Breath, from the Divine Centre magnetically projected, flows through the realm of which he is guardian. And here I would say, as in the case of Oriphiel and Anael, that, whilst Salamiel is a most glorious embodiment of the Divine Mystery, and therefore intimately related to the Eternal Arche, yet he is not to be thought of in a merely personal way, nor individualized to the extent of losing the divine universal significance of his presence as God's vicegerent within all the realm of which he is guardian.

The Divine secret is hidden in the Arche. The Arche is the magnetic Mystery of the spiral, the divine spiral.—That spiral, as expressed on the Divine Kingdom, is absolutely perfect and complete. As that sacred Mystery has to be expressed in more outward realms of manifestation, it must needs be accommodated. Before this Mystery the Initiate may well cry out from the depths of his Being, *Oh, the depth of the Mystery of the Love of the Father-Mother! Who is equal unto the fathoming of its deeps? Oh, the glory of the Wisdom of the Father-Mother! Who is great enough to receive unto the full comprehension of His most transcendent revealings?*

As the divine Initiate responds to the motion of the Breaths flowing through the Spiral, and accomplishes his ascension through the various arcs, the most sacred Mystery of the Most Holy One becomes more and more realized. For, as the

Soul ascends, the consciousness of the living stream of the Divine Mystery deepens as that Lifestream moves through the Soul's own corresponding spiral; and, through its motion, the Soul enters more fully into the conscious realization of its oneness with that glorious Mystery; and, as the sacred Bowl which crowns its spiral receives from out the Chalice of the Divine Love, there is a commensurate deepening consciousness and an ascension of the Being into the fourth sphere of the Divine World.

THE SPHERE OF RAPHAEL THE COUNSELLOR

Passing through the portals which admit the divine Initiate into the fourth realm, which is the sphere of Raphael, the Soul is participant of the Divine Counsel. For Raphael is the glorious Archangel of the middle sphere of the Divine Kingdom, through whom all counsels are issued ere they pass into the sphere of the Spiral Breath and the realm of Harmony and that of Divine Embodiment, through the gates of Oriphiel into manifest creation. For Raphael is the Divine Counsellor through whom the FATHER-MOTHER issues commandment unto the various glorious systems. For though each system has its own corresponding sevenfold sphere through which the ELOHIM act by means of Angelic vicegerents, yet the primary source of all Divine Counsel, is this sphere of Raphael. The Soul in its growth and evolutory acts receives counsel from this sphere, deputized unto it, and accommodated according to the degree of the world whereon the Soul is manifesting, and growing, and evoluting, and according to the degree of the Soul's own spiritual estate. But when that Soul, through Angelic and Celestial acquisition and attainment, becomes a divine Initiate, it can be addressed directly by Raphael, and led through his sphere. It is the realm of the Divine Wisdom. All counsels are related to the Divine Sophia. For all administration, Divine, Celestial, Angelic, Solar, and Planetary, is related to the Divine Wisdom.

The reader will thus glimpse the sacred mystery of the

universality of the realm represented by Raphael, and will know that the Soul who is a Divine Initiate and who is able to enter that realm and pass through the sphere which Raphael represents, moves in the very Sea of the Wisdom of God, and becomes conversant with the Divine Purpose as that Purpose is communicated unto worlds and interpreted in their manifestation. Within that realm the Initiate knows the Divine Wisdom by the process of realization. But realization itself is the result of the ministry accorded to the Soul and mediated unto it within Raphael's kingdom. And it knows that though Raphael is a most glorious embodiment of the Divine Mystery and the vehicle of transcendent Elohistic motion, yet he is not to be regarded in a limited personal and individual way, but rather as the concentrate exposition and power of the glorious Presence of the Father-Mother.

Through the most blessed education received by the Soul within the sphere of Raphael, the whole Being is enriched to such a divine degree that the Initiate attains the power by which the next sphere may be entered and possessed.

THROUGH THE PORTALS OF ZACHARIEL

Having attained a status so high and glorious as to be crowned with the radiant Wisdom of the Father-Mother as revealed in the realm of Raphael, the Heavenly and Divine Counsellor for the Father-Mother, the Initiate approaches the portals of which Zachariel is the guardian, and passes into the kingdom of the Presence. It is the third sphere, and is radiant with the glory of Him up into Whom all that is, is gathered, and out from Whom all that is to be doth proceed. As the divine Initiate is led through this realm, the consciousness grows and deepens within him that he is in the realm into which all things are reflected, and through which the Gods themselves know all things. For it is the realm of the Divine Omniscience.

In the realm of Raphael the Soul contacts and learns of the Divine Wisdom as expressed throughout the sphere of the Heavenly Counsellor, and issued to worlds as from the Divine

Commandant. But in its ascension to the realm of Zachariel, it becomes cognizant that it breathes the very atmosphere of the Omniscient ONE. And as it moves through that most glorious sphere of transcendent radiance, the consciousness within it deepens of the honour conferred upon it to be so empowered and graced as to be made participant of that knowledge which belongs alone to the heart of the Eternal Mystery we name the FATHER-MOTHER. There Zachariel will unveil, in such wise and in such measure as the Initiate may be able to receive, of the Eternal Mystery of the Omniscience of the FATHER-MOTHER. And the Soul will know that, whatsoever heights it may yet climb in the degree and intensity of the Divine Mystery within it, and howsoever vast may be its journeys through the sphere of Zachariel, and however great the wealth of knowledge it may gather in such journeying, yet it will always know that it is a child of the Eternal Mystery who has been gathered up in consciousness into the realm of Omnisciency for purposes of realization and ministry, and that it only touches that realm through its conscious realization of HIM Who is ever The Omniscient ONE.

THE REALM OF THE PARACLETE The sphere of Zachariel within the Soul is that of the Remembrancer. His ministry unto the Initiate in an individual way, is therefore Paracletic. He gives that aspect of ministry of the Indwelling Holy Guest or Ghost Whose operations within the Being are to ultimate in the Soul remembering all things appertaining to the Divine Love and Wisdom, according to the degree and the measure in which the Soul has realized the Divine. For it is only through such an individual ministry to the Soul that it becomes possible for the Initiate to ascend into the sphere of the Divine Omniscience. Zachariel officiates for the Initiate as the appointed High Priest, unveiling to him, as he is able to receive, the divine secret lying at the heart of the great mystery of Omniscience; and by such a mediation, Zachariel leads the Initiate from degree to degree of that consciousness through which the glory of the Divine Omnisciency can be beheld interiorly and soulicly realized. And by means of such a high priestly ministry, Zachariel brings the Initiate into that estate of realized Divine Life, as enables the latter to be quite at home whilst moving through the glory of the realm or kingdom of Divine Omnisciency. And the Initiate thus gathers power to ascend to yet greater altitudes wherein he may realize potencies in a measure far exceeding anything he has yet met on his way to the divine citadel of all Mystery of Being.

* * * * *

THE KINGDOM OF THE OMNIPOTENT

Having accomplished his ascension through the sphere of Zachariel and gathered in of the mysteries revealed there, the Initiate is so enriched and empowered that he may now pass through the portals of the second sphere whose guardian is Michael. The office of this Archangel is that of Omnipotency. He is spoken of as the Strength of God. Now, whatsoever of Divine Omnipotency has been met with by the Initiate on his high journey to the citadel of the great Mystery, when he passes through the portals of this realm, he enters into the stream of the Eternal Mystery which flows from the Divine magnetic Centre. For the second sphere is that of the great Sea, spoken of as a Sea that is like crystal, transparent and translucent, and so living that all things that have Life live by means of it. It is the sphere whence all Divine Potency proceeds unto all the worlds. It is the magnetic Sea whose action gives potency to all things. All power is derived from it. All Life is contained in it and sustained by it. It is the sphere wherein the secret of the mysterious Divine Love is contained. And no one can discover or know that secret until, as divine Initiate, the Soul passes through the portals of that sphere.

The Soul contacts the accommodated stream that flows from that sphere all through the journey. The more outward the realm, and the lower the degree entered into and realized by the

Soul, so is the intensity of the magnetic action of that stream accommodated. But as the Soul ascends and moves inward towards the Divine Centre, the magnetic action of that stream intensifies.

It is thus that an Initiate cannot be other than moved by the Mystery of the Divine Love. Though the term is a simple one, easily uttered in human speech, yet in that which it represents it is most complex, its ramifications great, and its accomplishments mighty. For all divine potencies made manifest in creation, have their origin in the motion of the secret elements of which Divine Love is composed, and are the expositions of the polar action of that Love. It is Michael who is the divine apologist for the Lord of Being. For Love in itself is the greatest and highest Divine Apologia. The mind, the reason, the intuition, touched by the sacred wand of Michael, move responsively to the magnetic motion of Love. And the heart, which becomes the chalice of His outpouring, knows verily that there is no other power in all the universe so great, so holy, so righteous, and so glorious.

HOW MICHAEL MEDIATES OF OMNIPOTENCY

The Initiate, having passed through the portals of Michael, therefore, finds himself in a realm of such glorious Love in its Divine motion, and in its creative, generative, fashioning potency, that only through all the Initiate has learnt on the way, is he able to endure to stand upon the threshold of that sphere and look upon the glory of it. And only as he is led by Michael, who is the very embodiment of the Infinite and Eternal Love in the Omnipotency of its motion, is the Initiate able to endure the tremendous magnetic effects upon and within himself, as he moves through the arcs or arches which mark the way from the threshold to the innermost of that sphere.

The reader who has been able to follow me thus far, will now be able to recognize how it comes to pass that, when a Soul is divine Initiate and ascends in its state through the spheres, its magnetic lifestream is not only intensely affected as it passes from sphere to sphere, but it also has this experience when it enters the sphere of Michael, that its magnetic stream must become one with that of the Mystery we name the FATHER-MOTHER. For Michael operating within a Soul, works upon and through its magnetic centre. This centre is the Divine Principle. It is the Arche. It is, therefore, the magnetic Love-centre.

Now the measure of a Soul's capacity to receive of that magnetic stream, to endure the motion of the Eternities which it contains, is the measure in which Love itself has been realized. For the Initiate can function within that sphere only in the degree in which the Love of which it speaks has been realized. Even the divine Initiate can cognize, recognize, appropriate and realize the Divine Omnipotency only in the measure in which the divine potencies of the Being have become one with the Omnipotency of that sphere. Thus, within the Initiate the realization of the Divine Omnipotency will be commensurate with all that he has gathered in and appropriated from the ministry of Michael, as that glorious one has communicated, in degrees of ever increasing intensity, the sacred Mystery of the Divine Love.

When a Soul is called upon for purposes of high ministry to lay down its attributes on the divine oblatory, it is Michael who stands upon the threshold of the Soul's corresponding second sphere, and addresses it as Ambassador for GOD. It is Michael who stands upon the banks of the Brook Cherith and doth minister unto the prophet. It is Michael who brings to the Soul, when in its aloneness it is realizing Elijah, the Bread energized by the Fire, and the cruse of Living Water. And it is Michael who overthrows Abaddon, or the powers and potencies and works of the Darkness, and calls the Soul who is awaiting the Presence by the River Chebar, to take its place in the great redemptive and regenerating work of the Divine Love and Wisdom. And it is Michael who leads the Initiate to the threshold of the first sphere of the Divine Realm, of which Uriel is the guardian.

URIEL: THE SACRED FLAME

The divine Initiate who would have his experience ultimate in the absolute oneness of his Being with the most sacred Mystery we name the FATHER-MOTHER, must needs pass through the portals of the realm of which Uriel is the divine and eternal representative. It is possible for the Initiate to be content to be a dweller and server within any of the preceding spheres, and be at one with the Divine Love and Wisdom as expressed within and through those spheres. It is possible for the Initiate to sense and appreciate the Divine Purpose revealed in the motion of those spheres, even whilst he is on his way to the very innermost. But if he would be all and in all, in and with and for the Eternal Mystery of Love and Wisdom, he must be prepared to partake of and become one with the Mystery expressed within the first sphere or realm of Uriel. For the Divine Man is seven-fold in his consciousness: his realizations are upon all the spheres. The glory made manifest within each in their ascending arcs, will fill his innermost Being, lighting up all the spheres of his consciousness, *even unto his knowing of the divine secret contained and hidden in the heart of Uriel.*

THE ALTAR OF HOLY FIRE

Uriel represents the most sacred Fire. He is the embodiment, as the Sacred Flame, of the resultant of the motion of the Eternal Spirit, as that most glorious One moves through the elements in their first estate. He is the corporate Presence of the Eternities, representing in his fashion the innermost aspect of Deity as the most Holy Fire. It is from him that proceeds the flaming sword which is said to guard the way. It is through his motion that the "tongues of living flame" can sit upon the Initiate's brow. It is through his energizing motion that the most sacred Mystery stream of Divine Love flows through the spiral of the Initiate, lighting up the seven lamps of his Sanctuary, thus giving to him the seven-fold Holy Fire and Flame. He is the Abrahamic home of the Soul. And when it is said that Abraham went out from the land of Ur, a great mystery is implied, relating to the Planetary estate and subsequent history. For Ur of Chaldee is related to the land of the sacred Fire. Through Uriel doth the LORD speak as the I AM THAT I AM. It is through Uriel the fire is kindled and kept burning upon all the Altars of the Most High. He is even of that sacred Fire which it is said the Seven Angels of GOD in obedience to divine command, filled their censers with and then cast upon the Earth unto its purification and healing.

The Initiate who passes through the portals of this first sphere, rejoicing to be welcomed by Uriel, and by him led through the realm in which he is GOD'S vicegerent, will realize that all which he has gathered on the way coming through the spheres, here becomes so energized that the Initiate, in all his potencies, elements, essences and attributes, becomes like the Divine. And if he can endure to pass through this sphere from its first threshold up into its Innermost Sanctuary, he will henceforth be, in a microcosmic sense, a living flame of GOD and for GOD. And though he will still retain his individuality and be cognizant of functioning through a personal vehicle for ministry, yet in his consciousness he will no longer be even individual, but one in the Absolute World, one with the Eternities, one with his LORD, one who in his consciousness is ever in the Presence of the FATHER-MOTHER.

THE DIVINE ANNUNCIATOR—GABRIEL

There is another great and glorious servant of the FATHER-MOTHER who is also one of the Divine Hierarchy and the vehicle of Elohistic ministries. He is known as the Archangel Gabriel. He does not reign in any of the seven spheres as vicegerent for GOD, yet all the spheres communicate through him. In his state he is transcendently glorious, and in some of his offices he becomes the Angel of the Presence. To the seven spheres he acts in the capacity of communicator. His office therefore is often ambassadorial as understood in the innermost realms. In his office he reflects into the various realms that which is to be accomplished through them and by them in their ministries unto systems, unto GOD's Hosts and Angels, and even unto the Human Soul. He is not the sum of the seven. The LORD alone in HIS seven-fold Elohistic Mystery is the sum of all. But Gabriel is the revealer of the Divine Purpose. *He is God's annunciator.*

It is thus that into all the spheres that which is to be accomplished through motion, activity, creative ministries, perfecting ministries, is communicated. And it is in the same sense, though in the lower degree of embodiment and manifestation within the Soul of a divine Initiate, that Gabriel announces the coming of the LORD. It is through the light reflected through the Being by him as the Angel of the Divine Countenance, that the Soul arrives within its consciousness at the knowledge of who it is, what it is, and the ministry it has to render for the Divine. He announces to the Soul as it passes through the various spheres, that which has come to pass within it. And when the Initiate has accomplished his journey through the spheres, it is Gabriel who announces to him that which the Divine Love and Wisdom hath purposed concerning his estate and the office which hereafter he may fill in blessed ministry for his LORD.

Thus the reader will understand how it comes to pass that Gabriel is the Archangel of the Annunciation, through whom the Divine Love heralds His approach in the day of most glorious realization by the Soul and manifestation of the LORD through such an embodiment as the Soul is capable of expressing. For it is thus that divine revelation and manifestation come.

THE FESTIVAL OF CORPUS CHRISTI

THE FESTIVAL OF CORPUS CHRISTI

A MOST SACRED MYSTERY Though the day appointed for the festival of Corpus Christi was last Sunday, yet the influence, and even the ministry, of that festival proceed through the week and culminate to-day. This is what is called *the octave* of the festival of Corpus Christi. Those of you who are familiar with the liturgy of that festival as sung and recited within the Church of Rome, will know the importance that is attached to the festival. And although it is celebrated in the Anglican Church, it is in a very minor degree in comparison with the celebration of the Festival in the Church of Rome.

As the term implies, it is "the Festival of the Body of Christ." It follows that great "Festival of Pentecost," wherein it is supposed that the Heavens were opened and that there was experienced such a baptism of the Spirit as had not been in previous ages; that, as a result of that baptism, all the intimate ones who were named Apostles of the LORD were specially endowed, so that they spake in tongues other than they were wont to do; and that the most marvellous phenomena accompanied this outpouring from the Heavens; and that, as a result of the witnessing of it, the Christian Church as known to-day took its rise.[1]

The festival of Corpus Christi, you will observe, is put a week afterwards. It celebrates the giving of the Body of the LORD for the world. But as the LORD is supposed to have ascended up into the Heavens to be for evermore at the right hand of the FATHER-MOTHER as the intercessor in high priesthood on behalf of the children of men, in order that a memorial of HIS Presence should abide; and, that that memorial should be so affected from HIMSELF that it would become even as HIS own Body, the sacrifice of The Mass was instituted.

It is thus that *the Host* takes its place as the first of all sacred things in the Sanctuary, and in the worship of the Roman

[1]*Vide* Article on PENTECOST, pp. 163-179.

Catholic Church. If you have read the liturgy appointed for the Festival, you will know the vast importance attached to belief in the reality of that memorial, in the outpouring of power from the Heavens upon that memorial, in the changing of the elements of the bread and the wine until they become the Body and Blood of the LORD, and cease to be merely memorial, but are now to be regarded as the actual living Substance and Lifestream of the Divine Mystery.

HOW THE CHURCH REGARDS THE MYSTERY

And you will also be aware of this outstanding fact, that the Church teaches that, as this memorial is the living exposition upon the earth, and is placed upon the high Altar of the Sanctuary, of the Lord of Being, therefore it is essential that everyone should partake of it; and, also, that whosoever partakes of it worthily, actually partakes of the Flesh and the Blood, the Sacred Substance and Lifestream of the Divine Christ.

It is thus that the multitudes have been held. It is thus that the Host is revered and worshipped. It is because of this cultured belief in the mind, and the effect of its motion upon the emotion of the heart, that the multitudes have been held through the ages. For they mean to revere the LORD, to worship the elements of HIS Being. They mean to partake of HIS Substance, and to drink in of the living Stream called HIS Blood. And whatsoever there may seem to be of superstition in the belief, yet, in the case of many, it is an enlightened superstition. For in their belief they hold that the LORD of Love has HIMSELF left this memorial, and that continually into it HE is pouring of HIS own Mystery; and that, through the presentation of it to HIM, it becomes so highly transmuted that the elements themselves cease to be symbols and of the nature of only an outward memorial, and that these elements become actually the Substance and the Spirit, the Flesh and the Lifestream of the LORD.

On such a festive day, the Mass assumes a higher aspect of meaning for the devout and enlightened worshippers.

And you may be sure of this, that where such a doctrine has been able to hold enlightened men and women through the ages, Souls enlightened and cultured in mind and heart (for the saints have been in the Church, and they are the most cultured in heart and mind, of all the children upon this world), there is something more in it than there doth seem to be; and that whatsoever there may appear to be of superstition has had a foundation of truth out of which to grow; and that even wrong belief is but a misdirection of the mind concerning great truths. For, as has been recently shown to you, all the great doctrines are of the Truth; it is the interpretation of them that has been and is at fault.

THE TRUTH HIDDEN IN THE MYSTERY

Now, the festival of Corpus Christi is a memorial service with a deep symbolical significance; indeed, with such a signification that, if the Soul pursues it unto its octave, it ascends into high Soul estate, high estate of consciousness, high estate of vision, high estate of realization.

The Mystery is true. The Body of the LORD was given for the world. But that Body is the Divine Substance out of which all things have become, and the Divine Lifestream that energizes all things.

It is also true that on rare occasions when the need arose in this world for what have been named *Theophaneia*, or Divine Appearings, Messengers were sent; and that the Messengers had to be, within the Heavens, the Manifestations in embodiment of the very Substance and the Magnetic Stream of the Divine Love and Wisdom; and also, that where the Manifestations had to come on to the outer planes, as in the case of the Master's appearing in the days of the Manifestation, the whole life had to be caught up into that Divine Realm where the Lifestream of the Divine Mystery could affect it, fill it, and pass through it in every degree of its constitution, for manifestation unto the outermost vehicle, so that that vehicle itself in its outer substance took on something of the glory and became the symbol of the Mystery of the Body of the LORD.

But the LORD is universal; and HIS Body is universal. HE is in all Substance, and HIS Lifestream flows through all. So to put HIM under the limitations of even so high a Servant as a Messenger, is to change the meaning of HIS Body from the Universal and the Absolute, into the relative, the individual, and the personal.

This is just what happened to this Sacred Mystery in relation to the Master and the memorial. He was thought of as the LORD. The body spoken of in the Festival of Corpus Christi, is the body of the Master,—except where the mystic souls perceive the inner significance, and only use the language as the symbol of the inner meaning.

THE MYSTERY ASSOCIATED WITH THE MASTER

The memorial came to be associated with Him (the Master) and with His outer body, through a misrepresentation and consequent misinterpretation, and, as a result, an entire misunderstanding of the words He was supposed to utter on the eve of His betrayal. The words were,

"*This is My Body which is given for you.*'
"*This cup is the new testament in My Blood,
which is shed for you.*"

It is the Body of the LORD that is broken for the world, even through HIS saints in their travail. It is the Life-stream of the LORD that is given unto the world for its healing, even in the outpouring of every noble Soul, every child of the FATHER-MOTHER who loves HIM and lives for HIM to bless others. And the same truth holds good in relation to the Master. Whatsoever of giving had to be made manifest through Him, it was the LORD HIMSELF Who was giving. You will understand this yet more fully bye and bye, namely, that you cannot give Love, Soul Love, Divine Love, without giving the Body and Lifestream of the LORD. For you give what has been given to you of HIMSELF; and every good and perfect gift cometh from HIM Who is the Great Giver, Who is our Substance and our Spirit, in Whom we live, and move, and have our Being, and apart from the consciousness of Whom there is no Life. There is no Life except it be in the consciousness of HIM, Whose Divine Flesh and Blood are in us.

And now we will look at what this festival in the Human Soul signifies, what it signifies for the Human Soul, what it signifies for the world.

The Body of the LORD spoken of as Jesus Christ the LORD, was a Body of glorious manifestation. The manifestation had several degrees, and those were in states. And in the unveiling of these degrees once more, I would answer a question not infrequently put to me concerning consciousness. It is this—*Wherein does the consciousness of Christ differ from the consciousness of Jesus, and the consciousness of the Lord differ from that of the Christhood and the Jesushood?*

THE BECOMING WITHIN OF THE MYSTERY

The festival of Corpus Christi is the festival of the becoming of the Body of Christ in us. It is the changing of our mortal states into immortal states with immortal conditions. It is the elevation of all the attributes within us, from the merely human degrees of experience, into those degrees which are represented by Jesushood. For a Jesushood does not only represent that which is pure and beautiful, gentle and loving and lovable. It represents the Divine Man in the degree of a human manifestation, wherein Life is lived not for itself, but for all the children of the FATHER-MOTHER unto whom that one can minister. For Jesushood represents the state realized as the blessed festival of the Body of Christ becoming in the Being's attributes. But as that Body is ever given for the world, no Soul can become a Jesus without giving himself or herself for the world in the degree represented by the estate of Jesushood. In the measure in which a Soul enters into the Jesus consciousness, realizing the Love that makes Jesushood possible and which clothes it with the radiance of the LORD, the Body of the LORD is broken for the world, and HIS Blood is poured out from the cup of that Soul.

The giving of the ministry of a Jesushood, is the distribution of the Bread to the multitudes. It is the mediating of the Body of the LORD, the reception of which brings purity. For no one can receive the Truth to hold it, without becoming pure like Truth itself. No one can receive the cup to drink of it, without being exhilarated by its contents and constrained to seek unto the realization of that to which it points and calls.

So that the festival of Corpus Christi is made manifest in every life that lives the embodied Jesushood. Such a Soul is eating of the Bread and drinking of the Cup. It is the Bread which is Heavenly Wisdom. It is the Wine of GOD, which is the Blood of the Lamb accommodated to the estate represented by Jesus.

THE TRIPLE DEGREES OF THE FESTIVAL

Now, in the measure in which a Soul becomes one with other Souls in breaking the Bread of Life unto them through its own attributes, and pouring out from the cup of its Being the Wine of the Divine Love, so that Soul expands in consciousness. Jesus grows in stature. From the first degree of manifestation He grows to manhood in the Grace of GOD. When a Soul so loves, it grows in the Grace of Jesus Christ. Grace is the beauty of Love. Its garments are the exquisite revealings of the Divine motion which gives the beauty of radiant Love.

As the Soul manifests, its consciousness grows more and more, until it learns to be one with all, to have a part with every Soul in that supreme Love. Here it enters a realm that is spoken of as cosmic consciousness. This is a term very loosely used in speech and writing in these days. All consciousness is cosmic in this sense, that we all derive it from HIM Who is at the heart of all things. But to possess in realization such a degree of cosmic consciousness as would be associated with a perfect Jesushood means that the Soul's consciousness, through a state of Divine Love made manifest through embodying and giving, through realizing and outpouring, has reached that degree of universality and of oneness with all Souls upon the earth; understanding yet more and more the Mystery of the fashion of a Soul—at least, understanding its attributes and its history; and, as the consciousness expands, taking in the whole planetary household, until in the perfect cosmic consciousness (as that term may be applied to the planetary estate of Jesushood), the Soul knows the world, the World-Soul, the Planet-Soul, and, in the fulness of that cosmic consciousness, can look through the planes which are invisible to those who look for objective phenomena in all things, and understand through that consciousness the Mystery of the Divine Fashion in the heart of the Planet, and the Mystery in some degree, though not in full degree, even of the Planet's Travail.

Jesus is a lover of Souls. He is a lover of Souls everywhere. He is a lover of all Souls, whatever their degree and whatever their state. Geography and race put no limitations upon the vision of that Love and the outpouring of that Love. For Jesus loves all and forgets none, according to His degree. That is Jesushood. He could not have the cosmic consciousness, even in a planetary degree, without loving all and forgetting none.

THE FESTIVAL IN THE STATE OF JESUSHOOD

You will understand then, how Jesus is said to have loved every one; how He cultured Love in His intimate ones; how He urged them to learn to love, assuring them that, unless they did learn to love unto the perfect Jesushood estate of manifestation in which the Body of the LORD could be broken for the world in the distribution of the energies through service, and the outpouring of the magnetic stream in the giving of Love, whilst they might glimpse the radiance of the Christ Realm (from which, from time to time, they received illumination), they would never be able to rise up into the octave which those

Realms represented, to dwell there, and to abide in the consciousness which must obtain there.

It was thus He urged that they should love one another. "Greater love hath no one than this, that one lay down his life for his friend." Ah, yes, for a friend! But then, are not all the children of the FATHER-MOTHER, so far as their relation to HIM is concerned, one's friends? For in high Jesushood, there is neither family, nor tribe, nor nation, nor people, nor race in the earthly sense. He is a Son of GOD in the first great degree of the Theophaneia, or the Divine Manifestation of the Mystery of GOD in an embodiment.

Now you will understand that unto the multitudes it is Jesus who is to be mediated as the embodiment of GOD—the Flesh of the LORD. It is the Love as expressed in Jesushood which, in the planetary sense, is a universal Love. It is like the Divine Love, loving all and forgetting none. It is not a loose sensuous love, full of earth-desire. It is the Love of GOD; therefore, it is pure; it is beautiful; it is Spiritual; it is Divine. It seeks and acts divinely, desiring only to give in the doing of those things which bear the impress of the Divine.

The world needs the mediation of Jesus. It is only when Jesus reigns that the world shall be redeemed. For redemption is the healing of all life through the reign of true Love. Perfect Love gives perfect vision; and it touches everything unto healing. There is nothing shut out of the Jesus vision. None are passed by in the Jesus Love. The Jesus ministry is withheld from none who seek it. Where the Jesus love reigns there is no stint of devotion. It is not confined to the sanctuary for one or two hours a week, and then no worship elsewhere. In Jesushood, every hour of the week is a worship of the Ever Blessed ONE. Though you may not bow before the sanctuary altar, yet from the Altar of your Being where HE Who is the Living LORD doth mediate unto you that ye may give of HIS Love to the needy, and thus mediate for HIM unto HIS children, ye may bow worshipfully, and adore.

Oh, you can make everything reflect Jesus, if only you will touch everything with the glory of the Jesus embodiment. And it is thus that Jesus is to reign. There is no other way. The world has had persons reigning for great ages; but since the days wherein the glorious Theocracy passed away and Israel as an Oligarchy ceased to administrate from Him, this world has known nothing but sore travail and the agony of conflict upon every plane.

THE FESTIVAL IN THE ESTATE OF CHRISTHOOD

Now if you will mediate of Jesus, being in yourself a memorial of the Presence of the LORD of Love Who is ever in the Heavens; if your own life expresses HIS Substance, and the magnetic stream of your love be as the Wine of HIS Own Heart, then those things that come to you in glints and gleamings in passing hours and in all too fleeting days, will come to abide with you. You will not only touch the Christ Realm of consciousness and realization, but you will gradually ascend into it.

The Christ Realm is one that relates you directly to the Solar Body, the centre through which the LORD of Being ministers unto this system. The Christ Realm is the Realm of Light. It is the Realm of *the abiding radiance.* It is the Realm of high illumination. It is the Realm in which all things become interpreted to the Soul who enters into it fully, and who acquires the power to function within it and reach unto the octave.

Christ interpreteth all things. But Christ is no man. The Christ may interpret all things to you through the LORD'S Servant; but you can understand the interpretations only in the degree that you enter the Realms to which they refer. You may glint them through the mind, and relate them, and correlate them; yet the full understanding of them can come only in the measure in which you enter the Christ Realm.

The cosmic consciousness of Christhood is as far beyond the cosmic consciousness of a Jesushood, as the Solar light is in excess of the reflected light of the individual members of this system represented by the planets of which our earth is one. For the perfect Christ consciousness is Solar. And even the Children of the Sun, the Children of Love, and Life, and Light—those Children who once knew something of the glory of that Body—have to return unto it again by the Divine Processional known as the Festival of Corpus Christi. They have to enter into and realize its first degree of manifestation in Jesushood as the living memorial; and then pass fully into the Realm of the Christhood, though occasionally touching it as the Love-motion carries the Being in the service of Jesushood wherein the Soul gives itself even to one, or the two, or the few, and then unto the many.

When the Soul enters into the Christ Realm to abide in it, that Realm abides in the Soul. It is always potentially there; but when entering the Realm, it is the meeting of two magnetic streams which are related to each other. As the LORD abides in Jesus through His wonderful attributes consecrated to the embodying of the LORD Life, and through the motion of the Love stream in its beautiful outflow in blessed ministry, so HE abides in the Soul through the Christ Realm, giving to it gradual increase of vision, and, through the vision, increase of consciousness, until the expansion of it passes beyond all the bounds of a world like this, (though this Earth is a great world,) and the Soul enters the Realms whence the glory proceeds by which all the Planet-Souls are illumined, and all the Souls upon them derive their energy and their illumination.

Therefore, Christ interpreteth all things in the history of the world, in the history of a Soul, in the history of a community, in the history of a nation, in the history of a race, in the history of a planet with its Hierarchy, such as this world is. For the history is known only within the Solar Body and is reflected through the Christ Realm; and from that Realm only can it be interpreted.

Therefore, you will understand what it means for Christ to be the exposition of the LORD, and for HIS Body to be given unto the world. It is the unveiling unto the Soul, in the measure in which it can enter into the Realms, of the glorious Mysteries associated with that Realm. And the outpouring of the Blood of the Lamb from the Body of the LORD, is the octave, or higher degree, of the meaning of the Divine Lifestream as that obtains within the Solar Realm, and ministers from out the heart of that Realm unto this world and all the System's members, and unto all the FATHER-MOTHER'S children in the measure in which they are able to receive of that magnetic stream.

So the Christ-cosmic consciousness is a Solar consciousness within the Soul, wherein the high Initiate, having entered the Christ Realms and risen up through the octave wherein the Festival of Corpus Christi or Body of the LORD is consummated, knows from that Realm, is illumined from that Realm, interprets from that Realm, lives in the consciousness of that Realm, is one with those who dwell within that Realm, even with all the glorious Angels and Archangels. And the Initiate feels the play of the great magnetic radiations spoken of as the motion of the ELOHIM, or voices of the Seven Thunders, which are concentrated within that Realm in manifold sublime embodiments for glorious ministry.

THE FESTIVAL IN THE ESTATE OF LORD-CONSCIOUSNESS

Now you will understand how Christ is of no man, no people in an earthly sense, of no tribe, or nation, or race. He is not even of any one world, in a world-sense. He is of the Logos, or the WORD of Divine Substance. He is of the LORD ADONAI as embodied and realized in that Realm. To no man does He belong, being without earthly parentage. To no people does He belong, for He is of no human race. Yet He belongs to all peoples, and to every Soul. Of no individual world in the system is He the Creation. Yet, if He were commanded to pass from one world to another, because He is of, and from, and for the LORD, He could move through those Realms. If one in such Christhood were called from out any of the embodied manifestations of the system of Sol, to enter the Divine Realm itself and abide for ages in ministry there, that Soul, having the consciousness associated with the Divine Realm, could live in it, move in it, endure the vibrations that play as the exposition of the glorious embodiment of the LORD's Body and Lifestream. For such a Soul would be one with such a Body.

Therefore, when we call you to follow Jesus Christ, it is no shibboleth of earthly belief, but the Voice of a transcendent vision, the outcome of profound realization. It is unto a Fountain of Being and of Living Force that ye are called. It is to participate in a Body of which you are a member. It is a Body vibrant in every part of it. It is so alive that henceforth you live not for yourself, but for that Body in its manifestation, in its giving, in its outpouring. Henceforth your life is lived for the Heavens. It is not Life in a realm of dreams, but Life in a Realm where the dreams are interpreted into everyday action. Whatsoever your ministry may be there becomes a ministry for GOD, a ministry wherein the Body of the LORD is broken unto the blessing of many, a service wherein the Lifestream of the Lord is outpoured unto their exhilaration; and still on and on, until your embodiment in ministry becomes perfect in its inspiration and its fashion.

It is a glorious ministry of attainment and outpouring, is this Festival of Corpus Christi. No ordinary ceremonial could ever express it. No belief could contain it. There is nothing superstitious about it. It is the sublime realization of the LORD within the Sanctuary of Being. It is the unveiling of the splendour of HIS Holy Mystery in the sublimity of its motion within the Soul, and the exquisite concentric exposition in concrete fashion of all that most Sacred Mystery stands for in the Life embodied.

It is the LORD Who doth these things. HE doeth all things well. You need have no fear of missing the mark if you dwell in the consciousness that HE is near you, and is about you;

that HE is, through HIS blessed ministries, encompassing and upholding you through HIS glorious One overshadowing and leading you into these blessed states and degrees of manifestation, even until you are so much one with Emmanuel that you know HIM; that HE is no longer apart from you; that HE is not even a Presence outside of you, though the Angelic World ministers from HIM around you, and HIS most holy Mystery named the *Cloud* overshadows you; for you are so much one with HIM that your life is lived consciously from HIM and in HIM; and all your Life becomes HIS own embodiment in you and through you.

THE OCTAVE OF THE FESTIVAL And you will not misunderstand this, that, in such a state, there is never any claim to be HIMSELF. There is never any claim by the Soul to be the LORD. There could not be any claim to be HIS Christ. For Christ realized in the Soul, is the state up into which the Soul is elevated. But GOD'S Christ in the Heavens, is the LORD ADONAI Who filleth all the Heavens—all worlds and all systems. Therefore, the more the Soul knows HIM, the less it knows itself in a personal and individual sense. The more it knows HIM, the more it knows that it is HIMSELF that is revealed in anything that is beautiful, everything that is true, anything that is equilibriated, so that it is exquisite in its motion, sublime in its vision, and divine in its breaths.

So you will understand that even in the Festival of Corpus Christi wherein the Soul has realized Theophaneia or the becoming of GOD within the Being, there is nothing personal, though the personal becomes a vehicle for the revealing. There is nothing individual; for the individual is swallowed up into the Supreme and the Absolute, though not unto the losing of its individuated expression. In its consciousness the Soul is always one with HIM.

Oh, when you know HIM, you know the Supremest, the most glorious of all Embodiments. If this world in its unfallen state was beautiful, beyond interpreting in language; if a

Human Soul is wonderful beyond compare in its fashion; how much more so is the Solar Body that contains them all, and all such embodiments in the system? And yet the Solar Body is but one transcendent celestial expression of HIS Glory. How, therefore, could we describe HIM Who filleth all the worlds? And how could any Soul attain to the consciousness expressed as HIMSELF? HE is Omniscience. Yet that of which we have spoken in the Jesushood and the Christhood as appertaining to the Soul, comes also into the Realm of HIS Presence in such fulness that, in consciousness, the Soul so endowed can pass from system to system, from Hierarchy to Hierarchy, from Centre to Centre, even until, through the becoming of HIMSELF in that marvellous octave wherein the Festival of Corpus Christi receives its sublimest realization, the Soul knows HIM *there*, derives from HIM *there*, is overshadowed by HIM from *thence*, is filled by HIS Own glorious Lifestream as it proceeds through all the Realms from *the* Divine Centre.

May this day be for you that octave of Corpus Christi wherein the Jesus manifestation will become sublime, so that the world will know that the LORD, indeed, has come again! And in your own inner Life, may this day bring some measure of that high Festival of Corpus Christi wherein the realization of the Glory of the LORD shall be so great that your Sanctuary will be flooded with HIS Glory, and you will behold evermore in HIS Light, that your Gates shall no more be shut, and that within you there shall be no more any thing begotten of the night!

If these things thus become unto you, they will be the prophecy for you of that still more transcendent realization we spoke of as the Solar consciousness, with its sublime ultimate being absolutely one with HIM, and one in HIM.

O Transcendent LORD! Who is equal to the unveiling of THY Glory even as THOU art expressed within a Human Soul and a world like this? How inadequate our speech is and our potencies are for the revealing of THEE as THOU shouldst be revealed, and as we would fain reveal THEE unto THY children.

Ever Blessed be THY Glorious Name, THOU Who lovest us all! As THY children are able to receive, THOU dost mediate unto them through THY Servant. We would ever bless THEE. We would ever worship THEE. Evermore would we adore THEE.

Ever Blessed be the Name of our LORD! Ever Blessed be the Most Sacred Name of that Mystery of our FATHER-MOTHER which HE has written within us!

THE SABBATH OF THE LORD

THE SABBATH OF THE LORD

THE PROEM OF CREATION

The word Sabbath means *rest*. The idea of the Sabbath, so far as sacred story is concerned, is associated with that remarkable proem of the creation found in the book of Genesis where it is said that God created the Heavens and the Earth in six days, and rested on the seventh; and that He called that seventh day "The Sabbath"—that is, *the rest*. There is but little, if any, mention of the Sabbath until Israel is moving away from bondage. According to the story of the deliverance of Israel from Egypt, the Sabbath is then named, and from that time on it occupies a large place in Jewish story. Though it is inwoven into the history associated with the Jewish people, as if it had been specially related to them; yet it was not, but belonged to the Mysteries held by Ancient Israel, and was of the Greater Mysteries taught by them. What that Mystery was we would here unfold to you.

To take the primary thought into consideration first, is to show that the word could not mean *rest* in the sense of cessation from all activity. For there is no rest in the Universe, such as we understand by it. In the Divine and Celestial Realms, the Powers "rest not day nor night." Even amidst the lower Realms of manifestation, that which may be accounted rest is also a time of unseen activity.

A SECRET FOUND IN BEING

The Sabbath of the Lord signifies something hidden in the very heart of universal Being, and is expressed throughout the whole of creation. That it does not imply rest even for this world, must be known to you, whatever uses men may have made of the term. For, on the Sabbath day, which was the seventh day of the week (not the first as we now account it), the earth rotated, and does rotate, just as on the other six days. Nor is her motion round the solar body in any whit changed because it is the Sabbath day.

Even in our own life there is no cessation. Life is begotten of motion. It is the resultant of the motion of the Breaths amidst the glorious etheric elements. Where there is no motion there is stagnation or crystallization, though many believe that where there is even crystallization, there is a certain degree of motion. When we rest the vehicle during the day or in the night watches, there is no cessation of activity, except in the sense that we are not active in walking or in serving with our hands; and if we sleep, the mind in its outer ministries is inactive; but the circulatory system proceeds just as in the hours of our activity, though with reduced motion; and even the mind is active elsewhere, and the Being is learning and serving. There are times when even the Being has to know rest; but at such periods there is no cessation. Therefore, the term Sabbath, most sacred as it is, must have other meanings than the idea of merely resting from activities.

We will glance, first of all, at the inner significance of the call of the Sabbath. There must be some divine meaning in it, however mixed the story associated with the Sabbath day has become, and however mistaken the notions of men and women in relation to GOD's Sabbath may have been.

PERIODICITY SIGNIFICANCE OF THE SABBATH

The call of the Sabbath to a time of rest, one seventh of every period, must have some spiritual, soulic, and divine significance. It had a large place in Israelitish history. There was the Sabbath day—the seventh day of the week. Every seventh year was a Sabbatical year. It would do the land good, even now, if it could be carried out. For in Jewish history the land had to lie fallow every seventh year. Provision was made in the previous year. Though the real meaning of the story, as we shall see, is mystical, yet if men understood the inner significance of things, even of the elements, how different everything would be, how different life would become!

Then in addition to the Sabbatical year, all the festivals, of which there were many, came to be spoken of as the Sabbath, "the Sabbath of the Lord," "the Festival of the New Moon," "the Sabbath of the Passover," "the Festival of the Passover," "the Sabbath of the Tabernacle," "the Festival of the Tabernacle," and other festivals we might name. Nay, so great was the ramification of the idea that it entered into the whole of the life of ancient Israel, and became also significantly expressed in the days of earlier Jewry when there was such a thing as the Jubilee; and the Jubilee was the year in which all who had had the misfortune to lose their inheritance, having had to sell it or to sell themselves and their families to serve, were, by the very proclamation of the year of Jubilee, redeemed. They were not only set free, but all that they had had to lay down was returned to them. And that was the crown of the seven times seven Sabbaths. It was a fiftieth Sabbath.

You will see the full significance of this presently, when we speak of the meaning of "the rest."

That we should be called to rest one seventh, must have its significance, even outwardly. If men and women would give a seventh of the day to the spiritual aspect of things, instead of scarcely even minutes, if any, to enter into the Silence and reflect concerning the Lord of their Being, to think inwardly and upwardly, to soar above the mundane conditions into the realms of Seraphic realization (and all can get up there in some degree), how beautiful the idea would be in having a seventh of the week for rest from a world activity. There was a time in our own country when it was thought that to do anything on the Sabbath, or seventh day, or the day that was set apart for the Lord (though in the western world the Sabbath is the first day), was most wicked.

THE BONDAGE OF FORMALISM

I remember well in the days of my boyhood in this life, the strictures passed where the least motion that did not seem consonant with the Sabbath was condemned. Yet the idea of the Sabbath as we know it to be, was so utterly inverted that those who blamed, were themselves in utter bondage, bondage to their tradition.

Their mistaken interpretations of what is beautiful, spiritual, soulic, Angelic, Celestial, of the Gods, and of the Divine FATHER-MOTHER, made them slaves of traditional beliefs.

Yet it would do the world good to have one seventh of the activities of the week directed otherwise than into the world in its material activities, in its wealth-seeking, even in its pleasure-seeking, in the human sense. Nor could men and women be blamed if, after the travail of the week in the work-shops, they sought the great Temple of GOD where the sun shines and the sweet breaths blow, desiring to hear only the voices that spake amidst the trees and the flowers, and through the visions that came to them there. For lovers of the Good could be in the very heart of the Sabbath amid the Cathedral glories of Nature.

Yet it would be good if men and women could remember, and put it into experience without any feeling of bondage, that to worship within the Sanctuary of their Being is Sab-batical; and also, that that wondrous, divine quality may be expressed within and through them in an earthly Sanctuary. For it is possible to convert into a veritable inner shrine where the Presence is, an earthly House of Worship. *But they must take the shrine with them.* The mere earthly fashion of the shrine does not make it a spiritual or divine shrine. The Sanctuary helps the inner motion to find expression and reali-zation before the shrine of the glorious One. But the realization is within. The outer symbol can only help the inner motion to express itself, and in that expression to realize itself.

That man should have been called to observe the Sabbath, and to keep it holy, must have an inner significance quite beyond any interpretation that is put upon the term Sabbath, historically or ecclesiastically.

It is through certain kinds of rest we gather nourishment and strength and recuperation, and thus are enabled to be fitted for the service that will call us. Even when the trees in the park, in the gardens, in the forest seem to rest, as in the winter months, there is no cessation of activity, though there is an indrawing of vital qualities, leaving just sufficient to keep life in the more outward expression of the form. But the inner spirit is in motion downward. It is in the winter days that the tree extends its roots and gathers nourishment out of the soil to quicken it and to strengthen its hold, and also through that ingathering to prepare for the day when the spirit within it may make manifest again in the exquisite foliage, and in bloom, in the case of flowering trees, and in the fructifying trees, to express the essences of that spirit in the fruits. And within our Being it is so in the time of real rest. There is no cessation from activity. There is an ingathering, an enriching, an upgathering, and through these, a preparation for wondrous manifestation.

This will become clearer if we look at the Sabbath in relation to the fashion of man.

MAN CONTAINS THE SECRET OF THE SACRED SEVEN

Man is built upon the principle of the seventh. He has seven sevenths. The great creative Spirits are seven. And although man is fashioned out of Divine Substance, the motion of those holy Breaths expressed as magnetic centres, results in the creation and manifestation of man. The creation itself, in that wonderful proem of the Book of Genesis, was a Spiritual, and Celestial, and Divine history. It was not a story after the order of the interpretation given to it in traditional teachings. It was a Mystical Drama of the Soul, presented in hieroglyphics.

In the world creation man is set forth in this fashion. He comes out of the great Deep. His elements are chaotic, apparently, but fashioned through the motion of the Divine Spirit, and brought into a state of high polarization, until he becomes individuated consciousness of a high order, with inherent potencies which enable him at last to come into the knowledge and the realization of the Sacred Mystery out of Whose Bosom he has been emanated by the process of Divine Generation.

Man is so fashioned that he is built up of seven. Seven is the sacred number. The Seven Days are in him. The sacred Mystery which is expressed as seven times seven, is in man. We shall have to speak of those seven sevens in terms that are not easily understood or even expressed. For it is easier to use terms than to make them so luminous that all may understand them.

From the central Principle of his Being, man has seven planes. Two are related to the outer, or the realm of manifestation. Such a realm extends beyond the physical. Man will have those two planes wherever he goes, to make manifest and serve. Then there are two related to the intermediary; and two to the inner; and then the seventh is that which is balanced in the innermost. His Sabbath is his seventh. It is the seventh day from the without inward. It is the day within him of the central magnetic Presence wherein he finds equipoise.

Every one of the seven planes has also its minor seven. There are seven degrees within each plane, and each plane has its Sabbath. Man has to learn, in every realm of manifestation, the seven great degrees of experience. He has to receive, he has to assimilate, he has to transmute, he must needs gain energy, he has to come into illumination and knowledge. He has to realize the potencies of all these in combination. Man is so gloriously fashioned that there is nothing left out of him. For, through those planes, he can contact all the realms. By means of them he can ascend in his estate of consciousness from degree to degree till he reaches the Sabbath. He can even move upward from one Sabbath to another Sabbath, that is, from the seventh of the outer to the seventh of the next, and from that to the seventh of the next, and so, inward until he comes to the seventh of his seventh plane.

From all this you may begin to see how the Sabbath is inwoven into our Being. You cannot get away from it. Indeed, to understand it and let it be expressed, is to fulfil the Divine Law of your Being.

THE SABBATH RELATED TO EQUIPOISE

Sabbath means rest. Rest means equipoise. If the Sabbath of God be in you, every plane will be equipoised. You will not have deflection here and there, and uncertainty how to go, and uncontrolled desire. All will be controlled from within. Ye will learn patience. Ye will learn forbearance. Ye will learn endurance. Ye will learn gentleness. Ye will learn to be strong in gentleness. Ye will learn true majesty, and yet with it be in a state of true lowliness. Ye will acquire power, and yet in the manifestation of it, be as tender as the Divine Love. Ye will attain to Divine Love realized. Love is in them all; and to learn Love, is to learn it in realization. In that Love, you come to know the meaning of God's Sabbath.

We have the two outer planes,—a vehicle for the outer, and the atmosphere through which the mind looks and operates.

We have the two intermediary,—the mind in its upper reaches, and the heart in its exquisite emotions through which Love itself looks out, and through which it pours its streams and reveals itself in blessed motion.

In the Innermost we have that which is of the Soul itself balanced between its magnetic Mind, wherein is the divine Understanding, and its radiant point, or centre, which becomes the magnetic centre of its Intuition.

And then, crowning these, we have that Sabbath, that Sabbatical plane which is balanced from the Spirit, and through which the Spirit has its motion in us, even down through all the other vehicles and planes, unto the outermost. But you will note this, that even if the inner be balanced and the outer be not balanced, the effect of the motion of the innermost reaching into the outermost only disturbs it the more until it is brought into balance.

And it must be so. For that disturbance which comes to the life (which you must have recognized from time to time), is not begotten of anything outside of you, but of some motion within you. It is the result of lack of equilibrium and equipoise, or that rest which is the Sabbath of the LORD. And so the motion of the Spirit disturbs the superstructure until it gets the balance; and as soon as the balance is restored, there is equipoise. How exquisitely beautiful is the Divine creation of a Human Soul right from its Spirit or the Innermost Mystery, through its magnetic will and its holy stream of Love operating through all its planes, so that when the planes and vehicles are all equipoised, they have entered into the Sabbath. For they have all obeyed the Divine Command. To obey the Sabbath is to get into equipoise. To obey the LORD and to keep HIS Sabbath, is to become equilibriated, balanced in your Being, balanced in your Love, balanced in your emotions, balanced in your thought, balanced in your desires, balanced in all your activities.

Such is the Sabbath of the Lord.

Here we see the inner significance of the term in its relation to the Soul, every plane having its Sabbath, its seventh degree, and the seven Sabbaths signifying that quality within it which brings the jubilee wherein the Soul enters into all it may have gone out from. It enters into its inheritance which belonged to it before "the Fall." And since the Fall, all the degrees are represented in the resurgence of travail. Through that Travail, the Soul again enters into its inheritance. Its inheritance is the Sabbath of the LORD. "There remaineth, therefore, a rest for the people of GOD,—" The Sabbath of the LORD is for HIS people. *It is as clear as noonday, that that which awaits the Soul and its planes and vehicles, is this exquisite balance of Being.*

And now we will bring this wonderful truth to touch the festival of the passing days of Lent, and those that will come when the Lenten time is over.

THE SABBATHS OF LENTEN DAYS It must have occurred to you, and to you especially who have worshipped in sanctuaries where such festivals are very specially observed, that there are seven Sabbaths covering the period of the Lenten season—

six Sabbaths during Lent itself, and the seventh as the crowning victory in the resurrection.

Now, why should there be seven? At one time Lent only lasted some forty hours. Then it grew in the Church to a few days, extending to a week, and then it became of forty days' duration.

Has it never seemed strange to you that Passion Sunday should be the fifth Sunday in Lent, and Palm Sunday the sixth, followed by the Resurrection on the seventh? We know, of course, with whom all such days have come to be associated. And you can see the divergence of the true inwardness of Lent from being a most sacred Soul-Mystery, to the merely personal equation of the Master who is thought of as the LORD of Being. And it may be discerned how such a divergence prevented the Saints themselves from discerning the inner, spiritual significance of the Mystery of the Seven Sabbaths. They represent, in the process of self-denial and contrition, confession and manifestation of good works and of service, reaching to the fifth or Passion Day, the Soul in its Sabbaths. They represent the growth and unveiling of the inner Being through self-denial, through beautiful consecration, through loving ministries, and hence the attaining to the Day of Divine Passion. When does the LORD's Passion become a reality within the consciousness of a Human Soul? When it is on the fifth plane. It is in the Ætheric Body that all real passion is borne. It is the fifth plane that has to respond to the motion of that passion. It is that Sabbath wherein the Soul is reaching unto the sixth degree, and when it is feeling the inner power changing it, raising it, and using it. It is the passion of Love within itself, oft-times giving it sorrow; not from the Divine, but because of the motion of the Divine within its Sanctuary enabling it to look out upon what it would consider its failures, its shadowed garments, the misdeeds and the mistakes it may have made in life; thus causing it to sorrow in its passion through the intensity of its desire to be beautiful for GOD. And that Day leads to the next stage, which we only name in passing,—Palm Sunday. That is the Day of the Soul's triumph. It is not the day of its resurrection. But it is the day of its entering into the consciousness, in the first degree, of the Presence. Then follows the seventh Sabbath of the LORD which gives to it the resurrection, the raising up of the whole Being into the consciousness of the Divine power.

Thus you may see how those old world Mysteries have come down to be expressed in ritual without the Church knowing their meaning. They have relation to the inner Being. They are of the Soul. They are related to the Master and the Forty Days of the Temptation in the Wilderness, the Forty Lives of the Travail of the Oblation; but not to Him alone. They relate also to the Soul in its travail and its return. And they express the Soul's journey.

And you will note this, that between the resurrection morning and the day of Pentecost, there is the recurrence of the seven Sabbaths. And, also, that the Ascension of the Master is supposed to have taken place between the fifth and the sixth Sabbath, forty days after the resurrection. And thus we have the forty days, and then the ten days; and these are full of significance.

THE SABBATHS OF THE REGENERATION

Now the second round of seven Sabbaths bespeaks the ascension of the Being. That round of Seven Sabbaths relates to its passion, its triumph and resurrection into divine power, and then to the ascension of the Being into high estate of the Heavens. The Soul ascends first of all between the fifth and sixth planes. When the LORD ascended from Galilee is a story told in allegory, setting forth how the LORD within the Sanctuary carries the Being to the upper planes of Galilee, and prepares it to make its ascent from a high mountain in Galilee—the realm of the mind. The Soul ascends, first in its thought, then in its vision, and afterwards it ascends in its states of realization of the Presence. This latter is expressed as Bethany.

You will note that in the three different accounts of the Ascension, one is from a high mountain in Galilee, and another from Bethany.[1] It is said that "He led them out as far as Bethany." And then there is that other account of the Ascension from the Mount of Olives. Mystically they are all correct, though historically contradictory. The first is from Galilee —the illumined Mind. The second is from Bethany—the Soul. And then these are crowned by the third from the Mount of Olives. The Mount of Olives represents a state of Divine consciousness in which the Soul knows divinely, and has the power to look out upon the past. Herein the Soul knows all things in the Divine Omniscience, though the measure of knowledge is contingent upon the motion and conditions of life upon this world, or any world upon which the Soul may be functioning.

And then there follows as a result, the baptism. *This is the Jubilee. It is the second round of the seven times seven.* It is the immense baptism that is the result of Divine consciousness. It becomes the Cloven Tongue of Living Fire. It is the realization of the Immanence. The Being ascends Godward. The Soul proceeds to realize on the threshold of the Divine Presence. That Presence is the Holy Guest. Henceforth the Soul speaks in the language of the Spirit's motion, with all the tongues of the sevenfold Spirit, till every plane is reverberant with Divine power and motion.

That is God's Sabbath. It is the Sabbath of the LORD. By that is meant, the perfect creation unto realization by the Soul. The crown of creation is the perfect fashioning of man unto the realization of the LORD's Sabbath. That is the day in which such equipoise comes to the Being that it realizes in high estate the Presence within it, overshadowing it, and encompassing it. The Encompassing by the Presence is a defence and an upholding; the overshadowing is of the nature of a companionship and an illumination; and the Indwelling is a state of oneness,

---

[1] *Vide* THE MYSTERY OF THE ASCENSION, pp. 103-123.

or at-one-ment. In the Divine World, this is for the Soul the real Nirvana, wherein the Soul, though it is not lost amidst the immensity of diffuse consciousness, realizes the immensity of the Absolute One Who is within it and around it, permeating all things, and filling all things.

It is the Sabbath of the Lord. And the Lord demands that His Sabbath be kept upon every plane. You must get polarized ere His Week of Sabbaths can be observed. For each plane has its own Sabbath in its perfect equipoise through polarization in Him. Thus, through its travail, the Soul shall know resurrection again into the consciousness of Him; and that shall be crowned with the high ascension of the Being, until at last you can stand upon the threshold of the Inner Worlds in the Presence of Him Who is your Lord.

THE SOUL'S TRIUMPHAL MARCH

The mystery of the Sabbath of the Lord deepens from the day of the Soul's awakened passion, unto the day of the Resurrection. Through the deep motion of the Divine within it, its passion of Love expresses itself in exquisite obedience and consecration. And these enable the Soul to enter into the consciousness named "the triumphal march" into Jerusalem. For although that incident is supposed to relate only to the Master, and did actually relate to Him in the Heavens of His journey earthward, it also and very specially has this meaning for every Soul who is approaching the consciousness of childhood to the Father-Mother. For Jerusalem in the unfallen days, was not only the Holy City of the spiritual earth-life, it was likewise a state into which the Soul entered as a realization. In this relationship it was the Jerusalem which is from Above. The Soul enters that Holy City riding upon an ass and the colt of an ass,—by which is to be understood, a purified mind and body; the purification being the result of the motion of the Soul's passion. And in the unfallen world this process took place, though in it there had not to be the healing that has to be accomplished as the result of the fallen state.

Palm Sunday," as it is called, is that Sabbath of the LORD within the Soul who is functioning upon the sixth plane, having attained that triumph which is signified by the entrance into Jerusalem. What is carried is a branch of the Tree of Life, signifying the measure in which such a Soul has been able to partake of the Mystery implied in the Tree of Life. And the garments strewn on the way represent the various degrees of the clothing of the planes from the Heavens. For the Soul must take all its garments with it, each plane having its own.

Now, in relation to "Passion Sunday" and "Palm Sunday," it might seem strange that the Crucifixion should take place after such a triumph. For surely there have been travail and victory! But the inner significance of Good Friday, or the day of the Crucifixion, is this: the very triumph of the Soul leads it yet further; and as it approaches the Sabbath of the LORD represented by Easter Morning, *it has to learn to lay down everything, even Life itself*. For there can be no entrance into the Sabbath of the LORD without such a sacrifice.

That is the meaning of Good Friday—the day of religious tragedy in historical Christianity; but for the Soul the day of that triumph wherein it has acquired the power to give itself absolutely unto its LORD for Divine service. And then the result of such a giving is seen in the early dawn of the seventh degree of the sixth plane wherein the Resurrection takes place. The Soul arises and enters into the consciousness of the Presence in the measure in which it is able to receive.

Now, this relates to every Soul who attains to Spiritual Christhood. There is no other way. But though it is so great a triumph for the Soul who seeks Christ, yet it must not be taken for granted that it is the ultimate. Indeed, there seems to be no ultimate in the absolute sense for the Soul. But what we mean here is related to the Christhood.

THE SABBATHS OF MORTALS AND IMMORTALS

As there are seven Sabbaths between the inception of Lent and the accomplishment of the Resurrection; so are there seven Sabbaths between that glorious realization and the attainment of that which is signified by Pentecost. And here we would briefly indicate that, whilst the first seven Sabbaths related to the Lenten period portray the path of the Soul in its motion towards the first great realization of the Presence, the second round of seven relates to a higher order of Christ-consciousness, and, consequently, to a more transcendent realization of that Presence.

The Lenten seven describe the passage of the Soul in its mortal state towards that point of contact with the Divine wherein it becomes Immortal.

The Pentecostal seven denote the Soul as an Immortal Being undergoing the Regeneration, experiencing The Ascension in its threefold aspects from Galilee, then Bethany, and then the Mount of Olives, culminating in Divine consciousness wherein its seven Sabbaths in the post-Resurrection experiences have upborne it into The Divine Jubilee, wherein it comes into the possession of all the inherent properties of the Eternal Mystery which are within it, and knows in high realization, *The Lord of the Sabbath.*

Now, in a remarkable way, whilst the first seven Sabbaths, which cover the Lenten period, relate to the Mortals, the second seven relate to the Immortals. In this way the Lenten Sabbaths are more directly associated with the children of this world, and the Pentecostal Sabbaths with the Elect People, or the Ancient Christhood. And, whilst in the path of the Return, the Immortals or ancient Christs of God, naturally pass through their Lenten period, which is the day of their sorrowful travail, yet they can now accomplish that, and are accomplishing it, in this life; whereas the children of this world, who are of the Mortals, take ages to attain to the resurrection state. And it will now be also understood what is meant by the appearances of the Master after the Resurrection to His intimate ones. That He did appear to them, and was with them for many days after what is known as His crucifixion in this world, is true. But the Theophaneia and Epiphaneia have relationship to the Soul's vision, and belong to those children who were of the Ancient Christhood. For it is only after the Resurrection that the greater Mysteries are unveiled. This was even so, literally, in the experiences of the Master's intimate ones; for it was long after the Roman Crucifixion, whilst they were dwelling amidst the Galilean Hills, that He taught them intimately of the Sacred Mystery of the Divine Love and Wisdom as revealed in the Oblation. And it was during that period that He also unveiled to them their own intimate relationship to Himself, and their ancient high estate.

THE LACK OF UNDERSTANDING IN THE CHURCH

How little the Church understands of the Sacred Mystery of the Divine Love and Wisdom, on the one hand expressed in the Lenten ministries and experiences, and on the other hand unveiled in those Sabbaths which are supposed to have come between the triumphant morning of the resurrection wherein the Mortal becomes the Immortal, and the entering into the very "whirlwind" of the Divine Breath as it moves through the whole Spiral of Being, during what is named "the Pentecost!"

See what the Sabbath of the LORD means for us! See how the Sabbath has been misunderstood and misinterpreted! See how, like all the other glorious, divine doctrines lying at the very heart of humanity, and in the very heart of Christ, that wondrous doctrine has been abused, how it has become a source of bondage, and of hurt, and of darkness to the children! As if mere outward observances could please the FATHER-MOTHER and make HIM gracious and generous towards HIS children! Compulsion has made it a day of falsities and mockery! That which is irksome is not soulic. That which to you is irksome, contains something for you that has to be healed, either in you, or in the thing that has to be done by you. There is nothing irksome in the Divine Way. There is nothing begotten of the Divine Purpose that is of such a nature to the Soul. When you realize the Sabbath of the LORD upon each plane, you love everything HE asks you to do; because HE never asks you to do anything that is not in perfect harmony with HIMSELF, and, therefore, from the innermost to the outermost, in perfect accord with HIS Sabbath.

It is a glorious thing to know the Sabbath of the LORD; a transcendent thing to know HIM Who is LORD of the Sabbath. And it is into that experience HE calls HIS Children.

THE LORD OF THE SABBATH

Now you will understand the expression, "*The Sabbath was made for man.*" Also that other saying, "*For the Son of Man is Lord of the Sabbath*"—a wonderful scripture that has had given to it outward relationships and interpretations; but, doubtless, the meaning of it is dawning within you. For the Son of Man is ADONAI within the Being, realized by the Being; and HE is LORD of the Sabbath. When the Divine in the man and in the woman, realizes the Son of Man, ADONAI, that One is LORD of the Sabbath. Do you not see it? That One becomes the reigning Presence in the Sabbath of the Soul. It is man as a Spirit, as an individuate Being out of the heart of the Great and Holy One, becoming regnant over all the universe of his own Being, Lord of all its Sabbaths, Lord of that Sabbath which is the crown of them all; and Lord of them all, because the LORD is there.

The Son of Man is LORD of the Sabbath. He is equipoised. He can command his planes and his vehicles to obey him, to be obedient to the Divine Law of motion. The Sabbath of the LORD, therefore, means for you also, realization of HIM, illumination from HIM, empowerment in HIM; praise-motion, worship, and the power of service; adoration, the garment of embodiment by which HE doth become revealed through all the Being,—in the innermost motion, the mind's thought, and its purpose; the Soul's willinghood, the love's sacrifice, the heart's desire; the mind in its outer activities, in its purpose and ambitions; and the body or vehicle of the outer manifestation, in all its sensory experiences.

It is the Sabbath of the LORD, HIS day of rest, of perfect equipoise, in and through the equilibration of every power within the Being.

What a life ours is! I hear you say, "Yes, but what a life of travail it is!"

I am not oblivious of that fact. But the travail is contingent; and it is not of the Eternal, except in the sense of the motion of the Eternities within you. I see the Life. I see the fashion. I see GOD's Mystery. I see HIS wondrous creation. I hear again the call of HIS Sabbath. I hear that call made to every plane. I hear the call to the Sabbath of each plane to combine in the perfect polarization and equilibration that come with *that Divine Rest* for which the Sabbath speaks. I hear HIM anew saying to you amidst your travail, "There remaineth, therefore, a rest for the people of GOD"—a Sabbath for you, if you will take heart, if you will not lie down by the way, if you will persevere, if you will strive to bring the planes into perfect equipoise, if you will let the Divine urge within you bear you forward. For, in the Divine motion, He will bear you upward. If you will let the Divine Presence within you affect your Life, He will make the waters of your experience lap the shores of your life in gentleness. And even at times when storm-swept, and those waters dash against the shores of your Being, HE will keep you. HE moveth through the storm. HE allayeth the storm. HE walketh upon the waters. HE commandeth their obedience. HE doth speak to you :—

"O My people! Enter ye into the rest that awaiteth you. It is rest of mind, rest from desire, rest from ambition, rest for all emotion, rest for your feeling, rest for all your love, rest for your yearning begotten of the Divine urge within you. This rest is found in the perfect realization of My Presence encompassing you, overshadowing you, filling your Sanctuary; thus making your Lenten days a

triumph of Divine Passion in the Life of the Resurrection, and your restored consciousness of all Goodness intensifying until the ascension of your Being brings to you that realization expressed in the Indwelling of My Holy One, who is most wonderfully revealed as the Holy Guest. For such realization is My gift to all who enter into the high estate of the Sabbath of the Lord."

O Wondrous Love, Who hath so fashioned us! O Transcendent One, Who hath so exalted us! In the motion of our Being only can we express before and unto Thee, what we feel and know of Thy Love.

May the days of each of Thy children here be crowned with Thy Sabbaths, even until each one knows again in high estate "the Sabbath of the Lord!"

THE MYSTERY
OF THE
ASCENSION

THE MYSTERY OF THE ASCENSION

TRUTH AND ITS MIS-INTERPRETERS

The Ascension is truly a sublime Mystery. It is related to those things which cannot be objectively beheld, or even mentally apprehended, though it can be both seen and realized.

All great doctrines are founded in Mystery. Mystery means that which is within the Divine Cloud, in due course to be unveiled and made manifest. *All great doctrines have their origin in great truths.* That does not mean that the true interpretation of them has been given; but that they are founded in the sublime Mystery we name the FATHER-MOTHER; and that each aspect of that Mystery has a true interpretation.

The great doctrines whose affirmation and interpretation have filled the ecclesiastical and scholastic world with conflict, have been the cause of the conflict, not because they were untrue or lacking in truth in any particular, but because the true meaning of them was not understood, and the wrong interpretation was enforced.

It has been thus with the doctrines of the origin of man; of man as a divine child; of the Soul as a miniature of the sublime Mystery of GOD. Even the doctrine of the growth of man and the evoluting of his consciousness, by which dual process he moves onward and upward until he attains that of which the latent divine potency within him testifies and is prophetic, even the prerogative and inheritance of divine consciousness, is true. But the interpretation of the growth and evolution of man has been sad beyond words to describe, through the misunderstanding of the nature of *Divine Substance and Spirit*, and the motion of the Divine through such Substance; and also through failure to perceive the way of the Divine in the fashioning of a life which is to bear the Divine Image of the Sacred Mystery in its likeness, and endure the vibrations of the Eternities in its motion. The doctrine is true; but the interpretation has been greatly at fault.

AS WITNESSED IN THE HISTORY OF MAN

It is the same with the doctrine of the Fall, that Planetary deflection which brought about a change in the polarity and conditions of the elements, in the direction of the breaths of the Planetary life, and ultimately involved all humanity. Through that Planetary change man has become a fallen Soul. For he is not, even to-day, where he was before the great Planetary change took place. Indeed, it is only in quite recent days that he has begun to trace his way back again to the Life of unfallen days. The Fall is sadly true; but the interpretation given to it is mostly that of the child trying to find the meaning of some mythical story. The truth is there. The Mystery, which is Planetary, and related to cosmic things, must needs be unveiled to be understood; and, when rightly interpreted, whilst revealing the shadows that fell upon this world and crept into the minds and hearts of all the children—and thus darkened their vision so as to make their life to be lived through one long night, unillumined, except in most rare instances when the Messengers brought some exquisite story of the Divine Love—reveals also the Majesty of the Love that never fails, never forgets nor withholds, but that gives unto the uttermost to accomplish its most sacred Purpose.

And so with many other doctrines we could name, such as the Incarnation and Manifestation, the Resurrection, and the Mystery of the Oblation or Sin-Offering. All these are true. But they need the right interpretation to reveal the glory of the Love and Wisdom of the LORD of Being.

And it is thus also with the glorious Mystery of the Ascension. It is a mighty truth, difficult to apprehend through the mind, and yet apprehendable to some extent, and not beyond the full understanding by a Soul that finds illumination from the King of Glory, and enters through the Everlasting Doors of Being, with all the Gates or attributes of the Soul lifted up until they are clothed with the Glory of HIM Who is the LORD.

We will look at this Mystery as it is expressed in historical belief, and then in relation to the inner significance of it and in relation to the Descent.

HISTORICAL BELIEF IN ASCENSION

In relation to the historical belief. If we look at the Records of the New Testament, we shall find there three distinct portrayals of the Ascension; and those three are associated with the departure from this world of the Master known as Jesus. For, in religious thought, the Ascension is generally associated with Him. He is the one who is supposed to have risen up from these fixed planes, and passed into the Celestial Heavens. The way of it as told in the Records, is indicated at the close of St. Matthew's Gospel, which is also confirmed by St. Mark's. In the Gospel of St. Matthew it is said that, on the night of the Passover Supper, the Master said to Peter and to the other disciples, "*After these events have come to pass, I will go before you into Galilee.*" And then it is recorded that after the Resurrection, the Master met them all in Galilee upon an exceedingly high mountain, and that from it He ascended into the Heavens.

When we turn to St. Luke's story we are informed that after the Resurrection, the Master met two on the way to Emmaus, one of whom was named Cleophas; that He conversed with them as He walked with them on the way to Emmaus; that on reaching that village, He brake bread with them; that they did not recognize Him, because He had appeared to them in a strange form. And yet there was some remarkable attraction to Him, *so that their hearts burned within them whilst He spake to them of divine things.* And then, as He brake bread with them, their eyes were opened, and they knew Him. Yet, immediately, He vanished from their sight.

A little further on in the same chapter, it is recorded that He met and had speech with His intimate ones, and then, later, He led them out as far as Bethany, where He was suddenly parted from them and carried up into Heaven. And the disciples went into Jerusalem, full of praise and blessing.

Here it is implied that there was an Ascension from Bethany.

In the fourth Gospel, which is considered to be the mystic or gnostic story of the Master, there is no record whatever, nor attempt in any way to record the story of the Ascension. And yet its message is the most inward of the four Gospels. The story closes after a marvellous soliloquy on the part of the Master (though it is recorded as if it were an intimate conversation between the Master and His most intimate ones): and that took place in Galilee. It is the passage wherein He is reported to have turned to Simon Peter and said,—"Simon, son of John (or Jonas), lovest thou me more than these?" Those of you who have read the Logia will know that the words were spoken in an hour of most intimate talk with the Heavens, and that they comprised a soliloquy spoken by the Master concerning Himself. But there is no reference whatever to the Ascension, as ecclesiastically interpreted.

However, on the morning of the Resurrection, as recorded in the fourth Gospel, there is the first indication that there must be *an Ascension of the Being*. For it is said that the Master met Maria Magdalene in the garden; and that when she came to recognize Him, He said to her, "*Touch me not, for I am not yet ascended unto the Father: but go unto my brethren and say unto them, I ascend unto my Father and your Father, and to my God and your God.*"

THE ASCENSION SET FORTH IN THREE WAYS

Now, it is evident that there are three ways of the Ascension set forth in the Records, so far as they related to the Master. There is one from Galilee, upon a high mountain there; one from Bethany, when He was leading the intimate ones as far as that little city; and one from the Mount of Olives, where it is said he was taken up into Heaven, and a cloud received him, the record of which, found in the opening of the Acts of the Apostles, reports that the Angels appeared and spoke to the disciples and said, "*Ye men of Galilee, why stand ye gazing up into*

Heaven? This same Jesus, which is taken up from you into Heaven shall so come in like manner as ye have seen Him go into Heaven."

These things are named, not to point out the apparent contradictions in the New Testament, of which there are many, but to seek for their meaning as apparent discrepancies. People read the Bible with the coloured glasses on which they have had given to them (speaking metaphorically) by their teachers, and so they see what they read according to the colour of the glasses they wear. But the work of the Servant of the LORD, is to bring forth the hidden meaning in the story, and unveil and show forth the glorious Mystery of GOD as HE was unveiled by the Master, and as the Records purport to reveal HIM.

In the interpretive settings of historical Christianity, as the Ascension was related to the passing from this world of the Master, it is believed that He had power to appear and disappear at will; that He did appear suddenly walking on the waters of the Galilean Lake, and also pass through doors into the midst of the disciples. Not for one moment do I even hint that apparitions, as they have been named, are impossible. Indeed, they can be and often are most real. I have seen into the Heavens many a time. The Occult world has been open to me, and amid the play of the Astral Elements I have beheld forms in the lower occult, and also within the highest. And, like the disciples who are said to have beheld on the Mount of Transfiguration other forms than that of the Master, namely the LORD HIMSELF transfigured, and the ancient Law-Giver in a Divine Manifestation, and also that most glorious prophetic embodiment spoken of as Elijah, so have I witnessed the glories of the Innermost Heavens.

But these things were seen from within. It was thus the intimate ones beheld the Transfiguration. It was through the opening up of their Being. The Master took them to an exceeding high mountain. That represented a state of great elevation of thought and desire. In that state they were able to enter into the Beatific Vision as given from out the Cloud of

Glory. It was thus with them when they came out of the Cloud, that they saw no one but Jesus only. Yet, although all such things are possible, it was not after the manner of that vision that the Master is said to have appeared and disappeared after the Roman Crucifixion and the Resurrection.

In the historical belief it is supposed that the Master underwent a process of change after the Resurrection. Between the Resurrection and the Ascension some forty days are said to have intervened. During those forty days, it is believed He underwent a process of change, wherein there was such transmutation of His vehicles as would accommodate them to the Heavens into which He would have to ascend, in order that He should be able to carry the form that was crucified by the Romans up into the Heavens, and that there He should be the great Human-Divine High Priest, with His body changed, but bearing upon it evermore the marks of the Crucifixion.

THE THREE ASCENSIONS MYSTERIES

Such has been the endeavour of the mind to explain a sublime Mystery. Through the Oblation being misunderstood, the Ascension became misinterpreted. For those stories in the Records which set forth the Ascension, relate to Teachings the Master gave concerning the motion of the Soul as it takes the three high degrees of the Ascension Life, the first of which is in Galilee. For it must needs ascend unto the LORD from the heights of its mind. Man has to climb out of the valleys on to the heights, in the path of his evolution; and in that sense he is ascending. But he is still a denizen of earthly conditions, until he ascends higher. When he reaches the Divine heights in his vision, in his great longing, in the motion of his Being, he is then capable of ascending in his understanding, even unto the comprehension of much associated with the Mystery of the Divine Presence. And there is no understanding of that Mystery, except through the ascension of the Being. There is no true understanding of GOD, but through the realization of HIS Presence within us. We can apprehend only through the Understanding that which we have apprehended within the Sanctuary of our Being, and according to the measure of our realization. That is the first great degree of Ascension. The attributes lift up their heads and glimpse the glory that streams through the Doors of the Everlasting World.

Yet, if the Soul would go further it must needs be led, not only into Galilee and unto the heights called the Hills of Galilee, which are the uplands of the purified mind, but it must be willing to be led *as far as Bethany*. For the disciple must learn at Bethany how to pour out the precious spikenard of his Being, and anoint the Christhood. To anoint the vision of Christhood and express his love for that vision's embodiment, is to have a further Ascension. For such an anointment is accomplished by the process of realization; because Bethany is the home of the Christhood where the LORD loves to commune intimately with the Soul.

"*And He led them out as far as Bethany*" that is, as far as they could go for the time being "and was parted from them." All that is of the outer vision passes away in the hour of high realization. Through that fuller realization there is given to the Being power and illumination to interpret all outer things.

You may therefore apprehend that the Ascension from Galilee is true; and that the Ascension from Bethany is likewise true. But they are to be understood in relation to the Soul, and not simply in relation to the Master.

THE MYSTERY OF THE MOUNT OLIVET

Then we have the further statement that He ascended from the Mount of Olives. In this instance it is recorded that the Angels came unto the Galileans who had been on the high mountain in Galilee, and who had also accompanied Him to Bethany. For the state of Bethany is not far from that of Olivet. Bethany was but a short distance from the Mount of Olives. And although the Soul might have to pass through the garden that was at the foot of the Mount of Olives, called the Garden of Gethsemane (the Garden entered into through the Soul coming into the vision of the Divine, and which becomes also the garden of sorrow in the Soul's travail), yet, when the Soul can climb to the summit of Olivet and ascend into the Heavens from there, it climbs into the state wherein it acquires the power to look out upon, and into, and through the past, and also forward and inward into the Eternities. *Because Olivet is the Mount of Recovery.*

It is said that the Master sat upon Olivet and wept over Jerusalem, looking out upon the history of the city and the people. It was too sadly true of Him. His sorrow was over the whole of the Planetary conditions, the fallen spiritual household spoken of as Ierusalem, and what had befallen all the children within her gates.

It is said concerning the LORD HIMSELF, that when HE doth come again, HIS Feet shall stand upon Mount Olivet. But HIS return is unto the Soul. Then HE shall reveal HIMSELF within the Soul. HE will illumine the Understanding. HE will recover for the Soul the remembrance of HIS Presence and the glory of HIS Love. HE will restore to it the state of Emmanuel. HE will make Emmanuel manifest through it. And in that hour the Soul will know even as it is known.

Thus the Ascension from the Mount of Olives has great Divine Revelation in it. It is a story concerning a momentous Soul event, the inner significance of which was revealed by the Master Himself.

WE KNOW GOD THROUGH LOVE, GOOD AND TRUTH

Such are some of the associations of the historical belief in the Ascension; and such is the spiritual interpretation, partially set forth, of those three great Soul events from Galilee, Bethany, and Olivet. All truths, to be of value to us, must have a particular as well as a general relationship. It is not enough for us to be told that GOD is, and to be commanded to believe the statement. *We must know He is.* And the only way we can know this, is by the process of realization. That process can be accomplished, because GOD is in us. The Mystery of our life is that of HIS own Mystery in us. We are made in like fashion to image HIM. The Eternal Principle of Love is in us, with its Good and its Truth. Thus are we made in HIS likeness. Love, and Good, and Truth, are in us; and we know GOD only in the measure in which these are realized by us, because HE is Love, HE is Good, HE is Truth. We cannot know HIM in any other way than by realization. And that is accomplished through the Soul becoming one with HIM. You do not know each other because you walk by each other's side, and have casual conversation with one another. You may do that for years without knowing each other. To know each other you have to get into rapport; you have to be able to touch each other's Being. And there are some who seem to succeed in doing that very quickly when they meet in the way, as if they had known each other for ages. They get into a realm which they have touched before. They touch where they can know.

So is it in relation to the knowing of GOD. You may talk about HIM and worship HIM outwardly, and yet know really nothing about HIM. You can only know HIM through knowing Love, and Good, and Truth. Goodness and Truth are of the quality of Love. They are its dual reflections. *For Truth is the beauty of Love, and Good is its radiance.*

THE ASCENT AND DESCENT OF THE MASTER

And now we will look at the Mystery of the Ascension yet more intimately, in its relationship to the Master in His experiences. It has been associated with His descent from the Heavens. For even the orthodox belief teaches that the Master came out from the Heavens for the purpose of the Manifestation and the Redemption; and that, when He passed away, He ascended again into these Heavens out from which He had come. That is a belief held sacred.

I would like to set forth, in the briefest way possible, two great aspects of this. The first is an endeavour to teach the truth of the Ascension which will be found in some of Emmanuel Swedenborg's writings; and the other is apocalyptically hidden in that most mystical apocryphal writing called "*The Ascension of Isaiah.*"

Swedenborg, in his message relating to "the doctrine of correspondences," also taught that the Master, whom he regarded as the LORD HIMSELF, came to assume humanity in the human form, in order that He might accomplish that which would have the effect of making possible the Redemption. He believed that, after the Roman crucifixion, the Master descended into the Hells to bring them into order. For it was shown him that the Redemption could be accomplished only through bringing the Hells into order. Nay more! It was borne to him that unless the Hells were brought into order, the Angelic World itself could not be saved from disaster, as the effects of the conflict between the Satanic forces and the Heavens were such, that the Angels themselves were in great danger of falling; that there were those of the Angels who had become, as it were, tainted. He therefore taught that the LORD HIMSELF went down into the Hells and wrought the miracle of bringing them into order; and then, after the Resurrection, the Master as the LORD so changed His Divine Humanity by the process of transmutation, that He was able to carry that Humanity with Him in His Deific ministry, even into the Inner Heavens, and in this sense, reconcile Humanity with the FATHER-MOTHER. So that He, being one with Humanity, but having exalted in His own estate that which represented Humanity, Humanity could become one with the FATHER-MOTHER, and all the Angels could be saved, and the Angelic Heavens healed wherein they had been wounded.

Sublime truths underlie the statements of Swedenborg, though expressed under great limitation. The LORD had to cause the Hells to be brought into order. But it was not done in the way Swedenborg thought. For the Divine LORD could not descend into the Hells. When HE brought them into order, HE did it through HIS Servant whom HE appointed. HE entered into the Hells only in the sense of HIS Passion filling that Servant who was chosen for the purpose and endowed to enter into the hell-states unto the extinguishing of the fires that were prevalent in the one time Angelic Kingdom of the Planetary Heavens, where, indeed, the very Angels and the Sons of GOD suffered, and where the evil conditions in their activity were of such a nature as to prove of dangerous and inimical character to the Soul's upwardness, and even necessitate the Solar body to effect yet greater changes in its atmosphere. That atmosphere is now known as the photosphere of the Sun. (Of that Mystery I may not now and here speak.)

It is remarkable how, in such a direct way, although under such a limited vision, even Swedenborg testified to the reality of the Oblation. *For the Sin-offering was a descent into the hell-states.* And of confirmatory value is his testimony concerning the Planetary Heavens and the Angelic World, although the Seer, through the limitations of his vision and understanding, associated them with the Angelic Heavens of the Divine World.

He also taught that the Redemption was the changing of the hell-states, and the redemption of the Angelic Heavens; that that was the real Redemption; and, consequently, a provision was made by means of it through the Divine Humanity of the LORD, by which all the children could return unto the FATHER-MOTHER in the degree in which they were ready.

THE VISION GIVEN UNTO ISAIAH

But we turn now to another aspect, which though contained in what is regarded as an apocryphal writing, nevertheless has the heart of a true myth in it. It is called "*The Ascension of Isaiah.*"

In that writing it is represented that the prophet Isaiah was carried away from the planes of this world up through the Heavens, even until he reached the Seventh Sphere, the Inner Heavens; that there he was made to see a great conflict between the Divine World and the forces of Hell. And in the writing there is portrayed what he saw. In the Heavens he beheld one who was a Son of GOD, and who came to be named the Beloved

One, chosen to descend from the Seventh Sphere, and pass through the atmospheres and the elemental kingdoms of this world, until he reached the Human Plane; and there to undergo incarnation for purposes of a Manifestation and a further descent; and that he might at last have power to descend into the abyss, and enter into conflict with the supreme power of Evil, and overthrow that power; and then, having accomplished the Divine Will, to return as conqueror, bearing with him Redemption for all the children, because of the overthrow of the powers of darkness.

In the story it is also shown to the prophet, how the one chosen would have conferred upon him the power to assume a form consonant with the various spheres through which he would pass; so that no one even in the Angelic World could recognize that he was in such exalted state in the Divine World, and that he was descending into the Hells; because they would have objected to such a work being accomplished; they would have objected to any Son of God going down into such states, and entering into conflict with the powers of Evil.

And so he descended, as it is set forth, until he reached the Earth-planes. But the Angels, being so veiled by this manner of descent, did not know of the humiliation until the days of his return when he began to ascend into the Angelic World and pass through it again, and through the Divine Heavens, even until the Seventh Sphere was entered.

Though "The Ascension of Isaiah," as an apocryphal writing, is supposed to date back to about the middle of the second century, yet the myth itself is considered by many students to have been pre-Christian, and to have had certain glosses given to it by Christian scribes.

You will note the great truths underlying that which Swedenborg gave in the eighteenth century, and that which was given in the second century in this apocryphal writing.

You who have read some measure of the Teachings given under cover of the Order of the Cross, now know the real meaning of the Passion of the Oblation, of the Burden-bearing implied in it, of the entering into the Hells, of descending to their states, of the conflict with them, of the conquest over them, of the blotting out of the graven images upon the Magnetic Plane, of the purifying of the Elemental Kingdoms, of the restoration of the Angelic Heavens of this world to such a state that now it is possible for all Souls to pass from these planes in the hour of their translation, and to enter those redeemed and restored circuli of the Planetary Heavens, to find in them pure homes with pure breaths blowing upon them and exquisite ministries rendered unto them, and that they can there breathe an air from the Angelic World itself which will enable them to rise still higher, even from circle to circle, until they stand upon the seventh plane of the Angelic Heavens of this world, and look into the higher Angelic Heavens and commune face to face with the Angels, aye, even to receive the direct, wondrous ministries from that Realm.

Note that in both the writings I have referred to, there was first a descent, and that the Ascension was related to the descent. The Ascension was a returning into the state that had been left for purposes of ministry. But the Ascension, as set forth in Swedenborg, is one wherein even the physical form assumed by the LORD is carried up into the Heavens, though of course, so changed that it is etherealized beyond all the substantiality of an outer vehicle. In the apocryphal writing, the Master, who is named the Beloved One, has given to Him the commandment to bring the Hells into order, and to overthrow the Prince of Darkness.

All these allusions must needs be understood metaphorically. For although we have to contend against great powers, at times, *there is no personal devil,* though there are still many evil embodiments. The devil is the spirit of negation in every one who has that attitude towards the Divine. *There is no personal Satan.* For Satan represents the deceiving influences and powers, anywhere and everywhere. The Prince of Darkness is the power which veils the vision, and takes the Soul into the night of sorrow and bitter travail.

After the conquest the Master is said to have ascended up "on High," having had the power given Him to do so. Herein He was able to lay down His life, and to take it up again.

ISAIAH, THE PROPHET OF THE OBLATION

In this apochryphal history there seems to be a reflection of the Ascension story. If it was of the second century, which is believed by many, and was attributed to and given the name of Isaiah, then it is a remarkable thing that the real prophet Isaiah did see the travail of the Oblation, and write of it as no other prophet did. How may we otherwise account for all the remarkable statements in Isaiah which are borne out by the Oblation?

Now, there is a profound and far-reaching reason why the Ascension associated with the Master was impossible. For, after the Roman Crucifixion, He dwelt in the midst of the Galilean Hills, teaching intimate ones concerning the Oblation. He came out from the FATHER-MOTHER. In His consciousness He knew the FATHER-MOTHER. He was a dweller in the Inner Heavens. He could talk with the Angels. His fellowship was with the Gods. The glorious Hierarchies were dwelling places within His consciousness. Yet, when He passed away from these planes, it was not to accomplish the ascension into the Seventh Heavens again. No; it was an experience far removed from those heights. *Oh, would that it had been so for Him, and that the Oblation had never been necessary! What a joy for Him it would have been, to have passed again into the Heavens out from which He had come!*

You will understand that there could have been no sorrow in His heart if that was to take place. How could He have sorrowed in the Gethsemane, even if He had a few days burden-bearing before such a transcendent and glorious return? How could He have sorrowed, as He is said to have sorrowed, in view of such an immediate event? He sorrowed in His travail because of the approach of "the Prince of the power of the air," the Prince of this world, His betrayer, His afflicter. For He had to enter into conflict with that power and the evil potencies out of which the Hells had been generated. He had to enter into these Hells, and live for long years in Gehenna—the Valley of the Fires; and in Gehinnom—the Valley of unspeakable Darkness.

That is the meaning of the Saying that, "He descended into the lower parts of the Earth," into the lowest states into which the children had gone. That He had to do in the process of blotting out the graven images within the Planetary Angelic Heavens. For the Heavens were denizened by evil creations, and those had to be swept out of the circuli of the Planetary Heavens. That was the work of the Oblation. Therefore, the Redemption was not something He bore to relieve men and women of obedience to the Divine Laws, in the sense of satisfying divine Justice; but something He bore because of the Supreme Love that is ever just and exquisite in its balance, and upright in the motion of its Righteousness. For the equity of the Divine Love is so equilibrated that it never misjudges a Soul; it is so Righteous that it must have all within its world balanced. And so that Love satisfied its own just judgment in sending Him to bear the burden by which the Heavens could be equilibrated. He was sent to be the vehicle of Love's own Passion, and to accomplish the destruction of the enemy by means of the blotting out of those graven images. Thus was changed the whole of the Planetary Heavens. The burden-bearing made them again Angelic in their state, so that the Angels could enter them, and the children come to dwell in them. Thus were they to become again, as in the former times, the many mansions or states provided by the Divine Love for His children in their spiritual growth.

THE ASCENSION AGES AFTER THE DESCENT

How little the Church understands (and we say this most reverently), about this Mystery of the Descent to this world, the Divine Passion in the Travail of the Oblation, and the Ascension! Nor does it appreciate what it would have been for Him to ascend up "on High," leading captive that which had been in captivity. It would have meant something more for Him than taking the body He had assumed for purposes of the Manifestation and Burden-bearing, up into the Heavens. It would have been something infinitely greater than taking that vehicle up through all the starry hosts until He reached the Presence of the FATHER-MOTHER. For, during the manifestation years, that glorious Presence was always with Him. He lived in the atmosphere and consciousness of that Presence. But it was otherwise during the ages of the Oblation. If the Ascension was at the close of the Manifestation, then it was the ascension of His Being in its consciousness into the glorious state wherein He was always with the FATHER-MOTHER, as at one time He had been, that wheresoever He was, He was in that Presence, and in such a transcendent state as could not obtain in Him whilst veiled in this world, even such as He had before this world or cosmic order arose. Such an Ascension would have been the most transcendent realization of that Indwelling ONE Who made Him Emmanuel, and Who was Emmanuel ever unto Him, GOD in high Immanence, the Radiant Dweller within His Sanctuary.

Such would the Ascension have been to Him. Such is it to every Soul who attains to the estate of Son of GOD. That high experience is not the passing of the individual from this world to some other world. For by the mere transitional experience to another Planet, the Soul would be no nearer the great secret, nor the understanding and realization of it, there than here. *The secret has to be realized within the Being.*

The Mystery of the Ascension was contained in the Master's own Teachings. He gave it unto His intimate friends. He showed them how to ascend unto the FATHER-MOTHER in their estate, to arise in their Being, to lift up their Heads and let their Gates be open unto the Glory streaming from the Everlasting Doors, the Doors of the Eternal World, that the consciousness of the Indwelling Presence of the King of Glory should be theirs. *That is the Ascension of Being.* That is the Ascension which brings the Soul into the consciousness of the Presence of the Indwelling ONE. That is the Ascension which brings the glorious vision of the FATHER-MOTHER. That is the Ascension by which is changed our vision and substance, until we become like unto HIS own glorious Body. Herein and henceforth we reveal ADONAI in our likeness to HIM.

And this is the only way in which we can ever reveal GOD. We may endeavour to interpret HIM through speech or writing; but we can never reveal HIM in speech or writing. He is revealed through embodiment. We do not reveal Love through simply speaking about it, and writing about it, and persuading others to believe in it; we reveal it through embodying it. To embody it we must have it. It is in such a possession and embodiment that GOD is revealed.

The Ascension brings to all who realize it, those glorious qualities.

THE RELATION OF THE ASCENSION TO THE DESCENT

And now I would for a moment or two speak of those things which the Ascension means in relation to the Descent; in relation to the Divine outpouring; in relation to the Galileans who stand gazing into the Heavens; in relation to the children nurtured in the Home at Bethany; in relation to the splendour of the Galilean Understanding—the mind illumined through the approach of the Divine Presence to it; and in relation to the Master.

The Master's ascension could not be accomplished in any of the Lives of the Oblation whilst He travailed. For the Travail was the process by which the enemy was overthrown and the Hells blotted out. Whilst the closing cadences of the tragic song of each Life were deeply minor, they were also full of hope; because He was permitted to return into the consciousness of the Jesus-vision and the realization of Spiritual Christhood. But He was not permitted to proceed further in the process of recovery, lest He should amidst the travail of the Oblation discover who He was and what He had been doing. For, of each Life it might truly be said that the time was not yet. But after the Oblation was fully accomplished, then was He allowed to return into the consciousness of the Mystery of the Travail. That was the Mystery into which the Angels are said to have desired to gaze, as stated in the Epistle to the Hebrews, but were not permitted, with the exception of those few of them who were appointed to minister to the Master during the ages of the Travail. After the Oblation was accomplished, there was not only the resurrection from the oblation states into some measure of Divine consciousness, and the bringing forth into blessed manifestation again within Him of the Jesushood and the Christhood; but there was the process begun by which He could ascend into the realms of vision of high consciousness, to know the FATHER-MOTHER again as once He had known that ONE; and to commune again with the high Angelic World, and to live in it.

ASCENSION NOW POSSIBLE FOR ALL

The Oblation has been accomplished. Of late days I have spoken to you of the Naronic Cycles and the closing days of the Travail, and also of the Return. Now, hear ye this. It is because the Oblation has been accomplished and the process of the Return begun, that it has been possible for the Heavens to give back to you these wonderful Teachings. And when I call them wonderful, it is not because my name is attached to the books as the Servant of the LORD. The Teachings are HIS. The Message is from HIM. I have nothing of my own. I know these Teachings to be true. I believe in them, and know them to be true, not as men and women believe and know religious doctrines which have received the imprint of some School of thought whose fiat lays claim to Divine Authority, but because I know them to be direct from HIM Who is the Truth.

It is thus that I know that the age of the Ascension is now, that the days of the Ascension are with us, that the Servant has returned from the work of the Oblation. It is the time for the ascending up "on high" again of the Soul. It is the day for the transcension of all that is of the earth, earthly; of all that is merely of the human, even though that which is truly human means a very sacred, angelic state. It is the ascension of the Being through the Angelic Heavens, ever upward, still upward, realization following after realization, each step onward and upward bringing new glories, intensified degrees of vision and attainment, until the Soul can stand upon the threshold of the Inner World. This is no Pauline message purporting to come from the third Heavens. Its source is not the Astral or Occult plane of this world, nor even the circles of Angelic realms of the Planetary Heavens—though these are now purified as a result of the Oblation. The Message is from the Seventh Heavens of the Divine World, and is at once an Angelic Message; a Celestial Message; and a Divine Message. It is the Message of the LORD of Being, with the call in it to you to ascend up out of all limitations in your state, until the mere earthliness of things disappears.

THE LIFE REVEALED IN ASCENSION

But that does not mean that earthly duties and claims will disappear, or that your vision will be so transcendent that you will not see them. Not so. *The true Mystic is the Soul who knows God, and whose ministry is beautiful, even in all earthly things.* It is not to be imagined that, as the Being rises, you will not have any more of these ministries. What I mean is this, that you will transcend their influence over the mind, and their power to hold down the Life; that in your Being you will transcend all the lower spheres, and reach the innermost; that you will stand face to face once more with HIM Who is the LORD, and know HIM again as the FATHER-MOTHER; and that from that altitude of consciousness, you will look down upon all the lower ministries, and touch them with new power.

But in looking down upon the lower estates and planes and the services to which they call, you will not consider them beneath the dignity of the service of such an exalted state.

The littlenesses of men and women in their thought and purpose upon the Earth-planes, when they think that any ministry is beneath the dignity of their life, could not obtain in the Heavens. *All true ministry is full of dignity: it is worship.* It is a truer worship than the mere singing of hymns to the Great Love. The LORD of Being rejoices in the exultation of HIS children in and through the worshipful song. But HIS worship is service. And the Soul who has ascended to that vision and entered into such a realization of Life, comes back to earth-planes in thought and purpose to touch everything, even the lowliest, until all service takes on the radiance of the very Heavens of realization from which the Being looks out and operates. For in Divine service, the serving one makes everything touched, take on the glory of the Heavens.

That is the concrete expression of the Ascension Life. It is the meaning of "ascending up on High" to serve HIM Who is our LORD. "Be ye holy, even as the FATHER-MOTHER is holy." Be perfect in your consecration. Be ye perfect embodiments after your order and degree, even as your FATHER-MOTHER in the Heavens is Perfect. HE maketh HIS Sun (Son) to shine everywhere, and HIS Rains of Blessing (HIS magnetic streams) to fall upon all Souls.

Unto what end should we ascend up "on high"? For individual delight? The delight would be great. It would be very beautiful. We should rejoice in it, and be rejoiced by it. But surely not for self-gratification. There is no gratification of self in the Heavens. If you are only happy when you are pleased, you have not found the secret of Life. If you are only beautiful to people when they do to you and for you what you like, you have missed the meaning of the attitude of the Divine Love. I am sure you understand the true way, and that the Ascension of the Being is not for personal gratification or individual joy. The Divine motive behind the Ascension is this, to be more like HIM in embodiment; to be more and more in HIS fashion in attribute; to have greater power to express, reveal, and interpret HIM; to have motion which is the true praise of HIM, wherein the whole Being gives itself in sublimest ministry. For to "ascend up on high" and lead captive all that has been in captivity, is to ascend with all our powers liberated so that we can bring them back for service as free and redeemed potencies, the once rich endowments of the Divine Love, the gifts of Love's sublime giving unto us; and that we may use these in blessed ministry, in lowly as in great things, in humble as in exalted estates. Let this morning be a day of such an Ascension for each one.

* * * * *

The Ascension of the Master was nothing outward. It was nothing that seemed even to violate the law of staral, magnetic motion. It was an Ascension of HIS whole Being, such as was in perfect harmony with the Law of the Soul's motion, even unto the realization in high estate of the most Sublime ONE'S Overshadowing, All-Encompassing, and In-dwelling.

Of like nature is all true Ascension.

O Majesty on High! How wondrous THY Love and THY ways! THY Servants would be filled with the consciousness of THY Love in its transcendent Power, even unto the Great Realization, which is THY gift to THY children in the day of their Ascension unto THEE.

Amen and Amen.

PART II

THE DIVINE ECCLESIA

THE BEGINNINGS OF HISTORICAL CHRISTIANITY

DIVINE REALITIES AND HUMAN CLAIMS

THE STORY OF PENTECOST

THE ADVENT OF PAUL

THE PRECIOUS STONE WHICH THE BUILDERS REJECTED

THE CHURCH OF THE LIVING CHRIST

THE SEVEN SACRAMENTS

THE BEGINNINGS OF HISTORICAL CHRISTIANITY

THE BEGINNINGS OF HISTORICAL CHRISTIANITY

The beginnings of historical Christianity are supposed to have been set forth in the book entitled "The Acts of the Apostles." I would speak of those beginnings, and preface what I may say to you, with these few sentences that ye may understand. It is not my ministry to take the books of the New Testament, or those of the Old, as a Biblical critic to examine them critically, weighing the evidence for and against their authenticity and the value of their contents; though it is necessary in the ministry to which I have been appointed, at times to unveil things that are not correct, and which are oft-times misrepresentations of the Master known as Jesus Christ, what He said and what He did, and even of the rise of what is known as historical Christianity. So you will understand that any apparent criticism of the book entitled the Acts of the Apostles which I find it necessary to make because of its claims, is not approached nor executed in the spirit of scholastic criticism. Far removed, indeed, must ever be our Message from such a spirit of mere criticism.

The Truth is in itself revealed. And although the Truth has to have its apologists, yet it can be looked at only from the within; for its value is there, and neither in the book in which it appears as a statement, nor in the name that may be attached to the statement.

The value of all spiritual story is to be found in the heart of it, in the motion of it, in the revelatory nature of it, in the power of it, and in the call that is inherent in it.

OUTSTANDING FIGURES IN THE ACTS

The Acts of the Apostles purports to set forth the passing of the Master from these planes, the founding of the Church, the order in which the Apostolate should be chosen, and how the apostles became endowed with power from on High. The book is concerned largely with two outstanding figures, one who was a friend of the Master, and the other who long after came into notoriety. Nearly the first half of the book is taken up with Peter, his sayings, his experiences, his acts. John, the most intimate disciple, has just a small portion; and James, John's brother, even less. And then there breaks upon the vision that one who became the morning star of historical Christianity,—for undoubtedly he was so accounted, and is considered such to this day. Paul is that star. The book is supposed to have been written by Paul's friend Luke, who refers to his former treatise, namely, the Gospel that bears his name. Luke did not know the Master nor the Teachings. He could only have heard the oral and traditional story. Sometimes he writes as one who has himself heard; and at other times as one who has seen certain things. In the latter portion he could write in this way more effectively; for he came to know and become the friend of Paul.

The book might have been written with a view to the development of historical Christianity; though, doubtless, no such thought was in Luke's mind. For he did not see what lay ahead. But the two great foundations on which historical Christianity has been built up are those of Peter and Paul. And although the whole of the Christian Church has been largely Pauline, as is evidenced by the influences of the Pauline teaching, yet Peter is presented as the great apologist for the Master, and as such, the chief teacher in the newly formed Church. Ultimately he is made the rock-foundation of the Church, and becomes the forerunner of the Pontifical Seat and Authority. In name and belief Peter is the head. But Paul was elevated for his remarkable theses found in the various Apostolic Letters which he wrote to the early Christian communities, and for the claims which he made as one who, though born out of due time, was called to be the chief of all the Apostles—called from the Heavens, and spoken unto by the Master.

You will bear with me, I know, in many things it will be necessary for me to say to you. How I know them must remain unspoken. But I do not ask you to receive them, unless you see the glory of truth at the heart of them, and feel the motion of that glory flowing unto you, and hear from out the heart of this Message the call unto that Life for which the Master stood, and to that ministry unto which GOD alone appoints a Soul.

THE MOTIVE BEHIND THE WRITER

One of the chief features lying behind the motive in the book was undoubtedly the endeavour to reconcile Judaism with the new faith, and also to gloss over, in so far as possible, the differences between the Brotherhood and the Teachings they had to give as members of the inner fellowships unto whom the Master spoke, and the interpretation which Paul brought with him unto them in his enthusiasm. For be it understood, Paul was a great Soul. He is still great. He could not be other because of his Soul constitution, and his previous attainments in great ages. That he was capable of mighty sacrifice for anything he took in hand, is evidenced by his toil on behalf of the communities which he raised, and those which he did not raise, but which he found in their early beginnings, and ministered unto, giving his idea of the Message of the Master.

The book has startling contradictions, one of the most notable, perhaps, being the description of Paul's conversion. That is given in two different parts—the ninth chapter, and in the twenty-second. There is yet a third account given in the Epistle to the Galatians which differs from the two records of that conversion found in The Acts of the Apostles. There are other things one could name, two of which are of vital importance because of the influence they had upon the early Church. I refer to the Ascension of the Master, and the Baptism of the Spirit. I have indicated to you in another place that there are three distinct Ascensions spoken of—one from a high hill in Galilee, one from Bethany, and one from the Mount of Olives.

Also, there is that most strange inconsistency in relation to the reception by His intimate ones of the power designated the Holy Ghost, and the story of Pentecost. Towards the close of the fourth Gospel it is said that the Master appeared unto the disciples after giving the demonstration of His resurrection to Thomas; that He breathed on them all, and said to them, "Receive ye the Holy Ghost. Whosoever's sins ye forgive they are forgiven, and whosoever's sins ye retain they are retained."

Here the apostolic endowment is evidently sent forth from the Master to them, and the power of the Highest comes upon them to give them the position of endowed and illumined Apostles of the Lord. But immediately you turn to The Acts of the Apostles you find they were not so endowed; that they were to tarry in Jerusalem until such endowment came; and that the Master told them that such endowment could not come until He left them. And then there is the description of the Ascension, speedily followed by the disciples meeting in the Upper Room; and those brethren who went back from Him, finding that there was going to be an institution, coming and meeting in the Upper Room, or the House of Mary, with the others. I may not say more to you here about this, for there is much in it that must still be veiled until the Heavens decree that it shall be made known.

Then there is the election of a new apostle to take the place of Judas who was supposed to have betrayed the Master. Immediately the eleven are led to choose certain members, and then to cast lots, after prayer, as to which should take the place of Judas—as if the Divine Love and Wisdom ever chose His endowed ones after that manner. The Master did not choose His friends by lot. The thought and act are pagan. No apostle could be chosen in that way, nor appointed by any man, nor any community, nor system. Apostles are God-begotten; and they are God-illumined. And those who are not, and who are only apostles appointed by man, whatever be their historical claims, are not illumined nor endowed from on High.

And though there is much in this also that we have to leave veiled, such as the tragedy in relation to the betrayal of the sacred Logia written by John the disciple in order to preserve the Sayings of the Master; yet it may be said that the beginning of the tragedy was the theft of the Logia, and the uses made of it, until the marvellous revelation given by the Master was so changed that none knew it, and the world has not seen it unto this day, though it is now being restored by the Heavens for those children for whom it was meant, because they are those who can understand it unto the embodiment to which it calls; that through that embodiment the revelation of what life is in and from the Divine may be given; and through that revelation a radiance shed over the world of the pure life, the beautiful life, the noble life, the lovely life—lovely because it is begotten of Love, absolute Love from HIM.

THE MASTER'S TEACHING ON THE CHURCH

The Teachings the Master gave to His intimate ones concerning the Church of GOD had nought to do with outward institutions. Just as they had the most intimate fellowship with Him, so it was possible to express that for which the Church stood through their meeting together. The intimate ones knew that the Church of GOD was the Kingdom of GOD within the Being. It was the superstructure of the Soul and the glory of its fashion. For the living Church of GOD was there—the Church where the Living ONE ever mediated. It was the Church where the high Altar was, where the Shekinah abode, where the glory of the LORD dwelt, where the resplendence of HIS Presence illumined the sanctuary, and where HIS cross was a living power, vibrant with the motion of HIS own Mystery, glorious with the radiance of HIS own auric outflow.

After receiving such intimate Teachings, those beloved friends of the Master could never have dreamt of founding churches as churches are understood to-day, nor as they came to be thought of in the first century. Even long after the Master had passed from them to take up the Oblation ministry, the little communities were still Brotherhoods. But during the betrayals that the Brethren passed through in their experience, these Brotherhoods came to be disbanded. There were those who entered the Brotherhoods to discover the secrets. These betrayed the things that were held so sacred, and then they betrayed the Brethren. And it was thus the Brotherhoods became disbanded and the Brethren scattered. It was a tragic *diaspora* for them and the Teachings.

There was a strange oral message going forth, a message such as Luke laid hold of; and those who had heard the Message at the feet of the Master felt they must counteract that oral presentation of the Message and the false interpretation of it; for it was not understood. So they were willing to be at the command of communities that would listen to what those had to say who had sat beside the Master and heard His wondrous Unveilings of the FATHER-MOTHER, and the purpose of the Divine Love and Wisdom for the Redemption of the World.

It was thus the first communities arose that came to be called churches, and that some of the intimate ones of the Master took upon themselves to mediate unto them, but not as bishops and priests, as the terms are understood to-day. They only sought to mediate, in that true priestly sense, of the glorious Love and Wisdom of the FATHER-MOTHER in the measure in which those who were willing to listen, could receive. It was in this way that there came into the historical records such names as John, and James, and Peter, and Phillip the Evangelist, as disciples associated with the foundation of the Christian Church.

But before the Brotherhoods were disbanded, many things took place such as are set forth in the opening of The Acts of the Apostles. And you will note, those of you who may have looked at the chronological setting of that book, that it covers thirty years, from the close of the year thirty-three A.D. to the year sixty-three.

SIMON PETER AS APOLOGIST FOR THE MASTER

Now in the endeavour to associate Peter with the founding of the Church in Jerusalem, of which for some years James was the teacher after the Brotherhoods had to be disbanded (for he sought to help those who desired to hear something of the Mysteries that were unveiled by the Master), Peter is represented as the apologist for the Master, especially on that great day of the outpouring, named the day of Pentecost. Of this latter event I have spoken in another chapter, and shown that there was never such an event; though there was a portrayal of that which would come to pass when all the children would hear, in their own tongue and according to the degree of their understanding, the Divine Message interpreted.

It is Pentecost now. It is only the beginning of the Great Work; but it is to go on until this world is healed through the ever increasing outpouring from the Heavens of the magnetic streams by which alone the Planet's life can be healed, and all the children helped back into the beautiful way. Though beliefs naturally grow up around ideas, yet the beautiful way is not the way of beliefs. For the way of beliefs oft-times, like Herod, kills James (for James is the faithful Life-principle within the Soul); and would destroy even John (the beautiful Love-principle), and always keep Peter in prison (for Peter is the Understanding).

It is said Simon Peter became apologist for the Master. And you will note, if you read carefully, how in two different sections of the book, his presentations of the Master and the purpose of the Manifestation are in harmony with the Pauline setting. For Peter is made the mouthpiece of the teachings that were disseminated throughout that part of the world; then they travelled west, and still further west, setting forth the Master, His betrayal, His crucifixion, His Ascension into the Heavens, with the authority of Peter but after the manner of the oral tradition and Pauline view.

Oh, the sadness of it all! Although it is said of Peter that he would deny the Master during the Three Days of the Oblation, which verily he did; yet at that time it was surely too early on for him to have forgotten what the Master said to him concerning the Burden to be borne. For Peter himself, in an indirect way, was to be a real ministrant or sharer in the travail of the Oblation. But, according to Luke, he just presents the Master as the Nazarene, betrayed, crucified, and as dying for the sins of the world; and assures his hearers that whosoever should believe this message would be forgiven. They would be healed. And it is said that over three thousand believed that day after his address; and then in another portion, many thousands.

It was a great betrayal. Luke did not know the Teachings of the Master. He wrote his book to try and make it possible for Paul's advent to be accepted by Gentile and Jew. For the acceptation of his message meant for Luke the reconciliation of these. Paul is the dominating factor throughout the book, from his first introduction. But in the first part of the story Luke had established the Church; and when Paul came he found communities of believers in the oral tradition here and there, and made use of these in his work.

THE GREAT BETRAYAL OF THE MASTER

Now in the advent of Paul there are clearly set forth such things as these;—that he stood apart from the Brethren; that he would not be one of them; that he visited them twice, or three times at the most; that he was never their friend, though he came into touch with James and Peter on more than one occasion, individually; that he went up to Antioch to them; and also met them in Jerusalem, it is said; and likewise that he travelled to Damascus and met them there. He claimed to be one born out of due time with special illumination from the Heavens; yet he was an untrained Soul, so far as the Message of the Master was concerned. He was one who had not heard the Master. He was one unto whom nothing of the Christhood and the Oblation had been unveiled. Yet he claimed to know the mind of the Master, and even to have had a vision of Him, to have heard His voice, to have been blinded by the light of His glory, and to have recognized Him and spoken to Him as the LORD. He laid claim to be the one who was chosen and called to be the Apostle of the Gentiles, and Christ's herald to the world of the glorious Redemption.

Yet he stood apart from those who, for several years, had been in intimate fellowship with the Master; unto whom had been unveiled the Passion of GOD, as expressed in the travail of the Oblation. Yet Paul would have none of what these friends of the Master had to say concerning the Teachings which the Master had given. Why was this?[1]

Luke so effectively glosses over two of the visits of Paul to the Brethren, the one called the Council of Jerusalem, and the other the Council at Antioch, that the difference between the Brethren and himself is made to relate to circumscision, and whether the Gentile Christians should observe the Mosaic Law. And the decision arrived at was, that as long as the Gentiles refused to eat the creatures which had been offered on the altars of the idols, they might go their way believing what Paul had to say to them.

What was it that was at the very root of the meeting of the Brethren with Paul, both in Jerusalem and at Antioch, and also in Damascus? It is one thing for a writer like Luke, who gathered information from hearsay, setting out with the endeavour to place Paul in a glorious light, to say that the controversy had relation to the bondage of circumscision in which the Brethren desired to hold all disciples to the Mosaic economy, whilst Paul desired liberation from that economy of all who would receive the message; but it is another thing to know that such a subject had nought to do with the visit to either Jerusalem or Antioch, and far from it in relation to the visit to Damascus. It had to do with the Oblation and the doctrine of the Redemption. The evangelical doctrine of the Redemption which has grown up

[1] *Vide* THE ADVENT OF PAUL, p. 183.

through the ages, came to the followers of what was called the New Faith through such letters as Paul's Epistles to the Romans, the Galatians, and II. Cor. where the Master as Christ is set forth as being made sin for the world, and as bearing the burden of that sin on Calvary.

It was thus the faith of early Christendom was directed to the Master in a personal way, and to the Mystery of the Redemption in relation to His Burden-bearing for the world during the hours of the Roman crucifixion. And the Resurrection was made a resurrection from the dead of His own body after the crucifixion; and His Ascension into the Heavens, to be a passing up to the Right Hand of the ETERNAL ONE to act as Mediator. And the western world has followed these beliefs, and still worships at the shrine of the Master. Men call Him LORD. They think of Him personally. They rejoice in the redemption He is supposed to have brought; but it is a redemption that He accomplished for them, and has nought to do with that most vital process of the Redemption in the Being.

When Paul met the Brethren they told him what the Master taught. But he would not have it. And so in his Epistle to the Galatians he writes:—"If any man preach any other gospel unto you than that ye have received, let him be accursed." And in the Epistles to the Romans, the Corinthians and Timothy, he emphasises that the Gospel is his gospel, to distinguish it from that given by the Brethren who knew the Master.

THE CHURCH IS PETRINE AND PAULINE

Since the Church is built up far more on the Acts of the Apostles and the Epistles of Paul, than on the Gospel Records which purport to be the story of the Master, is it any wonder that the western world has been under so great a delusion all through the ages concerning the Redemption?

Even unto this day the Christians, that is, those who are nominally Christian, and many, many who are truly Christian in the spirit of their life, in the love of their heart, in the reverence of their attitude, are still in the dark concerning the real nature of the Christhood and the Oblation. The whole world has been betrayed through the misrepresentation of the glorious Message the Master was sent to give. The misunderstanding and consequent misinterpretation of the Divine Passion in the Oblation is most tragic. In the Schools and the Churches, the lack of true knowledge of Divine Events is amazing. The Schools have written voluminously on the Sin-Offering; yet none have discerned the nature of the Oblation, its travail, the duration of it, its Burden, the Passion of it, its pain and sorrow, and its anguish through great ages. They have all confounded events essentially different, and related the Passion to the temporary hours of suffering on the Roman Cross.

When Paul visited Damascus, the last visit he made to the Brethren when they were in hiding, there were those who became incensed against him that he could persist in giving such a direction to the thoughts of those who would be disciples. And he is said to have fled from them. Yes, that is true. But there were other things which caused them grief. For he had held the Logia of the Master in his hands and read many passages. And he even took some portions of them away with him to work up into his own theses. These are found in his various Epistles in a fragmentary form. But in some instances, like the thirteenth chapter of I Corinthians, and a portion of the eighth chapter of Romans, considerable Sayings of the Master are almost fully given; yet so far as Paul's theses are concerned, these Sayings are quite apart from the things with which he is dealing.

Oh, that it had never been necessary for me to have said all these things to you. I am sure it must be difficult for you who know me best to understand such a criticism from me. But there is reason for it. I knew some of you desired me to speak on The Acts of the Apostles and its influence, and so I have chosen to respond to your request, and am moved to do so this morning. And now I would show to you that which the Heavens have done for us all, notwithstanding Paul's misadventure and Peter's triple denial, and the hushing up of the exquisite Message of Love the Master left behind to be voiced in the Teachings, and the silencing of the divine apology of the Love and the Wisdom of the FATHER-MOTHER given by John and his brother James. For those two noble interpreters taught the way of life and how to serve the Divine Love nobly, free from all the limitations that mere beliefs impose, or that institutionalism places upon the life. For James taught concerning the Life, as John did concerning the Love. Yet they are glossed over. They are lost in the New Testament. A solitary letter is attributed to James; and three supposed brief letters attributed to John. Of these latter the first seems the most important, though greatly changed. It contains vital Sayings of the Master which John heard in the most intimate hours. And the one letter of James preserved to us, though much corrupted, is a very practical counsel to those who would be disciples of the LORD of Love.

THE WITHDRAWAL OF THE MYSTERIES

The Great Love has not left Himself without a witness. The Mysteries were gathered up like "the Seven Baskets" and "the Twelve Baskets of Fragments" into the Heavens. They are let down again. The Children of the Kingdom, especially those who contacted the Master in the days of the Manifestation, have been like fishermen seeking for the real meaning of all the travail of the ages, and oft-times wondering how it came to pass that that Message of exquisite beauty founded in the Divine Love and radiant with the Divine Wisdom, could have become a Message to set the whole western world in conflict, school with school, community with community, race with race, and that, notwithstanding all the beauty of the Message in its Love and Wisdom, the effect has been nil upon the nations; that wars have continued through racial strife, communal strife, strife in every realm of experience. Oh, the Saints have travailed to understand how it has come to pass that where the belief in the Great Love has seemed to be strongest there has been the most dire betrayal of all that Love stands for. The witness to the reality of the truth given by the Master to the intimate ones who were scattered, and who were told by Him that they would travail through the night until he returned, is this very travail of the Saints of God in the heart of the Church, their travail oft-times being the result of the oppression of them within the Church itself. Their very travail is the evidence of the glory of the Message they were seeking to get back to. That they could not get there, testifies to the betrayal of the Message. The Sanctuary was dark; the veils were closed. They sought the Light in earthly sanctuaries in the hope that the veils would be drawn apart. They were the real Soul devotees throughout the ages in the Church, the blood-force, the life-energy, which was verily the seed or living power within the Church. But it was night with them. It was the long night of the travail that was foretold. The Teachings had been so changed and the presentation of them so materialized that the real Message had to be guarded and withheld until the close of the Travail, because at the close of the Travail the betraying factors would be lessened, the Planetary Heavens would be changed, the possibility of more intimate and more direct Angelic ministry would be realized. And so in the Wisdom of the Great Love, the exquisite beauty of the Vision had to be held back until the Oblation closed. And then when the Heavens were opened, what an unveiling for the soul to look back through the ages and see the play of all the militating forces; to look back, aye more, to stand back in those ages and witness the betrayals as they took place by those who should have known better; and such a betrayal as is set forth in the Apology of Peter wherein he says that the Master was received up into the Heavens to be seated at the Right Hand of God, there to be the Mediator for the race; when the Master was living in Rome, beginning the Travail whilst yet a child, but more than a child in the motion of His Being! (For the first Life of the Oblation was lived in Rome.)

THE RESTORED MESSAGE

But now to the great *Recovery*. What has the FATHER-MOTHER done for us? HE has restored the Christhood. Does that mean that HE has raised up Jesus, or raised up that One Who was known as Jesus? Is that the recovery of the Christhood? No. Is it that the LORD Himself has actually come from the Heavens to appear upon this Earth, and speak as the LORD unto the children of men? No. The LORD does not come in that way. HE is never a man. You might as well ask or expect the Universe to be gathered up into the Sun. The Universe is potentially in the Sun's potencies, as a microcosm. But not in the macrocosmic sense. Or you might as well expect the glory of that volume of Divine Elements which the Sun represents, to be gathered into this small body of the Earth, the land of Judah, the sphere of the Planet-Soul. If the restoration of Christ is not given in that way, then how? Through the unveiling of the Message. It is not of man but of GOD. It is the Word of the LORD. All who would be servants of it must embody it; all who would be revealers of it, must be filled with the glory of it; all who would interpret it must understand it; all who would know the power of it must open the flood-gates of their Being that the fountain of the Divine World may pour out into them all fulness.

The Oblation is accomplished, and the Heavens have unveiled the meaning of Christhood. They have revealed that the Jesus-life is the exquisitely beautiful life of Love's embodiment in everything—Love's embodiment in the beauty of life, in the graciousness of life, in the radiance of life, in the service of life, in the motion of life. Christ is coming back again as a state of consciousness within those who *will* to embody Jesus and radiate the glory that comes to them. For Christ is the Son of GOD within, making manifest in a state within the Being. Such is Christhood. The ETERNAL CHRIST is the LORD of

Being. When it doth please GOD to call forth HIS Son in you, it is HIS calling into manifestation of the Christ. HE is in you. But to call that Christ into manifestation, is to call you forth into a life so characteristically Jesushood, that it reveals the radiance of Christ. Christ in you is the glorious hope of the perfect realization of the Divine FATHER-MOTHER.

THE MASTER RETURNS IN THE MESSAGE

The Heavens have brought back the Message which the Master gave, and all those who once were of the Ancient Christhood Order may behold the vision and understand, and in understanding, return again into the states of Jesushood and Christhood. GOD'S Message is not simply in words. *It is a Living Message in the whole motion of Life.* If the Message be vibrant in you, it will make your life one with it. As part of His Message, the Master had to call intimate ones. He unveiled to them the Divine Vision. That Vision was betrayed. They were overtaken by the night.

You have all travailed to know again this Vision. You have loved Jesus; you did not know why. You have loved Jesus Christ, and very specially the LORD. You have prayed to the LORD, and you have longed for HIS approach to you. Your inherent love for the Divine sought to express itself, and you have had to learn that to love Jesus is not simply to love a man, but rather that which He represented. Has not the whole of the nominal Christian world professed its love for the Master Jesus? Yet look at the western world to-day. At whose shrine does it kneel and worship? Not at that shrine for which the Master stood. Even the Churches cannot bear to hear that their ways of life are impure; that in their eating and drinking they are still pagan; that their compassion is circumscribed by their own desires and the limitations of their vision. For they will not hear the truth that all the creatures must share in the glory of the Jesus-Life of compassion and pity. Why are the altars and the pulpits silent concerning this monstrous perversion of the way of Love that overtook the early Christian Church? Because those who are in authority as Popes, Priests and Teachers have no convictions in the matter. They have shared the great betrayal. They are within the darkness which that betrayal brought.

Even such as have felt that the way of life was wrong, have not dared to lift their voice in a nobler message because of the crucifixion it might lead to. The dread of the resulting ignominy and repudiation has made them fear to proclaim the Message that the Master gave of beautiful Jesushood, in so far as they knew it. What was it to Him that men and women went back from Him, or sought to follow Him in any personal way? It was to Him a great sorrow and a grief profound, that they would not endure to hear the beautiful Message in its full roundedness. Even His brethren, most intimate brethren, went back from Him. Yet they were present at the founding of the Christian Church after He had gone, and they shared in propagating the doctrine of His Ascension to a life that was Angelic, and Celestial, and Divine, according to the degree in which He could enter into those high and glorious estates.

This then, is the first part of the Recovery, *that the Heavens made it possible to declare again the resurrection of Jesus Christ the Lord; not any person, but the resurrection of Divine Life in the Being; the resurrection of the Vision of Soul-Christhood; the resurrection of the glory of the Lord Himself. The Lord is risen indeed.*

THE UNVEILING OF THE OBLATION

Then the second part is, that the Divine Love has permitted the unveiling and interpreting of *the Mystery of the Oblation.* It could not have been given to the world; for the world would never understand the motion of it. And the intimate ones have, and will still have, to learn it gradually. Even from them many things indeed have had to be hidden concerning it. For the Oblation was the ministry of the Passion of Love. It lies beyond the human understanding until illumined.

Have you never wondered what could be the real significance

of the saying,—"And when the night had fallen, He went out to accomplish that which the FATHER-MOTHER had given Him to do"? Oh, it was night for Him, a terrible night in its duration, motion, burden, passion, pain, and sorrow, and anguish. But it was a terrible night also for the Heavens. Yet all the while the LORD of Love, through HIS Heavens, has been revealing the exquisite beauty of HIS patience and unfailing tenderness, until this day should break wherein the glory of HIS own Love might be unveiled again, and the Mystery of the Passion interpreted to those who should be found ready, and willing, and able, to hear the wondrous story.

Such is the message unto you this morning, though the portrayal has but touched the hem of the garment. Notwithstanding all the betrayal, the delusion and its effects, the misunderstanding and consequent misinterpretation, and, as a result, misrepresentation; notwithstanding the night of the awful travail as the result, not only the bearing of the karmic burden of this world, but the perversions occasioned by the betrayal, the Great Love has found a way by which HIS Heavens are opened again to HIS children. You may again see the Angels of GOD descending and ascending. You may behold the glory streaming from afar; and you may see the glory near at hand. You may hear the songs full of divine harmony begotten of the rhythmic motion of Souls on the Other Side, and now beginning to be repeated on this side. You may glimpse and gradually enter into a great degree of realization of the Mystery of the Divine Passion, to reveal which the Master was sent, and to bear which He went out when the darkness had fallen, to travail unto the healing of this world, and the bringing about of this day. Oh, praise the LORD for HIS Goodness, and for HIS wonderful works on behalf of HIS children! For HE hath wrought mighty things whereof ye should be glad.

But in your new found joy of glimpsing the Vision, do not forget the call. If these things sit upon you only as knowledges, they will have no more power than if ye knew them not.

But if they become to you living factors, then your whole life will vibrate to the motion of the Heavens, and you will share now in the Divine Passion, the Passion of the LORD. This Passion will not be the burden-bearing of the travail of the Oblation, but the burden-bearing of sacrificial service unto the perfect healing of this world, and the restoration of all Souls unto the beautiful life and the consciousness of childhood to the Divine Love. That Love has never wearied. It could not weary, though it has grieved. That Love has never been withheld; it could not withhold. It is the Love that never faileth. Love Supreme is ever Divine in its giving. Its outpouring is without earthly measure.

I would that I could reveal my LORD to you as you should know HIM, and as HE is to me.

Alas, that historical and ecclesiastical Christianity should never have known HIM, from its inception even unto this day!

DIVINE REALITIES
AND
HUMAN CLAIMS

DIVINE REALITIES AND HUMAN CLAIMS

This subject is intimately related to that of the Mass; for those things which are implied in it lie at the very heart of the Oblation, and are claimed by those who minister in the Offices of the Mass, and Confession and Absolution.

ENDOWMENTS ARE FROM GOD

Our claim is in GOD, and HE meets it. If our attitude be true, HE meets all our needs. But we cannot lay claim to anything worth possessing and holding which is in any way apart from HIM. Nor may we lay claim to powers and offices which have not been HIS own wondrous gifts. Nor can we build up offices upon these planes, and then claim that they are GOD-begotten, and fashioned, and endowed. For all that is true is of HIMSELF, and from HIMSELF, and for HIMSELF. All that is true has its origin in HIM, has motion from HIM, and has manifestation through HIS children who enter into the consciousness of the Truth.

You will see and understand what is meant when we speak of the claims that are made in relation to the Mass and the Forgiveness of Sin. For the power that is claimed is a divine power that changes even the Eucharistic Elements. It is also a power that can appropriate great things to itself, and shut out others from sharing in these. It is the power of earthly, official priesthood. We might name it, as it has claimed to be through the ages, *viz.*, "Apostolic Succession," wherein the power of GOD-appointed office is held, and the arrogation of the further power of granting the Forgiveness of Sin.

It is true that, even as we have nothing of our own worth holding, and all that is true and beautiful in us is of the Divine, so is it equally true that it is HE who gives us, in a special way, gifts for ministry. But Divine endowments are never given irrespective of the qualifications of the recipients. For Divine gifts are an exposition as well as an endowment from HIM. They are the testimony to the Soul's growth in consciousness and power, in the beauty of holiness, in the realisation of HIS All-Encompassing and Overshadowing and Indwelling Presence. *All gifts from the Divine, are endowments through acquisition and attainment.*

Even as the flowering-tree needs the sunshine as well as the stimulating chemicals of the earth at its roots; even as it needs the breaths to blow through its arms and its leaves; so we need to draw from the great Deep of the sacred Mystery of Being, and to drink in continuously of the glorious magnetic streams which proceed from the LORD of Being as the Sun of our life, and to feel the wafting of HIS Breath through all the planes of our Being. We grow thus before HIM, and as we grow we are endowed. If we thought of the endowments as beautiful blooms, we would then understand that they are not stuck on, but are the exposition of the motion of the hidden life within the divine plant, even as it is in nature.

Gifts are acquirements. There is no artificial manufacture of gifts in the Divine World, nor of endowments. This will help you to understand some things I would say to you on "apostolic succession."

THE ARROGANCE OF HUMAN PRIESTHOOD

The claim to it is made through ecclesiastical venues; but then it is an old claim repeated in the nomenclature of the historic Church of the Christian Religion. For in all ages since historical religion became formal and official, and largely a mere creedal and ritualistic venue of power, this claim has been put forth. In the heart of ancient Egypt the priests claimed all power. They did so in the midst of Greece. They have done so in every religious motion. It has become, as it were, a system, not necessarily evil in itself—for many noble Souls are in the priesthood, and many have been through the ages in all countries and under all religious expressions; but the system became such as to lead to evil states and evil ways, and to claims which have been untrue, unjust, and oft-times oppressive.

Throughout the historical development of Christianity, the claim of the priesthood to "apostolic succession" is dated back to the times of the Master. It is supposed that to His intimate ones He communicated a power from the FATHER-MOTHER other than was resident in them; that He empowered them to go forth as ambassadors for GOD, and as His priests, forgiving iniquity, transgression, and sin. But the old question is raised which was spoken, it is said, in connection with the Master,—"Who can forgive sin, but GOD only?" And we get back to that always. For it is only the Eternal Mystery, we name the FATHER-MOTHER, Who can forgive sin; because HE is at the heart of all law. HE is in the breath of all true motion. HE is the exposition of that Mystery as Power. HE is the great Healer, as well as the great Fashioner of Souls. HE heals where the fashion has been hurt. HE heals where the attributes have been wounded. HE heals where the spirit has been broken. HE is the balm in Gilead and the Divine Physician there. For the balm in Gilead is HIS Love, and Gilead itself is the Divine Kingdom; and the Physician there is the sacred Mystery that has its motion unto, and into, and within, our Being. This will become clearer presently.

DIVINE POWERS NOT TRANSFERABLE

Now, all transference of power is through realization. The Divine Love has fashioned us in HIS likeness, with corresponding attributes; so that we are miniatures of HIS own sacred Mystery, containing the elements of HIS glory and the essences of His potencies. And when these essences through their motion, have fully expressed themselves, the fashion of the Being takes on Divine likeness, and the potencies realize themselves in most blessed and wondrous attributes, which are concrete expressions of the attributes of GOD. It is in this way that we are like HIM. But the attributes are not simply outer, nor are they mental. The mental and the physical are but the correspondences upon those realms of the attributes which belong to the Being, and which will belong to the Being, as long as the Soul has the consciousness of Being, and is an exposition of the Divine Mystery.

Now, even as the Divine Love and Wisdom can transmit to HIS children the magnetic rays of the solar body in which the earth and all the children share, HE likewise transmits influences and breaths through a glorious Angelic ministry which is rendered to this world, quite unseen and unknown to the vast multitudes. In this way HE transmits power, blessing, and joy. Being like HIM, we are not only receivers from HIM, but we have the power of transmission; we can give forth to others from out the auric potencies of our Being. We do it through our attributes. We do it through the atmosphere HE generates within us. We can give another Soul love; a broken life compassion; an oppressed Soul the wings of divine protection and pity. But we cannot transmit GOD in HIS qualities to anyone. We can only reveal HIM through the outflow of HIS own glory that is within us. We cannot transmit to another the divine power with which HE has endowed us. Our endowment being an attainment, something we have risen into, something that has become realized within us, we cannot transmit it to another. We can convey the knowledge we have; yet even here, we can speak such knowledge only in language which relates it to the realm of the mind. If we wish to get a Soul beyond the realm of the mind, we have to transmit that knowledge as embodied Love. And no language can interpret love but the language of attitude and action. It is true that you can lay your hand upon the head of another, and bless. Would that the children understood just this wonderful thing, that they can bless always; but not as superior Beings; not with any thought of superiority. That would nullify any blessing. There cannot be such thoughts of pride and vanity within the heart that understands the Great Love, and that knows that all things that are worth holding within the Being, are of HIM, and from HIM.

DIVINE POWERS MUST BE ATTAINED

True "apostolic succession" and GOD-given ambassadorial power, are the result of the realization of HIMSELF: the beauty of HIS Character, the potency of HIS Attributes, the joy of embodying and revealing HIM as the great Lover of Souls, the Interpreter in so far as HE can be interpreted, and the Giver Who gives without measure. And there is this measure in it, that HE gives to Souls according to the measure of their capacity. For the cup can receive only the amount of its measure. So the Soul can receive from HIM only according to its spiritual and divine status. But all that it receives can be truly apostolic. And everyone, even those in what are accounted the lowliest estates, understood in relation to spiritual attainment, can be ambassadors for GOD, revealers of GOD, interpreters of GOD, embodiers of GOD.

Now the "apostolic succession" is claimed, first, because of the intimate relation of the disciples to the Master; and those disciples are believed to have been appointed as apostles. A disciple is one who is learning, acquiring, and receiving. An apostle is one who, having acquired, has received authority, and is sent forth on ministry. It is believed that the Master communicated of the powers with which He was enriched, unto those intimate ones, and that they communicated them again to successors.

But you cannot thus make apostles, any more than you can force Souls to be disciples of truth. You cannot endow a Soul, though you may help a Soul through the gate into the temple whence endowment comes. You cannot communicate of what you have unto anyone by transference, but you can influence a Soul to come where its lamp can be lit and its fashion rounded, its attributes healed, its powers exalted, its Sanctuary illumined, its garments made translucent, where it may enter into the consciousness of the All-Encompassing Presence and the Power of the Overshadowing One, and, highest of all, the realization of Emmanuel, GOD'S Indwelling Presence.

If this power had been a reality on the outer planes, what a different history Christianity would have written! What a different history all the Religions throughout the world would have written! For, surely, no one can hold such a power without being conscious of holding God. And no one can hold God within the Being without the consciousness of holding the Eternal Good. And no one can hold the Eternal Good in consciousness without embodying the Good, revealing the Good, interpreting the Good, expressing the Good in every service of life. And in that Good there is no oppression, there is no condemnation, there is no repudiation, there is no false and arrogant claim: there is only Love triumphant.

THE PRIESTHOOD OF THE SOUL All Souls are priests if they mediate truly unto other Souls. The disciples grew into the knowledge of the meaning of true priesthood; yet it is never said that they were priests in an outward and earthly way. The human claim to this special power has revealed itself as unutterable failure throughout all the ages, and never more so than throughout the Christian era. And this wonderful "apostolic succession," which is supposed to have been communicated to the disciples from the Master, and handed down from them to their immediate successors, through the ages has excluded woman. She has not been considered a fit vehicle to receive this marvellous endowment, this mysterious, divine potency; this wonderful office; this mediatorial ministry. Yet the Master's Mother was, naturally, a woman. Some of His most intimate friends are spoken of as women, like Mary of Bethany, and Martha who served. Nay, it is said that out of the abundance of their love and what earthly inheritance they had, they ministered unto Him during the days of His sojourn upon these planes; as He made His journey throughout Palestine, including Idumæa and Peræa. And, indeed, it is recorded that the three Marys were at the Cross of the Crucifixion to the last; and it is also told of Maria Magdalene, as well as of that other Maria, that they were so intimate with

Him that they dared to anoint Him. At supper in the home at Bethany, Mary took a precious cruse full of unguent, so valuable that the fragrance of it filled the room, and with that she anointed Him. Then there is that other story of one who is supposed to have been another Maria, who entered the house of the proud-minded Simon (who, according to the story, omitted to extend to the Master the common courtesies), and stooping, washed His feet with her tears and dried them with her hair, and then anointed Him. And then, at the very close of the earthly days of that period, it is recorded that Maria Magdalene was the one who sought Him after the crucifixion, and who met Him in the garden, and who in the midst of her sorrow, thought of Him as only the gardener, the caretaker; but who discovered that He was her Lord; and that it was she who had the commission given to her to go and tell the wondrous story. It was of her that Ernest Renan, in his *Vie de Jésus*, said, that she was the first great apostle of the resurrection, and the author of the belief in such a doctrine. Yet not one of the women is included in the "apostolic succession." No woman, it is affirmed, can mediate of the Mass because of the nature of the potencies that are supposed to flow through it; nor be a priest in office as a confessor, and healer, and forgiver of sin.

Yet what would the world be without the love, the graciousness, the purity, the nobility, the blessed motion, the glorious self-sacrifice, the divine ideas and ideals of womanhood? What would the churches be to-day in their congregations and collateral ministries if the women were absent? Yet this human claim of a system of male priesthood is made. There is no condemnation meant of the men who have entered the priesthood believing they could devote themselves most truly to the mission of the One whom they have loved as their Lord. But the system itself is self-condemnatory because of its history. Much that has emanated from it has been most hurtful. And the claims it has made are arrogant and false.

Divine Realities are not after the manner of human

imaginings. Divine Realities are not communicated by outward office, nor mere ceremonial, nor any process of ritual, nor any affirmations of belief. Divine Realities are matters of realization. You cannot communicate Love to others, though you may love them into loving. You may give them of your Love in ministry, but if they do not want it to come into their hearts to move them, it does not communicate anything to them. You cannot give them the power of Love, though you may help them to come to the altar where their love can be fanned into oneness with the mighty Flame that will divinely consume them, and interfuse all their Being until they are as a living flame for GOD, full of divine motion, full of divine energy, full of divine warmth, full of divine giving.

THE REAL APOSTOLIC SUCCESSION

Apostolic succession is through the Divine Blessing. The Master could bless, and did bless; but not even He could communicate this power. Do you think there would have been a Judas in the camp, if He could have communicated this GOD-begotten power and transferred it to that mistaken one? If the Divine Love could transfer to all HIS children in this way, do you think there would be the tragedy of the travail which is found in the world to-day? Is GOD less than man in HIS Purpose, in HIS Love, in HIS Devotion to HIS children? HE has given to us the secret of true succession. In the Principle of our Being we are HIS. In the fashion of our Being we are like HIM. In the attributes of our Being we have the potencies by means of which we are able to express HIM. But to do this, the central Mystery of our Being must be in motion. Our fashion must take on HIS glory through that motion. The power must flow magnetically through all our fashion into our attributes; and thus, being enriched from the inner potencies through HIS motion within us, we become apostolic. Love is apostolic; it is divine in its giving. Love is apostolic in its mission: it is ambassadorial in its activity and its motion. Love is plenipotentiary : it has the power of mediation even unto healing.

I would help you to understand how you may come into the direct line of "apostolic succession." It is not a way without priesthood; for it is the priesthood of the Being. Nor is it without high priesthood; for it is the Archpriest of all Being who communicates the power. HE calls you. HE leads you upward. HE endows you. HE sends you as HIS apostles, HIS ambassadors. The Realities of GOD are of the Soul. To know how HE doth bless, the Soul must enter HIS Sanctuary where alone it can behold HIM unto realization, and know the real meaning of HIS glorious Cross in wondrous Fashion; that Cross, the imprint of which is upon the brow of every child of the FATHER-MOTHER. For it is inlaid on our altar, and woven into the very fabric of our Being.

APOSTOLIC BENEDICTION

Now, it is through "apostolic succession" that we are able to offer the Mass; for our Mass is the sacrifice of our Being, the living sacrifice of our Life, the perpetual testimony of HIS own Energy unto us and within us. HIS glorious Motion through us, and the living witness that HE is and that we know that HE is. We know that HE is through realization. HE calls us to mediate of HIS Mass. HE appoints us to embody HIM, making of our Life one complete whole for HIM. In the measure in which we are like HIM, so are we for HIM. Thus we reveal HIM, interpret HIM, express HIM, and generate the atmosphere that HIS Presence ever brings. It is thus all HIS children are to be embodiments of HIM, mediators for HIM as priests in high order; a kingdom of priests for HIM. And as such they are HIS venues, having the power to forgive sin. But they do not forgive sin in the sense in which the word forgiveness is generally used. The forgiveness of sin is healing. GOD alone is the Healer, but HE heals through HIS children. A heart is aching to be loved; you can heal its ache by your love. A life is faltering, shaken by the blasts that blow, into the swirl of which it has been caught; you can steady it and heal it by your love, your sympathy, your understanding. Through your love you can lift up one whom the world accounts fallen, and. whose Being anguishes in sorrow; and you can be the instrument for healing that sorrow, for allaying the motion that produced the anguish, and for the bringing back again to the life the beautiful garments of truth and purity begotten of an exquisite motion and consecration of heart and mind. You can raise up the fallen and the bowed down; make the lame and the crippled leap as an hart, and once more be full of the potency that brings joy. Even unto the impotent, those who have lost their power to seek unto the higher, and to go into the waters troubled by the Angels to find healing, you can accommodate yourself and help them through your love, your gentleness, your meekness of heart, your lowliness of spirit. But only by the strength of the Divine in you can you be healers. It is the Divine alone through your love Who accomplishes it. It is the Divine alone who blots out sin. You are only the medium for HIM to help to awaken, to encourage, to strengthen, to bring hope, to bring light to guide the life back to the consciousness of its childhood to the FATHER-MOTHER Who will accomplish the perfect healing, even to the blotting out and the removing of the very scars that the wounds have made, until at last there is perfect healing and complete wholeness. That is forgiveness.

MEDIATION FOR GOD

The way the Great Love has been presented in religious literature, even in the Bible stories, through the changing of the truth that was given, fills one with unutterable sorrow. How HE has been represented as pronouncing judgments and condemnations, and full of wrathful potency against HIS children! Oh, the Wrath of GOD (as stated in the Scriptures), was the Power of GOD manifested unto the blotting out of all sin, and the healing of all hurt, the casting out from the life of every evil and hurtful thing. The Master commissioned His intimate ones, men and women (and there were more women than men, even in those days), to be such mediators for the FATHER-MOTHER, to mediate for HIM unto Souls that they might feel and know the great reality. He asked His intimate ones to love one another, and to love all Souls; to give love, to be children of Love. "By this shall all men know that ye are disciples of your LORD, if ye have love one to another." So He asked them to mediate for HIM. And it is the same Message you are having to-day, and the same call. Is it not the repetition of that wonderful call of those far away days?

But in your response, make no human or personal claims. If you make great personal claims, family claims, national claims, racial claims, be sure you are not in "apostolic succession." The Realities are of GOD, not because men and systems claim them. The royal road is GOD'S road. There must be humility of heart and purity of purpose. There must be the Divine motion that makes you one with all Souls, because you are one with HIM. You must know that the lowliest Soul is HIS, even as those are who may be accounted higher in estate and ministry.

The power to forgive sin is HIS Power of Love in you. When you can take to your heart another whom the world would despise and cast out, aye, one whom all the ecclesiastical institutions would repudiate and condemn, you will know that you have touched the realm of real priesthood, without outer orders; that you are apostolic in your succession, and of *the Order of Melchisedek*—GOD'S High Priesthood. The human claims that are merely of the world-mind, or the mind turned earthward, are poor affairs in comparison with those Divine Realities which we can claim from the FATHER-MOTHER. Because HE calls us into the inheritance of them, they are our claim. We have the potencies that HE alone can satisfy. We have the capacity which HE alone can fill. We have the nature which is like HIS own. We have the attributes through which HE can be exquisitely revealed and expressed. They are HIS own sublime gifts to us.

Be ye true priests for GOD. Priesthood is a state of mediation. It is the mediation of Love, all-revealing, all-healing, all-triumphant, all-illuminating, all-regnant and glorious.

Unto this end may the gracious One breathe within you His Breath, even unto the making of you like Himself in fashion, and in the revealing of His Love in priestly service.

THE STORY OF PENTECOST

Oh, exalted One and most glorious, our transcendent Lord! As we have the power to enter in and receive from Thee, so guide us to the Within, and fill us from Thyself with Thy potencies, glorious and transcendent in their motion, and in their revealings of Thee! For thus we would be altogether Thine, to serve and embody Thee.

THE STORY OF PENTECOST

We are nearing Pentecost. It is a great Church Festival which stands as the memorial of a miraculous event.

The term Pentecost has come down from the heart of Jewish story. But the real meaning is far, far greater than can be compassed by any racial thought or religious ritual; and is immeasurably more spiritual and Soulic than can be expressed by any phenomenal demonstration of the approach of mysterious hidden forces from the Unseen World, and their manifestation to the objective vision as tongues of Living Flame.

THE CHURCH FOUNDED ON A MIRAGE

Pentecost is not only associated with Jewish story, but also with the real founding of the historical Church which has taken the name of the Christhood. For the arising and development of historical Christianity may be said to date from that supposed phenomenal outpouring which was the resultant of the meeting for prayer of the little communal body of intimate friends of the Master. Upon the day of Pentecost there is supposed to have been a marvellous outpouring of GOD's Spirit, so great and so deep, that the intimate ones became overwhelmed by it, then were caught up into other realms by its power, and were so influenced that it is said concerning them that they were moved to speak in tongues which they had never learned; and also that many foreign visitors to the Jewish Pentecostal Festival, heard them give utterance to strange things in their own tongue.

It is recorded that there were present Parthians, Medes and Elamites; dwellers in Mesopotamia, Judæa, and Cappadocia; Pontus, Asia and Phrygia; Pamphylia, Egypt, and Libya about Cyrene, and Rome; and down, as it were by a strange descent, to Cretes and Arabians—all of whom in their own tongues heard of the wonderful works of GOD.

But there is no description of what was said to the listeners to arrest them, and make them see, feel, and know that of which those intimate ones of the Master had come into the knowledge and realization. There is no reference to the sacred Mysteries they had been taught. There is no record except that Peter is said to have stood up, in response to the mocking voices of those who glibly stated that "These men are filled with new wine," and described what had taken place, and gave some slight outline of the mission of the Master and the Divine purpose lying behind it.

The glamour of the story has fascinated multitudes; but it is non-historical, except in a Soulic sense. It is entirely mystical; yet it has been miraged into the phenomena attendant upon an imposing spiritualistic or magical seance. The mere recital that the Master had come and lived, and given His life in some strange way to effect redemption for the world, and make manifest unto all Souls the holy purpose of the FATHER-MOTHER to redeem them, heal them, and give them a salvation that was a perfectly healed equipoised life, is no real unveiling of the Mysteries of GOD, nor interpretation of all the phenomena said to have been seen and heard. All that is told is simply an account of the miraculous after-effect of the Master's Life, Death, and Ascension, a response to the challenge that had been sent forth by the leaders of the people.

What was the day of Pentecost that so influenced the Western World as to lay the foundations of the whole of the historical fabric of Christianity? For the veracity of the author of the Acts is assumed by Christian historians, and the recorded phenomena are accepted by them.

Pentecost was a Divine Event in the form of prophecy. It was a prophetic story concerning that which would come to pass and be accomplished as the result of the Message which had been sent from the Heavens to Israel. And the accomplishment was to be in those who could receive the Message. But it could not come until the days of the Return of Israel: as is indicated in the previous chapter in "The Acts," where it is said that Angels appeared unto the disciples who were looking up into the Heavens and following the Master as He ascended, and that to the observers the Angels said, that in like manner should be the return of that One; and also in that day of the return, all Israel should be saved, and would come to know the Divine Message.

Even in this latter statement there is a strange perversion of a sacred Mystery in relation to the Ascension Life. As you will know, in the Church Calendar, Pentecost dates from the close of the Passion and comes seven weeks after Easter. The Ascension is supposed to have taken place forty days after the Resurrection, and the outpouring of Pentecostal Breaths ten days after the Ascension was accomplished.

PENTECOST AN INWARD SOUL EVENT

The term Pentecost is full of significance. Fifty has relation to the Jubilee. The Jubilee is a time wherein the Soul realizes its Divinity. It is the seven times seven unified into the glorious ONE. It relates to the Ascension of the Soul through all the degrees signified by the seven times seven. It passes into the high estate wherein it can enter the White Light, the Radiant Presence. And that experience is not for a passing hour only, but that the Soul may abide in the high consciousness of the Indwelling ONE. Pentecost is, therefore, the time of the Soul's Jubilee.

The Jubilee in Jewish story signified the time when every man and every woman had returned to them the inheritance of those things which, through misfortune, they had had to sacrifice, or of which forebears had been disinherited.

But that was only the social adaptation in Jewry of a spiritual law. Yet it brought many a blessing to the individual life, and put many a limitation on those who would have utterly crushed the life of families and made it almost impossible for there to be any return into the lost inheritance by those who once were the inheritors of outward blessings but had been so unfortunate as to lose them.

But the real Jubilee was significant of the Soul's acquisition of power; the gradual ingathering of spiritual forces; the drinking in of the Breaths of the Heavens, ever more and more deeply as the Soul rose from Kingdom to Kingdom, from Realm to Realm, from Sphere to Sphere, and from Angelic to Celestial states of consciousness, and still on even unto Divine consciousness, wherein the crown of the Sacred Seven was attained, and sevenfoldness of Life realized.

During such a period there is ascension of the Being. The real Ascension, which was related to the Master, signified the Being's ascension, and not the passing of the Master from these outer planes up into any of the Celestial Systems. The Ascension did not require any such phenomenal demonstration. If His passage from the Heavens to make manifest upon the earth was unseen by the world, (even if we could give you no other assurance)—then, reasoning by analogy, you may rest assured that His passing from these outer planes was equally unobserved by the human eye.

PENTECOST RELATED TO THE ASCENSION

That was not what took place. Nor was there any such Ascension at that time on the part of the Master.[1] It could not have been, for He was leaving His intimate ones to go away to take up the burden of the Oblation. To do that great Work necessitated His going away from them and descending from the Christhood, expressed by Him as *the laying down of His Life*. This was a movement which of necessity prevented His intimate ones from being always with Him. For whither He went, they were told they could not follow; but He said He would return to them when the work of the Oblation was accomplished.

In the Scriptures it is recorded that He ascended from a high mountain in Galilee. In another portion it is stated that He led them as far as Bethany and was parted from them; and then, in the Acts of the Apostles it is said that He ascended from the Mount of Olives. Taken literally this could mean that there

---

[1]In an earlier address I have spoken on the Ascension, but here recapitulate the three-fold story because of the bearing of the Ascension upon the Pentecost.—*Vide* THE MYSTERY OF THE ASCENSION, pp. 103-119.

were three Ascensions. Whilst outwardly that could not be, yet mystically they are all true. They are stories of attainments as degrees are taken by the Soul in the advanced path of its Initiation. For the Being must ascend from Galilee, the realm of the Mind known as the Understanding. For GOD is not knowable through the Mind, though at all times HE is observable, and the Mind learns much through understanding the mystery of GOD's glorious manifestations.

But if the Being would know the inner things, it must needs ascend from the Mind into the realms of Divinity. And Bethany is the House of the Christhood. It is the realm of Christ-consciousness. It is the place in the Soul's story to which the LORD loves to come, and where HE loves to dwell. It is the coming of the Being into that abiding consciousness of the LORD Presence with it, around it, and even over it. It is the place where the Being contacts the living LORD, to sit at HIS feet and learn continually from HIM.

Olivet is the Mount of Recovery which is accomplished as an ascension after the degrees of Galilee and Bethany have been taken. For there is no way into the realm of Omniscience, that kingdom whence all things can be revealed and unveiled unto the Soul, but by the high mountains of Galilee, and the Home in Bethany, and then the summit of Olivet.

Thus it may be discerned that the Ascension is intimately associated with Pentecost in a most inward way. For there can be no real Pentecost to the Being except by the process of ascension. If Pentecost stood for external things only, for an outpouring of sweet Breaths from the Angelic worlds, then there would be no need for ascension, though there would be need for receptivity, understanding, and reciprocation. But far more than that is meant. Upon the multitudes these influences are to be poured forth; but by the intimate ones of the Master something greater is to be entered into. And it is to these latter that the mighty power comes. It is said to have come as a rushing, mighty wind, filling all the house where they were; and as a result there appeared upon their heads Living Tongues of Fire.

PENTECOST SPEAKS OF THE JUBILEE

Without Ascension there is no Divine Realization. We may realize the beauty of the world when we are amongst the flowers and the trees, and away from the world-distracting noises. In such hours we may come to know something of the peace of God even amid Nature. But the peace of God in Nature is not that Peace which even the world-distracting noises cannot disturb, which is realized through the equipoise of the Being and the finding of the Lord as a Presence. Though we may feel the joy of the Angelic Life amidst the sweet and beautiful embodiments of the Divine Love and Wisdom in Nature; yet to realize the Angelic world, is something greater. And so, one must go within oneself to find that world through the Angelic Love and learning the Angelic Wisdom. To know God in the majesty of His embodiments, is an experience vastly richer and more real than to look up into the stellar Heavens and behold the unspeakable and glorious revealings of His Majesty. They are there. Yet His Divine Majesty, whilst revealed in the glory of the Stellar Heavens in a measure that must surely impress the Mind, has to be known within the Being as a Presence, ere the Divine Motion can be realized as a rushing mighty Breath.

We know the Divine only in the degree in which we ascend from state to state. Thus Pentecost becomes the crown of the Ascension. In relation to the Soul, it speaks of that which is to be. Concerning Israel, it is the prophecy of the days in which we are living. It is a great indicator of that which is to be accomplished as the outcome of the call of the Word of God. The coming again of the Message is to awaken within the Being the memories of the past, by showing to the vision the real Life, the transcendent Life, the Divine Life, whose motion is God-begotten, and whose circumference is nothing less than the full-rounded expression of Divine Love and Divine Wisdom as a true exposition of its glorious hidden Principle.

That is the Life which reveals HIM in everything—in the inner motion, and in the expression of that motion of the Spirit as it flows from the centre to the full circumference of the Soul's power of manifestation. *It is of this that Pentecost speaks.*

Pentecost signifies that which is yet to be. It is the prophecy of a re-ascended Israel. It is a vain dream, a dream begotten of the dark night throughout the ages of Historical Christianity, to imagine that there was such an outpouring of the Spirit, from the Divine World, as that which is recorded to have taken place on the day of Pentecost.

THE NATURE OF THE ETERNAL SPIRIT

What is Spirit? Can it be poured forth? How is it poured forth, if it can be given? What are its venues? How does it reveal itself?

The Spirit of GOD is the mysterious motion of HIS own Presence within the Being. It is not even the Divine *Aqua* as understood in an atmospheric sense, that can descend as gentle rains upon the earth beneath, or even be outpoured as the mighty showers.

What is the Spirit of GOD? IT creates. IT re-fashions. IT re-formulates. IT changes. IT transforms. IT transmutes. And IT can, through ITS mighty motion, cause great blessings to fall. But the blessings are not to be confounded with ITSELF.

WHAT IS THE SPIRIT OF GOD? It is HIS own Sacred Mystery within us. It is the vital Life-stream within the arterial system of our Being, that has its correspondences in the arterial system of all the bodies, even through to our outer vehicle. It is that Life-stream which gives Life to all our substance. And when that stream is poured forth, it is not sent in any devious way whatever, but enters the bodies fashioned to receive it into their arterial systems, through which it can flow unto the quickening of the whole Being. For the inner body, as well as the outer body, has also its Life-stream. Aye, even the Innermost Sanctuary has flowing through its Divine Substance this Living Stream.

Love is power, and has its influence; it generates atmosphere. Though the atmosphere is the result of it, yet it must not be confounded with itself. The atmosphere is an effect of Love's motion.

Love gives itself in gifts. The gifts are full of the vibrancy of its own Divine potency and motion, and they speak of the beauty of Love and its power. But the gifts are not the Love; they are only the tokens which reveal that it is there. And it is thus with the Spirit.

It is said that when the day of Pentecost was fully come the disciples were all in one place; that they were with one accord gathered together; and that, in that state there came to them this magnificent revealing of the Heavens in the marvellous phenomenon for each one, in the nature of a mighty rushing wind which filled all the house where they were communing.

We will look at that statement, though a little differently from the usual interpretation of it. *There can be no Pentecost without Accord.* They were all in one place with one accord. Naturally, that is thought of in a communal way in relation to the disciples. What is meant is, that the individual must be in accord. He must be unified and equilibrated. All his attributes must be in harmony. They must be in one place—*in the one state.* Their seat must be in, and their sphere of operation must be from the Sanctuary of His Presence—*the one place,* "the upper room" of His dwelling. There must be unification in the Life. There must be accord. Mind, Heart, and Being have to be one in the purpose of Life. If the Heart should be seeking to worship, but the Mind yearning to go out in its earthly ambitions, there could be no accord; there would be no harmony. If the Heart should be yearning to realize the influx of the Life of the Innermost Realm, but the Will in its operation through the lower mind be desirous of accomplishing something for itself in the outer world, then there would be discord between the outer and the inner; and the inward and upward motion of the magnetic streams of Life, and the purpose of the Will in its operation through the mind, would be at variance. Under such circumstances there could be no Pentecost.

No outward influences can bring us the Pentecostal state, unless the state be within us. The outward influences can contribute to the uplifting of us; but the inward state is one realized through accord in our attributes when conflicting elements are healed, and there is harmony and oneness between the innermost and the outermost, thus giving accord right through the Being from the central Principle to the circumference.

THE EFFECTS OF INTENSIVE BAPTISM

For what is Pentecost? What is this mighty rushing Breath that comes to the Being, and reveals itself as a tongue of Living Fire upon the head? It is the great realization of the intensive motion of the Divine Mystery Breath within the Being, when the Soul and all its vehicles can endure its pleromic influx. It is the resultant of being in Divine Accord. It signifies a state of Divine Unity. It is the fruitage of perfect Love. In such a state there is real full-rounded consecration to the Divine Will.

With Pentecost there is Divine motion through all the vehicles. The Divine Presence within sets the Divine Breath in motion in such measure that it flows through all the vehicles. And in its upward flow, it manifests as a tongue of Living Flame. It is the energizing and illumining power of God within the Being. It is the Sacred Flame arising out of and resting upon the Golden Bowl.

Fire is the symbol of energy and illumination, and also of transmutation. In this latter sense there is an apparent destructive aspect. Yet God is never destructive. It is true to affirm of Him that He is "a consuming fire." Nothing that is out of harmony with the states and conditions His Laws create, can abide the day of His coming. He is as "a refiner's fire." When He enters the Being, all the elements which are impure and out of harmony with His Sacred Flame, are consumed in the way; that is, they are changed and transmuted. If that did not happen, the very Chalice would be broken through His power within it. When the Divine Mystery fills all the Being, it is as if the Breaths of the very Heavens were rushing through it, and the Eternities were uttering their voice and making the whole fabric vibrate to, and be in unison with, the Eternal ONE.

It was thus that, as the glorious resultant of the motion of the Breath, there appeared the Living Flame. And it is said that it sat upon their heads as a cloven tongue. Such was the resultant manifest to the Heavens and realized by the Baptized, of the Divine Motion within the Being.

The flow of the sacred stream we have named the Divine Spirit through all the vehicles, issues in the upgathering of them, and in their perfect equilibration. The effect of the combined potencies in motion within the vehicles, is a flame of light. In such a life the intense aspiration of the Being becomes the Soul's Ascension, and the Living Flame is seen arising out from the Sacred Cup whose correspondence in the outer body is called *the pineal gland*.

Its twofoldness speaks of the upward motion of the Flame within the Spiral, and of the downward motion of that Flame as the Stream of Divine magnetic force flows from and returns unto the inner Heart, whose systaltic action gives Life to the vehicles.

All these things are wonderful in the beauty, power and purpose of them, when you understand the Divine Love and Wisdom they reveal. And a Soul who is always Divinely Overshadowed has that understanding. The Sacred Flame is upon his head at all times, though it be unseen and unknown to men. There are no external phenomena associated with the motion of the Divine Mystery within, other than the phenomena to be found in the circumference of life, and which are expressed in the exquisite motion that reveals HIM in every act, in every attitude, and in the Service of Being.

And what this means for the Soul it is not easy to portray. It tells of the exaltation of the Being—though that one will ever be conscious of being in lowly estate in relation to the Divine.

It implies the exaltation of the Being to that realm of sublime realization where it will always have the consciousness of the encompassing and overshadowing Presence; and where, through greatly intensified consciousness, the Soul will come at last into yet higher degrees of the realization of the Indwelling Presence, and will live as in that Presence wheresoever it may be, in this world or some other world, in the Heavens above or in the beneath of the earth. The Soul will live and serve for HIM who is its Life. It will be even as HIMSELF in an accommodated form, revealing HIM in blessed ministry unto some of HIS children. *For such is the meaning of Pentecost.*

THE PROPHECY OF PENTECOST TO BE REALIZED

But there is a further meaning in the Mystery which now may be understood. It is the meaning of the message that has come back to the world in the re-habilitation of the Message of the Master in these Teachings wherein are set forth the Jesus, Christ, and LORD states of consciousness, manifestation and ministry; for such is this Message that at last is to win all the world back to the estate from which it went out. It interprets all the world's motion, the Divine Heart of all Souls, the Vision behind all religious endeavour and expression, and even the cryptic meaning hidden in the nomenclature and liturgy of religious devotion in all lands.

It is the Day for the rehabilitation of the glorious Christhood, because it is the Day of the Return. It is the Day for the coming again into one place and being of one accord, of all the Children of the Kingdom. It is the Day of the re-gathering of the Children of Israel. It is the Day of the Master's return to the Galilæans. But it is far more than that; for it is the Day of the LORD in HIS second coming. Were not all those who heard the Message, Galilæans? Were they not dwellers amid the uplands of Galilee, the land of the illumined Mind? They were Nazarenes. To follow the Message the Master brought, the disciple had to be a Nazarene. To know anything at all about the motion of the Divine Presence within, to understand that Presence and be His consecrated child, the Soul must be Galilæan.

It was thus the intimate ones were Children of High Illumination. They were dwellers in the Nazarene state. They were all Galilæans—those who had been in Galilee with Him of whom they spoke.

It is true that when they spake of the Message, the ONE of whom they spoke was not the personal Master, but the Living LORD. The message they had to give was the Message the Master gave; but it was the Message of the Living GOD. That Message HIS most intimate ones did not confound with the Master, though it had association with Him in the embodiment of it, the form of it, and the travail of the Oblation. Yet the Message itself was always the LORD's Message, and not thought of by them in any personal relationship to Him. He was to them the Beloved One who was the Servant of their LORD.

THE RETURN OF ISRAEL TO CHRISTHOOD

It is the Day of the Return through the Message. It is the Return of the Being to that glorious vision. It is the Day of the Ascension. of the Soul. It is the hour of the triumph of Love. It is the Day of the Ascension for all Israel.

Pentecost is said to have come ten days after the Ascension. Now, ten is the number of the first great degree of Christhood. Therefore, Souls who ascend into the Heavens in their state, rise into that glorious degree of high Christhood, wherein the Radiance will for evermore shine within them. It will be found by them to shine ever more and more unto the perfect day of HIS coming—that is, the perfect day of the Divine *becoming* within them. For GOD *comes* in the Breaths; but HE *becomes* through changing the fashion of the Soul in its ascension in consciousness unto HIMSELF as the result of the motion of the Divine Breaths.

Now, just look for a moment at this story, even in the imperfect form in which it is given in the Acts of the Apostles, and see if there be not a yet deeper and fuller significance in the event of Pentecost. We have a description of those who heard the disciples speak in tongues unknown to the speakers, though each man heard in his own tongue. But the reference is not to languages spoken by men and women; though that is the interpretation usually given to the event. The inspired and GOD-endued ones spake the language of the Soul in varied vernacular. Their speech betrayed them. It revealed to those who could understand and veiled from those who could not, the sacred Mysteries. To the latter it was an unknown tongue. The Tongues were the gifts of the Spirit. They were the resultant of the motion of the Spirit within the Being. Their Tongues or speech revealed the motion of the Living Flame.

THE MINISTRIES OF ISRAEL ARE MANIFOLD

Now, consider this part of the story wherein it is recorded that there were dwelling in Jerusalem devout men and women of all nations:—Parthians, Medes, and Elamites; dwellers in Mesopotamia, Judæa, and Cappadocia; Pontus, Asia, and Phrygia; Pamphylia, Egypt, and the parts of Libya about Cyrene, and sojourners from Rome, Cretes and Arabians; and these heard of the wonderful works of GOD in their own tongue as the Mysteries were unveiled by the endued ones. How the glamour of the supposed miracle has miraged the Truth! For these terms are all mystical. The terms were made use of to embody mystic things.

The Parthian means, a partaker of GOD. He is one who mediates of the Divine Mystery, who has held that office and therefore is ever a Parthian, or one who knows GOD. He has the shaft or power of GOD, and his glance is full of the Radiance.

The Mede represents the Medo-Persian Kingdom, spoken of as the realm of Cyrus, where Cyrus reigned. Cyrus means the Sun, and is related to the Christhood. It is He who gives power to Israel to return unto the Land of the Temple of the LORD.

The Elamites are "the aged ones." Therefore the Elamites indicate the patriarchal souls who are crowned with ages of spiritual story, and who have been as arch-fathers and arch-mothers in the world.

The dwellers in Mesopotamia, since the word means "the land of streams," or of flowing waters, relates to those seekers who make their dwelling places amidst the streams of God, those streams which are at last to nourish the very desert.

The land of Judæa is the land of praise, and the real Judah is the House of praise. So the dwellers there were those who loved the Divine rhythmic motion which is Praise.

Cappadocia is a combined word meaning "the glory of the Mind illumined," and thus the reference is to illumined minds who dwelt in the Land of the Light.

Pontus represents the bridge that crosses the river; but it also means "the Great Deep." Those who can move within its waters are the dwellers there. It is Asia-Minor.

Asia is the land of the Spirit's ministry; the Asiatic parts of the Being are those which bring through the ministrations of the Spirit into concrete expression.

Phrygia is the country and state of the Seekers, those who are ever seeking to know the Mysteries, that they may embody and interpret more and more beautifully the Divine Life.

Pamphylia relates to the lovers of fame, those who love to make themselves famous. It is a matter of course that there are Souls even in an unfallen world who love fame; but not for its own sake. They seek fame because they have to minister in that realm in the offices of great Teachers, great Artists, great Scientists, great Administrators. With wrong direction, of course, many may seek fame for fame's sake and merely to be famous. But that is not worth the endeavour. To be famous in the sense of embodying God without thinking of fame at all, is the way to be truly famous; because the influence of such is abiding. It does not pass away with the flight of the ages.

And you will note that Phrygia and Pamphylia (although the punctuation follows Pamphylia) take in Egypt. Now, Egypt represents the outer life, the manifest life; and it is there that Souls seek for knowledge, and that they seek to be even famous. It is there that they strive to acquire fame and power. A Soul may do it beautifully. It may strive to be famous in the sense of becoming divinely beautiful and gifted; not to minister to pride and vanity, but to be so gifted that the right use of the gifts can contribute to the blessing of many. That is the way to be famous on the outer planes.

And the parts of Libya about Cyrene. These are the parts of the lower mind's activity of which the word Cyrene is the symbol; and Rome is the realm of muscular activity where the Cretans and Arabians also dwell. These Cretans are those who live chiefly for the sense-life. Paul is said to have called them "slow-bellies." The Arabians are those who dwell in the desert places, amid the arid sands of spiritual death.

THE TEACHINGS MEET ALL SOUL NEEDS

Here you have a revealing of the meaning of Pentecost. It is the outpouring into the Being of the Eternal Potencies. Thus the dynamics of Life are raised even to the Divine World in those who have realized the motion of the Spirit. And through all these, the peoples in their various states shall hear this Message concerning the living LORD of Being, as the LORD Christ in Jesus manifestation through HIS children. And it shall go forth from the rivers to the ends of the earth. The Rivers of the Divine Love shall bear it, and the Streams of the Divine Wisdom reveal it, till all Souls shall know it in the degree in which they are able to receive of it. The Parthians who once mediated the Divine Mystery, shall be arrested at once, because the Messenger in the Message speaks as one who knows the Mystery of the Divine Love and Wisdom. And those who are Medes and Elamites will understand that the Radiant Presence is ever their Sun, even as when they were ancient Zoroastrians and worshipped the Sun as the LORD of Being. As Medo-Persians they will understand the symbol of Cyrus who was their Christos. For Cyrus is the Christ under whom there is accomplished the great liberation of Israel from out the land of Babylon, and the return to their own land to rebuild their Sanctuary and reinstitute the Law of GOD; and then to rebuild Jerusalem until it has become once more The Holy City of the LORD.

Thus is the Message of Pentecost unto those who were children of the Sun, though they now be dwellers by the streams of the desert; Souls who love the glory of illumined understanding, who would seek to minister in the land of Phrygia, and even along the path of the Pamphylians; and those who would seek to do those ministries that are accounted outwardly famous works, though they are, when true in vision and rightly accomplished, but the reflex of the great Divine motion within the Being.

WHO IS READY AND EQUAL TO RESPOND?

Such was to be the Day of Pentecost. And it is now beginning. The mighty rushing Breath in the Within can be heard. It can be felt there, if there be Accord. If all the powers are gathered into *the one place* where that Breath can come, even the inner Sanctuary of Being; if there be a real uplifting and indrawing, a true Ascension of Being; then there will be such a baptism, the baptism that is to accomplish for every one of the children of the FATHER-MOTHER who has won unto the glory of HIS Presence, the ability to speak to Souls in their own tongue, to so understand such Souls as to accommodate the Message for them, and interpret it truly unto them.

Here is a vision of life and ministry for you. You sing, "*Oh, for the living flame!*" But though you thus pray in song, it will not come down from the Heavens to you. It is the resultant of the Divine motion in you. Oh, for the living flame that burns upon GOD'S own Altar, means the Spiral Flame upon the Altar of your Being. It can only burn through HIS motion in you; it is its resultant. It is within to be yours; for it is HIS gift to you. It is the power to embody unto the revealing of HIMSELF, even in the innermost, and right through all the estate of your Being, even unto the desert places, till the desert places again rejoice and blossom with the rose of Life, the emblem of Love, the revealings of Love, the motion of Love. It is a vision of that time when you will love to sense and understand divinely the real meaning of even the outer life, and make it beautiful and sweet, wholesome and pure, an embodiment worthy of a child of GOD whose fashion reveals the majesty and glory of the Divine Love, and the beauty of the Divine Wisdom.

Oh, come up with me to the Inner Room! Come up to the Room of perfect Accord! Come up to the Altar within the one Place of HIS Presence, HIS dwelling place, and there abide to pray! Ascend in state. Here there is felt the mighty motion of the glorious Breath. Here there is entered into the transcendent vision of HIMSELF. Here there is realized the power of HIS sacred motion in the mysterious Tongue of Living Flame, even HIS energy within us, HIS energy pouring itself forth into and through the Being.

THE ADVENT OF PAUL

THE ADVENT OF PAUL

It is St. Paul's Day in which the Churches celebrate his conversion. Of the man I would speak to you. My theme will be a further elucidation of the theme of last Wednesday evening which was concerning *Human Claims and Divine Realities.* Those of you who were present will remember that the Claims referred to had relation to divine gifts in apostolic succession; and that there was shown the contrast between them as claims and the great Realities.

I take it you are all familiar with your New Testament, first in relation to the Gospel stories, and then in relation to the Pauline Letters.

THE APOSTOLATE AS TOLD IN THE GOSPELS

Now in the Gospel stories it is set forth that those whom the Master is said to have chosen, concerning whom we spake intimately last week, were not chosen only to follow Him, but to receive the Message He had to give; and that, as a result of the reception of that Message, powers would come upon them from the Highest; that is, through their receptivity of the divine motion caused to play upon them through the unveiling of Life's Mystery within them, and the great Purpose of the FATHER-MOTHER concerning this world and all HIS children, they should rise up in consciousness into states of realization wherein the most heavenly endowments would become their possession. For, as He taught them, the potencies of all such endowments were not only latent within them but greatly cultured, and needed but the touch of the Divine Hand to set them all in divine motion again, through which they would come into high realization.

To those intimate ones of the Master it did seem most wonderful. They were well aware, although they loved to bask in the atmosphere of His presence in which they found the atmosphere of the Angelic and even the Divine Worlds as these encompassed Him as the result of the magnetic motion within Him, causing His auric outflow to be unto them as Angelic streams, that He could not transfer to them any powers, nor give to them principalities. For powers were divinely gifted to the Soul These were resultants in the Being gained through attainment; and all principalities, realms of dominion, and regnancy, were the gifts of the FATHER-MOTHER.

Yet it was wonderful to be so filled with hope that they would be worthy successors on these outer planes, embodying that most glorious Mystery of Love and Radiance which it was His honour and joy to give them. Nor did this hope depart from them even in those days of most intimate fellowship when shadows seemed to fall upon the threshold as He unveiled to them the necessity for the Work entitled the Oblation. They were still full of hope that it might not be necessary for Him to bear such a burden, though He often sought to impress upon them that it was necessary for Him to leave them for a time.

THE INITIATES HIS TRUE SUCCESSORS

It was thus they came to know by the path *via dolorosa*, that GOD'S way is not man's way, nor even the way of the Children of the Kingdom when these do not see beyond the immediate perspective with limited circumference and horizon that only takes in the things that are immediate in the sense of nearness. They had themselves to learn (for they could not, for a long time, accept His statements about this *via dolorosa* which He must needs pass through) that GOD'S way of telling HIS Message to the world was not after the manner of human concepts; and that they were to be the transmitters of that Message even as they had been the receivers. So their hearts were filled with hope. How long that hope in its full splendour remained with them, we cannot speak of now; for it would bear us far afield in many directions; and elsewhere I have spoken of the total eclipse of that hope.

Now in relation to apostolic succession, believed in by so many, in order that ye may understand such claims, it is well to remember that it is most natural to think that the intimate friends of the Master who knew most about Him, must surely have known most about the Teachings; that they heard these as they listened to Him; and saw the states of His own glorious Love and motion; that they witnessed many things of which they could not speak and which could not be chronicled; that they had hours of such intimacy with Him which might not be unveiled to the world. You would have expected, naturally, that if there had been any succession at all named apostolic, they would have been truly the recipients and the transmitters.

And it is said in the New Testament stories that "He breathed on them and said, Receive ye the Holy Ghost"; also that He counselled them thus; "Go ye into all the world and preach this gospel to all creatures, baptizing them in the name of the Father, Son and Holy Ghost." And still following the story in the Records, we read that He said further unto them, "Whosoever's sins ye remit, they are remitted; and whosoever's sins ye shall retain, they are retained unto them."

From this you would have thought their qualification was supreme if there had been such a thing as "apostolic succession." And yet the dramatic situation of the "Day of Pentecost" has to be introduced in order to crown them fully with apostolic powers. Taking for granted, as most of you will have done in other days if not in these, that that story was as it is represented to be, you would think that they were endowed sublimely and supremely for the work of the transmission of power to the world; and that, if such a thing as "apostolic succession" could have any existence whatsoever, from the hour when He breathed upon them it must surely have been divinely and fully imparted.

And yet the great drama that was to have been accomplished as the result of the Manifestation, even as men and women have dreamt of it, could not be continued, notwithstanding the rich endowment bestowed upon these beloved ones, without the adventure of another coming upon the scene with equal and even greater claims. The new comer knew not the Master; nor did he share in Pentecost. He is a Jew of the Jews. There was no hurt in that, for all the children are the children of the FATHER-MOTHER. But he calls himself "a Hebrew of the Hebrews," a Jew of the Jews, that is, one steeped in Jewish rabbinical lore. His name is Saul. He sits at the feet of Gamaliel, a well-informed teacher, not only in Jewish lore, but in Roman Law. He hears the story of the Master. It arrests him. It arouses in him something he does not understand. It is an oral tradition; for at that time there were no written records, except the two that were held by the Brotherhood,—the real story written by the intimate disciple Matthew, and another, which formed a companion, of such Sayings of the Master as were to be held in writing, called *The Logia of Ioannes.* Saul heard the Story of Ioannes through the oral transmission. It is said that annoyance and anger were aroused in him by the Story. He says of himself that he went out determined to suppress the new movement, and to hale men and women and take them to prison, and have them condemned unto death.

ON THE WAY TO DAMASCUS

The drama changes. Saul is on his way, it is said, to Damascus on a mission of persecution. And on that way he beholds a light, and he hears a voice. The light he claims to be the radiance of the Heavens, and the voice the voice of the Master Jesus. It might, indeed, have been a light shone forth from the Lower Angelic World to arrest a mind that was great and a heart that had many noble qualities, to stay the hand in wrong service and the feet from following a false direction. It might have been a voice that spake from out the Cloud of Glory, calling a Soul up into the regions of realities and away from the rabbinical lore of Jewry that had become as lifeless leaves; calling it away from seeking for knowledge that in itself brought no exaltation of Being, and no empowerment for the embodiment of GOD.

It might have been such a Light that shone, and such a

Voice that spake. But all the subsequent motion reveals that it could not have been. Few will be able to hear this unto the receiving of it. Yet the day is hastening when the Church must learn the truth. That call was the hour of triumph for those who had sought to make the Manifestation impossible; who were out to defeat that Manifestation as a revelation of Divine Childhood in its true nature and embodiment as Jesushood and Christhood. It was the triumph of the enemies who sought to overthrow the Master himself all through the days of the Manifestation, and who were determined to pursue Him, and would have done so had He not always been so veiled that they could not find Him. For, if His intimate ones did not know Him when they met Him in the way during the Lives of the Oblation; if even the Angelic World did not know Him as He trod the planes of the world bearing the Burden of the Passion of the LORD, except those specially appointed to minister directly unto Him (for even the Angelic World had to be closed during that period), you can see how it was impossible for any who were other than friendly, to know who He was and where He was, as He trod out the winepress in the Oblation.

It is self evident that the call of Paul was not a divine call, but a call of the occult world; that the voice which spake to him could not have been that of the Master, for at that time the Master was in the first Life of the Oblation and in the heart of Rome. These things are not amongst the New Testament Records, for they were not then known. But now we know them. During the period covered by Paul coming on the scene and making his claims, and the great inception, and development of early historical Christianity, the Master was in Rome bearing His first Life of Burden. He was then carrying the first "tree" of the many "trees" of the Passion of the Cross, where the LORD HIMSELF—not the Master, but the Divine Potency in Him, the Divine Motion in Him, the Divine Love in Him that was as a consuming fire—moved amongst men upon the earth as a Tree, the Cross, bearing the burden unto the healing of the Planetary Heavens and the blotting out of the awful states upon them to make the Redemption for all the children possible, and to ensure at the close of the Oblation, if not before it, some degree of the ascension of all those Souls known as Israel, whom He came to seek unto the finding of.

THE PASSING OF THE TRAINED INITIATES

Now, as this new star breaks upon the firmament of human thought and rises above the horizon and ascends to the zenith, the stars of the firmament whose light had been rekindled by the Message, and who had been divinely endowed for the purpose of carrying the light of that Message to the whole world, grow dimmer and dimmer, until they become changed from stars of the first magnitude to be stars of the fifth and even sixth magnitude; whilst the new star, Paul, fills the heavens with the brilliance of his personality and the glamour of such a message as he has to give to the world. Even the glory of Peter on whom the Church has built itself throughout the ages, grows dim before the splendour of Paul. And in the story told by the writer of the Acts of the Apostles, it is said that Paul rebuked Peter. It is well to remember that even Peter, concerning whose going to Rome tradition is quite uncertain, though it is claimed that he founded the Papal See through which now all apostolic succession proceeds, is superseded. For the apostle of the New Testament is Paul. There are four Gospel Records, and then the Acts of the Apostles. In the Gospel narrative the disciples have a place, and some of them share in the first act of the drama of the Acts, until Paul arrives to fill the stage and turn the drama with its several further acts, into the story of his missionary journeys. From thence he fills most of the New Testament with the Epistles to the Romans, first and second Epistles to the Corinthians, the Epistles to the Galatians, first and second Thessalonians, Ephesians, Colossians, Philippians, Philemon, Titus, and first and second Timothy—thirteen Letters in all. We have all these books, and in addition the Epistle to the Hebrews, which many have attributed to him, and which bears his name in the New Testament. And though there are wonderful things in these books, strange "sayings" seemingly inserted quite apart from their context, like so many in the Old Scriptures which are found separated from the context and the subsequent narration, these profound Sayings were borrowed from the Teachings of the Master, and do not belong to Paul. For, by the time the Epistles were written, the manuscripts containing the Sayings of the Master had been found and taken away from the Brotherhood. For the first Gospel story issued to the communities of Christians that had arisen through the oral tradition, was that of "The Gospel of the Holy Twelve," which was largely compiled from the two stolen Records. That record is almost contemporaneous with the first of Paul's Epistles.

THE MASTER'S TEACHINGS CHANGED

It was thus that the wonderful, secret Teachings given by the Master came to be handled by those who did not understand them, and who had not known Him. And they so presented His Sayings, that unto this day they are not understood in the New Testament. Where is Jesus in the New Testament, except in the name given to the Master? Where is Jesushood and all that He stood for? It is so mixed up in a general way with other elements, that the reader cannot distinguish it. Where is the meaning of Christhood to be found, that high state of consciousness into which the Master called those intimate ones? It is related to Him personally in such a way, that, to think of Christ, the reader must think of the Master in the person, instead of relating Christ to the LORD of Being. The Master was in the state of Christhood; but when He asked the intimate ones to behold Christ, it was not Himself He referred to, but the glory of the Indwelling CHRIST Who was to clothe them with HIS own radiance through the motion of the divinity within them. Through contacting that One they were to be clothed from on High. They were to be garmented with that radiance and rise into real apostolic power. CHRIST was to endow them with the powers of ambassadors. Those sent forth from the Divine World came with a state of consciousness of that World in themselves; and it would be so with them that they might carry the Message of the glorious redeemed Jesus-life, and the vision of the splendour of Christhood unto the House of Israel.

From all this it may be seen that the Church itself is built upon Paul and his Epistles, though it takes the name of Peter. It is Paul who laid the foundations of historical Christianity, and his writings have been its directing genius. And though he did not intentionally mislead the whole western world, yet through his dominating mind and the misdirections that took place in him, and the strange illusion which overtook him, he caused the historical disaster to the Message.

FAILURE OF PAULINE CHRISTIANITY

Is it any wonder that Christianity is said to have failed? Men and women have been carried away by a glamour of religious vision, human claims and presentations, rather than the exquisite beauty of the Divine reality whose foundations are of GOD within the Being; whose superstructure is from GOD, of the nature of Jesushood. To see Jesus, is to see the vision of a Life of beauty begotten of Divine Love. To follow Jesus, is to follow the vision of Life unto the embodiment of it. There is no other following of Jesus. It is this the western world has not understood. It is of this Jesus the Church still seems to know nothing. It worships a name only. To follow is to walk in the same footsteps as the Teacher, to pursue the same path as the Guide, to have the like vision as the one who unveils, to have the same exquisite motion, the same wondrous, holy purpose as the Leader.

And in like manner is it with the discipleship to the Christ. To follow Christ is not simply to revere the Master or any servant. You may do that if it cherishes and comforts the heart to revere His memory. There are many people who revere His memory who do not follow the Christ He revealed. They know no more about Christhood to-day than they did when first they believed, because they relate Christhood to the person of the Servant, and see not that it has relation to the superstructure of Being, to the inner Sanctuary of the Soul, to the glory of divine realizations by the Soul, to the wonderful mediatorial ministries within its Sanctuary.

Christhood is a state of conscious realization of divine vision and potency. It is the knowledge in realization of the Overshadowing and Indwelling One. These are the divine realities the Master taught His intimate ones. They are the divine realities that were lost through the mirage. Alas! that the mirage should continue! But it is manifest throughout Christendom. There have been many revivals during the Christian era in this country and elsewhere, where wonderful experiences of illumination and power have been claimed. Then all the new influence has passed away, like a fleeting breath of wind after it has shaken the leaves upon the trees, leaving no permanent results of the embodiment of Jesushood and Christhood.

It is necessary to distinguish between religious emotion and true religious motion. For religious emotion may never pass beyond the outer circle of the emotional spheres; whereas religious motion is related to the great Spirit within us that has nought to do with mere beliefs and dogmas, nor even with ecclesiasticism, but with the Kingdom of GOD which is within. Here it is not implied that Souls may not worship in the Church. But mere outward worship and beliefs and revival of phenomena, and all such manifestations and embodiments, are not to be confused with and mistaken for the motion of the Divine Spirit in us making for the realization and embodiment of the exquisite Jesus-love, and the radiance which is beyond all telling, even the Light of Christ. For the Jesus-Love and the Light of Christ are not passing phases in the realm of emotion, but Divine estates that fill and hold the Being. There is great emotion, but its motion is of the Great Deep. When the story of the Light comes, the Light itself must shine within. The Light of Christ is the radiance begotten of magnetic motion within the Being. It is the Christ's motion within. It is of the Christ in you, the glorious hope of the perfect realization of Jesus, Christ, and the LORD, conscious states of Being wherein you will know HIM Who is LORD of all.

If only the New Testament could be put into the fire of purification and have all its false elements consumed away, then there would issue forth those things which the Master spake, separated from all the elements which are found associated with them as the result of the Pauline betrayal; and that all men and women could see with the understanding, and receive with the heart, the glorious Message which He gave to Israel and the world, and unto which He called His beloved ones that they might embody it and be GOD'S ambassadors!

THE RETURN OF THE MASTER IN THE MESSAGE

Many ages have risen and set, and Christianity is much, in a sense, where it was centuries ago. But there is this difference in the present time; the Message that was so changed as to be beyond recognition even by the Sons of GOD themselves, those beloved intimate ones who once knew the Christhood, is being restored again, and is calling Souls unto the Jesus Christ estates of Life, as in the days of the Manifestation. That Message will now prevail. The Oblation has accomplished this. It now calls Souls unto the embodiment and the realization of the blessed estates of Jesushood and Christhood, and for those who can go so far, even the LORD consciousness. As the Master called in those far away days, so the Message has to call to-day. It is the same Message though given under different conditions, and surrounded by different circumstances. It is the same Message of the Soul's inherent, divine inheritance, which when unfolded, gives to the recipient the consciousness of living in the ever most Blessed ONE.

And the path unto the way of Love and Light and Life, is by the wondrous way of Jesus, Christ, the LORD. For a man must know Jesus before he can know Christ. Have no vain dreams about this Life and this Message. You must know Jesus, the purified life, the life of compassion and pity, of Love majestic and lowly, of potency mighty and gentle, of Love that learns to love all and fails towards none; Love that gives without measure, and does not complain in its giving; Love that is willing to be even as the Divine; Love that fills the Being with such a motion that it is irresistible; and it *must* go on to know Christ, the glory of Love itself in its radiant potency within the Being. *That is Christ*. It is the motion of divine power in you that brings illumination, until all the Sanctuary is radiant with HIS Radiance, and the Soul comes at last to know everything in the Light of HIS Countenance. And we can know the LORD only through this Christhood. For the LORD is not a man, but a Presence. HE is not even an Angel, though HE has HIS Angel. HE is not even an Archangel, though HE has HIS glorious Patriarchal Angels. HE is not just one of the ELOHIM, but all the ELOHE in one.

And HE can be known. There is no glamour where HE is. There is no uncertainty where HE is known. The Message where HE is known, is not as a reed shaken by every passing breath that is contrary to itself; it is steadfast. And by this Message are ye again called in this hour. Ye are called away from the human claims to the Divine Realities; away from the paths where you sought outwardly to attain the powers that can come to you only from within the Being, as the divinity within you unfolds and expands, and brings you into the realms of realization; ye are called to come back to Divine Realities where there is perfect certitude, real knowledge, most blessed light, transcendent vision of glory and enrichment and power that enables the Being to take the flight of the Spirit into the regions of the ever Blessed ONE. And yet the Message calls you to remain as little children in your spirit. For you could not get up there, if the Being is not as a little child in its Spirit. Christ in the Soul is mighty yet lowly; full of majesty that is also exquisite tenderness; crowned with divine dignity, yet ever the little child of HIM who is the LORD of All.

These are the Realities unto which you are called. Without them there is no attainment such as we have spoken of. With them all things become yours. Nor can Paul, nor Cephas, nor Apollos, nor any other claimant who may have written and spoken, deprive you of the Divine Inheritance.

Paul had a great heart; he has suffered greatly through his error. His sorrow was indeed great when he awoke to know that the real persecution of the Saints of GOD, was not simply the haling of men and women who had accepted the oral message that had been handed down to them, and the causing of them to suffer; but that the real betrayal of Jesus, and of the LORD, was the betrayal of the Message which he understood not, in giving a message that was foreign to the Message of the Master.

How know we these things? Are they not all known in the Divine World, along with the Travail of the Oblation? Think you these things are of man? They are of GOD. Unto Paul would we send great Peace and Joy, and to all who went his way, piling up the Burden of the tragedy of the Passion of the LORD. Peace unto all who in their mistaken motion made that way such a *via dolorosa* for the Master, as none but the Gods could understand!

Unto you HIS Peace, and the great Realities which bring that Peace as an abiding inheritance and fill life's cup with the Joy that is yet a stranger in this world, but which is of the nature of the Kingdom of GOD.

O Divine Lover of Souls, our FATHER-MOTHER, how shall we ever express all that THOU art for us and unto us in THY giving? How shall we ever tell the story of the LORD'S Passion, and the Mystery of THY Love in the Travail?

Yet would we give ourselves unto the following of this way wherein THOU mayest become again made manifest upon these planes unto this needy world, even in the manifestation of THY Jesus, THY Christ, and THY glorious Lord-Presence within us for evermore.

Amen and Amen.

THE PRECIOUS STONE
WHICH THE
BUILDERS REJECTED

THE PRECIOUS STONE
WHICH THE
BUILDERS REJECTED

THE MASONIC STONE OF HISTORY

The Stone which the builders are said to have rejected is generally associated with the personal Master. He is thought of as the foundation and chief corner stone in the Temple of God. With Him has been associated the whole superstructure of the Divine Temple; for He has been accounted the foundation upon which men and women must needs build in order to attain a place in that Temple. The builders are thought of chiefly in relation to those who were at the head of the Jewish and Græco-Roman administrations, and who on the one hand, had to do with empire, and on the other, with the priesthood. And as the Master was thought of as the foundation stone on which humanity was to build, and the chief corner stone, representing the completion and perfect expression of all angles and heights; so the rejection of Him by the builders is chiefly related to the Jewish and the Græco-Roman powers. And especially is it thought of in relation to the priesthood of the times in which He lived.

It is amazing that, after so many centuries of the historical development which passes under the name of Christianity, it should not even yet be perceived what was then meant, and what is now meant, by the terms *Foundation Stone*, and the *Chief Corner Stone*, and what the rejection of that Stone laid in Zion means.

The builders in relation to the Christian Institutional development, were those who laid the foundations of the superstructure of the Church. They claimed to understand the personal Master and the Divine Teacher. They claimed to know the Divine Mind in relation to His Church. That which was to have become a glorious concrete expression through individual and communal life and fellowship, was turned into a concept of a Church having the insignia of Christ, but without understanding Christhood; claiming indeed the very signature of the Master as authority for the erection of a great earthly system, but without knowing Him; proclaiming belief in Him as a personal saviour, king and priest, as well as prophet and redeemer, but having no true understanding of these blessed estates and ministries; claiming that the Eternal Life of which He spake could by belief alone be come at and found unto realization; and claiming to have the power to give unto all who came within the Fold, the White Stone with the Unutterable Name upon it, as an inheritance, and the Glowing Stone through priestly administration.

RELATING THE STONE TO THE MASTER

All through the ages of that historical development, the claim has been made that the Master as the Christ was the foundation of all true belief; that He was in the Church; that it was His Church, and was the outer vehicle through which to express the travail of His Soul, and the glorious revelation of God given by Him. Even in the departures that came in later ages wherein many symbols were used, the claim was still made that the Church was the Church of the Living God, founded in Christ, and as established by the Master; that it was the venue of His voice and His speech to the world. Unto this day it is still thought by the vast multitudes who form the communities of the Church universal, that He who was the Master, the burden-bearer as well as the healer in the sense of being the redeemer through the Cross has directed His Church universal from the Heavens, ministered unto it, and administered through it. And so its claims have gone on from age to age; condemning those who have dared to stand outside its pale; but all the while *rejecting the stone laid as the foundation of Life* by the Divine Love through His Son.

Oh, the sorrow of it! The tragedy of it! That there should be such a night of darkness where the radiance of the Sun of Glory is claimed!

The builders were those who created the great religious

institutions. And here I do not mean, the Churches and the Cathedrals, but the institutions which have stood for the Teachings of the Master, and have continued throughout the ages since the Churches' foundations were laid by Paul, until these days. For those institutions claimed to be the treasure houses of that Foundation Stone, that sublime Divine Mystery. And, with rare exceptions indeed, those institutions have believed and proclaimed that unless the Soul came within their folds, it could not attain unto the possession of that Stone, and must needs be considered by the Heavens to be a partaker with those who had rejected the Christ.

If this be tragic, it is also pathetic. If it brings anguish, the anguish is begotten of the very pathos of the situation. For, though the Church called by the name of Christ in the European nations, from Armenia to this land, and in the far west and south where the manifestation is great in buildings, in beliefs, and in ritual, testifies of the Christ historically, and the manifestation reveals the Church in its earthly power and dominion; yet through the whole historical development, that which has been claimed by the Church, and affirmed concerning those who rejected it in its claim, *was and is the inversion of the truth.*

THE MASTER UNVEILED THE STONE

The Master was not the Foundation Stone, but the interpreter of it. The Master was not the Chief Corner Stone, but the unveiler and manifestor of its sacred Mystery. Nor was He the White Stone with the Mystery Name engraven upon it; though He knew that Mystery, and could, when occasion required, break the seal. For thus could the Mystery become revealed.

Our consciousness of the tragedy deepens when we look through the ages and see how the Foundation Stone has been rejected by those who profess to be the builders upon it, and how little they and their successors have understood the inner meaning of the Chief Corner Stone. The whole Church has yet to learn the distinction between the personal Master and the Christhood; the distinction between personal embodiment and individual expression of the Divine Mystery, and the cosmic CHRIST. The builders of the great institutions have yet to learn that the secret of the Foundation Stone is not to be had their way at all, though many within the Church have touched that Stone through divine desire, through Godlike feeling, through true Soul emotion in their prayer, in their aspiration, and in ecstatic visionary moments. For the Stone which the builders have rejected is, on the one hand, the living Christ as the Glowing Stone in sacrificial ministry; and, on the other, the White Stone of the Soul's inheritance of high consciousness in the Temple of the FATHER-MOTHER.

THE REJECTION OF THE STONE All who refuse to go in the way of Jesus Christ reject the Stone. All who refuse to build upon the foundations of Love, and make concrete the radiance of Love in the life of Love, reject that Stone.

All Souls build. They build individually, as well as communally. They build within and without themselves, as well as in the great institutions. They build in religious thought, and feeling, and ministries. But how few in their building grasp the significance of the terms, Jesus, Christ, and the LORD! How difficult it is even for the Children of the Kingdom in these days of the Return, to apprehend and grow to comprehend, the length and the breadth, the height and the depth, embodied in these terms, Jesus, Christ, and the LORD! Other foundation can no man lay than that which is laid, even Jesus Christ. But you will now understand that Jesus Christ is not the historical Master. Jesus Christ is that Life which He realized within Himself, and revealed through Himself, and expressed in all the ministry He gave, and interpreted in the Teachings concerning the Soul's ultimate estate.

The Foundation Stone is none other than the LORD of Being as the Great Love. Upon that Love men and women must build. They cannot build wood, hay, and stubble upon it, for its Flame would consume such a structure. They must build with the golden Love of the Being, the silver of illumined intuition, and the precious stones of living virtues. For the gold is the symbol of the giving of Love to that mysterious Flame, that wonderful and inexpressible Glowing Stone, who is the LORD of Being; gold to be used for exalted service; gold that can be beaten out into the most exquisite forms; gold that never tarnishes, wherein there is no alloy. And the silver is nothing less than pure Faith, touched by that Glowing Stone, mercurial in its potencies and its ministries: for silver is of the vision, and the glory that accrues through it to the Soul. Thus the building upon the precious Stone, is with the gold of Love, the silver of true vision and true action, and all the precious virtues, opaque and transparent, the shielders and the veilers, the revealers, transmitters, and reflectors; for they are the precious stones of the Being's divine attributes. All the precious stones are from HIM Who is at once the Sardius Stone or glorious ONE, and Whose glory must needs also be veiled, as with a Jasper stone.

THE FAILURE OF MANY BUILDERS

The stone which the builders despised and rejected, was none other than the real Christhood. The institutions took the historical name. They took all the historical associations. They took the supposed historical stories. But they rejected all for which the apparently historical stood. They rejected the full-rounded pure way in life. They would have none of it; although Souls did arise from time to time proclaiming it as the true way. The early centuries reveal a fearful betrayal of Christ. There were Souls who cried aloud to other Souls, within the increasing darkness, as is testified to by many of the writings of the Apostolic and post-Apostolic Fathers.

But the builders, speaking generally, failed to understand. They would not permit such teachings to obtain and prevail. Thus has it come to pass that Christ has never been in Christendom, except as a personal leader to be believed in and followed, after the manner of the historical and traditional interpretations given concerning Him.

The real Stone laid was the Mystery of GOD in the

rebuilding of the Temple of the Christhood. It was and is the Masonic Stone; for the word *mason* means builder. All masonic ritual and symbol, in their first beautiful meanings, implied building, on the Foundation Stone of the Christhood, the beautiful Temple of God in the Soul, which is the real Temple of Solomon, the Divine Man.

That Foundation Stone is great in its effect upon life. To the Soul who builds upon it, it becomes none other than the Glowing Stone from the Altar of God. In its touch upon life, it makes everything pure and beautiful. When it is applied by divine ministrants, it gives the Being the consciousness of the healing power of the Great Love. When it is understood by the Soul, it reveals the glory of God in His sacrificial ministry for His children. When appropriated by the Soul, it energizes all the Being, filling the very life-stream with the potencies of the Fire, or Sacred Flame of God.

THE GLOWING STONE OF CHRIST

The Stone which the builders have rejected is a Glowing Stone. It is the sure foundation of the Radiant Life. The Stone which the western world needs to have thrown into its midst is this Glowing Stone. It is the Mystery of God in Christ. It is this interpretation of the Father-Mother Love as expressed in, and revealed through, the estates of Jesus Christ. Through such glorious revealings, the Divine Love draws the Being on to realize Jesus, until the state of Jesus reigns through all the world of the Being, lifting every attribute up to that yet higher estate named Christhood, wherein the regnancy is of Christ, and the Life is crowned with the Light of Christ, which is Love's radiance: and then by the combined dynamic forces contained in the estates of Jesus Christ, lifting the Being still upward and farther on to the consciousness of the Eternal One, named the Lord, wherein the Glowing Stone becomes part of the very Being, and the Being receives in perfect fulness of expression that White Stone whereon the name of the Mystery is written, that Name which none knoweth but those unto whom it is revealed.

The Stone which the builders despised and rejected, is the Stone which has been, as it were, thrown from the very Heavens once more into the midst of the great city built up upon other foundations. It is the great city spoken of as Babylon; the city full of great misdirected potencies, strange superstructures, astonishing inversions, most sad and pitiable perversions and tragedies unspeakable resulting from the subversion of all for which the Divine Stone stands. Into the midst of that world of thought, of emotion, of commotion, of contrariety, of mighty opposing forces, where the great earthly superstructures have been reared in the name of the Sacred ONE, that Stone is once more projected from the Heavens. It is to change the Astral Sea. It is to transmute the elements. It is to affect the emotion, and change its commotion into harmony. It is to touch the fabrics which have been built upon vain dreams, until these all pass away. For all inversions must pass, all nightmares must cease, all shadows must flee away; aye, even the long and most dark night of the Soul must give place before the dawning glory of the radiant sun.

THE WORLD'S NEED MET IN THE MESSAGE

That which the world needs for its healing has been bestowed from the Divine World; though few yet know of its coming, or have come to understand the gift, or even that the gift has been given. Even the Children of the Kingdom have yet to learn the real significance of the coming from the Heavens of that precious Stone, GOD'S Glowing Stone. Yet how is the world to know of that Stone? How are men and women to distinguish between the historical story with its historical, personal Christ, and the living gospel of the Foundation and Glowing Stone? Only through realization, and as a result of the inheritance, building; and as the outcome of the building, manifestation; and through the manifestation, radiation; and through the radiation, the revelation of the real meaning of Jesus Christ.

The Soul can build only as it has capacity. A man can rear, but only according to the powers within him. He cannot express the Foundation Stone, except through embodying it; nor reveal the Glowing Stone in any other way than through manifesting it.

What then is to be the distinguishing feature of those who are to possess that Stone, to know that Stone, to build upon that Stone? How is the world to perceive that that Stone is quite different from the stone supposed to have been built upon through the ages? How are Souls to understand that the superstructure to be reared upon it, is not the superstructure of historical Christianity such as has been loudly proclaimed in these last days as having failed to touch the world to finer issues? How are Souls to know that that Foundation is verily a Stone of Living Fire, whose motion gives Life wheresoever it is; whose Fire gives energy to whatsoever it touches; whose potencies consume evil when they come face to face with it; and whose Radiance makes for the everlasting day when the dark night shall pass away for ever? How is the world ever to know the Truth? How is the false superstructure ever to be changed? How are Souls to be won to build upon that Foundation Stone the gold, and the silver, and the precious stones of spiritual and divine Being, if it be not through the recovered Inheritance by the Children of the Kingdom, of the White Stone with the Unutterable Name and the consciousness of the FATHER-MOTHER within them, and by making manifest again unto all men and women, the holy estates of Jesus, Christ, and the LORD?

The Foundation Stone is the Christ. The Glowing Stone is Christ, macrocosmically understood, and individually realized; and the White Stone is Christ within the Soul in high Christhood estate of LORD-consciousness, wherein the Mystery of GOD can alone be realized.

THE FOUNDATION OF OUR TEMPLE OF BEING

If you would understand more and more the reality of the Vision of HIM Who is as the Sardius and the Jasper Stones, then you must build upon the Foundation HE hath given. If you would possess the Glowing Stone which is ministered from HIS

Altar, then the very Fire of HIS Presence must energize all the powers of your Being. If you would understand its application to Life, then you must be in Love with the ways of Jesus Christ.

That Stone makes alive the life that was accounted dead. That Stone transforms and transfigures the whole Being, till Life is radiant with the very glory of GOD. It is the Gift of GOD to him who overcometh: It is the glorious endowment of the Soul with the Glowing Stone containing the Sacred Name. It is realized Divine Christhood. Other foundation can on man, nor any school, nor any system, lay. None but the LORD of Being can lay such foundations as these. And to build upon them, is to build the most glorious Temple, the wonderful House of the Living GOD. To build upon them is indeed to attain ultimately unto the realization of the Temple of the Divine Man. And to attain unto that House, that sacred Edifice, that state which is expressed as a Living Temple, is also to know the sure foundations and the blessed consummation, and likewise the right angles of the foursquare Divine Estate. The chief corner stone has four right angles, and, in its fourfoldness, expresses Divine attainment by the Soul. For that which becomes the Foundation Stone, grows to be the Glowing Stone, and becomes the Chief Corner Stone in each angle. In the Temple of the Soul, such is the realization that is gifted by the Divine Love and Wisdom to the one who attains.

Beloved children of the Great Love, be ye builders on that Foundation. It is of the Christ-Spirit and the Christ-Life. Be ye the inheritors of the Glowing Stone; it is the Divine Mystery of Love. It will make you to be vessels full of healing, embodiments of power, and centres of radiance. It possesses the dynamic force to raise you even to the Divine Threshold where you will come into the perfect fulness of the power of that White Stone, and henceforth have within yourself the consciousness of the Eternal Mystery.

May it never be said of one of the beloved Children of the

Kingdom of the Heavens, that, because of the travail of these times, they knew not the Day of HIS coming; that they could not behold with the understanding, nor enter into the realization of the great Gift of the Heavens bestowed upon them in this recovered unveiling of the reality of Christhood, and of the coming again of the LORD of Being in beautiful manifestation and sublime ministry in the holy estates of Jesushood, and Christhood, and the Lord-consciousness.

As ye once were, so be ye again. Be nothing less than Living Stones of the Temple of the macrocosmic household of the Christhood, sent for blessed ministries unto Souls. And unto this end make consecrate all your powers, chase away all the shadows, and dwell in the Radiance shed by the Glowing Stone of HIS most holy Presence. Surely unto many it should become the Divine Vision, even the Vision of HIM Who is the glorious Sardius and Jasper Stone!

THE CHURCH
OF THE
LIVING CHRIST

THE CHURCH OF THE LIVING CHRIST

We hear much and, if we so desire, we may read much concerning the Church of God as that sacred Mystery is expressed in this world. To pursue the study of the Church of God historically can only lead an earnest student into a realm of confusion, unless that student has the true vision of all that the Church of God really is, all that it is to the individual, and all that it should stand for to the community. There is a confused sound of voices in the whole world concerning the Church of God; but there is no confusion where the true vision is held, as to its meaning, what it is, how it becomes, the nature of its manifestation, the scope of its activity, the quality of its motion, and the possibility of its full inheritance.

THE INTERIOR NATURE OF THE CHURCH

The Ecclesia of God first expresses a Divine Principle and then a manifest Life, followed by a dual motion bespeaking the motion of the Eternal Spirit, testifying through its motion, and especially through the glorious resultant of its dual motion, of the universal nature of the Church of God. And I would take you along with me this evening that we may look into the heart of the great mystery which is couched and deeply veiled in the very term, *The Church of the Living Christ.*

Now you will recognize that Christ is first a Principle and then a manifestation; that the manifestation is the estate of *Christhood*, as the exposition of Christ as a Divine Principle. For the Christ of God is in everyone in the Principle of the Being. The potential Christ is the hidden Divine Principle. It is the secret of God in the Soul. God is a Mystery. He is, therefore, a secret—though He may be realized, can be realized, is to be realized even until His secret becomes known to the Being.

The Church of the Living Christ is the Divine Principle in

the Eternities. It is revealed in all the Heavens. In all high embodiments of the Divine Mystery there has been an ingathering of the Divine Elements, and such a polarization of them gives to the Soul and the world-embodiment, a wealth of potency which expresses itself as consciousness; so that through consciousness, the Soul rises into the heights to know the Mystery whose Principle is within, and thus realizes the secrets of God.

The Church of the Living Christ is therefore the Divine Principle in us; and in that Principle we have God's Mystery which we name God's secret. Therefore, we have in us the Life of God. And the Church of the Living Christ is, in its first exposition, *God-likeness.* And God-likeness is a wonderful thing. The thought is overwhelming in its greatness that we can be like God, having the qualities of the glorious One, endowed with the attributes which reflect the glory of the Eternal and ever blessed Father-Mother. Yet it is even so. For, unless there were present in such perfectionment the Divine Potencies and the Elements and the motion caused by the Divine Breath within, the Soul could never realize the estate wherein it could know the Church of the Living Christ; for that is to be in the fashion of God, and have God-likeness.

THE PRINCIPLE AND MANIFESTATION OF THE ECCLESIA

From this you will understand that the Church has nought to do with anything on the earth, though venues may be used upon the earth through which to express that Divine Organism. But the Church is not of those. It is of the Principle within. It is of the living Presence within the Sanctuary of Being. It is of the Mystery of God Whose secret is within us. And every Soul who realizes even in a limited degree, something of the Love and the glory of the Love of the Father-Mother, has come within the gates of the new Ierusalem, the Holy City. For that Holy City is a state of Life, and the realization within the Being of those elements which constitute a Soul a member of the Church of God. And, potentially, every Soul is a member of the Church of God. Were it not so we never could become members.

The Divine FATHER-MOTHER does not create out of nothing. How the very thought that the Divine Love and Wisdom created all things out of nothing, ages ago misled great men and women, and imbued them with the desire to write philosophically about it! It has seemed difficult for some to understand how it comes to pass that the FATHER-MOTHER is All Being, and that all things are created out of and from HIMSELF. It is a great Mystery; and the mind has to bow before it, and learn to be lowly and humble; and the heart has to acquire trust in the reality of it, ere the Soul comes ultimately to realize and to know. To know GOD as universal Being is to dwell evermore in the consciousness of HIS Presence and in the consciousness of HIS ensphering, and, through the ensphering, as one consciously upheld by Divine Elements and sharing in Divine Motion. As the Being rises, there comes the consciousness of HIS abiding Presence as the overshadowing and indwelling ONE, so that the Soul is never away from HIM, never out of the atmosphere of HIS Presence. And then it becomes one with that atmosphere. What is meant here is more than atmosphere, but I have to designate it in a term that you may understand. It is an Ætheric Radiance. To become one with that Radiance means that it enters into the Being, interfuses the whole Being, fills every vehicle, and becomes the motive power in the arterial system of the Being, and makes the Soul absolutely one with HIM Who is its LORD.

Such is the Church of the Living Christ. It is not built upon a Christ of mere belief, a dead Christ, a historical Christ who has failed to redeem the world. It is reared upon the foundations of a living Christ, Who is the living Principle within the Soul, the Divine Secret within the Being who feels the motion of the living GOD ensphering and overshadowing and filling the whole Sanctuary. That is the Church of the living Christ. Ecclesia is generally interpreted as a community of Souls who form the Church of GOD and express GOD through belief, and worship, and service. But the Church of the living Christ within the Being is the Divine Ecclesia. *It is the calling out or process of the unification of all the potencies and elements and attributes of the Being, polarizing them so perfectly that the Life becomes a God-likeness, assumes the fashion of the Christ, and reveals the Christ glory, the Christ Life, the Christ Radiance, and the Christ Love.*

This is the Christ who saves the Soul of a man or a woman. This is the Christ who is yet to be Saviour of the world, revealer of GOD, interpreter of HIS Love and transmitter of HIS glory. And HE accomplishes this through the community of all the elements, potencies, and attributes having accord in a state of divine oneness with HIM Who is the LORD.

CHRISTHOOD THE MANIFEST ECCLESIA

Now you will see and understand that such a "Church of the Living Christ" in us, has for its manifestation the estate of Christhood. It is first a realization, and then a manifestation. There is first the Principle, and then through the motion of the Principle, the manifest Life. There is first the GOD-likeness in the fashion within, and then there is the GOD-fashion in the exposition without. You cannot have the motion of GOD within you without feeling it. You cannot realize HIM in the Principle of your Being without your Principle, through its magnetic action, desiring to express HIM in and through every vehicle and attribute, making every potency a power for HIM, every element a vehicle through which HE can reveal HIMSELF.

The Church of the living Christ is the manifestation of Christhood in and through the individual. Christ is no man, no person, except in the sense that He is related to the Divine Hypostasis and Pneuma, Substance and Spirit. In the Eternal World He is the exposition of the motion of the Eternities in their embodiment and interpretation of the Eternal Mystery. All through the Heavens there are expositions of that Mystery in Christ embodiments; and the Soul, having the qualities within itself of that Mystery in its manifold potencies, elements, and attributes, has also the power to express the Christhood.

For the Christhood is the manifestation of the Divine glory in and through a Soul. You will readily understand that the Divine glory cannot fill you without revealing itself. You cannot bottle up the divine power within you. Nor would there be any desire to do so.

Though it be true that the Divine Wisdom ever governs the Divine Love in its manifestation, it is never shut up in the sense of being withheld, where there is a counter magnetic attraction, something in juxtaposition to it, drawing its magnetic streams.

Thus is it with the Soul in whom the Church of the living Christ has become realized. And such is the Christhood that is to save the world. The historical Christhood has failed; the living Christhood could not fail. It has been from lack of the living Christhood that the failure has taken place. Where Christ lives within the Principle of the Being and in the consciousness of the Being, and in the motion of the Being, expressing through that motion and attribute and potency the very glory of God, Christ is revealed. And it is such a revelation that the world needs, such a revelation that alone can save the world.

Whither I am leading you, you will presently see. It is to a happy land, yet one full of grave responsibility, grave in the sense of great, divine burden, even the burden of the Divine Cross within the Being.

THE ECCLESIA COMMUNALLY EXPRESSED

The Church of the living Christ being first Principle, and then the manifestation of this motion in a glorious Christhood, the Christhood of the individual life reveals itself also in the communal life. It is said that like attracts like. But opposites oft-times attract each other. Two positive poles do not attract each other, but a negative and a positive do. There is a dual repelling power in two positives poles. There is a dual constraining power in two negative poles. But with the positive and the negative there is unity, there is unification of potency; there is oneness. Now, just as in the human individual exposition of the Church, so in the communal life, there is the Divine Motion. It is centrifugal and centripetal. Centrifugal seems the stronger word, but the measure of the centrifugal force is the measure of the centripetal motion. A Soul's power for outgoing and creative acts, and revealing testimony and power to embody the glory of the FATHER-MOTHER, is dependent upon the centripetal motion. In the measure in which you go inward to the realm of *the Silence*, the realm of the Presence, and realize the Presence, so do you gain power for centrifugal action. Many are anxious to manifest their centrifugal power before they have learnt how to direct and make manifest their centripetal forces. Your power to give lies, not only in your love that desires to give, but rather in what you possess. And you can give only that which you possess. And you come to possess through the centripetal motion. Your inheritance is through the inward and the upward motion. Your realizations come in that way. And you never realize through the outer aspect of the centrifugal motion. I have qualified it, you see, calling it the *outer* aspect, because centripetal motion is also centrifugal. It is active, but it is the inward motion. This dual action I would speak of as the Cherubic motion when it is Godward; and as the Seraphic motion when it is from GOD in ministry outward. And the measure of our power to reveal HIM seraphically, and to give the glowing stone from off the altar of HIS Holy Presence, is the measure of how we cherubically learn at HIS Feet. Thus, if you would give to the world in the coming days in a divine centrifugal sense, such a creation of the Church of the living Christ as the world has not seen, then it must be through the intensification and the steadfastness of your centripetal motion, your Godward, Cherubic desire, worship and service, in the innermost. The word service has come to have relation to outer activities to such an extent that the Children of the Kingdom have even lost the consciousness of the inward service through which there is the upbuilding of the fabric of the Being that is to be made manifest. For you cannot give the revelation of the Christ in manifestation unless you have it in the within.

Oh, what a day it will be for this world when all Israel has heard the Divine Call and magnetically responded to it within the Deeps of their consciousness, and with joyful alacrity for their LORD's service; and when men and women see the old Religion in a new manifestation, in its true and real manifestation, with the old creeds raised from the dead to become living attributes, the old beliefs so vivified and changed in their interpretation and made radiant with the light of the Heavens as to reveal the FATHER-MOTHER as HE was meant to be revealed; and when they understand that the Church of GOD is the Church of the living Christ, the glorious Divine Principle of the Being in sacred motion, responsive ever to the motion of the Presence who enspheres the Soul, even until the individual life takes on the very fashion of GOD in its potencies, in its elements, in its attributes, in its vehicles; and, wheresoever it goes, is in such GOD-likeness that the GOD-given atmosphere of the Presence is generated! That will be a glorious day when it is understood and realized what is meant by being in the fashion and likeness of GOD.

THE MANIFEST UNIVERSAL ECCLESIA

Now, we have spoken of the Principle and the manifestation in Christhood, and of the dual centrifugal and centripetal motion; and now as the glorious resultant of these we have a Church Universal. It is a Church of Universal Being. It belongs to the realm of Universal Being. It is also the Church of true comprehension. It is not a Church comprehending, in the outer sense, all the religious sects in the world, and asking them to fall into what might be called a line of uniformity. It is not a Church of comprehension in name only. The Church of the living Christ is Universal. It is of Universal Being. And it is all-comprehensive. There is no limitation to it within the radius of the Divine Atmosphere, which means the circumference on the outermost sphere of the Angelic Breaths, the Angelic

Love, and the Angelic Wisdom. For the Church of the living Christ has all the qualities within itself. It has within itself all the Altars that you meet on the way. It is not materialistic; it is highly and intensely spiritualistic, for it is of the Being. Its symbols magnetically vibrate as the result of the play of the atmosphere of the living Christ, as that is breathed out from those who embody Christ. There is no bondage to symbol; there is no bondage to outward altars; and there is no bondage to unexpressed formations. There is a recognition of the beauty of GOD in HIS Universe amid the symbols which are far flung wherever HE is truly made manifest. And the Church of the living Christ is so comprehensive that there is nothing shut out from HIS ministry. It is to express in the most perfect way from the innermost to the outermost, from the highest to the lowliest degree of manifestation, all that the Divine Love and Divine Wisdom stand for in the exposition of the FATHER-MOTHER in and through a Human Soul, and through a community of such Souls. Therefore, there is no self-seeking in the Church of the living Christ. There is no littleness of mind. There is no dimness of vision causing a lack of apprehension of the truth that lies behind all the language of symbols. For the symbols form a language, even as the symbols of our speech have been inwrought, as it were, into a language, every character of which is a sign and a symbol.

Now you will see whither I have been leading you. The Church of the living Christ is a Divine Principle within the Being. Its manifestation is the likeness of GOD. GOD is the Divine Love and radiant Wisdom. The life that would manifest HIM must be the embodiment of that Love and the exposition of the glory of that Wisdom. That Church gathers into itself for ministry through its Cherubic motion, its service, its lowly Altars, its higher Altars, its highest Altars. The Soul thus gathers on the way. Even the community of the Christhood must also gather on its way. The centrifugal power of that Church in the coming days, will be exactly commensurate with the true extent of all that the language of symbolism and the language of true worship has brought into the treasure-house of the Being of the individual, and the Being of the Church communal. To heal the world of its darkness, to heal it of its sorrow begotten through its misdirection and all the multitudinous mistakes which have smitten it, the Church of the living Christ must be able to interpret all things; and in that interpretation it must reveal the perfectionment of the FATHER-MOTHER'S Love and Wisdom as expressed in the glory of the living Church of the living Christ within the Human Soul, and in the communal life of all such Souls in fellowship.

THE RETURN OF THE MANIFESTATION

It is the day for the manifestation of this Church of GOD. It is the day for the realization of such a Christhood in the individual and in the community. It is the day when the FATHER-MOTHER HIMSELF is to become manifest to the world again as the FATHER-MOTHER Who understands HIS children far better than they understand one another or themselves. And HE calls to them to follow on unto the understanding of HIM, wherein they will the better understand themselves, and then ultimately, through being healed in their understanding as well as their desires, they will come to understand yet more fully and beautifully the sacred Mystery of HIMSELF as HE has implanted that Mystery in the secret Principle of their Being, having hidden HIS secret there for them in due time to discover. For no one can discover that secret for, nor uncover it to, another. HE HIMSELF does that as the Soul rises up into the consciousness of HIS overshadowing and all-encompassing, wherein there is such an eventuation as gives to the Soul the realization of the Divine Secret.

Oh, beloved ones, how I would love to see you and all the noble children throughout the world who are awakening, arising and coming forth to make manifest within the Holy City of the redeemed Life and the radiant Christhood! How I would see, through you individually and communally, and through all the others who have passed before me in vision, in thought, and in blessing, such a manifestation of the Church of the living Christ, that there could be no doubt any more as to what the Church of Christ stood for, what the Church meant, the kind of Life it expressed, the nature of the Life it experienced, and the redeeming, healing, exalting and regenerating power of its ministry rendered for GOD! For it is the yearning of my Being that you may be helped to a larger vision, to a nobler understanding, to diviner concepts of the FATHER-MOTHER and HIS Holy Purpose in the world, and that you may understand what has lain for years hidden within me as I have ministered to you. The yearning is Divine. It is a continual prayer in its desire. And I would have it become to you a continual blessing. For that which I would bring to you individually, I would rejoice to behold as a glorious manifestation of my LORD in such communal fellowship, worship and ministry, as would truly express, and reveal, and interpret, the divine meaning of the Church of the living Christ. I would have the communal Life reveal wherein the Cherubim minister Godward, and the Seraphim minister from GOD Soulward, wherein the Altar ever has its sacred Shekinah, and Sacrifice overshadowed by the Divine Shekinah; and the Altar Lamp ever burning, full of the living Flame of HIM Who is said to be a consuming Fire, which surely means nothing less than the Sacred Fire upon the Altar of our Being.

Bless the LORD with me, ye who are HIS saints! Bless HIS Holy Name within the Sanctuary of your Being, and in the greater Temple of Life! Bless HIM Whose gifts are so wonderful, Whose Love is so full and enriching, and Whose glory hath made the night pass away and the Day to dawn, whose glory shall know no dimming, whose circuit shall know no ending.

O my FATHER-MOTHER, for this hour THY servant would bless THEE!

THE SEVEN SACRAMENTS

BAPTISM

CONFIRMATION

HOLY EUCHARIST

PENANCE

EXTREME UNCTION

HOLY ORDERS

MARRIAGE

THE SEVEN SACRAMENTS

The seven *Sacraments* are seven Offices to which the great historic priestly institution, the Roman Catholic Church, with its various offshoots, attaches great importance. However veiled the inner significance of these Offices may be within the vision of those who fill them, yet to them the outer observance is vital to the Soul. And by the insistence of the heads of the Church upon the outer observance of the Offices as essential to the Soul's redemption and regeneration and heavenly assurance, millions have been held in bondage to belief in their sacramental value, and the necessity for their outward observance. These seven Sacraments are, *Baptism, Confirmation, Blessed Communion, Repentance, Extreme Unction, Holy Orders, and Marriage.*

Taking the outer titles, the first three seem to have the most intimate association with those who are accounted the faithful. The fourth might be applied to everyone in this fallen world. For where wrong is, there is also sorrow; and those who love the true, the beautiful and the lovely, could not do other than sorrow if they did wrong, and essay to return to the true way. The fifth is a sacrament in its outer office related by the Church to the anointing of the sick and offering prayer on their behalf, and to the administration of the Blessed Sacrament of the Body and Blood of the Lord officiated and mediated unto those who are passing from these planes to the beyond. The sixth is, to the Church, purely ecclesiastical, since it relates to the Holy Orders of the priesthood, from the office of High Priest to the Cure, with the other offices which have grown up out of monastic and conventual ramifications. The seventh sacrament in the Church's thought is related to the union of men and women in the sacred bonds of Marriage.

BELIEF IN THEIR EFFICACY

It is quite true that to all of them the Church attaches vital importance. Through superstitious belief in the outward ritual of the first three, the millions have been and are held. For they are taught that not to be baptized by the Church is to lose their right to a place in the Church, and also in the Heavens; and that it is necessary that the baptism be confirmed when the recipient has attained sufficient age of understanding when individual and personal responsibilities can be taken up and borne. For Confirmation is the seal of the Baptism, and also the token which admits the postulant to his and her first Holy Communion. There may be deviations from this practice of Confirmation in these latter days, but what we have stated is the original thought behind the sacrament of Confirmation, and in most of the Anglican churches Confirmation precedes the first Communion.

But of whatever value the outer Office may be to the postulant, and however sacred the Office may be held by the Church; and though all of the Sacraments have been sadly brought down and materialized, yet they have a real meaning, a divine significance, a soulic ministry. For, in reality, they are not of the nature of outward offices. As Sacraments they belong to the realm of the Soul. Indeed, in their native air, they are absolutely free from all outer ecclesiasticism, and are of the sphere of the Spirit. They are intimately related to the Elohistic ministry as that is expressed through the great Archangels, and then through the Angels in offices of lower degree. For the seven Sacraments correspond to the seven great Arcs, through the magnetic stream of which the Soul must needs pass on its way to the realization of its inherent divinity. Each Sacrament forms the keystone to the arc or arch of the seven realms into which the Soul passes in its pilgrimage of divine childhood from the Human estate up into the Divine estate. They are thus great steps of ascension, representing degrees of consciousness entered into and possessed by the Soul unto full realization. Without these Sacraments the Soul could not contact, and enter into, and pass through the realms of Oriphiel, Anael, Salamiel, Raphael, Zachariel, Michael, and Uriel. And only unto such as have passed that way is the

Archangel Gabriel sent. In lower degrees of Soul experience than those for which the Sacraments in their full significance stand, the ministries of the Elohim through the octave of the glorious Archangelic Hierarchy are deputized and accommodated according to the Soul's degree of realization and the realm within which it is able to function.

That the reader may glimpse something of the wealth of sacred story hidden in the casket of each of the Sacraments, the Heavens herein unveil the Divine Mysteries they contain.

* * * * *

The Mystery of Baptism

DIFFERENT KINDS OF RITUAL

As an outward office the Sacrament of Baptism will be readily apprehended if not understood. Connected with the time and place of the outer office there are diversities of opinion, and also regarding the intrinsic spiritual value of the rite. There are those who believe that only adult baptism should be administered, although the opinion in the Church is almost universally Pædobaptist. Of course, there are those who repudiate all ritual of the outer office.

Considering the claims which have been made concerning the value of baptism, whether to infants or adults, and the utter manifest failure of any results from the office which may be truly said to express the redeemed and regenerate life, it is indeed surprising that anyone can have faith in the effectual soulic nature of the outer office. For the baptism of the infant is generally regarded as an office which confers upon the infant a change of state by which it not only becomes a child of the Church and so one of the faithful, but also a child of God. That such a high blessing has not been conferred through the office, is made most manifest by the history of the whole western world where such a belief has reigned for great ages, and where the office has been duly rendered. Through infant baptism alone by means of the office of the Church, the world in its western races and nations and peoples and communities and individuals should long ago have been redeemed and regenerate, if the rite had been effectual.

Yet baptism is one of the most sacred experiences into which the spiritual child enters. It is an office divinely appointed, the liturgy of which is vital to the Soul. Baptism is a sacred rite. It is an office of the Church of GOD. But the Church of GOD is the root principle and exposition of the Kingdom of GOD. Now the Kingdom of GOD is within the Soul. Therefore, the Church of GOD is there also. And the priests who administer the baptism unto the Soul are Angelic. They are the LORD's servants in the office. The consecrated water which they apply from out the sacred bowl or divine laver, is none other than the vibrant Truth concerning the Divine Love and Wisdom, as these are expressed within the Soul in its constitution and its realizations. It is that Living Water that makes the life pure, and which, in its purifying ministry, crowns the life with the sign of the cross. For the cross is in GOD, and the child-Soul is imaged after the likeness of GOD. And the baptism of the Being with the vibrant waters from out the sacred basin of the Divine Heart, brings into that Soul's consciousness its childhood to the FATHER-MOTHER. It is that great Initiation wherein the Soul becomes conscious of itself as a centre of divine potencies, elements, and attributes. The baptism is the hour in which its childhood first becomes realized. Henceforth it is one of the faithful; for its faith, or perception, becomes active. Henceforth its name is written within the register of the Divine calendar of Souls, signifying that it is a member of the living Church of God, and a citizen of the Heavenly Kingdom. In the day of its baptism the Soul receives the new name—a name ever to be hallowed unto it, written upon its forehead, which signifies the crown of its spiral, the full meaning of which it will come into as it ascends the golden staircase in its divine pilgrimage.

NECESSITY FOR THE SACRAMENT

It is therefore true that such a Sacrament of Baptism is an absolute necessity for all Souls; for all must ultimately be baptised with the waters consecrated by the great High Priest and taken from out the sacred Bowl. The reader will understand, if he follows on, seeking to know the Angelic and Divine estates, that without such a baptism there is no real awakening of the divine consciousness which is inherent and latent in the Soul. And he will also come to know that, though the baptism in its first degree is as the sprinkling of the child with water and the making of the sign of the cross upon it, yet, bye and bye, the baptism becomes so great in its measure that it is in its effect upon the Soul as if absolute immersion took place.

Thus may be recognized the truth underlying the sprinkling of the water, and also the immersion in the baptistry or in the river. But the illumined will perceive how the things which are essentially Soulic, Angelic, and Divine, have been brought down to be circumscribed by an earthly ritual, and have assigned to them only an outer ecclesiastical significance.

The Great Love accommodates HIS ministry unto the Soul. Herein is HIS Wisdom most exquisitely revealed. Through HIS Angelic Hosts the waters are outpoured. But the Soul is not immersed in the first degree of its baptism in the stream of living Truth. It is so mediated unto, that, like a little child receiving the few drops of the earthly water in the outer ritual, the Soul receives the *aqua vitæ* from the priestly Angelic hands. It is at first, the baptism unto full purification of life. It is the writing in its first degrees of the signature of the Divine Name upon the brow of the Soul. But the baptismal act in its initiatory service is only the beginning of the office wherein there is mediated unto the Soul such a fulness of the waters of Truth, that, bye and bye, the whole life becomes absolutely immersed. In that day the Soul knows the living force of Truth within itself, in its enriching, sustaining, and exalting power. And in this way it becomes, in the seventh degree, a citizen of the

Kingdom of the Heavens, and a child of the living Church of God—one bearing the Divine Signature.

* * * * *

The Mystery of Confirmation

APOSTOLIC TEACHING CONCERNING

In the Apostolic Church, as set forth in the Acts of the Apostles, it is said that the leaders went about confirming the new converts. By this ministry it is to be understood that the teachers confirmed or established the taught in their beliefs. This is the only kind of "confirmation" spoken of in the New Testament. It had, therefore, nothing to do with the baptism of children, nor with children as such, but only with the Jews and the Gentiles who had accepted the new faith.

In later ages the idea of Confirmation took another departure. It became associated with baptism, and was the crowning act of the office of Baptism wherein the baptized child received a special benison, and where the god-parents who had undertaken the responsibility of spiritually as well as temporally looking after the child, should occasion arise, were relieved from the burden of their vows. For in Confirmation, the baptized child had become a youth or maiden of sufficient years to shoulder the burden of individual responsibility wherein they were answerable for the way they lived. But Confirmation was not only the confirming of the baptismal act by which the child was made a citizen of the Kingdom and a member of the Church; it was also that high sacramental act by means of which the great gift of the Holy Ghost was in a minor degree received. The Blessing given by the High Priest or Bishop (for it is the Bishop who confirms), conferred upon the confirmed one that most holy gift. And through many ages, even unto this day, where the practice obtains in the Episcopal Church, the sacrament of Confirmation was and is the prelude to the reception of the youth and maiden at the high Altar, and the communicating to them, through the symbols of the bread and wine, of the elements of their first Communion with the substantial LORD.

In the Roman Catholic Church, the child of seven years is admitted to the Holy Eucharist. There it first partakes of the Body of the LORD. And by means of this Sacrament it is bye and bye prepared in itself for the Sacrament of Confirmation, wherein it is believed to have communicated to it, by the Bishop or high Priest, the Holy Ghost.

THE REAL CONFIRMING IS WITHIN

Whilst such outer offices may be most beautiful, and whilst a real spiritual mediation may be accomplished through them, wherein there is vouchsafed ministry of healing and strengthening and encouragement, yet the great reality lies afar off from the merely outward office, which, alas, is not infrequently rendered in a most perfunctory and lifeless way. Confirmation is a most sacred rite. It is soulic. It takes place within the sanctuary of the Soul. The ministry is Divine, and the ministrants who mediate for the Divine are Angelic. The sacred act of Confirmation is that whereby the Soul is confirmed or established in its spiritual estate. It is the sacred hour wherein the Soul makes manifest its high childhood to the FATHER-MOTHER. It is the hour of revelation through its embodiment of how fully it has received and applied unto itself the waters of Truth with which it has been baptized, first in the lesser degrees and then in the greater. It is the event in its history wherein there becomes revealed within it the deep consciousness of the significance of the Divine Signature written upon its brow. It is the Sacramental Act composed of many minor acts, wherein the Soul knows itself to be, not only in its latent potential life, child of GOD, but wherein it has become such a lover of the Divine Truth that that which was communicated unto it in Baptism as a gift from the FATHER-MOTHER, becomes divinely confirmed. Henceforth it is established in its life. The white garments, such as adorn the Saints, become its garments. It is henceforth in its embodied life, as Jesus. Upon its attributes the Sacred Name is written, and through ministries the Love and Wisdom of that Name are revealed. To pass through the blessed ritual of the Sacrament of Confirmation, as that obtains within the Heavens, is for the Soul to have its feet set upon that Rock of Ages whose foundations are immovable, immutable, eternal. To have the consciousness of Confirmation from the FATHER-MOTHER through HIS beautiful Angelic ministrants that the life in its consecration is acceptable, is indeed to know something of divine joy.

How sacred that hour is within the sanctuary of the Soul's Being in which there is heard the Voice of the LORD speaking unto the Soul through the Angelic cohort, saying, "Well done, good and faithful one," the reader may now glimpse. And if he would enter into the full realization of all that Confirmation means, he will follow the way thither. And if he does so follow, he will come to know the glory of life as that is crowned from the Angelic World by the Divine Hand, preparatory to the exaltation of the Soul into intimate communion with the LORD.

* * * * *

THE MYSTERY OF HOLY EUCHARIST

ITS THREEFOLD SIGNIFICANCE

In the Roman Catholic Church this office is spoken of as that of the most Blessed Sacrament of the Body and Blood of Our LORD. It is, as an office, the kernel of the Mass. The Communion is mediated unto the postulants from the high Altar after the ritual of the Mass. By means of this latter, as has been more fully dealt with in the preceding volume in the section on The Mass, the elements of the bread and wine, mingled with water, are changed into what is accounted to be the actual Body and Blood of the LORD. A like belief obtains in the High Anglican Church, though not quite so strongly accentuated. In all the Churches, the office is Eucharistic;

though in the Low Church and those sections of the Church named Non-Conformist, the Sacrament is regarded as a fellowship of the communal life wherein, through the symbolic acts, there are commemorated the Last Supper supposed to have been partaken of by the Master and His intimate disciples, and the events which followed.

That which is celestially signified by Holy Communion is most truly sacramental and eucharistic and communal.

It is sacramental in that it is one of the most sacred acts of the Soul on its way to the high realization of the divinity within it.

It is a most blessed Eucharist, a ritual of Soul motion expressive of profound thanksgiving unto the Great Love.

And it is a living communion with the realm of Realities.

That which is signified in the Communion is the natural spiritual resultant of the Divine Baptism with the waters of living Truth, and the Confirmation and establishment within the consciousness of the Soul of the Divine Name written within it. It is the sacred ritual by which the Soul appropriates in most real experience the sacred Substance of the Divine Mystery we name the Body of our Lord. For, to partake of the Body of the Lord is to receive yet more fully into the sanctuary of the Soul's Being of the Divine Ætheric Elements, such as it took its fashion from when it was created and generated, and crowned with individuate consciousness as a child of the Father-Mother.

THE DIVINE SACRAMENTAL ELEMENTS

To partake of the Body of the Lord is therefore to partake of the Eternal Truth, which, in the Baptism, was mediated unto the Soul as the vital knowledge which will purify and exalt the nature. For that same Truth in the more inward realms, is spoken of as "the Bread of Life" and "the Body of the Lord." And to partake unto great fulness of that sacred Mystery is to ingather of the Divine Ætheric Elements for the upbuilding of the Soul's constitution, and the erecting of it even unto the heights of Divine Estate. For it is only through such a reception and partaking of the Divine Mystery that the Soul can endure that altitude of consciousness wherein it becomes crowned a Son of GOD.

And in the process of sacramental ritual by which an elevation of state takes place, the Soul drinks of the most sacred Cup filled from the Divine Chalice which contains the Blood of the Lamb, the Lifestream of the most Sacred Mystery.

This is what is meant by drinking of the Blood of the Son of GOD from out the Cup of the LORD. And in that most blessed sacramental act, wherein the Soul receives so great an involution of the life-giving power of the Eternal Mystery, all the Divine Ætheric Elements which were ingathered and upgathered through the partaking of the Divine Substance or Body of the LORD, have a motion given to them which ultimates in the Divine Signature written upon the Soul *becoming luminous*, and therein testifying of the Soul's attainment. And in this experience, it enters the first great degrees associated with the manifest realized life of a Son of GOD.

The reader will herein apprehend something of the wealth of most sacred Soul-story and divine motion hidden in the outer ritual and symbols associated with what has been termed the most Blessed Sacrament of the Body and Blood of the LORD. Indeed, the innermost significance of the most Blessed Sacrament is something realized only when the seventh sacrament becomes fully accomplished. For the Mass, which ultimates in the sacred outer elements becoming changed into the actual Substance and Blood of the LORD, is actually the process by which dynamically the whole of the elements of the Being are exalted in their state by the operation of the law of transmutation, *till the whole Being becomes a living sacrifice or embodiment of divine elements offered for service.*

The most interior signification of the most Blessed Sacrament, is nothing less than the realization by the Soul of perfect oneness with the Body of the LORD, and, therefore, with the LORD Himself. It is thus that the experience is a Divine Sacrament and most Holy Eucharist; a most awe-inspiring Communion with the LORD of Being; and a fellowship Angelic, Celestial, and Deific, because the Soul shares the Angelic ministry and joy, and also the glory shed within the Kingdom of the Gods, and, transcending these, the Glory of the LORD HIMSELF filling the whole temple of the Being.

* * * * *

THE MYSTERY OF REPENTANCE

THE SORROW OF THE SOUL IS SACRED

The Protestant Churches, except the highest Anglican, have doubted whether Repentance was a Sacrament. Indeed they have rejected five of the seven Mysteries as sacraments, retaining only Baptism and the LORD'S Supper or Holy Communion. But the word sacrament is now the Latin form of that which in the Greek meant "a sacred thing." And even taking the ordinary conception and interpretation of the doctrine of Repentance, it cannot be otherwise spoken of than as a sacred act. For surely the turning back from the goal of a wrong road, to seek the right road and its goal, is a sacred purpose of the heart and action of the mind. And should the word Repentance be taken to mean something more than a turning back, such as deep sorrow for all past mistakes, surely the heart's sorrow over the life's failures and mistakes, iniquities and transgressions and sins, is a most sacred motion! For such heart sorrow would lead to the welling up of the living streams of purified and deep and noble emotion. And such an experience would be a palpitating evidence of the Soul's awakening and arising, and its onward journeying in the upward way that leads to the City of GOD. Therefore Repentance even as sorrow over the past, is a Sacrament. And it should ever be so regarded by the Soul who enters into such a state, and by the observer who knows of the Soul's return.

Though it may seem strange to affirm it amid the heavily shadowed beliefs of the Church and the world, yet is it the living truth that *the Sacrament of Repentance, in its inner significance, has nought to do with a fallen world at all.* For it forms one of the seven great links in the chain by which the Soul itself is anchored from and to the Divine, and by means of which it ultimately arrives at its Divine Haven. For the Sacrament of Repentance is deeply interwoven with that of the Communion of the most Blessed Body and Blood of the LORD. It is the profound experience which overtakes the Being of one who would become a living member of the LORD'S Body, a vibrant stone in the sacred house of the Living Church, and an illumined citizen of the Kingdom of GOD.

The Sacrament must needs be entered into as a state, and partaken of as a realization, by the Soul who would stand in such a relationship to the FATHER-MOTHER.

It speaks of that divine motion within the Being wherein there is revealed the most exquisite lowliness of mind and heart.

It is an interpretive state of the Soul who is ascending, revealing its consciousness of the awful purity of the Eternal ONE, the ineffableness of HIS glory, the resplendence of HIS radiance, the Divine transparency and translucency of all things upon which the Soul looks, and into which it enters.

For who could stand on the threshold of exalted vision, even such as becomes the gift of GOD to the Soul within the Angelic World, and not feel, in a comparative but most real sense, as if only One were pure, even that ONE Who is LORD of all?

THE GATEWAY TO DIVINITY Truly the Sacrament of Repentance is not only a saving grace whereby a sinner, out of a true apprehension of sin and also of the limitless Mercy of GOD, returns humbly and sorrowfully from the wilds of life to the pure and true and narrow way that leadeth unto Life Eternal; but it is supremely that most saving grace without which a Soul could never receive the unction of the Holy ONE, but by which it prepares itself for that unction. It is that Sacrament which must be partaken of ere the Heavens absolutely trust the Soul with the secrets of GOD. The graces which accompany it are those of lowliness and humility. Without these realized by the Soul, there is no further inward and upward journeying into the Kingdom of the great revelation, and the mystery of the Church of the First Begotten. Therefore it will be seen that the Sacrament of Repentance is not only something for the poor, returning, sin-laden one, but it is a sacramental gateway through which those who have attained great estate must pass ere the innermost sacred mysteries can be communicated and entrusted to them.

The Sacrament of Penance in the Roman Catholic and Greek Churches includes *contrition, confession, satisfaction, and absolution*. But the Divine Love and Wisdom never penalize. There is no such thing in the Divine administration as penal servitude. Along the whole way of the Soul's growth and evolution, Divine Judgment is exercised. But Divine Judgment is not penal. It is segregative: it separates for purposes of Soul enrichment.

In the Inner Spheres whither the Sacraments lead, the Soul arrives at that estate of consciousness wherein it may be entrusted with the Divine Secrets. The Way of Penance must be trod. It is the sacramental act wherein the Soul takes up the full burden of the Cross. The Soul accepts it gladly; but it is divinely imposed. It is a voluntary *penance* or burden of the Cross, yet it is commanded. It is a sacrament of supreme trial, and shows by the manner in which it is celebrated, and the extent to which it is entered into, the capacity of the Soul, and the measure in which it may be trusted with Divine Secrets. When the celebration is full and complete, then the Soul is one with the Divine Cross within itself, and with whatsoever burden the Divine Love may ask it to bear upon its Cross.

The Sacrament of Penance or Repentance, has a significance relating to the Soul's Divine Estate. And it obtains throughout all the realms where embodiments of the Divine Mystery are to be met with.

* * * * *

The Mystery of Extreme Unction

A MODE OF SPIRITUAL HEALING

The Sacrament of Extreme Unction is, in the Roman Catholic and the Greek Churches, an office of anointing. It is founded on some professed scriptures, especially that in the closing verses of the first chapter of the epistle attributed to St. James. It is the anointment of the sick. Prayers are offered on behalf of the needy one, and the holy oil is applied to the troubled parts. The office is believed to bring unction to the afflicted, relief to the pain and healing to the parts.

But the Sacrament has yet a deeper significance when, in addition to such prayers and communion, there is also the administration of the most Blessed Sacrament of the Body and Blood of Our Lord. This part of the office is specially fulfilled in the case of those who are known to be "passing over." For in the faith of the eastern and western churches, it is believed to be an office vital unto the Soul in the day of its setting out on what is oft-times spoken of as "its lone journey."

We would not take a ray of hope from any mind, nor drop of joy from the human heart; and if such a sacrament contributes to the hope, and the joy, and the healing of one Human Soul, let us rejoice that there is such an office through which it may be helped.

But surely there is a more profound meaning, and a yet greater significance hidden in the sacrament of Extreme Unction, than the Church gives as its interpretation and belief. That which is *extreme* relates to a proximity to the extremity, and that which is truly unctuous relates to hidden power. It is said in the New Testament scriptures concerning those who truly believe, that they shall receive "the Unction of the Holy ONE." To receive the Unction of the Holy ONE is, therefore, to receive divine anointing. And the divine anointing is not only unto the full salving of all the elements and potencies and essences of the Being with their concrete attributes, but it is also to be endued from on High with the dews of the Divine World, which drops are the distillations of *the aqua vitæ* of the River of GOD. To receive Unction from on High, is to be endowed with the Holy ONE; and to be so gifted, is to be the possessor of the Indwelling Holy Guest, and to have realized the Omnipotency of HIS Presence.

Herein the reader will see the intimate relationship between the Sacrament of Penance and that of Extreme Unction. The Sacrament of Penance is that wherein the Soul takes up its cross absolutely, to bear the LORD's burden upon it. Divine Penance is herein, not affliction, but sacrifice. It is not self-imposed pain with a view to reward or self-glorification, but the sublime act wherein the Soul not only desires to share, but actually enters into the suffering resulting from the Divine Passion.

The Sacrament of Penance is therefore the Soul's appropriation of the burden of the Cross wherein it becomes redeemed and redeemer. And having taken that step, it is qualified for the Sacrament of Extreme Unction. For though the Soul is always debtor to the Divine Spirit, as that Holy Mystery moves within the sanctuary of the Soul's Being, and through all its planes, yet it is only when it approaches the portals represented by the sacrament of Extreme Unction and passes through them that it enters into that estate of life wherein it has the consciousness of divine empowerment. It becomes more fully endowed of the Holy Ghost, with profounder realizations of the Indwelling Guest; and thus it enters into that further baptism of the Holy ONE of which the first baptism was the prophecy. In the baptism by the water of the regeneration and the renewing of the Holy Ghost, it becomes awakened to a sense of its high calling. Then it receives the divine urge to proceed yet further inward and upward, being confirmed on the way and established in its life, and fitted to enter into the joy of the first degrees of real union with its LORD, in becoming partaker of the Heavenly Mystery of the LORD's Body and Blood, wherein it comes to realize, with a fulness of degree greater than hitherto, the awful sublimity and purity of the most Holy ONE; and is so impressed and filled with divine motion that it partakes of the succeeding Sacrament, unhappily named Penance, and becomes henceforth one of the divine burden-bearers in this world, and one of the glorious cross-bearers wheresoever it may go, bearing the burden of most blessed ministry for the FATHER-MOTHER. And thus it is prepared for the Sacrament of Extreme Unction, or that baptism which comes to the Soul in the extremity or ultimate of its Spiral. Henceforth it is endowed with Divine Unction. It knows; it understands; it is endued; it is illumined; it is crowned for regnancy; it is clothed with power.

The Sacrament of Extreme Unction is therefore that sacred experience wherein ultimates are realized, and the Being, in consciousness, becomes so interfused with the breaths from the Divine World that it knows henceforth the meaning of the Crown of Life, and becomes a partaker of the Mystery of the Holy Guest. It is the fifth Sacrament of the seven. It gathers up all the preceding ones. The power indicated in each one is herein realized. It becomes great in the realm of the Extreme, in the Kingdom of Ultimates. It is anointed with the power of the Holy Ghost, that is, it is illumined from the Indwelling Presence Who clothes it with the power that is from on High, and enrobes it for regal service. In this baptism all power is bestowed. The Soul *passes over* in the sense that it ascends into the realms of the upper airs wafted from the Divine Mystery, having the power to function there.

Thus this most holy sacramental process which came to be related to the sick and the suffering children upon the earth, and the anointing of them with oil, and the praying over them for the divine blessing, and the administering unto such as desired it, and especially those who were passing over, of the comfort of the sacramental elements believed to be those of the Body and Blood of the LORD, was and is nothing less than the great sacramental act by which the Soul becomes so GOD-endowed, that henceforth its potencies touch the realm and partake of the mystery of Omnipotency.

* * * * *

THE MYSTERY OF HOLY ORDERS

It is only after the Soul has been a sharer in the great sacramental act known as Extreme Unction, and has received anointing from the Divine World by means of which high illumination fills the sanctuary of the Soul, so that the individual has become endowed with the unction of the Holy ONE, which is the anointing of the Holy Guest, that the Initiate is ready to fully understand and participate in the Sacrament of Holy Orders. For this sacred office is not to be confounded with the merely human orders sought after by men and conferred by some authority, individual or collegiate. For, as we shall see, to be a participator in the offices of Holy Orders is to be a divinely ordained Soul for some special form of mediatorial ministry.

In the Roman and Greek Churches representing the western and the eastern sections which hold the validity of the Seven Sacraments, there are seven orders of ministry implied within the Holy Orders, and these are all sacramental. There are four minor and three major. The four minor are related thus—the Door-keeper, the Reader, the Exorcist, and the Acolyte. The three major are the Deacon, the Priest, and the Bishop.

Though there are many other offices in the Church, some of which are held to be important and connected with other ministries, yet these seven comprise what are considered to be the sum of the Sacrament of Holy Orders. Originally the four minor offices were intended to lead up to the three major. We will look at them individually.

THE OFFICE OF DOORKEEPER The office of Door-keeper does not appear on the surface to be one of holy importance. It is true there is no ordination service held over it; nor is there any supposed transference of power from the Bishop to the Door-keeper. Yet the minor offices are appointed from the Bishop who in a mystical sense is a high representative, as we shall observe.

Door-keeping is a most important office. True, it may be rendered in a perfunctory way, and noisily by the Door-keeper, or by those whom he admits into the sanctuary. But door-keeping is a most important office. The sanctuary, even to its outer gates, should be regarded as sacred. The Door-keeper should see to it that none enter other than reverently and with due respect to the sacredness of the house. For that which is signified is something far, far more than the Door-keeper of any earthly house at its western door, its northern door, or its southern door. In some great sanctuaries there would be a Door-keeper at each.

The office of Door-keeper is a divinely appointed one, and has relation to the Soul as a Sanctuary, the precincts of which are most sacred. And the office of Door-keeper has its true interpretation in the Soul having acquired the power of guarding its Sanctuary from intrusion, opening it only to those elements which may be admitted to share in the processional life of the Soul in its acts of adoration and worship, praise and blessing. For the Door-keeper guards the Sanctuary as well as admits to it. Nay more; even as in masonic lodges the door-keeper has to hear the password and behold the sign made by the entrant, so should the Door-keeper of the Sanctuary. Thus, all the elements which have no sign of the sacred meaning impressed upon them, no articulation of the secret password of the mystery of the Soul itself, should be refused admission.

Now you will understand the psalmist when he wrote, "I would rather be a door-keeper in the house of my God, than dwell in the tents of wickedness; for a day in Thy courts is better than thousands of days outside of Thy house." It is no mean office to fill. It is no humiliating position to hold. When the Soul can through its prescience, its love, its understanding, its power, be a Door-keeper of the sanctuary, it has verily attained to high estate. It knows the blessing of the great Bishop of Souls. It has realized something of the joy of serving even at the outer gate.

Nor can a Soul proceed further until it has learnt how to be a Door-keeper in the house of the LORD; to guard its western door against the material world's intrusions; to guard its northern door from hurt through the mind's wrong states or pride of heart; to guard its southern door from those things which would hurt its divine emotion, and, through that emotion, cause deflection and consequent misdirection to its entire passional nature, which is the divine magnetic Love stream within it. There is also the Door-keeper of the sacred screen; but that belongs not only to the major Orders, but to the Divine Realization within the Soul, after the major Orders have been passed through. For then the Soul acquires the power to open and shut the gates of the Innermost Sanctuary.

The symbol of the Door-keeper is the Keys; and these are handed to him in the hour of his appointment.

THE OFFICE OF READER

The Holy Order of the office of Door-keeper is to be crowned with that of the Reader. The symbol of this office is the codex or sacred manuscript appointed to be read. He may share in the outer lessons, but he may also in his ministry have the office of comforter and instructor. In the Episcopal Church there are Lay-readers. The office does not confer the power of the administration of the Holy Eucharist, nor that of the Confessor; but it gives to the Reader the power to interpret. At first it might seem as if it were not an office of great importance. How casually even lessons are read in the Sanctuary! Yet, like the Door-keeper, the Reader has a divine origin and a divine appointment. No one can read the sacred codex wherein, written with the very fingers of God, are to be found such glorious stories of the Mystery of His Love and Wisdom as are found gathered up into the superstructure of a Soul. How few who would be great within the Sanctuary in filling its offices, are even Readers in this respect! For to be God's Reader means that the codex handed to the Soul is in a language it understands, which it is capable of reading, and which in its reading it is capable of interpreting. How few can even read the codex of the Divine Mystery expressed in the flowers and the trees; in the human story of the Soul's travail, even the fashion of a man or a woman, let alone the glorious fashion of the Divine within the Sanctuary! Yet the true Reader has this high office given to him that he may interpret the glorious expositions of the Love and Wisdom of the Father-Mother as these obtain within the Sanctuary west of the inner veil.

The Reader is not a prophet. He has not got there yet, but he is on the way. The prophet is an illumined one; not only illumined by the power to interpret through understanding, but illumined directly from the Divine World with messages still unwritten, so far as knowledge is concerned. If to be a Door-keeper in the house of God be a great office to fill, an office crowned with divine dignity, what shall we say of the Reader who is able to interpret within the sanctuary much concerning the Love and the Wisdom of the Father-Mother for the comforting of Souls, the enlightening of Souls, the strengthening of Souls?

Thus, though the Reader is not yet accounted worthy to be a Deacon, he is on the way to the High Altar of God; and, in the measure of the fulness of his consecration in filling his office, so shall the higher office become a realization.

THE OFFICE OF THE EXORCIST

Following the office of Reader there is one with an unhappy association through the term applied to it, namely, the Exorcist. That office in the Church is given to one who is supposed to have the power conferred upon him of exorcising evil spirits. Though the office is far removed in the Church's thought from that of mediatorial priesthood, yet the ministry seems to partake of the nature of divine mediation. For who could exorcize evil, casting out evil spirits and changing conditions, but one who had power over evil to repel or transmute it? Now evil conditions are only changed truly by the power of goodness and truth. Darkness is dispelled only through the inshining and onshining of light. The things that are hateful can be conquered by Love alone.

Now, even taking the office to mean just this exercise of power in exorcizing evil states and entities, powers and principalities, the office is surely a high one, GOD appointed and endowed. Yet there is more in it than the word would convey; for the term has been used occultly. The Exorcist was the healer, the mediator who could change the conditions. His office is third on the way to the innermost. He stands outside the sacred screen that divides the Holy of Holies from the outer courts. He challenges any elementals or individuals, the presence of which causes contrary vibrations. In the Soul system the Exorcist is the Being, the individual within the Sanctuary having the power to cast out evil, the power to change all conditions that are wrong, the power to heal the elements, the power to cause evil forces to be in abeyance, and at last to become obedient to the Law of Christ who is within the Sanctuary.

To the Exorcist there is given, as the symbol of his office, a Book of Sayings. These are not occult mantrams to be recited in monotone. It is the Book of the Sayings of the Divine Love and Wisdom which contain the power of transmutation. The true utterance of Divine Sayings permits the inherent quality of the divine magnetic potency to express itself in vibration. The book is full of the Sayings of the Divine World, and the Soul must needs learn them for their inherent quality, and come to understand their inherent divine potency, and acquire the power to bring forth from them that magnetic force by which atmospheres can be changed, hurts can be healed, opposing conditions can be brought into harmony and inimical breaths wafted away. The office of Divine Exorcist is the office of healing within the realm of the mind and the heart. To fill that office well is to be a Healer for GOD, ordained of HIM, though the greater ordination services have not yet become associated with the lowlier office; but the office bears the imprint of the Eternal Mystery of Love and Wisdom, and is apostolic and redemptive.

THE ORDER OF ACOLYTE The office of the Acolyte is intermediary between the minor and the major Holy Orders. The Acolyte is permitted in his office to pass through the gate into the inner sanctuary. Having acquired the power represented by exorcism, redemptive in its ministry and apostolic in its blessing, the Soul is able to proceed through the gates into the inner sanctuary to serve there before the high altar. Whatever there may be of formalism and what we might term mere earthliness in the office of the Acolyte as that place of sacred service is filled by many within the eastern and western Churches, yet in its inner significance the office is most sacred. The symbol of it is the candlestick and candle, with tapers. When the Acolyte is blest unto the filling of the office, these symbols are given to him. They bespeak his ministry, which is to attend to the lights in the Sanctuary, to replenish the sacred lamp before the high Altar, so that it shall be kept burning as a perpetual flame. And he also lights the six candles upon the high Altar. At times during High Mass and in the processional within the Church, the Acolyte may have the office of holding up the train of the high Priest or the arch-officiate in that sacred service.

It is a symbolic allegory of the Soul in its first ministries before the high Altar. Having acquired the power of opening and shutting the Sanctuary as Door-keeper, making true use of the keys or powers necessary for such a ministry; having learnt how to read and interpret for itself the Divine Love and Wisdom revealed in those exquisite forms within the Sanctuary and its marvellous fashion, and also the revelations of the Divine Love and Wisdom in the world exterior to itself; and having thus acquired the necessary Love-power and light of Wisdom to be in the office of Exorcist, and having filled that office unto the acquisition of an apostolic power, redemptive in its motion and full of sweet healing, blessing and guardianship, and thus of defence within the Sanctuary, the Soul is gifted from the Great Love with the office of Acolyte—one accounted worthy, because in a state of readiness, to mediate before the high Altar in the more outward aspects of the worship-service. For before a Soul can attain to be a Deacon and then Priest within the precincts of the house of the LORD, it must learn, like Samuel, to attend to the lamps of the Sanctuary. The Acolyte lights the six great candles upon the high Altar. By that is meant, the lamp within each plane must be lit. Nor must the lamp with the Ruby flame before the high Altar be permitted to burn so low that it becomes extinguished; for that flame in the Sanctuary is the symbol within the Soul of the most sacred Lamp with its glorious living Flame of the Spirit before the canopied Altar of HIS Presence Who is Our LORD of the Host. In devotion to this ministry and the high consecration of the Being, the Acolyte may even touch the hem of the garment of the great High Priest, and uphold it; for it is the garment signifying all that the Cross stands for of righteousness and equity. Blessed is that Soul who is an Acolyte indeed, who ministers within the Sanctuary, and keeps aflame the lamps before and upon the high Altar. For, as the crowning office of the four minor offices in Holy Orders, it leads to yet greater experiences, responsibilities and ministries.

THE OFFICE OF THE DEACON

The first of the three major of the holy offices is that of Deaconship. There have at times been recognized two aspects of this office, called the Deacon and the Sub-Deacon. Where the two obtain, the symbols are these: The Sub-Deacon receives the paten and chalice, water-cruet and napkin; but the paten and the chalice are empty. In full Deaconship the symbol given is that of a copy of the Gospels. The ordination is by the Bishop, for the Deacon is a minor priest. Yet he may not fill *the Office of the Mass* and celebrate it; nor yet be a Confessor. These offices belong to full Priesthood.

The Deacon serves before the Altar in assisting the Priest. He is a carrier or bearer of the holy vessels within the sanctuary. His paten and chalice are empty, but he bears them to the one who can fill them. He is also a Reader, but his readership is within the inner Sanctuary, so that he can read the Gospel for the day.

The office is full of profound significance for the Soul: it is most holy and sacred. Even as the Soul must learn to be an Acolyte through ministering in what might seem to be temporalities but which are of vital moment to the Being, so in the office of Deacon the Soul must acquire the power of sweet willinghood to bear the vessels of the LORD, which are ever sacred, even though for the time being they may seem to be empty. The Deacon has to guard those vessels. He cares for them. Thus, the one who would be Deacon before the high Altar, must keep sacred his paten or receiver, which is his Mind, and his chalice, the container, which is his Heart. And he must learn how to interpret GOD'S gospel, reading the meaning of the divine glad tidings; in other words, he must become an interpreter of Christ, and a revealer of the Christ lowliness of mind and humbleness of heart, willing, if need be, to have his vessels empty for the time during which he fills the sacred office of assisting before the high Altar. For it is to the Divine Priest he brings his vessels and his book to be blest. He brings the book to have its pages illuminated with the Light of the Christ glory, and the paten or Mind, to have put upon it the sacred Bread (which represents the Divine Wisdom as knowledge broken from the Heavens to the Soul); and his empty chalice, even the Heart emptied of all self, and everything that is of the earth earthly, that it may be filled by the High Priest with the sacred contents of the Wine of GOD.

The office of Deacon is thus seen to be most holy. In the inner Sanctuary it is the first degree the Soul takes in that Priesthood which ultimates in Priesthood after the Order of Melchisedek. Nor can any Soul proceed further until in its motion it has processed through all its Sanctuary, carrying reverently and gladly the sacred vessels ere yet the High Priest has enriched them with the sacred Bread and Wine. For there is no way into the Holy of Holies other than that of perfect willinghood to do the Will of the FATHER-MOTHER, even in the lowliest offices associated with a true mediatorial ministry. What a wealth of blessing would be upon and within the institutions which claim to be representative of the Church of the living GOD, if all those who are in the office of Doorkeeper, Reader, Exorcist, Acolyte and Deacon, realized the holiness of their Order!

THE OFFICE OF THE PRIEST

The Priest is a mediator for GOD. It is his office to unveil the Mysteries. In addition to the garment given him significant of his holy office, he has presented to him as his symbol the paten containing the sacred Bread, and the chalice full of the holy Wine.

As Deacon he must have come to know the meaning of the Christhood; as Priest he has now to mediate of that Mystery.

As Deacon all his powers were laid before the Altar of the Most High for ministry; as Priest all his powers are in motion in mediatorial service.

It is his office to unveil the sacred Bread, and also the holy chalice of Wine. In his office he has to mediate directly of the living Substance of which the sacred Bread speaks, and to give of that most holy Lifestream of which the Wine within the chalice testifies. It is his office to break the Bread of the Divine Wisdom unto the needy Souls of the FATHER-MOTHER'S children who hunger for the Bread of Life. He has the honour of pouring out from the chalice of the Heart, the Wine of the Divine Mystery of Love. His *paten* or Mind, must ever contain the Bread of Heaven as the realized Divine Wisdom; and his Heart as the sacred chalice, must have its pulsation through the power of the Divine Love, as that magnetic Lifestream flows out from him in blessing unto all to whom he is privileged to mediate in ministry for the FATHER-MOTHER.

It is thus he can truly celebrate the sacred Body of the LORD of Love, and Life, and Light. It is thus also that he can be a true Confessor; not only as one who has to hear of the travail of Souls as they outpour their sorrows and temptations, but as a Divine Confessor, one who confesses by his very mediation that he knows the sacred Mystery of the FATHER-MOTHER as represented in the most holy Presence spoken of under the imagery of the Host, or the Bread and the Wine of most blessed sacramental nature. Knowing the sacred Mystery himself through realizing that fulness of life of which the most sacred Host speaks, he is able to dispense unto the needy, giving them such counsel as brings healing to them, and comfort, even the comfort of the Holy ONE, as he tells them of a Love that is unwearying, beautiful in its purity, and sublime in its sacrifice. As a Priest of the Living ONE, he doth thus cause to be blotted out from the ways of the children all sin, all wrong doing, all hurt, and all shadows resulting from the hurt and the wrong and the sin.

Such an one is GOD-appointed. He is a servant of the Bishop of Souls. He is in most Holy Orders. Of no man is his appointing, nor from any school or college or system doth he derive the power with which to fill the holy office. He is of the college of Divine Presbyters. He is one of GOD'S anointed.

What a glorious world this would soon become if all who profess to have been ordained Priests of the Living GOD within the outer Sanctuaries to mediate unto the children of men, could realize what their office means, and come into a divinely endowed inheritance of such a true Soul Priesthood! The Sanctuaries would become Angelic Homes, the scenes of Cherubic and Seraphic ministries upon the earth. The glory of the LORD would fill the Sanctuaries, and the Cloud of HIS Radiance would abide upon them evermore. By means of such a ministry it would come to pass that the children of the FATHER-MOTHER would soon cease to be as sheep without shepherdhood, roving amid strange pasture land, impoverished in their souls unto the uttermost because of the dearth of spiritual provision. Henceforth they would become as the sheep of the various folds of the FATHER-MOTHER, wisely because divinely shepherded, resplendent in Love and Wisdom because nourished from the green pastures of HIS Love and Wisdom. And upon the gates of the city of Life in this world there would be once more imprinted in terms of living flame, the Holy City of Ierusalem.[1]

THE OFFICE OF THE BISHOP

Just as a realized Deaconship is crowned with the higher mediatorial office of Priesthood, so is the server before the High Altar of the LORD named the Archpriest. An Archpriest is one who in the ascent of life has taken that divine scholastic degree wherein the realization of the Divine Love and Wisdom is of the intensity and resplendence of the Innermost Realms. For the Archpriest is the chief Presbyter or Elder.

Now, a Bishop is a shepherd. He is not only in a general sense a shepherd of Souls. The Deacon has to learn to be such a shepherd, and the Priest yet more so in his mediatorial office. The Bishop's shepherdhood is that of directing those who are in the lesser degrees of shepherdhood, ministering unto them

[1]The office of Woman in the Priesthood is dealt with under the Sacrament of Marriage.

and unveiling still more of the Divine Mystery of Love and Wisdom. A true Bishop is a Revealer for God.

The Bishop is the shepherd of the Priests and the Deacons and all who are in Holy Orders. His general mediation has, therefore, to be through the intermediaries, from the Priest down to the Doorkeeper. On the earth-planes, when a priest has attained such a standing that he is accounted worthy by those in authority to be chosen for the office of Bishop, and ordained to that sacred ministry, there is made over such an one by the metropolitan Priest or Archbishop, the Sign of the Cross, and there are given to him the gifts of the office, apart from the robes which are significant of the office, a ring and a staff. The ring signifies his seal, and the staff his power of administration. Herein is unveiled a great and glorious Soul mystery. As the combination of the seven Orders is spoken of as the Sacrament or Mystery of Holy Orders, so is the Bishophood the crowning experience of all. It is an estate entered into by the Soul. It is a realization within the Being. It is the full resultant of being a perfect Doorkeeper, Reader, Exorcist, Acolyte, Deacon and Priest. It is the polarized exposition of all the elements of the Being upgathered and focussed into what we might term the divine apex or radiant point, wherein the divine mystery of shepherdhood becomes possible as a realization for and by the Soul; and the transmission of the divine power through the Soul is made manifest in a shepherdhood wherein the Divine Love and Wisdom find exquisite embodiment and revelation.

A SHEPHERD OF SHEPHERDS

When a Soul becomes shepherd for GOD, and therefore one ordained to the high office of a Bishop of Souls, it has given to it the ring and the staff. The ring symbolizes the Soul's marriage to the LORD. It is that first great act which culminates in the seventh Sacrament of Marriage being fully realized. The ring is the sign of union. There must be such union even in Priesthood; but in shepherdhood, as in the office of Bishop, the union is more fully entered into. The ring is the seal of the office. It is, under the imagery of symbol, the transference to the Soul of the right of that shepherdhood which can seal or impress upon all the pastoral ministries rendered through the office, the insignia of the LORD. Whatsoever such a Bishop of Souls does, bears upon it the imprint of the Divine Presence. The seal is put upon his finger, which means that power is given to him in his office to reveal the Divine Authority. His staff is the rod of power by which that authority is exercised. The imagery means that to such a Soul there is given, as the result of glorious realization within the Being, the Rod of Aaron the High Priest, which is the rod of divine power. But that power is none other than the Omnipotent Love, which is ever beautiful, redeeming, healing, enriching, uplifting, enlightening, transforming, transfiguring and glorifying. It is that rod of the Divine Omnipotency of the sacred Mystery of Love which, expressed within and through the sacred office of a Soul's Bishophood, can confound all the earthly magicians or wonder-workers amidst the elemental, communal, commercial, political and national conditions. It is the rod that can blossom with the most exquisite flowers even in the land of bondage and amid the desert conditions. It is the rod that can divide the elemental seas of opposition classed under the general term as the Red Sea, and make a way for captive Souls to find their liberty. It is the rod that can bring out of what appear to be stony circumstances and adamantine conditions, living streams of divine potency. It is the rod through which there is revealed, even amidst the most trying wilderness journeyings, wherein are the fiery serpents of false desire of heart, and will, and mind, *the flaming cross* by which all hurtful things become healed. For the Bishop's staff signifies the power of that sign which is made over him in his ordination wherein he becomes for the LORD an embodiment of the office of the Sign of the Cross. For he is a member of the Inner Temple, an interpreter of the most holy mysteries. He should be, according to the degree of his Bishopric, God's Emmanuel, Prince of the Heavens, revealer unto God's Priests in the various degrees of their office, the meaning of divine shepherdhood.

THE FAILURE OF THE CHURCH

Herein it will be seen how far the Church has failed to interpret the divine meaning of the sacred offices implied in the sacrament or mystery of Holy Orders. For, to the reader it must surely now be made manifest how otherwise is the whole system of ecclesiasticism become than after the divine pattern, the divine purpose, the real intent of the Lord of Being; and how the Church, operating for ages amid the darkness, though making high claims regarding its origin and its powers, has but built up a great earthly system, associating with it the Heavenly symbols and offices, but materializing them all at the expense of the Kingdom of God and the Kingdom of the Heavens; and how the sad betrayal has come to rob the Soul of its divine birthright even whilst claiming to give to the Soul a right to citizenship in the Heavens.

Oh, that all the Archbishops, Bishops, Priests, and Deacons, and all in the minor Orders, could realize the inherent soulic sanctity of the office they hold and fill—a sanctity begotten of realized spiritual grace and power, and where there is also illumination, and no mere outer sanctity resulting from the creation of the false and earthly atmosphere which has come to surround all the offices, and accompany them wheresoever ministry is rendered through them!

* * * * *

The Mystery of Marriage

THE CROWNING MYSTERY

The crowning act in the holy mysteries named the Seven Sacraments, is that of Marriage. The term has come to have quite an earthly association, though the Church has endeavoured to preserve the sacramental nature of the experience. Marriage in itself seems to be an event which belongs entirely to the Human Kingdom, and is entered into as such an experience by men and women. Even the Church has no higher vision of it. For, though it speaks in mystic terms of Souls being married to the LORD, what it means is simply the consecration of a man or a woman to a monastic form of life wherein there is special ministry rendered to and on behalf of the Church.

The human aspect of Marriage dominates the world. Though the event has been named something sacramental and appertaining to divine mystery, yet the beginning and the circumference of the idea are related to an outer experience between men and women. Indeed it is almost entirely circumscribed by what has come to be unhappily called "the sex problem." For Marriage, in the outlook of men and women, is confined to the thought of physical union, though along with such there may also be union of heart and mind in sweet and tender fellowship.

But a perfect marriage between a noble man and a beautiful, gracious woman, would be a union of Soul, of deep spiritual purpose of heart, of profound emotion, of mind or unity in outlook, as well as union through the body for purposes of the sacred office of the generation of children. There is no more sacred union upon the earthplanes than a perfect marriage between such men and women. Where the Soul's hope is full of the light of divine vision, and the heart, mystically understood in its systole and diastole motion, fills the whole stream of the emotion with the magnetic force of a love redeemed and purified; and the mind with its splendid attributes is full of heavenly purpose in all its outlook and activity, there is no such thing as a sex problem; for the outer union is beautiful, and, after its order, perfect as an exposition of the union of mind and heart and soul. For Love seeketh not its own in any self-regarding way. It lives always unto the exposition of itself through ministry unto the beloved object or objects.

Such would be the marriage state between men and women

in a redeemed world, and such marriage is of divine origin as we shall see. How far the world has wandered from the true standard; how far the Church itself has failed to understand the mystery it has included in its Sacraments, and, consequently, misled the world, will be unveiled.

THE TRUE MARRIAGE IS A SACRAMENT

Marriage is verily a Sacrament. It is of the most sacred Mystery. As a mystery it belongs to the very constitution of the Universe, and, therefore, to the constitution of man. The mystery is expressed within all the Spheres, Divine, Celestial and Angelic. Therefore, it is not to be wondered at that it should find its correspondence upon the Human Kingdom. That the glorious mystery has been most fearfully misunderstood and misinterpreted, and, consequently, betrayed, is made manifest by the dark and most hurtful shadow which lies athwart the world's threshold, filling the minds and hearts of the children of the FATHER-MOTHER with such degraded views of the divinely constituted and instituted sex complements and co-relationships as are derogatory to the glorious CREATOR-FATHER-MOTHER out from the Bosom of Whose Love all things beautiful have proceeded. For if there be any shadow or hurt or bitterness begotten of what has come to be spoken of as "the sex problem," these things are the results of a great betrayal of the Divine Love and Wisdom, and are parts of the catastrophic effects which befell this world when it was overtaken by what is known as the great Descent, or fall from high estate.

Marriage is a most sacred mystery belonging to the Divine Nature. It expresses the union of Divine Elements and Spirit. It is revealed as a consummated event in the manifold embodiments of the stellar Universe. The glory of the mystery is revealed in the Divine World in the most sacred term we give to the Eternal Mystery we name the FATHER-MOTHER. All creations are the result of the marriage of the Divine Elements and the Divine Spirit. They are the exposition of the glorious purpose of the FATHER-MOTHER, and of HIS dual motion through the vehicles, expressed as Hypostasis and Pneuma. Even the birth of a Human Soul is a resultant of this marriage of the Divine Hypostasis and Pneuma. For a Human Soul is generated elsewhere than through that union we speak of as earthly parenthood. For, just as the body of a human child formed in the womb of the mother, is the result of the union of the elements in the father and the mother, the one representing the Spirit force or creative energy, the other the beautiful Divine Substance to be energized, so is a Human Soul generated amidst the Divine Ætheria and fashioned out of it, by means of the action of the Holy Spirit. For it is in the womb of the Eternal Mystery that a Soul is generated. Even the Soul who comes to take up residence in the vehicle provided as the result of human union, is created there. For the Soul is a resultant of Divine action. In nature it is of the Divine. In patrimony it is from the Divine, and it contains within itself the creative Elements and Breath which belong to the Eternal Mystery. Thus the Soul itself is the result of the marriage of Divine Substance and Divine Spirit; and from its inception it is a divine child, containing potentially all that will enable it bye and bye to pass through marriage in its divine intent within all the Spheres whither it goes in its consciousness and its realization, even until it attains that estate or inheritance of power and understanding and perfect willinghood wherein it can be absolutely married to the LORD.

THE DUAL NATURE OF THE SOUL

In its constitution the Soul contains the Divine Elements in their negative and positive states. These express themselves in centripetal and centrifugal motion. *The Soul is, therefore, in its constitution, patronic and matronic: it has the paternal and maternal qualities.* By means of the action of these, according to the degree of the estate of its consciousness, it becomes married and unified. When the Soul has fully attained, it is married to the Spirit. This means that all its elements and essences are magnetically upgathered into a centre of unity by means of which it enters into high spiritual consciousness or oneness with the realm of the Spirit. And from this experience, wherein it becomes a living Soul or one whose consciousness has risen to touch the realm of the Spirit, it proceeds inward and upward in state. And thus its estate or inheritance increases in the measure of the Soul's realization of that which has been gifted to it. And in this process, between the first degree and its ultimate Nirvanic or perfect realization of oneness with the LORD, it passes through the experience of what we would term marriage. In its journeying it enters into and passes through the experience of the unions which take place in the lower Angelic World.

It is by a process of this nature that it attains to be as the Angels of GOD in Love and Wisdom, and as a Son of the Gods in cosmic consciousness (celestially understood), and realizes the fulness of the estate wherein it becomes a Son of GOD. In this latter experience it becomes absolutely married to its LORD. The whole journey from its first awakening to spiritual realization until it reaches the crown of its evolution, is a process of unification, wherein the Soul's whole Being becomes more and more divine in the intensity and expanse and height of its realization. In this process the mind becomes unified with the outer life, and the outer life with the mind, in a manifestation of what is pure and beautiful, what is true, and what is of equity and righteousness. The outer life and the mind together become unified with the divine emotion expressed through the heart, so that there is another stage reached of the marriage of the Soul. And as the various degrees of such an experience are passed through, heart and mind and life become one with the Soul in its highest aspirations and most spiritual vision. Here the perceptions and the understanding are unified or married, and become one with the Soul. And then as the result of the unification and consequent marriage of all the glorious elements associated with the body, and the mind, and the heart, and the Soul as a sanctuary with its heavenly mind wherein are contained the perceptions, the understanding, and the reason, there is an upgathering and fresh polarization upon a yet more inward kingdom; so that these become unified to *the real will*, which is the divine magnetic centre of the Being. For the Soul seeking only heavenly things through its perceptions, understanding and reason, and the expression of these through the motion of the Love-lifestream and the purpose of the mind, together with the desires of the body, arrives at that degree of its evolutory motion wherein even *its will* can be laid on the Altar. For *its will* is the divine Principle within it by which it makes divine choices, and through which in the ultimate it becomes married to the LORD. For a perfect Soul marriage is that union of the divine will in us with the Divine Will expressed in the Holy ONE Who Overshadows us. When the Soul enters into such a realization, henceforth it lives only and absolutely in the Divine, from the Divine in its individuated life, and for the Divine in all its ministry. It lives in the Divine, for in consciousness it is one with the LORD; it lives from the Divine, for it is in consciousness an individuation of the glorious Mystery, and an exposition of that Mystery in its fashion; and it lives for the Divine, for its life is an individuated embodiment of the most sacred Mystery we name the FATHER-MOTHER. It has become of the Theophaneia, though not yet in the special sense, which happens only when a Soul is chosen to be a special Messenger. But that Soul's very substance becomes like the Divine Substance in its magnetic states; and in the Soul's fashion and the spirit that energizes it, is the Holy Breath, produced through the Holy Indwelling. For it is the resultant of the motion of the Eternal Mystery through the Soul's Spiral.

In such a glorious state, the Soul is patronic and matronic. In its patronic ministry it uses the centrifugal mode, which, on the outer planes, would be expressed as the positive and masculine; in its matronic ministries it uses the feminine mode, which may be spoken of as the negative and centripetal. The Soul is thus dual in its motion and its manifestation, even as the FATHER-MOTHER is said to be dual, for the Eternal Mystery is not only potentially in the Soul, but divinely realized. The Soul is thus both male and female. The male aspect is the divine motion as creative Spirit within it: the female aspect is the glorious Hypostasis which enables it, through the energizing motion of the Spirit, to know Divine Motherhood as well as Fatherhood.

Great is the Mystery of the Living ONE Whom we name the FATHER-MOTHER, even within the limited compass of an individuate Human Soul.

THE PAULINE BETRAYAL OF WOMAN

The Sacrament or mystery of Marriage has, therefore, a significance more profound than the Church has yet come to understand. Though it has designated Marriage a Sacrament, yet it has related the sacramental act chiefly to the union between a man and a woman. And where it has sought for a more mystical interpretation of the sacred mystery and applied it to the individual, it has circumscribed the full exposition of its meaning to the outward consecration of a human life to some form of monasticism. For, in the Church's teaching, the Soul that becomes married to her as priest or as nun for purposes of ministry, is accounted as one married to the LORD. And the highest and most sacred vision given to a Soul is that of such a consecrated union with the Church in priesthood, or monastery, or convent. Following upon the Pauline teaching that marriage has within its sacramental nature something of the Mystery of GOD, the Church has become utterly Pauline in the place it has given to the woman. For even in her marriage to the LORD as expressed in her consecrated conventual life, as well as within the sanctuary, she has to be silent. Nay, in the Church's teaching concerning human union, it has emphasized that the woman must not only be silent in the Church, but obedient and subservient to the man. Though the Church has cherished the most glorious sacrificial ministries of lovely women in lowly and high earthly estate, yet it has not accounted them worthy to be interpreters within the Church of its own mysteries, nor mediators before the high Altar as Priests of God. It has done as Paul advised should be done; it has made the woman silent in her ministries, and subservient to the pride of man. And in doing this in relation to the woman, it has but outcarried into the realm of the human unit that which it has done in principle in relation to the realm of the Spirit, as that realm, through the Spirit, became manifest within the Soul. For it has silenced the Intuition, of which woman is the exquisite symbol with her heavenly perceptions and soul motion. It has exalted the man to the depreciation of the woman, even whilst it has courted the woman's ministries in order to fill its sanctuaries and render the greater part of its outer ministries. It has exalted the male principle in the priesthood, and dethroned the female principle. It has thus blighted the glorious flower of a perfect priesthood, by depriving woman of her true estate as sharer with man in the divinest of ministries before the high Altar. And this action on the part of the Church, so essentially Pauline, has been the outcome of the Church's own darkness as to the nature and constitution of the Human Soul, man and woman. It has accounted her the more fallen member and the least worthy, though it has exalted her in the Holy Mother, and worshipped her as high mediator with her Son. It has accounted the Holy Mother worthy of such a priesthood as would give her the approach to the Lord Himself, to receive from Him that which she could mediate unto the needy. Yet within the Church itself woman is accounted unfit to render any of the offices associated with the Altar services.

WOMAN IS BY NATURE A PRIESTESS

This attitude on the part of the Church has revealed, and still reveals, the darkness which fills the sanctuaries where the light of the glory of God is supposed to be radiated. For it is thought that the functions of a woman, apart altogether from the fallen state, are such as to unfit her for priesthood. It is believed that in priesthood there is a divine transmission of spiritual force, and that the constitution and functions of a woman militate against such a ministry from the Divine World.

Here I would say to those who may read these words, that no man is fitted to receive the empowerment which the Unction of the Holy ONE doth give, unless he be pure of heart, and of mind, and of body; that such a power as is supposed to be transmitted through the Priest, having been conferred upon him first, would unman any Priest whose heart was not in a state of Divine Love, and whose mind was not in a state of equipoise in that Love, and whose body was still unredeemed and knew nothing of the process of regeneration.

Nay, more than this would I say to the reader. It is only through the woman mode and motion, and, therefore, the divine feminine of a Soul, that the Divine can be apprehended and entered into as a realization; for it is the Cherubic motion. And until that be accomplished, the Seraphic motion, which is the positive, cannot take place; for it is through this latter motion that the Being becomes filled from the Divine, as the result of the Cherubic realization, with that divine power which enables the true Priest to embody and make manifest the Divine Mystery, and to transmit in blessing some of the divine power. Yet it is only the blessing of such a power that can be given, for no Soul can do more than receive the blessing until it has attained.

Therefore in a perfect priesthood there must be man and woman. The woman is the glory of the man, even as the man is the crown of the woman. In this sense the man represents the understanding, as the woman does the intuition; but the man, being the centrifugal force, also symbolizes the motion of the Spirit of the LORD, and it is unto the LORD Who is the Spirit in us the woman in each Soul has to render perfect obedience.

THE REALITY VEILED BY TRADITION

With the light of the foregoing it will be seen how far away the Church has gone from the divine ideal. It may also be recognized how great was the Pauline betrayal when the woman was silenced in the Church. Of this latter there is still a vestige in the tradition that the woman must not enter the sanctuary uncovered, whilst the man should not enter the sanctuary with his head covered. The head is the symbol of the understanding. It speaks of the mind. But with the understanding and the mind, there is also the Intuition, and it is the Intuition that is still covered in the sanctuary.

Many things might be written on this aspect of the sad betrayal with its subsequent tradition. The spiritual state of the world, or, rather, its lack of spiritual estate, is the saddest, most pathetic and tragic commentary upon the Church's darkness, the inferiority with which it has clothed woman, and its mistaken interpretations of the sacred meaning of marriage. It has made a sacramental act, in the case of many who have entered into outer union, of that which in motive and purpose was void of all that is truly sacramental; for most of the unions in the world to-day between men and women are the result of physical and social, commercial and racial attractions, and not such unions as could be truly spoken of as divinely sacramental, wherein the Divine Mystery of Marriage found exposition and interpretation.

Even the true nature and uses of the Life-forces by men and women are little understood. Physical science has said much concerning the Life-forces, and in its way has endeavoured to enlighten humanity. A pure physical science might do much more than it has yet accomplished, to heal many of the grievous states which still obtain in men and women, the prevalence of which through long ages has thrown a deep, deep shadow across the very threshold of the relationships between men and women. For the Life-forces, which are creative, are related to the Eternal Mystery, though they may seem to be operative only within the area of two human lives who have entered into union upon these planes. If many of the great evils in the world, and a multitude of the sorrows by which men and women are most obviously afflicted, can be related to the uses and abuses of the creative Life-forces, such states and experiences obtain, not because of anything inherently evil in sex constitution and in the Life-forces, but rather because of the fearful degradation of men and women in their uses of those beautiful attributes and forces, resulting from an entire misconception of the constitution of man as a spiritual Being.

Man is GOD-endowed. In his potencies he is of GOD, and in his creative energy like GOD. Though in such lowly degree, contrasted with the Infinite and Eternal, yet he is a perfect expression of the Eternal Mystery in his Divine Principle, and nucleolus, and nucleus. For the Arche or apex of his Being, is of the nature of the Eternal, and is the Divine Principle. What I have termed his nucleolus represents the inner sphere of his motion, usually spoken of as the Soul; and the nucleus represents the intermediary and outer spheres of his activity wherein he makes manifest, creating and fashioning according to the degree and the intensity of motion of his Divine Principle, and in harmony with the character and form of his desire and vision.

Being so divinely endowed, man can create from the outer realms, named the physical, to the inner realms which are accounted spiritual. Through the male and female Life-forces, forms of a human order can be generated. Though man cannot create a Human Soul, nor give the Divine Principle and its nucleolus, yet is he so gifted that he can generate the vehicle to be inhabited by the Divine Principle with its nucleolus or Soul, and thus give to the Soul the nucleus through which to make manifest upon these planes.

Man has also the power of mind creations. He can make use of the elements, bringing them into combinations, and, like the artist, fashion them in such a way that they represent divine ideas or earthly ideas. It is thus that the human mind reveals its inherent potency for conquest. It learns through its creations, and in many respects conquers the elements.

But man has also the power to create in the Soul-sphere within the realm represented by the nucleolus. He can generate atmospheres. He can magnetically affect conditions. He can create inner forms. When he perfectly attains, man has the power to generate even as the Angels in their high unions generate within the spiritual spheres.

THE LIFE-FORCES AND THEIR USES Now all these are the outcome of the motion of the sacred mystery we name the Life-forces according to the realm of their operation. For the Life-forces upon the outer planes are the exposition, within the realm of the nucleus, of those forces operative within the realm of the nucleolus and the Divine Principle. Herein the reader may glimpse the sacred mystery, and know how true it is that even as it is in the above or within, so is it in the beneath or the without. And the reader may also come to understand that, in a perfect union between a man and a woman, when the process of generation takes place, there is something more accomplished than a mere physical exposition of the uses of the Life-force on the outer planes. For in perfect union there is effected such a meeting and blending of the inner elements of the Being, as will affect any child to be born through the vehicle generated.

With this sacred view of the constitution of man and woman, and the nature of the masculine and feminine Life-forces as representing Spirit and Substance in their outer expression, it will be understood what a sacred thing a true marriage is; that such marriage is not simply the result of legal union, but is constituted in that act wherein two Souls enter into inner as well as outer union for purposes of creative ministry. And it will be recognized that where the expressions of love are pure and beautiful, there can be no mere self-seeking on the part of the man or the woman unto the fulfilment of earthly desire; for Love is Divine and, like the Divine, seeketh not its own. In its fulfilment there is no self-regard, no acquisition or attainment for itself alone. It is of the very nature of Love to think for its object. The radiant centre whereon it is focussed is the first and last thing in its vision, so that all its action is unto the blessing of the object.

It is into this high estate of life that all the children of GOD who would liken HIM in their embodiment, must enter. For HIS children must reveal the fashion of HIMSELF which is within themselves, not only in the realm of the nucleolus and the Divine Principle or Soul-kingdom, but also in the realm of the nucleus or heart, and mind, and body states and ministries. There is no looseness in perfect Love. It has the freedom of a GOD in its potencies; but it has also the wisdom of a Son of GOD in its ministries. It has the power to give always; but it has also inherent in itself the power to withhold. It has the power to lay down its life and to take it up again; but in the laying down and even in the uptaking, it hurts not its object or objects. It is like GOD Whose fashion it bears and Whose Mystery it is.

Thus, a GOD-endowed man or woman will be rich in that Love; and in all earthly relationships into which the man or the woman, or both, may enter, the mantle of that Love will be ever in evidence, and the fruits of that Love will be ever manifest. *For even in such lowly degrees of life as may be found expressed in the outer realms of manifestation, the Marriage of the Soul to the Lord may be revealed.* For the one who is married to the LORD can accomplish even the lowliest office if it be of HIS appointing, and accomplish it full of the consciousness of oneness with HIM, of being in the stream of HIS magnetic motion, of living in the realm of the Divine Principle which is of the Eternal, and thence operating through the realm of the Soul, and the Heart, and the Mind, and the Body, into the spheres of the outer ministries, even there making manifest the sublime dignity of Marriage to the LORD, even there revealing the Divine Omnipotency in the perfect exposition of HIS Love.

Here is a Sacrament indeed of union sublime and glorious with the LORD of Being, wherein the most sacred Mystery of the FATHER-MOTHER finds high realization within the Soul.

Here is consummated the meaning, through the realization within the Being, of all the degrees of Marriage, or union, from the outermost to the innermost.

Here is realized within a Human Soul in the beneath, all that obtains and prevails in the above.

Here in the outer realm of manifestation is expressed the motion of the Innermost Worlds.

* * * * *

In the Seven Sacraments the Seven Greater Mysteries of the ELOHIM are couched. In their innermost significance they become seven most Sacred Caskets, golden in their elements and Divine in their fashion, containing the Sacred Scroll whereon are written THE DIVINE SECRETS.

Thus, the Seven Sacraments or Greater Mysteries, have their relationship to and correspondence with the Seven Archangels, and their Realms and Regnancies.

Oriphiel:	The Baptism with Truth.
Anael:	The resultant Harmony or Confirmation.
Salamiel:	The Low Mass—the partaking of the Divine Substance and Breath.
Raphael:	The attained Understanding of the Divine Wisdom.
Zachariel:	The Unction through the Anointment by the Holy Breath, which is the Baptism of The Presence.
Michael:	The full Realization of the Power bestowed upon one who has attained to be a Son of GOD.
Uriel:	The High Mass—The Divine Union wherein the Being becomes One with the Divine Mystery.

PART III

THE RENASCENT PATH

A REDEMPTIVE RENAISSANCE

THE SEVEN THUNDERS

THE HEALER, MANIFESTOR, AND REDEEMER

THE DIVINE PASSION

THE OBEDIENCE OF CHRIST

OUR LORD AND OUR LADY

SANTA MARIA

A THREEFOLD MYSTERY

A REDEMPTIVE RENAISSANCE

A REDEMPTIVE RENAISSANCE.

Great is the meaning of the Divine Renaissance. It is renascent Redemption. The beam of healing is in its motion. Its light reveals the true Jesus-way wherein is found the pure and noble Life. The Message makes manifest God's Way of Renaissance; the unveiling of this theme will uncover some of the inimical forces working for the overthrow of the Christhood, and the defeat of the Divine Purpose underlying the Manifestation and the Oblation, and thus to make a true Renaissance impossible.

THE RENAISSANCE.

What has been termed the Renaissance will be familiar to those who have read the history of the fifteenth and sixteenth centuries, and especially to those who have studied the revival of Italian Art during that period; and, indeed, its revival in other countries also. At that period there were three great aspects of motion. There was the desire to find something concrete in Art that was truly beautiful, since the Church and the State did not supply it. There was also the effort to find a culture of mind and taste which did not appear to exist outside of certain eclectic Schools, by means of a revival of what is called Letters—that is, literature in its higher aspects apart from anything spiritual. And with that dual motion outside the Church, there was also a great effort to effect a spiritual change from within the Church itself.

Whilst those who sought to bring about a renaissance of Art and Letters, were largely within the Roman Church and involved in its priesthood, worship and ministries ; yet they felt there must be freer avenues through which to express themselves and to arrest the thoughts and ambitions of those who longed for progress, and to culture in those who were able to respond a deeper love for the beautiful, even though it took largely, and sometimes only, an architectural direction.

And the same objective obtained in relation to the finer culture. There was the endeavour to study again something of the wisdom of the Greeks ; to renovate the Church, if it were possible, through Greek Art and classic literature.

FAILURE OF THE RENAISSANCE

We know how the endeavour failed. Art and scholasticism, however brilliant, could not of themselves effect spiritual changes. Within the Church itself there was the great desire to find something purer than its expression of religious life. Many of the things in it were considered to be corrupt. Indeed, viewed from a pure and lofty standpoint, all its glorious symbolism and the interpretations given, might be spoken of as sad degradation of Soulic and Divine meanings. The mistaken direction of the activities of the Schools, and the Priesthood, and the Higher Powers in the Church was so serious, that the results were appalling.

But these three motions, each of which was spiritual and had the same end in view, had to contend against great difficulties. Obstacles of every kind were placed in the way. The result was that the three motions, though pure in their purpose and inception, had misdirection given to them. Thus it came to pass that even the revival of Art and Letters and Religious Devotion, eventuated in hurt unto many. They certainly failed to accomplish all that was hoped for. Indeed, instead of the movement issuing in a true Renaissance, it failed to lift the Church into a larger Life and purer Vision of the LORD of Love and Wisdom, and the lovers of Art and Letters into a nobler outlook upon Life itself, and service unto mankind.

* * * *

In this connection it is not necessary to dwell here upon those who led in these movements. The history of the Medici is well known to students of those times, and especially that of Lorenzo the Magnificent, whose power for good or ill was almost superhuman. But, as the religious motion was the greatest contributing factor in what was to follow as the result of the contention of Art and Scholasticism with Religion, one familiar name should be mentioned. Fra Girolamo Savonarola appeared in the midst of the conflicting spirits. He seemed moved by the Divine urge which a message for his times gave him. At Brescia and then in the Cloisters and Church of San Marco, Florence, he poured forth his Soul in a call to a purer life. Later he became the dominating voice in the counsels of the city, and poured forth prophetic utterances in the vast Duomo. At first his call was to a purer and nobler life, and in respect of this he fearlessly challenged Rome itself. But political intrigue and ambition enmeshed him ; and his failure to accomplish the great spiritual purpose of his earlier message led to his betrayal and martyrdom.

Such may be said to have been the beginning of the renascent motion in the heart of Italy. Its effect was felt in other lands, especially in France ; and it travelled also into the heart of the Teutonic states. At first it did not much affect Britain. There had been an endeavour to revive religious thought and life and worship by one, in many respects more notable than Savonarola, about a century before Savonarola was born. For John Wycliffe had a motion within him which was divinely begotten. He made a supreme endeavour to get the Church into purer ways, up to loftier vision, and to bring to the people more enlightenment regarding the Truth of Life such as might be understood even from the Records of the Old and New Testaments.

For the people did not know. The Church made its great claims, and the people, being kept in ignorance, bowed to the authorities. The Church affirmed its beliefs as dogmas : the people, being unlettered and without knowledge, accepted them. The Papal See proclaimed that it had the Keys to open and shut the doors of the Kingdom of Heaven; the people did not know otherwise, having been nurtured on superstition, so they accepted that authority, and bowed in fear and trembling.

Even in Britain the like things prevailed, although not to the extent that they did in France and Italy. For it is well to know that though this country was under the regnancy of the See of Rome for so long, it never stood in quite the same relationship. It always claimed a certain degree of freedom. Consequently, there were those always ready to resent any encroachment of the powers of that central authority. This explains much in the history of England. The Renaissance did not affect it as it affected Italy and France and certain German States. Yet the desire for a more spiritual exposition of religious life and faith and worship, became even greater within many of the children in this land.

We will now look for a few moments at the motion of that spirit which is associated with the Reformation.

The Reformation.

The Reformation on the Continent undoubtedly owed its inception to the motion that began with the Renaissance. In this country it began with Wyclif in his endeavour to give the people the Bible. Whilst Savonarola was working in Italy to accomplish a reformed Church and Priesthood and social state, Wyclif's followers were working in this country to the like end. The story of the Lollards, who were like the Huguenots, is a story that moves the heart; for even in a great country like this, it was not easy for its leaders and teachers to receive the Truth such as these children were able to reveal and interpret and embody. For the Church and the State persecuted them.

THE THREEFOLD MOTION OF THE REFORMATION

Whilst there were those who a little later arose in Britain like Cranmer, Latimer and Ridley, and others who might be named; on the Continent the great moving spirits who were first in the field were somewhat earlier. In Florence there was Savonarola; in the Teutonic states a quarter of a century later, Luther; in the French and Netherland states, Calvin with Zwingli his great forerunner, who ultimately dominated the Swiss Confederacy; and in Spain, Servetus who opposed the Church authorities, rejected the doctrine of the Trinity as propounded and interpreted by the Church, and as a result had to fly from his country.

Around these it might be said that the great motion of the Reformation played; for it was centred in them.

Here is a fitting place to postulate this question: Was the Reformation really a true spiritual Renaissance? We have no hesitation in saying that it utterly failed to effect any such thing even in Britain.

In Italy it was a call through Fra Girolamo Savonarola to a purer life, a nobler vision and service, to be expressed concretely within and through the Church. For in its inception and purpose it was purely spiritual, though later it became sadly mixed up with political ambition and domination, and religious jealousies.

In Germany it was the repudiation of the Church that had not listened to the message of Savonarola. For, but for the Indulgences that were sold broadcast, Luther might never have arisen to become for Germany the apostle of a reformed religion. Alas! that he also should have permitted himself to be betrayed into becoming a minor and local Pope. For his attitude and pronouncements were echoes of the spirit and voice of the Roman See.

A kindred motion affected Calvin, who was of French origin, and may be said to have represented the French aspect and motion of the Reformation. When he turned from the Roman See to seek for a more spiritual interpretation of life, the dawn of the first ray of real spiritual hope seemed to break upon the world. But, alas! Where he got to we shall see presently.

About the same year as Calvin, Servetus is said to have been born in Spain. From his early days his mind grew in an expansiveness of vision, his heart in its motion craved for something purer and nobler than the religious life he saw around him, which was given as the exposition of the Divine Idea and Ideal in the Church. He questioned the truth of many things the heads of the Church taught, with the result that quite early on he had to flee from his country and seek refuge abroad, first in Germany and then in France. He was persecuted from country to country. And as it is recorded historically that he took up a position accounted most heretical even by Calvin, who surely himself was an arch-heretic, he suffered martyrdom for the things he held sacred. Alas, that history should have to indicate and tradition to emphasize, that Calvin and the heads of the Swiss Confederacy brought about his martyrdom! But he laid great and deep foundations in his "Restored Christianity."[1]

His message influenced many of the saints of God when they were seeking for a live Christianity.

OCCULT EFFORT TO DEFEAT THE OBLATION

The Reformation was not a real spiritual Renaissance. It was a tremendous conflict generated from the astral world. Those Souls who were used in it should have been the very foundations of a restored Christianity; Seers of God who were seeking for a purer and a nobler vision and embodiment of religious life. The opposing astral powers used them as the vehicles through which the motion might cause its mighty waves to break upon the shores of human thought in such a way as to set all who were involved in conflict with one another.

What the Church considered heresy was orthodoxy to those who held the heresies. But those who held heretical beliefs, and to whom what they held was the Truth, alas! became in their turn persecutors of those who differed from them. The conduct of Calvin towards Servetus, is an outstanding illustration and confirmation of this most sad betrayal of Love and Wisdom.

The whole story of the Reformation is like a history of conflict on the astral-occult planes, working downward and outward to these planes. If Savonarola be taken as a forerunner of Luther, Zwingli, Calvin, Servetus and others, in these we

---

[1] CRISTIANISMI RESTITUTIO.

have a representation of the new movement for the liberation of the Church from the ultra-domination of the hierarchy at Rome, the gaining of freedom of speech and thought for all seeking Souls, and the purification and redemption of the social and national life. For, if the Divine Intent behind the motion of the Spirit in these Reformers had been accomplished, the Redemption would have been realized by many, and the Christ-life would have been more easily attained to-day.

It is not easy for those who worship at human shrines to see what happened. It is well that you should know that for which Luther stood, that mission to which he was called but which he misinterpreted. We have to see that which came to Servetus in its true light in relation to the Soul and God. We have to read Calvin along with Servetus and Luther in the light of the motion of the Oblation, and the resultant in the Teachings to-day. And although we have named no great one in Britain contemporaneous with these three, yet there were those who were influenced through the teachings of Calvin and Luther.

Luther had deep in him a consciousness that that which the Church represented in relation to its beliefs, claims, and its Mass, was somehow not right. He read the Bible in monastic seclusion, and especially the New Testament, and discovered passages therein that seemed to be food for the strange motion within him. Those passages had relation to Faith. He read that we are saved by faith, and not by works lest any man should boast. This he found taught in the Pauline Letters. So he proclaimed warfare against works as taught by the Church.

It is quite true the Church attached importance to its own authority, to the beliefs it imposed, and to salvation by means of the Mass, and high or low degrees of attainment according to the amount of the works of supererogation which the individual might accomplish.

Luther on the other hand proclaimed that Souls could come to God without intermediate mediation ; that all they required was a "living faith" in Him; and a belief in the meritorious sacrifice of Jesus Chirst. He taught that salvation came in this way, and that it was of grace by faith.

LUTHER'S LACK OF ILLUMINATION

But Luther made his great mistake in misinterpreting Faith. He did not understand what Faith meant. For he simply interpreted it as another intellectual concept of the Divine, and a belief in the Divine Fiat in relation to HIS Mercy.

But that is not Faith. You may hold all the beliefs the world has ever had without having any true Faith. You may have great Faith and know nothing about those beliefs. For beliefs as such are quite separate from Faith.

Faith is a quality of Being by which the Soul perceives heavenly secrets. Faith is the substance of things hoped for, the spiritual and Divine substantial that lies beneath and behind all things.

Faith is therefore that power of perception which enables the Soul to read through things, and see their heavenly motions and relationships. Aye, it is even more. As it was written of old time, "Faith is the evidence of things not seen." It is the assurance through knowing. It is that power in the Being by which the Being apprehends. By Faith it is no longer a matter of belief. There is a degree of realization. Belief in any direction is not evidence of anything. But perception unto the knowing of a thing is sure evidence. We can know GOD only through perception and never through belief. He is apprehended by Faith. We can know HIM only in high estate of realization through Love. There is Faith and Hope and Love. Love is the first and the last. It is the greatest of all. For Faith itself is begotten of a real Love. For none who will not learn to love can do Divine Work. Not only will such an one fail to do the works of supererogation, but even that work by which the Soul can grow. Only those who love can come into the true perception of heavenly things and understand Divine Secrets.

Luther certainly apprehended a great truth, but mistook the meaning. He laboured by day and by night, preaching and writing new religious views he had adopted, and proclaiming against the edicts of the Church authorities. He did effect great changes in Germany. But I would ask you this, and with deep respect and reverence for the Teutonic peoples who are of a gifted and noble race: Has the Lutheran Church made the Germanic peoples a spiritual race, a nation with spiritual vision, a people understanding more and more the reality of the Heavens, the transcendency of the Life of the Soul as in vision and realization it stands before HIM WHO is its LORD? The answer is most obvious to the Seer.

Though the revival of Letters had remarkable results in the Teutonic states, and laid the foundations of the great educational systems of Germany, yet spiritually the nation was left where the Italian and French peoples were left, notwithstanding the apostleship of such Souls as Servetus, and the travail of the saints in the monasteries and conventuals, and even those in high priestly mediation who desired diviner states and nobler expressions of the life of the Church.

THE TRAGEDY THAT FOLLOWED CALVINISM

In Geneva Calvin chiefly laboured, where he was safe under the protection of many friends, and shielded under the shadow of Margaret of Navarre. Though his greatest work was written at Basle, yet it was from Geneva he issued his interpretation of things. He repudiated the Church; but he sought to found another church. He repudiated papal authority; but he made of his Institutes an authority that has had disastrous results through the succeeding ages upon the minds of many peoples. He was caught up by the Pauline confused message of predestination, till it became the root message in his mind. All he had to teach emanated from and gathered around that awful Pauline interpretation of the doctrine of predestination. He taught the doctrine of Original Sin under the terms of "total depravity." He wrote, "*Men are not all born equal, for some are pre-ordained to Eternal Life, some to eternal damnation!*"[1] How any one could have taught such a doctrine who himself must have witnessed,

[1] CHRISTIANÆ RELIGIONIS INSTITUTIO.

notwithstanding the fearful states that prevailed spiritually, nationally and socially, many angels in the way, angels even in human form, it seems most difficult to imagine. He taught the particular doctrine of Election; that as all men had sinned, God had, in a sense, reprobated them. But He had decided from all eternity to elect a certain number out of the reprobates, and find a way of salvation for them. That way was through His Beloved Son dying for them. For in all the Calvinistic interpretations of that Work it was only accomplished for the Elect People, without any consideration of or relation to all the rest. And then he taught the Final Perseverance of the Saints; that because they were predestined from all eternity, God foreseeing what is named the Fall, and the becoming totally depraved, of the whole of His creation, He decided to heal a certain number of them by the work of a Redeemer. And to make His purpose absolutely assured, it was arranged that His Grace should find them unto all fulness, and that there should be absolute perseverance, called the "final perseverance of the Saints." It was an assurance that each one would find his and her way back to the Heavenly Home.

Calvin glimpsed great things. He even perceived that there was a true meaning to the Theocracy. But the enemy opposed to the restitution and establishing of the Christhood, did to him what was done to Luther. The great Soul was betrayed into misconceiving and misrepresenting the Divine Love and Wisdom. And he wanted to institute that his Church should be the head in all temporal as well as spiritual affairs, and its laws binding. I have shown you when speaking of the Divine Theocracy and Oligarchy that such is the true Divine Government of an unfallen world. But there were elements present in Calvin's conception which were far from those belonging to a Divine Theocracy.[1]

Servetus also glimpsed great things. Calvin was a stoic, Servetus was essentially human. Calvin was an un-named

[1] *Vide* Chapter on The Divine Government, pp. 457 to 475.

Pope, Servetus was a Brother of the Race. Calvin was exclusive, Servetus was universal. Calvin repudiated Rome, but laid the foundations of another form of domination equally disastrous; Servetus also rejected the Church's authority, but he laboured for a restoration of the Christhood. Though an arch-heretic himself, Calvin proclaimed Servetus worthy of death because he was believed to be a pantheist and a unitarian, one who did not believe in the Deity of the Master, Jesus Christ. And yet, as I would now show you, viewed from within, those three represented most glorious aspects of the Divine Message. The success of the enemy lay in this, that the opposing spirit made use of them by making them get into conflict with each other. In this way was the message perverted and changed, and the issues confused. The astral world made use of their differences to veil the vision that had come, in order that the children should not be able to rise into the Christhood. For the motion of the Reformation was Divine; but the reception of that motion by the channels of it, and the direction given to its streams, was part of a great occult effort to defeat the Oblation in its redemptive and blessed results.

I have indicated to you what Luther apprehended but misunderstood; and what Calvin saw but did not understand.

THESE TEACHINGS ARE FOR THE ELECT

In these Teachings of the restored Message to-day, "predestination" is as prominant as in the most ultra-Calvinism. But not after the manner of Calvin's interpretation. For what is predestination but the philosophical aspect of destiny? Predestination is, to be destined beforehand. You cannot conceive of predestination and a fallen world as a part of it, in the light of Absolute Omniscience. Otherwise you are reduced to this state, that of questioning the Blessed FATHER-MOTHER, out from WHOSE BOSOM all things have proceeded, and WHO in all HIS creations could not make anything other than beautiful in fashion and purpose, beautiful as an exposition of HIMSELF, if HE foresaw everything, including the Fall, why HE did not prevent it beforehand. And if it were even so, why predestine the few only? If the few could be saved, why not predestine *all* to know again the joy of Life in the FATHER-MOTHER?

The doctrine is monstrous, and terrible has been its effects. For it has afflicted many countries. It misled certain sections amongst the Teutons. It pervaded, and does so to this day in a modified form, Switzerland. It pervades great sections of the English race. And it has blighted the north part of Britain. The religion of Scotland became a religion of beliefs from which real worship was excluded. Even unto this day the sanctuaries are but preaching-stations, and the people lack the true vision of HIM WHO is Ever Glorious. For the blight of Calvinism was carried from Geneva to Scotland by the ministry of John Knox.

Knox is one of Scotland's greatest heroes. Doubtless he was a great man, of iron will like Calvin, and capable of great sacrifices. But also like John Calvin, his arrogance was equal to that of the then Roman Pontiff, and his misdirected zeal was the cause of unspeakable persecution throughout the land. He did for Scotland what the Roundheads of Cromwell later tried to do in England. By his addresses against the papacy, he so worked into a state of fury the unredeemed mobs, that they destroyed many of the truly beautiful sanctuaries and monastries. Indeed, the only notable House they left intact was Glasgow Cathedral.

It is quite true that his work did for Scotland what the Renaissance did for Germany; it laid the foundations of National Education. But spiritually it threw the people back for ages. For even unto this day Religion in Scotland has not recovered from the effects of the blow then struck by the enemy under the guise of religious freedom.

England and Wales also suffered severely from the blighting breath of Calvinism; but there were other streams whose motion mitigated the effects of Calvinism, and alleviated the stress caused by its imposition.

THE DIVINE PURPOSE IN THE REFORMATION

Now I would show you what the Heavens meant by that which was set in motion as the result of the Work of the Oblation in as far as it had been accomplished up to the thirteenth and fourteenth centuries, and on from the fifteenth to the present day.

Faith was to be restored. Real spiritual vision was to come back again. That was the meaning of the threefold motion. The Church had no spiritual vision though it had much devotion. It had many in it who were the Saints of GOD, and who travailed for its healing and preservation. But faith became just another aspect of intellectualism, repudiating the most sacred works as of no account in salvation. Yet man cannot get anywhere without works. Of course, if he merely works to get reward, then the motive is impure. In the earthly and outer life, it is necessary to earn the wherewithal for living upon these planes. But if one worked for GOD merely for increase, the motive would not be right. Yet there is no growth without works. Growth is by means of good, noble heart-works and mind-works. No one can grow without doing what is beautiful, true and noble, spiritual and angelic. If a Soul would grow Divine, it must learn to do things like the Divine. That is the meaning of living like the Divine, growing in Love, in the personal from one to the few, from the few to the many; growing from the communal into the tribal, from the tribal to the national and the racial, and still loving all Souls.

To Love Souls divinely! Ah, that is an attainment worth striving for, a realization to be most diligently sought after! The Divine Loves all and passes by none. You cannot grow without working. The very endeavour to grow to love divinely, is a work. You may say, How can one work to love? In this way. When you meet obstacles in the way of your loving in this or that service to the Divine, then cause the obstacle to move away. Chide yourself until the obstacle melts away. Do not imagine for a moment that you will grow in Love unless you make the obstacles yield to you. Overcome them until they do not exist for you.

There are no works of supererogation as understood in the Catholic Church; yet when a Soul reaches certain states of consciousness, it seeks to work the more. But the labour is not merely for its own growth, or the expansion and deepening of its consciousness. The labour is for GOD for HIS children, irrespective of the thought of growth. When a Soul reaches any high degree of Celestial or Divine consciousness, it never thinks of growth for its own enrichment, for all its labours are consecrated acts for the FATHER-MOTHER in service unto HIS children.

Here may be unveiled the inner significance of the wonderful motion that came to Servetus and Calvin. Servetus had a glimpse of what was called pantheism. He saw that all things came out of the Bosom of the FATHER-MOTHER; that HE is expressed in all things; that HIS Spirit is in motion through all things. Thus Servetus sought to bring GOD into beautiful Immanency. GOD was in the Being; therefore to grow in consciousness into the status of Emmanuel in the Being, was fulfilling the Divine Law of growth. Servetus was repudiated and martyred by those who should have befriended him and welcomed his message. Yet his message was not to be silenced.

Calvin saw only the Will of GOD in high sovereignty. And in that vision no human child was a Son of GOD, except by that special act of grace which GOD bestowed upon those Souls who were of the Elect. Wherever a Soul had to go it must go, having been predestinated. It could not help itself. It could not save itself. Its God-like desires were of no value to it unless it had been predestined and chosen.

PREDESTINATION A GLORIOUS REALITY

We know that all Souls have had a high destiny; that their destiny is to be children of the FATHER-MOTHER; that all are meant to realize that childhood, to rise into the consciousness of the Divine Presence. We know the destiny of a Human Soul, because we know it has the Divine potencies within it. We know that the Arche is within the Soul, and that further Mystery of GOD named the Amen. The Amen in sevenfold fulness, is potentially within every Soul. We know that the Human Soul is *the Sanctuary* upon the Earth where the Divine Presence loves to dwell, where HE shows HIMSELF, gradually unveiling HIS Own Mystery as the Soul is able to receive of HIM, until the Sanctuary of Being is lit up with the glory of a light unknown except in that wondrous world of realization. We know that man was fashioned to bear the Image of God. In this respect we would take the opening of the Shorter Catechism which Scotland has failed to understand the significance of, or it would have repudiated long ago the fearful darkness imposed upon it by the deep shadow of Calvinism!—"Man's chief end is to glorify GOD, and to enjoy HIM forever." We glorify HIM in being true children to HIM. We show forth HIS Glory by expressing the splendour of HIS Own Sacred Mystery through our attributes and in our embodiment. We reveal HIS Glory when we love divinely. We glorify HIM when in our tenderness we are angelic. We reveal HIM when in our ministries we are selfless. And we enjoy HIM forever in that we become more and more like HIM.

Surely it were mockery to affirm such a transcendent experience for man generically if, because he was outside of the few Elect ones, he was reprobated before ever he made his appearance upon the Earth! How could any man enjoy such Life in God, with the shadow of reprobation hanging over him?

Of Theologians who are the products of the Schools may it still be said that with their eyes they see yet read not the meaning of GOD; that with their ears they hear but understand not the language of Divine Motion in all things, and very specially in man—HIS Child; and that, though many of them have great minds and even greater hearts, yet they fail to discern the Way of the Divine Love and Wisdom; and that, because of their sad limitations, they have perpetuated the long deep shadow which ages ago the opposing powers threw across the threshold of the Divine Love and Wisdom.

There is only one way in which we can enjoy GOD, namely, through being like HIM. GOD is not a person in the human sense. The word translated "person," is hypostasis. GOD is Divine Substance and Spirit in all things, and therefore in us. And because of this there is *a becoming* of HIM within us in concrete embodiment. *Becoming is Realization.* He is Pneuma and Hypostasis in the Absolute, the Eternal Spirit and Substance. And every Soul has HIS Substance and Breath, and thus becomes a sharer of the Divine Mystery of Being.

Thus HE is revealed in the Human Estate, even as in the Angelic and Celestial, in the glorious Hierarchies of the Gods, in the Son of GOD, and in the Only Begotten One, the ADONAI.

Calvin saw something of this, but he failed to apprehend its significance. The truth of predestination, and through that predestiny, the Divine dignity of the Human Soul, he did not apprehend. He failed to understand how a Soul is "Predestined from all eternity." From the beginning of Soul creation, it was predestined. From the day of its inception, its generation, its fashion, its manifestation, it was destined to be an embodiment of the Glorious One. It is a most high honour. Never let down that dignity within you by word, or act, or failure to embody, or through the withholding of your blessing. But ever uphold that dignity through being alert at all times, ever ready and waiting to accomplish the Will of our FATHER-MOTHER.

It is not necessary for me to dwell upon the frightful heresy of Calvinism in the light of the Divine Love and Wisdom, and especially on that perversion of the tragic story of this world in what is named by Calvin "Original Sin" and "Total Depravity." Surely it was the work of the betrayer to present such a view! Had it been so, there would have been no Human Souls on the Earth. They would all have become demoniacal in their state. And, whilst there are many evil elemental spirits still, yet where spiritual feeling is in the Soul, there are desires for the higher, the nobler, and the more beautiful. And so there is hope for the Race. For *all* must at last come up in state into the realization of perfect Childhood to the FATHER-MOTHER.

"Original Sin," as it is called, whereby all men become sinners, had to do with the Planetary Descent, of which I have often spoken to you. That was the result of a terrible mistake. That all the children became involved more or less, it is true. Even the Christhood members were drawn down by it amidst their wondrous ministries of Love unto the children of this world. But it was a Planetary Descent. And it was not foreknown. Divine Omniscience is not understood.

All the children of the FATHER-MOTHER, whether they be in Human embodiment, or Celestial embodiment, or in a Planetary exposition of HIM, have that which is of the very nature of perfect Love, namely, the liberty of the Children of God. They have the power to choose. The whole universe is full of contingencies, though it is rarely that a world goes wrong as this world has done. How it went wrong is dealt with in another chapter.

ANCIENT ISRAEL THE ELECT PEOPLE

With Calvin's doctrine of "Original Sin" there was associated the doctrine of "Election." He took the Pauline statement that GOD had chosen a people out of this world. But he gave to it the narrowest of interpretations, and made GOD unjust. What a great truth the doctrine contains this Message will show you. The Elect Tribes are a reality. They have always been GOD'S Peculiar People. They were a chosen Nation, but not gathered out of this world. They were of another system, but were sent here as a Nation of Priests. The word priest means one who is a mediator. They were in high priesthood, having an inner mediation for the manifestation and interpretation of GOD unto the elder children of this world.

The Elect People are therefore the Sons of GOD for whose manifestation the groaning creation waits. They are Ancient

Israel, the People whom the Heavens chose to send here. They were not chosen out of this world or any other world in preference to other children. They were of the Sons of God in their estate, and were asked to come to render special ministry. And they were chosen because of their gifts. They were appointed to the high Office of Manifestor to this world in a period of its need in spiritual evolution, long before there took place the great Descent that has been described as the Fall.

Therefore, the doctrine of Election is true. There is a Peculiar People. There are Souls in this world to-day who are of the ancient Christhood, members of the communities of the Sons of GOD in the days of high illumination, members of the Schools of the real Divine Illuminati in other days, real Israelites who are born such from the GOD in them, and not after the flesh, nor bloods, nor races, nor the will of man. You cannot create a Son of GOD by any creed, any will, any fiat of man, or human authority, or racial descent. It must be the growth of a Soul into high consciousness of the Ever Blessed One. That is the Divine way by which the Soul attains to be a Son of GOD. These Souls are still upon the Earth. Many of them are upon these planes now. And there are others who, having passed over, are hastening back again to embody and make manifest the glorious Faith, the Faith that gives illumined understanding. Such Faith is illumination in the Being ; a knowing of the Substance of the Divine Realities. It is a Faith which in itself is the living evidence of its Source and of its Message.

That is the Faith the Sons of GOD possessed. They knew divinely the reality of the Message they brought. They perceived divinely the realities of the Inner Worlds. They were the Elect Children. They were Israel, not after the Jewish concept of that great people, but after the Spirit of GOD. They were begotten and born of GOD. The God-Principle in them was brought forth into high conscious manifestation. Therein was their Sonship to GOD microcosmically embodied.

FOR ISRAEL CAME THE MANIFESTATION

According to Calvin, these were the Elect who were to be delivered by a Redeemer. For them there was to be a particular Redemption. And there is a great truth in this; but oh, the sad perversion of the interpretation given to it! For though the Oblation was first for them, and their arising was to be its first fruitage; it was also a Planetary Burden unto the Redemption of the whole world, including the elemental kingdoms of the Earth. Therefore, it was not only the bearing of their sins. No; for they have themselves had to partly bear the effects of the world's sin. Indeed, their age-long travail was begotten of the world's sin. They were the Saints of God who travailed through the ages. Their very blood, their Divine Life-stream, their energy, their Soul motion, became the seed of the Church, the power which kept the Church alive as an institution. But for their devotion, their spiritual aspiration, the wondrous giving of themselves, their absolute self-emptying oft-times in sublimest sacrifice, the Church as an institution could never have endured throughout the ages, because of the terrible darkness within it and the awful perversion of the Holy Things it professed to hold as most sacred. Nevertheless, the Oblation in its purpose and outworking first affects them. It opens up for them the Planetary Heavens. They are now able to ascend into higher states of consciousness.

It was for Israel, the Sons of GOD, that the Manifestation was made. The Master came to seek unto the finding of the lost Children of the House of Israel. Only they could understand HIS estate as Jesus, and as Christ. And they only could even apprehend dimly that HE was in the Lord consciousness. For only one who had been in some degree of high Christhood, could recognize a Soul who was in that state, and apprehend in such an one the LORD consciousness. And even as HE came to seek them in the days of the Manifestation, so was the Oblation made specially for them to effect their liberation. It was not a bearing of their karmic burden only, but the blotting out of the Planetary karma (wrought by many of the Earth's races long ago) through so changing the conditions, that the Sons of GOD might be able to arise, and the Planet's children find Redemption as the result. For the Redemption is dependent upon the ascension of Israel. Unless Israel arises there can be no Redemption for the world. The Sons of GOD must come back to this Planet. They must come back into that Sonship in their estate. They must reveal HIM through embodying HIM. They must again speak of HIS Love as a living force within them through the language of the Divine motion of their Being. There is no utterance so great as the language of the motion of the Being. For that motion passes not only into words and through them, but it vibrates in every act. It pours itself forth through the motion of the individual Soul by day and by night. For in the night watches even, the Christ-Souls minister for God.

* * * *

THE REAL RENAISSANCE IS AT HAND

There are with us in these days all the elements of a Divine Renaissance. These Teachings will ultimately revivify Art. Notwithstanding all the modern expositions of it, Art is still largely garmented in the grave-clothes in which materialism buried it. But the day is hastening when the Message will touch Art to higher issues so that it will come forth into manifestation, not only conformed to the Divine Ideas, but become an embodiment of the Divine Ideals in fine Art, and formative Art, in motion and in rhythm, in tone and colour.

And the Message will also touch all Letters. There will be a process of expurgation of the evil things which contaminate, and a bringing back through the Sons of GOD of the vision of what this world might be, could be, was meant to be, is to be, aye, what it must be if all the Sons of GOD return into the consciousness of their Christhood again, and become the embodiments and revealers of HIS Glory.

And the Message will effect a Divine Renaissance of Religion. It is to make religion concrete, apart altogether from matters of belief. The things of belief will come to be true. They will be purified and illumined. Devotion will be begotten of Love. The devotion of Love gives the atmosphere. Worship is the aspiration and service of Love. The children must be taught how to worship GOD without fear; to have no dread of HIM. No one could truly worship GOD and at the same time be full of the dread of HIM. You could not adore GOD and be afraid of HIM. You would never have the qualities to embody HIM, if you dreaded HIM. For to adore GOD is to embody HIM. Real worship is a service, and service is a delight. It is not a toil. We never toil for GOD. There is no toil in GOD. The Soul who serves GOD, even if it be unto the uttermost capacity of the inner and outer strength, is never conscious of toiling. Labour is service, and true service is worship. Every act is a worshipful act for HIM, a declaration that HE is first and last in the Soul's Life, the Supreme ONE. And thus shall the Soul who knows HIM speak—*He Whom my Soul and my Being loveth, possesses my Being; it is His*, and so any service of mine is HIS. It is begotten of HIS Own motion within me, and is its resultant in and through me.

It is now the Day of the long delayed Divine Renaissance. That which was meant to be preparatory, was made into a cause of conflict and persecution and even hatred, in Italy, Germany, France, Spain, the Netherlands, Switzerland, and this country.

No one who has inward vision can speak, for instance, of Calvin and his disciples, without thinking of conflict; nor of Luther, without knowing how far afield in relation to the true Faith his disciples have gone. They have added to the vast multitude of those who have missed the way of the true vision.

Where amid the ostentatious ceremonial display of most sacred verities, though they be only in symbol, in Italy and Spain and parts of France, and now even in this country, can the great Reality of a living Christhood be discerned? Or where in Germany, Switzerland and the Netherlands, amid the wealth of intellectual concepts, dogmas, and creedal statements, may be found a true interpretation of the Nature of Christ, a living exposition of a Son of God, or a worthy view of God in the glorious revelation of His Love and Wisdom in the work of the Oblation?

In Romanism and all its allied branches, there is an outward and symbolic Calvary without any true understanding of its profound mystery; and in Calvinism and Lutheranism and all the expositions they give, there is an intellectual Calvary at the foot of which hosts of evangelical idolators worship, but which, like the Roman Calvary, has failed utterly to heal and redeem the world.

The measure of the complete failure of the Reformation is the measure of its distance from all that a true Divine Renaissance must ever be.

THE RENASCENT CHRISTHOOD

Now, it is the time of the New Birth. That Life which is to be divinely renascent is becoming. The Sons of God are returning. They are arising. All who can hear the Message of the restored Teachings will come first; and then all the children as they are able to receive it. The new birth will come through the new vision of God, and of His Love and Wisdom. It is a vision that interprets all things and illumines everything. You cannot touch an epoch of history which the new vision does not illumine. As we look through those ages to which we have directed your own vision and of whose struggles we have spoken, the Travail of the Oblation in Italy, Spain, France, and in Britain, passes before our vision with all its sorrow, pain and anguish. We see how the opposing factors sought to make the return from the Oblation impossible; and if that return could not be prevented, then to make the return of the Sons of God and the restoration of the Christhood impossible. The opposing forces sought to destroy the new efforts to restore the vision, and to make impossible the embodiment of its Life, by means of the great centres of conflicting thought and desire, purpose and authority.

But this Message interprets them all. And it will also unveil, bye and bye, the meaning of the fresh endeavours in this age to confuse the real Message with many claims which are on the surface not unlike it, but which at the best are only partial, and indeed are side tracks if not actual perversions of the Ancient Wisdom and the Message of the Living Christ. For even these are the manifest efforts of the enemy of the Christhood to make void our Message and confuse the Divine Issues, and make impossible the arising of all the Christ-Souls as a glorious resultant of the tragic Travail of the Oblation. *For the opposing powers would nullify the work of the Divine Love's Passion.*

And now, one word on Calvin's last great doctrine which he entitled "*The Final Perseverance of the Saints.*"

In this statement you may see the Redemption and the Regeneration. It is there implied that the saints as the children who once knew the Divine Things, because of the Oblation having been accomplished, should triumph over all the opposing forces. And that is quite true; for the Heavens are open to them. The Planetary Heavens are purified; they are able to ascend into the Angelic Fellowship. They are able to triumph now over principalities and powers that were once in the high places unseen, but which have been cast down to the earth,—which latter is the meaning of many of the conflicts that are proceeding on the outer planes to-day. They will triumph because they are the Sons of GOD, the Souls who were in Christhood (as the word Saint means), those who were GOD's Christs; the ancient Israel; GOD's Sons who offered themselves sacrificially, and who, in the unfallen days, became individually GOD'S Mass to the children of this world.

With this triumphant note we conclude. For no height in the realm of occult principalities and powers; nor depth in the motion of all the subtle and evil opposing forces; nor length nor breadth of the mighty play of the contrary breaths blowing along these planes; nor any seen or unseen power, shall separate us from HIM Who is our LORD. We shall all triumph in HIS Love; for HE is with us. We shall all get back to the true Theocracy and Regnancy, HIS Sovereignty and Government, HIS Sublime Reigning One within the Being. And the whole fabric of the Temple of our Being will be HIS venue for blessed embodiment; and all the communal Christhood shall again be one glorious, vibrant Body of Manifestation, clothed with HIS Omnipotency to effect the Redemption of this world.

Need it be asked of you, would you be of this Divine Renaissance? Would you know the Renascent Life of GOD within you? Unto that end are ye here!

* * * * *

Oh! Transcendent and Most Glorious ONE! Most Wondrous LORD of Love! How impoverished is our gift of tongue and speech in the light of THY Glory and the fulness of THY Love for all THY children!

May these THY children come into a larger vision of THEE within themselves.

May they indeed know the wonders of THY Love unto them, the Glory of THY Stooping unto and for them.

May each one realize this dawning of THY Glory, and as they have never yet realized in these days, THINE Overshadowing and THINE approach to be the Great Indwelling Presence, until each becomes for THEE as THY Emmanuel.

THE MYSTERY
OF
THE SEVEN THUNDERS

THE MYSTERY OF THE SEVEN THUNDERS.

THE ADVENT SEEN FROM WITHOUT

We are in the season of Advent. The Advent is associated with Divine Manifestation. The Manifestation, glimpsed in so far as it can be through the histories, is associated with the coming of Him Who came to be known in the western world as Jesus Christ the Lord. In this season there is great anticipation. There is always a quickened motion during Advent, though it is largely manifest on the outer in relation to the materialistic aspects which men and women associate with the Manifestation.

The anticipation heralds the day of the commemoration of the Advent or coming of the LORD. It is of the annual events and comes year by year. Its procession has been through the ages. Yet the glory its celebration has been supposed to shed, has left the world much as it found it. Certainly the world is far from being healed, though the message was supposed to heal all Souls.

The season of Advent is considered to be a time for great rejoicing. No doubt the people do rejoice after their fashion, and in the degree in which they are able to enter into the traditional life of the west. Yet, whilst there doth seem joy and mirth even to hilarity, it is a season strangely marked and full of a mockery that is accompanied by the acts and the cries of tragedy.

It is a season of supposed exultation when the Being ascends to hear the Angelic Song repeated, and to join in that Song of Hope and Triumph. Yet it is the season of the darkest time of the year, for the atmosphere becomes heavy with the fumes begotten of riotous living.

It is supposed to be a commemorative season, a commemoration of the coming of the Prince of Peace, and a joining in the song of the Angel of the LORD who heralded the Message of Peace to the world. And yet, whilst the songs are sung within the sanctuaries, and chorale expositions of them doubtless given in public, there goes on a great warfare against the creatures. There is the inhuman slaughter of them, for they are compelled to lay down their lives in order to make the carnival of Christmas a success for the children of the west. The inhumanity of man towards the creatures stands revealed at the season of Advent, wherein far beyond one million innocents are slaughtered by Herod, the King of the astral powers, and his court of false desire, tradition, custom, and habit.

Such is the amazing preparation throughout the western world for the celebration of that season which should bring real rejoicing and exultation and commemoration, compassion and pity, and Love triumphant.

Is it any wonder that amidst such mockery and tragedy the Message the Master is supposed to have given to the world, has seemed to fail?

Is it any wonder that thoughtful men and women whose very Beings yearn for the true and the beautiful, should question whether there ever was a Manifestation such as the Churches believe in, and whether such a thing as the Advent is possible?

That it is possible, and that it took place we know. That it is to take place many times we also know. But that you should understand what it is that takes place is the supreme thing, and that I would endeavour to show you.

THE ADVENT SEEN FROM THE WITHIN

The Mystery of that Word uttered by the Seven Thunders is associated with GOD'S Mystery. The Divine Mystery of Life finds its manifestation and exposition, in embodiment. It is the very Mystery of Incarnation.

But you must understand that that term which has come to have merely an earthly meaning, has something far farther reaching in its meaning than could be held within the confines of human thought in relation to human embodiment. For Incarnation signifies the coming into the Flesh. Therefore, it means the becoming formulate of some-one in the higher spheres for embodiment. But wheresoever there is embodiment there is also that which corresponds to what is humanly understood as Flesh. There is the Substance that takes fashion through the motion of the Eternal Breath.

For a little time, in order that it may be more clearly set forth what is meant by the Advent upon the Earth, let us pass from these planes into the Inner Realms. Come up all who can (and all can in some degree come up), and, as far as you are able, witness something of the Incarnation process within the Divine World itself.

For the LORD HIMSELF doth come first as a Breath. The LORD is not a man. HE is not an Angel. HE is not even an Archangel. HE is neither Cherubim nor Seraphim. But all Cherubim and Seraphim, Archangels and Angels, and all HIS children called Human Children, are expositions of HIS glorious Mystery. They are meant to be embodiments of HIS Love and radiators of the Light of that Love as Wisdom.

Even in the Divine World the LORD (except for purposes of manifestation unto many) does not assume what is called the anthropomorphic form, the fashion of the Human Realm. HE is all perfect form; and HE can make manifest through all, according to the realm of the manifestation, and the sphere of that realm, and the degree of the manifestation required.

Now when the Angels of the Innermost Spheres celebrate the Advent, they celebrate *the becoming* of the Sacred Mystery in their presence, the making of it manifest in some concrete form unto their vision. For they behold the LORD through that vision. They receive HIM in HIS coming to them, through that vision. HE is in all the motion of the Inner Worlds.

That which Cherubim and Seraphim represent, HE is. Yet HE is greater than they; but they do represent HIS motion. Where the Soul sees HIM in vision, HE is as Radiance; HE is Divine Splendour; HE is in concrete Embodiment. HE takes the fashion known as ADONAI. HE thus becomes supremely the highest Angelic embodiment in the Divine World; and the Soul sees HIM and receives from HIM.

Here we must pause to let the yearning of our Being express itself. O glorious World! O Transcendent Vision beyond revealing through language or pictorial and symbolical representation, capable alone of interpretation through the motion of the Being as the Soul endeavours to make the vision concrete within itself, and make of it a living factor! For Vision is useless unless it becomes potency unto us and within us. And, in this way, even those in the Inner Worlds enter into ever increasing states of realization; for there, there seems no end to the profundity of the Realization of the Sublime Mystery.

HOW GOD BECOMES INCARNATE

Through the Vision and the Realization the LORD becomes. HE thus becomes formulate within; HIS motion becomes in the Soul's consciousness. HIS Glory becomes the Soul's Divine Atmosphere. HIS Radiance becomes the Soul's Auric Light. HIS Fashion becomes in the Soul's fashion. HIS potencies become manifest throughout the Being, until the Soul who has had the Vision, gradually entering into the Great Realization, becomes GOD Incarnate.

Is it not wonderful that GOD, the Sacred Mystery in the Substance of our Being, in the Lifestream of our Being, becomes incarnate in us, so that we become as Gods, having received so much of HIM, being so much one in HIM in consciousness, knowing HIM so truly and fully in realization that we become HIS embodiments?

That is the meaning of the Mystery of the Gods.

That is the meaning implied in "the Son of GOD."

That is the status of the Sons of GOD.

That is the Mystery of a Soul becoming a Son of GOD.

* * * * *

The Advent takes place in the Heavens.

It is a Divine coming, and a Divine becoming.

The LORD comes through all ministries; but HE *becomes* only within the Being.

In the ministries, HE reveals HIS motion in coming. In His becoming, the Soul is up-borne in a Divine Mass. For the process of the Divine becoming in a Soul, is the process of a Divine Mass. The Being is up-borne through the Vision unto the Realization. The Soul becomes changed in its substance even from glory to glory in status. It is a Divine transformation unto transfiguration, through the offering up of the vehicle, to be filled yet more fully with the Mystery, till it becomes the LORD'S Body, in so far as the individual can become HIS Body in the sense of being HIS perfect vehicle for service.

Such are the Souls who are sent into the Celestial Spheres, the visitants to Celestial Hierarchies, bearing with them from out the Eternal, the Will of the FATHER-MOTHER.

All that is meant to take place here is but a reflection of all that takes place there. It is a lower degree of the exposition of a Divine Incarnation.

MANIFESTATION UPON THE ANGELIC REALM

Now, when the Advent is to take place in the Angelic World itself (for we have to distinguish between the Angelic World of the Divine and the Angelic World of a Planetary system), the LORD comes as in the Divine World, but in different formulation, and in different degree of manifestation. Yet HE comes. HE comes in the motion of the Spiral Breath. HE becomes concrete in that World as a Sun. When the LORD approaches, it is always as ineffable Light. And that World which is always full of radiance, is more fully flooded with Light at that time. Everything becomes more intense. The Angels have to witness the Advent. It is in part their education. It is a process of revelation to them. It is a part of their service unto their LORD.

When HE approaches as ADONAI in high embodiment, the whole Angelic Heavens are full of joy and gladness. Their song is resonant of the great hope that there is to be a yet fuller representation of the Sacred Mystery of the FATHER-MOTHER. When the ADONAI approacheth, the Heavens are intense with the flow of magnetic streams. Every one is anticipating the coming of the LORD. And then HE comes, appearing as a glorious Sun, like the Angel whose face was radiant as the Sun. HE comes through the Divine Heavens in the approach of those Heavens to the Angelic World. HE comes through the individual and the communal embodiments. HE reveals HIMSELF as the Radiant Presence. The Angels behold HIM as the Glorious ONE.

And Oh, what joy there is there! And what reverence! What worship! What exultation! What triumph!

When HE comes, HE comes to reveal yet more fully HIS Love and HIS Wisdom. But the purpose of revealing HIS Love and HIS Wisdom is not only that they might know more about HIS Love and Wisdom, but rather that through the embodiment of the Love and the Wisdom in that higher estate, they might become the more fully equipped to be the vehicles for HIS Divine Incarnation through HIS Indwelling in their Substance.

Thus the vision of the LORD within those Heavens gives to the dwellers there such magnetic streams, that the substance of their Being becomes enriched and their own life-stream quickened. All their potencies are intensified in state and increased in power, and their fashion becomes more and more the fashion of their LORD. HE comes to them as the Radiant Presence; HE becomes within them the motion of a living power. All the potencies in true motion find true polarization, and generate HIS Power. HE becomes their energy. Their garments grow more beautiful and luminous. Sometimes you may wonder if there could be anything more beautiful than the raiment of an Angel. Yes, even in that world everything is comparative. The Angel may grow more and more beautiful, the raiment increase in its iridescence till it is wondrous in its radiancy, having the power of translucency and transparency, revealing HIS glorious Mystery in the degree in which it may be revealed within the Angelic World.

Thus is the Advent celebrated there. For there it becomes the Christ-Mass. The Angels can know CHRIST, the Eternal CHRIST, only in the measure in which they themselves become the Angelic Body of the LORD; their substance, their spirit, their potencies, their attributes HIS vehicles.

O transcendent vision! O glorious World! where our hearts long to dwell again for a time to witness such Advents as the coming of EL ADONAI, the Mystery of the FATHER-MOTHER in radiant embodiment, and the becoming of that Sacred Mystery within the Being of each one!

And you will note this, *His coming is heralded; but there is no heralding of His becoming*. You will observe the difference. HIS coming is heralded through HIS approach; HIS becoming becomes manifest. It requires no heralding. It is manifest in the Being and through the Life.

You have all known something of the glory of that Life in other days set forth in such Advent. It is the Angelic exposition of all that goes on in the yet more inward worlds, of which there has been given to you a glimpse in this hour.

THE ADVENT UPON THE EARTH

And now we will look at the Message as it is expressed through the Divine-Angelic World and the Angelic World, that Message which is said to have been uttered by the Seven Thunders, but sealed up for a time. We will look at it as that Message relates to the Soul upon the Earth.

The Advent upon the Earth is associated with the coming of the Divine LORD HIMSELF. It is thought of as HIS appearing upon the Earth, of HIS coming under great limitation, and being born as a human child into this world. It has, therefore, been associated with the coming of a Messenger, the vehicle of the Christhood Manifestation being the outstanding Messenger of all.

This anthropomorphic idea of GOD, of HIS coming, of HIS manifestation, of HIS dwelling with HIS children, has led men and women to worship the Messenger in the personal equation, and to regard HIM as the Incarnate ONE.

To become a vehicle for the Glory of the LORD to fill and reveal through, the Soul must know that Angelic World where HE appears in glorious revelation unto HIS children, and becomes within them unto high embodiment, and radiant manifestation through them.

Nay more. Such a Soul must not only be in touch with the Angelic World and know it, entering into its Life, realizing the motion of Being that is there expressed; but the Soul of the child who can be the LORD's revealer upon the earth-planes in high estate as understood in the Advent, must also know how the LORD comes even in the Divine World.

How is the Advent accomplished within a Human Soul?

Even as it is in the Divine World.

The LORD comes to the Soul as a transcendent vision, when the Being is looking into the heart of the Eternities. And such a vision is not to be confounded with clairvoyant vision, however beautiful this latter may be. In the vision of which we speak, the Soul sees, with open understanding, and with the perceptions unveiled, the glory of that Sacred Mystery we name the FATHER-MOTHER. The Soul witnesses the unveiling of that Mystery in high embodiment, in Cherubim and Seraphim, in Patriarch, Archangel, and Angel, and in the Angel of the LORD. Through that vision the Soul is filled with exultation. It is up-borne upon Seraphic wings even to the Altar of the Living Flame, the Sacred Mystery of the FATHER-MOTHER. The vision becomes concrete. It grows into realization. The Soul realizes that Holy Presence. The most Sacred ONE is no longer confined to a Soul-vision, but is contacted by the Soul. The Servant not only sees HIM, but touches HIM. The Soul not only touches the Mystery, but handles it, tastes it, drinks of the contents of the Cup of the Eternal Life-stream.

In this experience the Christ-Mass is set in motion. The inner Substance of that Being is made vibrant in every part of it through the touch of the LORD. The Life-stream of that one in all its motion pulses forth the Sacred Mystery throughout the whole arterial system of the Being.

THE MESSAGE THAT WAS SEALED UP

Thus, the Soul who is chosen to be the vehicle of an Advent is in large measure part of the universal Body of the LORD. In the degree in which that Soul has realized HIM in HIS sublime Fulness, it becomes HIS vehicle, HIS Body of incarnation. The LORD is incarnated. HE, the LORD of all Being is in the flesh—the substance, and in the life-stream—the blood, which is the Divine magnetic stream within the Being.

That is Advent; it is the real coming of the LORD. That is the Divine appearing; it is the becoming of the LORD in the substance, the potencies, the attributes, and the fashion of the Being.

But that Sacred Mystery could not be revealed through *any* outward form used by the Soul. Such a form has to be accommodated to endure the vibrations playing upon it and within it through the Divine Motion. For the Advent is Divine Motion. It is the motion of the Heavens within the Being. It is the motion of the Eternities within the Soul. It is the meeting of mighty waters of the Deep of the Eternal Mystery. Thus it is the Message of the Seven Thunders, the Divine Motion within the seven planes of consciousness, of which those Thunders are the exposition.

The Message that was sealed up is the Mystery of the Incarnate ONE within HIS children, the Mystery of the Eternal FATHER-MOTHER.

* * * * *

HOW THE ADVENT IS REALIZED

The Advent has come again. But it cannot be understood or glimpsed even, by following any man, woman, or any system of an earthly concept and formulation and embodiment. It can be understood and known only through high realization. In this

Message it has come back and is present with us. The Message of the Seven Thunders can now be unveiled to those who can reverently receive it. It is the Eternal Mystery of the FATHER-MOTHER, that HE is in your own substance to become manifest; that in the Life-stream of the Lamb HE is in motion within you, giving you Life and power through HIS magnetic stream which is at the very heart of you; that the sublime purpose of your creation is that you should be HIS embodiments; that the great Advents, those outstanding Divine ministries, only take place for the purpose of awakening HIS children to the realization of HIS own Eternal Mystery which is in the very Sanctuary of each of them.

This is not Pantheism as that doctrine has been traditionally stated and understood; but it is that Pantheism wherein GOD is All and in All in every System, Sun and World, and within our Being. HE is our flesh and our substance; our blood and our life-stream; our potencies and our attributes. These are HIMSELF in manifestation and exposition.

It is always an Advent when HE can become again incarnate in HIS children for glorious manifestation.

That was the Book whose contents were not to be chronicled by the Seer. It was the Book which the Angel held. That was the part that was most sweet to the One Who took it and ate of it. But there was a part which became most bitter, even as the Angel said it would.

The Mystery of the Incarnation has remained veiled throughout the ages. Notwithstanding all the libraries of human thought written concerning it, it has never been understood. The exquisitely beautiful Teachings given so long ago by the Master, were so materialized as to be beyond recognition in their relation to the Soul as the vehicle of the LORD. And so the Message, like the fragments of the Mysteries that were gathered into baskets and preserved through being taken up into the Heavens, had to be taken up by the Divine World, and its secret preserved unto this day.

Men and women have sought to get at the Mystery through ritual, through worshipful motion, and through symbol. And these venues can all be most beautifully serviceable. But they mistook the symbol for the reality. Indeed, they wanted to compel the symbol, by means of the operation of occult powers, to become the reality which they sought, and for which their Soul hungered and thirsted. This is part of the Mystery lying behind the ceremonious celebration of Mass. It is at once its materialization and the exquisite inner motion of the Being seeking for the substantial Mystery, yet looking for the power of the realization of that Mystery elsewhere than whence it could come.

So in this day it hath been appointed by the Heavens that you should know that the Incarnation is GOD in your flesh—the very Substance of your Being; and in your blood—the Life-stream of your Being. This is Divine Incarnation. It is HIS Own Motion within you. HIS motion doth give all power of pulsation to your Life-stream. HIS motion doth give your Life-stream the power to move and flow through all your substance, until HIS glorious Mystery floodeth the Sanctuary of your Being, and bringeth you into the vision of HIMSELF. And through glorious embodiment HE doth bring you more and more into the consciousness of the realization of HIS Own Emmanuel, HIS Immanence, HIS Dwelling within you. For this is the true Immanence of GOD.

THE MOTION OF THE SEVEN THUNDERS

Such is part of the Sacred Mystery of the Seven Thunders. These Seven Thunders are but the great intonations resulting from Divine Motion within the seven planes. In the Divine World they represent the motion of the ELOHIM, each Thunder being the action of an ELOHE. The ELOHIM are the Seven Spirits of GOD.

And when the individuate Soul becomes GOD'S incarnate vehicle, the ELOHIM speak through all the planes of the Being. Their motion is felt throughout the Spiral of the Soul. The

Soul knows HIM upon all the planes of its own sacred constitution.

That other part of the Sacred Mystery which was to be kept hidden and sealed up for a time; that part of the Book of GOD which became bitterness unto the Seer after the exultation and rejoicing in the incarnate realization of the Divine Mystery, was the Oblation.

The Scripture speaking of it, is full of meaning. It is one great hieroglyph of most sacred Mystery, wherein a Soul becomes GOD'S vehicle within the Divine Kingdom, a Body for the LORD of Being to manifest through.

It is not the coming of that Soul to this world which makes the Advent. The Advent has been accomplished in that Soul great ages before within the Divine World. That Soul knows the Advent within the Angelic Kingdom. And when it makes its advent on to these planes, it comes with all the glory of those Heavens within itself, and has the consciousness of HIS presence in the Sanctuary of its Being.

Thus, when the LORD of Being makes manifest through that Soul upon the earth-planes, it is through HIS Own Message. It is not through the vehicle as such; though the vehicle will, indeed, send forth streams which are true revealings of HIM, and must ever be in accord with HIM. But it is not the vehicle that is the incarnation. It is not the body that is the exposition of the Advent. It is the Being, and the Message in the Being. The Being knows; the Message testifies. If the Message be not a living testimony of the reality of that Presence within the Being, then it is not HIS Message.

THE BOOK WHOSE MESSAGE WAS BITTER

And now, this further part of the Message may be unveiled to you. It is that other part which made the Soul so full of bitterness. It was not a bitterness against anyone. It was not that kind of bitterness. Such would have been Divine Tragedy. It was the bitterness of Soul crucifixion, of conscious Soul limitation, of conscious Divine aloofness, as if the Divine were withdrawn. Though it only appeared to be so, yet it was felt as reality. It was like an aloofness from the Great Love, even the seeming hiding of the Great Love HIMSELF from the Soul.

There is nothing more bitter to a Soul who has known the Angelic World and its radiant life and ministry, and who has passed upward to the threshold of the Divine World and beheld the vision of the Radiant Presence, and heard the Alleluiahs there, and realized HIS Holy Mass, than the Cup which that Soul has to drink when it has the consciousness of being, in its vision, far from HIM Who is the LORD, in its realization and its potency, because of some ministry it has had to render, or because of some tragedy that has come to it during the rendering of that ministry.

But that which appears to be bitter to the Soul as it eats of the Divine Mystery yet more and more, becomes changed. Though the Oblation was a special ministry, yet is this wonderful truth also true for every Soul in this world of bitterness, this world of wrong direction. When you have eaten of the Book, then in the measure in which you have partaken of its Mystery, you will have felt something of the element of bitter aloe, sometimes even of gall. But that is only a temporary experience, a resultant of your partaking of the Divine Mystery, and the outworking of it within you through those realms that are out of harmony with the Divine Motion. It may be because you have been out of harmony in your own inner planes and in your inner attributes and your divine potencies, as the outcome of your age-long history.

But the writing or message in the Book will make you beautiful again. It will turn everything that is bitter into the waters of Elim, making Life divinely sweet. It will restore to you the Manna of the Gods and the Cup of Angels in the Divine Heavens. It will give you to share the sublime Life of Patriarchs, Angels, Cherubim and Seraphim, aye, even to partake of the Cup of the LORD from HIS Own Hand.

THE ADVENT AS THE PONTIFICAL MASS

The Advent is the Mass. But it is the Mass of the Soul. In it, GOD becomes realized within the Soul; and all the Being, through HIS becoming, is offered unto HIM.

Now children of the FATHER-MOTHER, you may witness the glory unto which HE HIMSELF hath called you, even unto becoming the Body of HIS Incarnation, the Temple of HIS Indwelling, the Sacred Substance and Spirit of HIS Own Mystery offered in high combination as HIS Mass, the Christ-Mass. It is the offering up of your Being to be HIS Christ-embodiment for HIS ministry.

This is the meaning of Advent!

How wondrous is the Love of the FATHER-MOTHER that hath called us unto so high an estate of consciousness and glorious realization, that we should be not only HIS children but HIS servants; that we should not only embody HIM, but offer daily and hourly the Mass of HIS Mystery within the Temple of our Being, and through the sacrificial service of our Being, make sublime manifestation of HIM!

O Wondrous Love! O Love Transcendent! Beyond all our telling, art Thou! Beyond the possibilities of our revealing are Thy Glories!

How shall we ever be able to unveil to Thy children the exquisite beauty of Thine approach, and Thy motion; Thine approach unto them, and Thy motion within them?

Yet we would have all Thy children know Thee. For to know Thee is to love Thee and understand Thee, and all that Thy Love is.

We would have them hear Thy Voices in the Seven Thunders, even as Thou hast, in the exquisite beauty of Thy condescension, permitted the Mystery of Thine Incarnation within Thy children to be unveiled again.

And we would ever praise Thee, and know Thine Overshadowing, and Thine Indwelling.

THE HEALER

THE MANIFESTOR

THE REDEEMER

THE HEALER, THE MANIFESTOR, AND THE REDEEMER.

The treatment of this subject is in answer to a question. The question sought for an explanation of the operation of the law of transmutation through the Manifestor and the Redeemer, in the ministry of healing.

But in dealing with the differentiation between the operation of that law through the Manifestor and the Redeemer, lest there should be confusion, it is necessary first to deal with the ministry of the Healer.

There may be the ministry of healing without that of the ministry of manifestation as a Manifestor. And there may be the two-fold ministry of healing and manifestation, without the fulfilment of the office of Redeemer. But in the office of Redeemer there is manifestation and ministry of healing, though the distinctive service may not be obviously that of Manifestor and Healer.

THE HEALER.

NEGATIVE AND POSITIVE ASPECTS

Now, a Healer is one who ministers to the vehicles of the body, or the mind, or the heart, or the Soul. The work of a healer can be both negative and positive. The negative aspect is but a tentative ministry; whereas the positive is the real ministry. To merely negative is not to heal. It may introduce the law of suspension. The operation of conflicting and opposing forces may be suspended for the time being. And such a ministry may be invaluable both to the healer and to the one ministered unto. But it is in the positive aspect of the ministry that real healing comes. For, in that aspect, there are set in operation forces which make for the restoration of the vehicle through the healing of the part that has been and is afflicted.

In neither the negative nor the positive aspects, however, is the real law of transmutation touched. It may be said quite truly, that changes are effected; but transmutation is more than change. It may be rightly affirmed that entirely new aspects come in the way of thought to the one being treated, and, through that thought, changes are effected within the vehicles; but such changes are not to be confounded with the operation known as transmutation. This will become clearer as we proceed.

The distinctive office of a healer is to negative through change of thought, and to build up, through that change, new conditions. The upbuilding of new conditions does not necessarily mean the transmutation of the old, but rather the building of a new fabric of thought and purpose, of desire and feeling, of intention and motive, and even of love within the Being. As the one healed grows stronger through the thought, and the purpose, and the purified motive, and the exalted desire, and the deepening of the love, power is acquired by which even the old conditions that may be lying in abeyance in the vehicle or vehicles—in the mind or the heart—untransmuted, may be probed unto the perfect healing of them through the transmutation of the very elements, and, in some instances, the very substances.

But this work is of a higher order than that of the ministry of the healer understood in the general sense, whether it be in relation to the outer vehicle, or the superfine vehicle behind the outer, or the atmosphere or vehicle of the mind, or even that body which is named the emotional or etheric body, and is the true spiritual envelope of the Soul.

THE REALMS TOUCHED BY THE HEALER

It is well that ye clearly understand that a healer, through the power of negation, can suspend the operation of militating influences, and even elemental powers. It is thus that the one being healed can be better dealt with in a positive way, through the negativing of conditions which are present and operative. By the positive ministry, there can be transmitted from the Healer to the sufferer, even magnetic streams.

Now, as has been said by me, this process of healing can be in the outer body, in the intermediary body, in the mental atmosphere, or in the emotional or etheric body. And such healing is a beautiful ministry, a wonderful ministry, whether you call it mental healing, spiritual healing, or Divine healing. For all true healing is Divine, even if it be operating on the mental plane. Only it must be recognized as such to be truly and soulicly effective. It is a wonderful ministry, and is a manifestation of Divine power operating through the healer. And in that sense the healer is a manifestor; he is a manifestor of the operation of the Divine Spirit. For it is the motion of the law of God within the Being and through the Being unto the healing of many.

Yet such manifestation is of the nature of general manifestation of spiritual life and of spiritual law, though expressed through a special, concrete form of ministry. But such a manifestation is not to be confounded with The Office of Manifestor.

THE MANIFESTOR.

What is a manifestor? He is a healer, also, though those unto whom he manifests may have to fill the office of healer in a more obvious way than it is given him to do. He has come for the special purpose of revealing the Divine attributes. But he does not do this simply as a healer. He has come to unveil God through the unveiling of the attributes, and especially to unveil the Mystery of God as Love and Wisdom.

A manifestor is not simply one who makes manifest the great Divine potencies for the healing of the bodies and minds, and even the hearts and Souls of men and women. The manifestor comes for the healing of the Soul. He comes to unveil the meaning of Divine Love, the Omnipotent Love. In that sense he is the manifestor of the most glorious Divine potencies, all of which are gathered up into the Mystery of God Who is in him. That is his great Office of Manifestor.

Have men and women come to know God through the discovery of the operation of great forces in nature, or in running through human history along the merely historical lines? Have they come to know GOD through any of the ministries which have had relation to the healing of bodies and minds? Even the great Revivals which have been associated in the minds of their expositors, workers and healers, chiefly with the claims of marvellous cures for body and mind, have apparently left no great permanent consciousness in humanity of a Divine Manifestation. All such scenes in the history of humanity have been as evanescent stars, the passing showers of meteors, luminous for brief moments and then evanescing into the great darkness.

A MANIFESTOR IS A DIVINE HEALER

Only through the manifestation of Divine Love and the radiance which that Love sheds, can Souls know what GOD is; how GOD would appear if HE were formulate and could be met in the way as other Souls are met. HE is formulate in HIS children; and it is within the Sanctuary that HE must be met by them. There is HE to be found of them. And HE is found that HE may be manifested through them. The great meeting of GOD within the Soul is come at only through the realization of that for which the Manifestation is made, namely, the Divine Love and Its glorious Wisdom.

If there be such potencies in a manifestor, how do they operate in relation to the Law of Transmutation?

The manifestor does not ostensibly go forth to heal. He embodies and unveils. He radiates, though not necessarily calling into operation the law of transmutation. The atmospheres will be changed, because he will bring his own atmosphere, which all those present will feel. And the atmosphere into which he enters must become one with his atmosphere, or it must recede. This latter is mostly what happens; the atmosphere must go because it is out of harmony with the new conditions. It flees, as it were; and that which would have otherwise been vacuum, is filled with the atmosphere proceeding from the manifestor.

The manifestor comes to heal. But the healing accomplished may be far from the Being. It may be outward. But the manifestor knows that, whilst the outer healings have to be accomplished, and whilst such work must needs be done, that true and permanent, spiritual and soulic and divine healing can be accomplished only through the healing of the Being, by giving to it not only the atmosphere of the very Heavens, but also a vision of GOD wherein the Divine Love is embodied. *For a Manifestor is the embodiment of Divine Love.*

THE LAW OF TRANSMUTATION What is to be manifested? That GOD is Love; that GOD is Wisdom; that HIS Life is Love, and that HIS Light is Wisdom. A manifestor may be endued with power from on High for purposes also of transmutation. And indeed he is, or she is, by the very constitution of the Being and by the realization entered into, and the nature of the manifestation. From that one there proceeds that which, under certain circumstances, sets the law of transmutation in operation. But that may be in a general way. For wheresoever a manifestor goes, all that is inimical and evil, and all the breaths that are generated through evil states, flee away. Even those who possess them, and desire to hold them unto the manifestation of them when opportunities arise, flee from a manifestor. They flee in their state; in desire; in feeling; in purpose. But they may also get into direct opposition. They may manifest militating powers, and seek to make the manifestation impossible, because they love it not.

Those elements which are said to be unconscious, will feel the effect of the radiating divine potencies of the manifestor without his speaking, or willing even to the healing of them. And they can be changed and often are changed. And those in whom evil has found a place, but who desire that the evil no longer find an abiding with them, and who are moved to finer issues through the manifestation, do not flee. The evil in such as these can be changed and transmuted. It is changed within themselves as they are affected by the potencies flowing from the manifestor; and more especially from the vibrant message of The Divine Love that he has to give, and the radiance of the Divine Wisdom he has to unveil.

For even in a manifestor, the great power is not in the personal and individual vehicle; it is in that for which he stands, that which is made manifest through him. His healing ministry, therefore, is a healing yet more inward than that of the healing accomplished in the office of healing, speaking generally; for Souls can minister as healers to the bodies and the minds, and even to the hearts of men and women without necessarily accomplishing in them healing to the very innermost of their Being. Indeed, they may be healers because of the inherent potency in themselves, their own heritage, their state of growth and attainment, and their march homeward to the Great Love, without being equal to "the Office of Manifestor." For one is chosen for that office, only when the Life is specially equipped for it, and all the Soul's attributes are endowed from on High.

And here I would say to you in passing, not to be discouraged by this latter saying from me; for it does not mean that your manifestation of life is not beautiful, nor that you have failed to be radiant. It is doubtless both beautiful and radiant, an embodiment of the Divine Love and a revelation of the Divine Wisdom. I am sure this is true of you in the degree in which you have realized. What I implied concerning the manifestor is, that *the* Manifestor is sent for the unveiling of the Sublime Mystery of the Divine Love and Wisdom, and has a special Vocation. And little, indeed, do even the Children of the Kingdom in the present day of their Return realize what it means to be in the Vocation of a Manifestor.

THE REDEEMER.

A REDEEMER A SOUL HEALER

The redeemer is a healer, yet not necessarily a healer as that term is understood by many. The redeemer is a manifestor, yet not necessarily a manifestor as interpreted in the light of the glorious Manifestation. The healer is a manifestor of divine potencies operating within and through him. *The manifestor* is the concrete embodiment of those forces. The redeemer is the veiled repository of those forces, all of them operating within and through him, giving him the power of the special office of "redeeming back." And this redeeming back is not simply the healing of the vehicles, the equipoising of the mind, and the bringing of equilibrium to the affection. It is also the perfect healing of the Being by a process wherein there takes place the re-polarization of all the elements and magnetic streams of the Soul.

Now, it is through the redeemer that the great Law of Transmutation has its highest and deepest manifestation. And if the office be a great one, such as in the Oblation, its extent is world-wide. But then, the Office of the Oblation was a very special work, as you will now understand.

THE OPERATION OF THE LAW OF TRANSMUTATION

Yet those also transmute who are in the office of the redeemer in lesser degrees. The healer negatives, and gives positive direction, and even imparts in a positive way at times, power. Oft-times the heart of one in the state of the redeemer can be as the Sacred Heart from which the very radiance of Love Eternal flows as a potency for healing. Such an one can nourish the heart that has become so impoverished that it is most difficult for the suffering one to live upon these planes. Through such a redeemer, the Divine Radiance in a qualified measure, can pour itself through the various centres unto healing, and accomplish the transmutation of the hurtful elements in the sufferer. Within the redeemer (and this is true in a less degree of great healers) the whole Being can be so infused and interpenetrated, first from the chalice of Being, then through the etheric body, and then through the mental atmosphere (there being no longer an astral body as that vehicle is understood, nor a mental body, since both are transmuted into radiant elements of Atmospheria), and then through the body of the outer manifestation, until the radiations of the very Heavens can pour themselves through all the Life. Then the touch transmits power and confers healing, and, in doing so, transmutes the conditions and changes entirely the elements in the body of the suffering one.

It is a great mystery. No man of himself has that power; nor woman of herself. It is the heritage of the redeemer, even only through the Divine Manifestation within. For such a redeemer is in a state of manifestation, though not in the same sense as a Theophaneia. There has been within the Being the realization of all that a manifestor stands for; though there is no direct office and service such as are understood in the sense of the Divine Manifestor.

POWER TO COMMAND THE ELEMENTS

And then the redeemer has also the power of speaking to the elements and commanding them so that they change in their conditions and become purified; and these, having regained the power of right direction in their motion and polar action, are restored to their primal qualities and service.

The redeemer's ministry, therefore, is primarily to change the elements and to redeem back; to change them even within the Soul, and bring back the elements of the Being into the perfect state.

In doing this the redeemer may meet with conditions which necessitate another form of transmutation, an echo of that tremendous process we speak of as the Oblation. There are elements which can be negatived in their operation. They may be suspended. There are elements which can be driven back by the power of the Divine within, but without being changed; though they will have to be changed some day. There are elements which can be changed, transmuted, and raised almost immediately. To transmute truly in the spiritual sense is not only to change the elements, but to raise them from their fallen state to their true realm. It is a process of divine dynamics. It raises the elements to a higher degree of Life in the individual, in the outer body, in the astral body, in the mental body, and even in the etheric body.

But there are elements which cannot be changed in that way. These are of such a nature that they cannot even be negatived, though in the case of a Soul filled with the power of GOD they are kept at arms' length, and are driven back from that one. For such an one will be guarded by thought, by love, by aspiration, by prayer, and by blessing.

There are also elements which are not obedient unto the healer. There are elements which, though they will flee from the manifestor, come back again when the first opportunity occurs. A Divine Redeemer has to meet those elements, attract them, hold them, absorb them into the vehicles, suffering while the process of transmutation is taking place, and then eliminate them from the vehicle, because they cannot be retained. For the Divine Redeemer may not build up from such elements; therefore, he must eliminate them.

You will see the profundity of this ministry. You will understand the wealth of the Divine call to souls, and the ministries into which the Children are again entering. You will understand that healers may be manifold. They may be simply healers, or they may be in double office. They may deal with the outer aspects only. They may minister unto the mental states; or they may deal with all these, and also with the first great spiritual conditions operative upon the spiritual body.

And you will understand this, that in such a ministry, there is to be the manifestation of Divine Power. All true power is Divine. But in the manifestation of such power, it is to be recognized that it is from the FATHER-MOTHER. Wrote one of old time, "Oh, that men would praise the LORD for HIS goodness, and for all HIS wonderful works!" Oh, that all the Children would praise the LORD for all HIS loving kindness unto them, and for all the gifts with which HE hath enriched them! I would that you give HIM the praise and blessing for every beautiful office HE has asked you to fill in ministry for HIM. Let your Soul praise HIM in the manifestation of HIS Divine potency through you, unto the healing of many. Vaunt not; boast not; but ever acknowledge HIM and be lowly.

DIVINE LOVE THE POTENT HEALING FACTOR

You will understand that, whilst in these latter days there is to be no re-appearance of the Manifestor such as took place in the days of the Manifestation when the Vocation was a special one for the unveiling of the Mystery of the Divine Love, and the showing forth of the Radiance of the Divine Wisdom in a way that was most distinctive, and also as a preparation for the Office and Burden of the Oblation; yet there is to be manifestation. There are to be manifestors who understand the Law of Transmutation in relation to their own ministry. These are to manifest Divine Love. For Divine Love is the potency that will kill hate. But it will not be by a process of negation. You will never destroy hate by negativing it, any more than you will change your desires by negativing them. That is not the way of healing and redemption. By that process you only suppress them for the time being. Suppression is not healing. Suppression is not transmutation. Suppression is the power of negation. It puts the states in *Helan*. You cannot create life by negation; for negation is only the manifestation of power for the suspension of the operation of that which has wrong direction, or which is militating against the life. Its exercise is, therefore, only temporary, until the positive elements come into true motion.

Negative through positive qualities.

Destroy hate through love.

Destroy jealousy through trust.

Destroy enmity through the spirit of friendship wherein true love is made manifest.

Destroy evil in every form by its opposite, namely, the positive manifestation of the good.

It is the only way in which you can change unto true betterment, all the elements, all the conditions, all the thoughts, feelings, desires, and passions of men and women; the only way in which to elevate their minds, to ennoble their hearts, to enrich their vision, and to exalt their desire nature. The only way in which you can bring God to them is to make manifest His potencies.

The manifestor transmutes. This is mostly done unconsciously. It is not a transmutation which necessitates the absorption of the elements into the vehicle. It is transmutation by the power of the radiations from the Being.

The manifestor may heal. He may be a healer. In these days of the Return it must be so. The transmutation of the conditions is the changing of them, and the exaltation of their state.

I will illustrate my meaning in this way. Consider what is called human desire, which is looked upon by many as absolutely wrong and hurtful. That desire must be the expression of something inherent in the Being. If it seeks to find its fulness in outward sensuous things, then its direction is a mistaken one; and if it has to be healed, if anything concerning the desire has to be transmuted, it is through gradually elevating that which is in itself holy, and which is, indeed, in its very nature Divine. For in its quality it is of the Love of God. It is the potency of the Divine Mystery in a Soul. If it has had wrong direction, then it has to be elevated from degree to degree, and changed in the process. In the change the purpose is purified. Through that purification the operation is on a higher plane. Thus the feelings of the desire-nature are exalted, and the force transmuted and changed by Divine power operating dynamically through the thought, the purpose, the will, the love; thus still changing and transmuting upon yet higher planes, and elevating the Force in its motion, even to the very Divine Kingdom within the Being.

The work of the manifestors and healers will be great.

Redeemers are fewer. In one sense the healers are the redeemers, and in a yet larger sense the manifestors are redeemers. But we use the word in its more limited signification. The redeemer can meet the elements, face them, fear them not, touch them, handle them, take them into the hand and crush them, in the process of which they are changed through absorption into the body; re-changed there by a Divine transmutory process, and then passed off. But this is a great mystery, which it is not easy to unveil to you.

AN INSTANCE OF THE REDEEMER

Here I should love to give you just one simple illustration that took place in the healing of a serious affliction.

In treating a most difficult condition, the healer became conscious of something not only abnormal, but most exceptional. And something that was upon the needy one came to the hand of the healer. It came in a form that revealed its evil nature. It came as an embodiment of that evil. It was a vampire, an evil afflicting elemental. No one but the healer could see it. No one could know that it was there, though the sufferer had been heavily oppressed by it; for it set up strange trouble in the vehicle. As the healer proceeded with his work, the evil thing came away; for it was nothing physical. It was an evil astral elemental, and of such a nature that it could be absorbed. For it was fluidic and magnetic. Indeed, in order to effect the healing, it had to be absorbed. In this instance the healer was also a redeemer. Through his hands he absorbed the evil thing, changed the elements and transmuted them. He thus delivered the sufferer and destroyed the evil states. So changed were they that those elements could not re-form into another evil state.

This is but to illustrate what a redeemer oft-times has to do; for it is the only way in which some of his work can be accomplished. There are those things which are not responsive to negation, nor to any ordinary methods; things which would flee before the power of the Divine Manifestor so as not to be destroyed or changed to better states. In the instance stated, the evil form was magnetically held and drawn out of the body. It was the only way to accomplish the healing of the sufferer; for it was an elemental, and the redeemer had to change the whole of the elements of which it was composed.

Therefore, understand that the Office of the Divine Redeemer is allotted to very few. For it is of the nature of the Office of the Redeemer in the Oblation. The redeemer's office is a vocation full of the gravest danger to the peace of mind and the comfort of the body. For oft-times the very states of the sufferer must needs be taken. The only way to relieve them and so be able to accomplish healing in them afterwards, is through taking away the elements and changing them. In this way the healer can take fever into his body; for it is the outcome of evil influences. The redeemer can thus take into his own body the evil states and conditions, and change the elements. He does not simply take the atmosphere around the fever. He takes the magnetic states which produce the fever; and he feels the fever in his own vehicle, during the process of the transmutation.

In these latter days there have to be redeemers to meet the needs of the children; and there may require to be such for a long time. But when the healing of all the children has been more fully accomplished, the Office of the Redeemer will cease for Israel. But it will not cease for the world until such time as the healing has proceeded far enough to enable the vocation of the redeemer to be withdrawn, for then all the rest can be accomplished through the manifestor and the healer.

IN DAYS THAT ARE COMING

Unto the healing of the world, therefore, the life of manifestation is absolutely essential. To embody the Love of God, and the Radiant Wisdom of God, is high manifestation. And even if it only drive back the wrong conditions for the time being, it nevertheless changes the atmosphere, and enables Souls to breathe afresh.

But it will do more than that. It will provide new conditions, redeemed elements ever growing more beautiful and greater in potency. It is in this way that the world is ultimately to be brought back in its consciousness to the feet of the FATHER-MOTHER. You will, therefore, understand what transmutation is, and that it is not simply the negation of elements, nor even their change. These prepare them for the transmutory process. The negation is the suspension of the operation of the elements in a certain direction. There are some you might destroy in their operation, but if they were not changed they would re-form in some other direction. Merely to change them is but to change the conditions which they generate. But to transmute the elements is to change them in their constitution, and thus enable them to be elevated. Thus, in the vehicles—the outer vehicle, the mental vehicle, the etheric vehicle—the elements can be enriched through the action of the law of transmutation. As has been said to you by me on several occasions, what is known as the astral body, the superfine constitutional body within this outer body, becomes so changed in nature, that its substance can at last be transmuted; and it ultimately becomes part of the spiritual body. That is the meaning of *indrawing*.

When one sent from the Heavens has accomplished his ministry and is to be withdrawn, the intermediary vehicles having all been changed from the states in which they had to be put for ministry, become transmuted, indrawn, and nothing vital to the Being is left behind.

And more than that. With such a transmutation, the Being passes immediately after the withdrawal, far beyond the Planetary astral and occult realms, being conditioned to function upon the Angelic Kingdom, and, according to the degree and estate of the Soul, the higher Angelic World; there to be enriched in what is called rest, though it is not rest as sleep, but rest for nature from the strain of ministry; and to be ministered unto as Elijah is said to have ministered unto His prophet in sending the dove of His Spirit to comfort, to enrich, to fill with the great joy.

Whatsoever the future has in ministry for you, must depend upon your response to the Divine call. But that call does seek for HIS children, states of blessed manifestation, and vocations of beautiful ministries, in and through all of which wonderful healing will be brought to the world at large, and to many of the elder Souls in particular.

* * * * *

O Most Holy, Most Ever Blessed, Thy children would adore Thee. Thy Love Sublime has found us. Oh, that it had found us unto perfect fulness from Thee!

How beautiful unto us Thy Wisdom is! Thou leadest us even as little children are led, until we can run and mount and soar. Thou carriest us ever in the Mystery of Thy Love. We adore Thee!

Oh, that we may indeed be Thy Manifestors, and Healers for Thee! And shouldst Thou lay upon us the burden of Redeemer, giving to us the sacred Vocation, may we be willing to share the burden of Thy Love even in this thing; knowing that Thy Love is our power, our strength, our defence.

The Angel of Thy Presence abide with all Thy children here, and minister unto them from Thee.

THE DIVINE PASSION

THE DIVINE PASSION

In ecclesiastical festivals to-day is named Passion Sunday.

It is well to understand what is meant by Passion Sunday, and especially the Divine Passion.

The general use of the term passion is far from angelic; and except when postulated of the LORD HIMSELF, far removed from the Divine Idea.

Passion as known to the human understanding is generally related to intense physical desire, or to anger.

But passion in itself is a divine quality in the Soul.

And it is well to note this also, that, whilst there may be omnipotent power where passion obtains in the Divine Fulness, there is no stoicism. GOD is not a stoic. The Gods are not stoics. Their power is not expressed in self-repression, and through that repression a negation that affects even unto annihilation, what has been named Desire. Theirs is the power to contain and retain until the hour of command proceeds for them to give forth.

SOUL PASSION A DIVINE QUALITY

Passion in itself is, therefore, a divine quality. It is of GOD. It is Godlike. The passion that is wrong is where the heart has had misdirection in the motion of its emotion, so that its desires obtain and seek their realization irrespective of the Divine motion; or where the mind, becoming full of resentment, becomes also full of anger, and may express it in words or in deeds, or indeed silently in an attitude that is so positive that it hurts those against whom the anger is held and directed.

Such is human passion as understood by the mind. But that is a perverted use of the term. It is a degraded interpretation of the Sacred Passion, and represents a fallen estate.

The Divine Passion is of the nature and constitution of GOD. It is in the Divine Elements of the universe; in all Souls, God-embodiments, Angelic embodiments, and all Human embodiments. So that Divine Passion in a Soul is a sacred thing. Therefore, we can postulate it most reverently in reference to the Divine Mystery as the Passion of our LORD.

We will look at the sacred Mystery of the Passion in relation to the Master; then in its relation to the Soul; and then in its relation to the Redemption.

THE PASSION OF THE MASTER

The relationship of the term is usually associated with the Master in His sufferings in the Gethsemane, and in His Burden-bearing on Calvary. In the Churches' outlook it is composed of the Temptations in the Wilderness, the Days of the Trial, the Hours of the Sorrow in the Gethsemane, the betrayal and threefold Trial, and the Crucifixion.

His Passion is, therefore, thought of as the period in which He bore the Burden of the world's sin. In the Scriptures that Passion is set forth in many *Sayings*, in a number of *Allegories*, and distinctively, in two which have most especial significance—that of *the Anointing at Bethany* in relation to Himself; and that in *the House of Simon* in relation to the Return and the recognition of the LORD Presence. The Passion is set forth in both stories of the Anointings as an outpouring of the Soul, the Anointing of the Being, the consecration of the powers for service; the one *the going down*, the other *the coming back;* the one the consecration for the Work, the other the Travail when the work was almost accomplished; the one signifying that which was to take place, the other giving a glimpse of the effects upon the Soul of all that took place.[1]

How little the Church understands the things it believes in relation to the Passion of the LORD, even as expressed in the Master, which was only an aspect of it for special ministry. For that Love which in its intensity becomes Passion, is always expressed in consecration, in anointments with precious spikenard, in the sweet breaths that flow from it when the

[1] *Vide* "LIFE'S MYSTERIES UNVEILED," pp. 273-288, and "THE MASTER: HIS LIFE AND TEACHINGS," pp. 561-590.

sacred cruse of the Being is opened; that Love which is willing to endure unto the uttermost for service. For in the measure in which a Soul can endure in service as it is moved by the Divine Passion, in that measure is the Passion revealed which is the LORD's Passion. And that Passion, in the exquisite beauty of its motion, reveals the effects of a world ministry, and Soul travail with its pain and sorrow and anguish.

It is not our purpose to impress these latter upon the mind unto the making of it sad. But in the portrayal of the Return of a Soul Who had been carried so far as the Master was carried by the Passion of the LORD in HIS Purpose to redeem, it necessarily means the unveiling of that Passion in its pain and sorrow and anguish. And yet it is Love Triumphant alone that can endure pain without speaking of it, without purposefully revealing it, without accounting it too great a thing to endure for the Love that loves so divinely; without measuring the sorrow of its cup, and thinking that it was too great to drink of, and the bitterness of it too intense to endure. The Passion of the LORD moving within a Soul, gives that one power to endure all things, all pain and travail, sorrow of aloneness and loneliness, and the anguish begotten of the consciousness of an afarness from the Homeland—the Home of the Divine Presence that is loved beyond everything else, except the service given to the hands, and the feet, and the head, and the heart, and the mind, to accomplish.

Such is the nature of the Passion of the LORD.

THE STATIONS OF THE CROSS

That Passion is observed ecclesiastically during this period, and in some instances very specially in what is known as the Stations of the Cross. The Stations of the Cross, ecclesiastically, represent the various stages of the Master's journey into Jerusalem, the Travail in the Gethsemane, the betrayals, the trials, and the bearing of the cross, with the culmination in the Crucifixion.

In the service of the Stations of the Cross, when it is fully observed, there is processional worship and adoration; and before each picture representing those Stations, there is a pause, and the utterance of sacred story, some part of which is suited for the occasion and blessing.

But the Stations of the Cross have a far deeper significance than the merely outward experiences which have been related to the Master. Those twelve stations (there are sometimes fourteen and even fifteen presented), have relation to the twelve states through which the Soul passes as it journeys towards the Holy City. It has to learn how to endure the Passion of the Divine Love in each state, and to make HIM manifest through each state. It has to learn how to adore the Great Love, not through the Master, nor through any picture of the Master, nor in the mere thought that He suffered here and there, and in this way and in that way; but to adore that Love which moves in all real, inner experiences; the Love that leads us from Station to Station, making us to pause and reflect, to bow humbly and adore, to praise and to bless and to worship, and learn how to serve through such experiences.

When we know the great Reality, the innermost significance of the Divine Passion, how great is the littleness of all the outward, perfunctory service where the inner significance is lost!

Before each Station the heart may say to itself, O heart of mine! are ye willing to drink of the cup that is here symbolized? Are ye willing to endure the Passion of the LORD to the extent that is here spoken of? Are ye willing to take up the burden of the cross that lies still further on? If so, then grow strong unto that end; make your sacrifice complete and absolute.

The Stations of the Cross obtained in the unfallen days. But they were not painful Stations such as they are now for the Soul in its return into high consciousness. In those ages they were not associated with the pain and sorrow and the sometime anguish experienced now by the Soul.

The Stations of the Cross are within you. They are your attributes, not one of which can escape the Cross; not one of which must be without the insignia of the Cross. For to have an attribute perfectly purified and consecrate, is to have the Glory of God filling it. And His Glory radiates through the Cross. It is the Cross of Being, the Cross of perfect uprightness, of perfect balance, of exquisite equilibrium. It is the Cross that calls the Being upward, ever upward even unto divine polarization, wherein it becomes one with the Ever Blessed One.

Do not be afraid, therefore, to pause before your attributes and ask whether this Station in its pictorial representation (that is, as to its quality, its power, its purpose, and its desire), is a true representation of the Cross of God within the Being.

FROM OLIVET TO CALVARY

The Stations of the Cross for the Master are represented from Olivet to Calvary. They are the degrees of the descent from high consciousness to the estate in which even the least of His brethren were found. His Stations were unseen to the observer, unknown to all but Himself and those in the Heavens who were appointed to watch Him, and encompass Him, and minister unto Him.

From Olivet to Calvary has a more profound significance than any outward expression can reveal or interpret. It has a far more transcendent significance than the world has ever dreamt of. For in that transcendency it revealed the Passion of the Lord. It was the Lord's Love, the Lord's Motion, the Lord's Desire, the Lord's Purpose, the Lord-Potency within Him. Of Himself, He said He was nothing; but in the Lord of Being, He touched all things. From Himself He could do nothing; but through the Motion of the Lord of Being in Him, all things could be accomplished. Therefore, it was the Divine Passion in Him. It was no human passion in its measure, but the Passion begotten in the Eternities, whose motion filled and moved His Being to go from Olivet (on the summit of which the Lord's Feet are placed) to Calvary, the circle where the Crucifixion took place; the circle within which all that was dead was to be made alive again; the circle wherein superstition, and unbelief, and materialism obtained, all which things had to be healed and purified, and the powers that caused them broken and thrown out of the circle.

Now you will understand something more of the meaning of the Passion of the LORD as it came to be expressed through the Master, and that all that has become associated with Him must ever be interpreted in the light of the Divine Indwelling, and the Divine Motion through Him. Any Love He had, must ever be related to the FATHER-MOTHER WHOSE Love it was that was in Him. However great the individuated expression of it as the vehicle of that Love, it was the Love of the FATHER-MOTHER, and must ever be so related and spoken of. It is the FATHER-MOTHER Who doeth all things. The LORD of Being alone is the Regnant One, the Conquering One, the Triumphant One, the Omnipotent One, the Omniscient One. HE alone is the Redeemer and Saviour.

There are some lovely old hymns which I have often longed to hear you sing. But just because of the terms made use of throughout them, to express the Soul's motion, and because the world's thought has been so greatly betrayed by means of such songs, one cannot sing them. Even the Children of the Kingdom have been so deeply wounded through the constant allusion to and the worship of Jesus, that the Vision of their Lord has been obscured by means of the personal equation of the Master. And even the terms which He used to express His Mission, but which were applied to Him as personal names, bring up to their consciousness His person, and eclipse, or at least veil for the time being, the vision of the Glorious One, the FATHER-MOTHER: my FATHER-MOTHER and your FATHER-MOTHER.

Such is the Passion of the LORD that, when it is expressed within and through a Human Soul, it must ever be related to HIM Who is the LORD. Whatsoever there is of that Passion in you, it is of HIM. And if you would glory in it, you must glory in it in HIM alone. But you may not glory in that you have such a Passion. When the Soul is divinely enslaved there is no consciousness of it in the merely human and personal sense. But the more that Passion is in you the more will you think of HIM. The more you are moved by it, the more you will be moved to HIM. The more HE reigns within you the less will your self-conscious persona reign. HE will reign through your persona and make it radiant with the Indwelling Glory of HIS Presence.

How little, indeed, do all the merely individual claims of possession and power seem in comparison with that claim for HIM Who is our LORD, Who filleth the Soul with HIS Own Glory, giving to it the consciousness of HIS Presence in such measure as it can receive, until it rises even into the Eternities and dwells there in consciousness where, though there is still the personal equation, it is swallowed up; there is still the individual manifestation, but it is clothed with the grandeur of GOD.

THE RELATION OF THE PASSION TO THE SOUL

And now we will look, for a passing moment, at this Passion in its interpretation for the Soul, the Passion of the LORD, the Divine Passion as it relates to the Human Soul.

We glimpsed when speaking on the Sabbath of the Lord something of the motion of that Passion which comes to the Soul upon its fifth plane. And here I would, by way of clarification, say a word.

The fourth vehicle from the outer is the Etheric Body, and the fifth is the Soul itself. The Passion of the LORD takes place in the Soul. But its manifestation is through the Etheric Body. And the fifth plane is the plane of Soul-consciousness. When the Passion of the LORD makes a Soul travail because of the intensity of its motion within the Being, the travail is between the fifth and the sixth planes. But the floods set in motion by that travail of Passion, beat upon the shores of the Etheric Body. That is why the heart is so much affected, even to the outer planes, in those who travail. And at such times it would seem as if, physically, there was something wrong, when it is only the effects of the inner travail. It is the result of the vibrations of the innermost coming through and acting upon the heart, perhaps seeming to affect its function. Approached and judged of from the without, it would seem most serious. But that cardiac condition can be understood from within.

The Passion of the LORD is an upward motion in a Soul on its journey home to the realization of the Divine. It is always present; for it is of the Mystery deep-seated within us. It is in the Arche of our Being, to be fully expressed in the Amen, when the Divine accomplishes the perfect fashion of the Being. It is the Life-stream which flows through the Being from its very inception, but which, as higher consciousness is attained, becomes more intense both in its magnetic power and in its motion. And when the Soul reaches a certain status, it enters into a full consciousness of that inner travail in an unfallen world; and it is very specially so in this world as at present constituted. And this motion proceeds until the Soul reaches the Sabbath of the LORD, which is the perfect polarization of all the elements and essences and their elevation into the consciousness of the Divine Overshadowing One.

But then that Passion has an earthward motion. The Soul that realizes becomes the vehicle of that which has enabled it to realize; so that the Life-stream which flows into it and through it commands it by its very motion, to earthward ministry. But that does not imply that the Soul is meant to be once more a little child upon the earth, finding life's chief delight upon the earth-planes. Rather is it henceforth to be a Soul touched from the Realm of the Gods, in whom is the motion of GOD HIMSELF, one going forth to serve for HIM. In the process of its upwardness the Soul has to learn to serve, and to serve under others for its learning. And as it grows older it has responsibilities given to it. Thus does it learn how to serve, and to teach others how to serve by showing them the way. And when it has attained a certain status and is sent earthward, having received its mission, it may be asked to go alone, absolutely alone, and thus know the great aloneness of one dwelling in the consciousness of the Presence, whilst ministering, living and serving no more for itself, but only for that Self Who is HIMSELF our Life, even the LORD of all Being.

The Passion of the LORD is the Divine Love filling the Soul until the motion of that Love becomes irresistible, and the Soul cannot help itself. It does not want to; but it could not if it did. In the measure in which it loves, in that measure does it serve. In the measure in which it realizes the Divine Overshadowing to that fulness does it long to be more and more like the Ever Blessed One, and to be the vehicle of the Divine World's outpouring for the manifestation of that Passion through every Station of the Cross, through every attribute, adoring, worshipping, praising, blessing, giving regnancy, and glory, and honour, unto the FATHER-MOTHER. The Passion of the LORD is the Divine Life-stream in you. It is the Divine Love-stream that flows through you. But ye are as yet like little children if ye think in a merely personal way of this; and ye must needs grow from childhood up through youth and maidenhood into manhood and womanhood of an Angelic order, and then to be Celestials, and then on even to realize the Divine manhood and womanhood.

And if you love divinely, you will be unconscious of it. Yes, actually unconscious that you love divinely! To some it may seem an extraordinary thing any Soul could be unconscious that it loved. But such a Soul is not unconscious that it loves when it has an object before it on whom to pour out that love. And this describes your state; for then you do not live in the consciousness of being filled with love, though you may be a fountain full to overflow. But the streams of your love will flow from you when the needy, the thirsty, and the weary appear.

In the measure in which you love HIM, in that measure is the Passion of the LORD in you. And in the measure in which that Passion is in you, so will you be more and more conscious of being just HIS; that HIS alone is the Voice that commands you; that henceforth HIS is the Presence you bow before and worship full of the consciousness of HIM Whom you adore; and that nothing matters in the human sense; that you are HIS absolutely in Being; in Soul, Heart, Mind, Vehicle, and Attributes, from the innermost to the outermost. In this state you are willing to undertake a journey if it be necessary, and you are asked to do it, from Olivet to Calvary.

THE PASSION AND THE REDEMPTION

Now, in order that what I have said to you may be more clearly apprehended by you, we will look at the Divine Passion in relation to the Redemption.

To-day we are still in the Divine magnetic stream, celestially understood, which the Planet approaches, enters into and passes through, during its Vernal equinox and its Autumnal equinox. The Mystery that is so lowlily and beautifully expressed in the Divine Passion-stream within a Human Soul, is indicated in the Celestial Realms in that Life-stream through which the Planet passes twice a year. For it is the day on which the Planet is supposed to cross the ecliptic. The recurrence is in the third-fourth weeks of March for the Vernal, and the third-fourth weeks for the Autumnal in September. The Divine Ecliptic is the Plane of the Divine Kingdom, Celestially expressed, and is a magnetic stream in whose wealth of vibrant energy the Planet once moved. That stream relates to the Divine Mystery. And although in mathematical Astronomy the crossing of the Ecliptic would be considered in a mechanical way, and remarkably calculated, yet it is recognised scientifically that the Planet is strangely disturbed prior to its ingress into the stream during the period of its crossing of the Ecliptic, and also during its egress from the stream. And although to the scientific mind it might appear as if it only took an hour or two to effect this crossing where the orbit of the Planet intercepts the ecliptic, we know that it takes a very much longer time; that it takes fully a week to approach, a week to pass through, and a week to gradually retard in its motion, until the normal motion of the Planet is restored.

And although it is known scientifically that the Planet is greatly disturbed at that period, there is no true, scientific explanation of the cause of the disturbance beyond the general statement regarding atmospheric pressure. And yet for ages, in a strange way, the equinoctial gales have been spoken of as being set in motion at this time, though coming to this land from one to even three weeks afterwards; and that those gales are generated through certain magnetic motion as the result of the Planet's entering into and passing through the stream of the Ecliptic.

But that which is named the Ecliptic is in the very centre of a great Stream that flows from the Divine World equatorially through the Solar Body—the Stream in which the Planet at one time moved to a very large extent, but now can enter only twice a year. The Mystery of that Stream is, indeed, a part of the Mystery of all Celestial things, and of the Divine motion. It is a living Stream of Divine Potency that magnetically affects the Planet as it approaches it at both the Vernal and Autumnal periods. It is a Stream that affects the whole Planetary constitution as the Earth passes through it. From the outer to the innermost, and from the innermost to the outermost, great things are accomplished. It is because of the outermost conditions of the Planet itself that it has to hasten through it. But that Stream passes through all the planes of the Planet. It enters not only the atmosphere, but passes through what once were the Four Atmospheres of the Planet, to the outer planes. It enters into and passes through the elements of those planes, through the water of the seas and the lakes and the rivers. So great is the magnetic flow, it passes to other unseen planes, even those at the heart of the Planet, and nourishes them. This Stream's magnetic potency is the source of the new power acquired by the Planet to enable it to continue its journey; for in the Stream of magnetic Ætheria, new propulsion is given.

The Planet-soul is a Divine member of the Celestial Hierarchy and was at one time in Divine Estate. It is not even now as it seems to be. There are hidden planes; planes unseen to the outward gaze; planes that cannot be known from the without. And that Stream passes right to the very heart of these, rushes up the Spiral of the Planet, and then diffuses through the planes. It disturbs them; but only unto the accomplishment ultimately of their redemption, the healing of all their elements, the equilibration of all the planes, the purification of the Planet's atmospheres, and the restoration to perfect balance of all its magnetic centres, all its centres of polar motion, and even its Divine Pole.

Now this magnetic Stream has never been thought of as having relation to the Passion of the LORD, except in an indefinite, occult way. Occultists have sometimes thought of the Passover as having relation to the Planet, not at the equinoxes so much as at Christmas time and in mid-June, in the perihelion and aphelion periods; but some have also associated the Passover with the equinoctial periods wherein the Planet crosses the line.

But that Stream of the Divine Ecliptic has relation to the Divine Mystery—*the Mystery out of which all things have become.* That Stream has relation to and reveals the Divine Motion, the Motion by means of which all things are begotten. That Stream has also relation to the Life-Principle, the Magnetic Centre without which no one could realize the glorious Presence. That Stream has likewise relation to the Mystery of Being, and therefore to our own Being. We drink of that Stream. In the measure in which it fills us, we become polarized and equilibrated. And in a celestial sense it is the Mystery of the Divine Passion expressed in and through the Celestial Realms for ministry unto this world.

Now, that Stream affects men and women just as it affects the Planet. It affects all things in some degree. If the Soul can receive it, the Soul is enriched. If the Heart can endure it, it is strengthened. If the Mind can bear the play of its power, it will become purified and equipoised. If the Body can receive it truly, it will enable the individual to accomplish more speedily the purification and the regeneration of the Vehicle.

On this Passion Sunday we are in the very midst of this Planetary Stream, this Divine outpouring, this glorious Celestial and Divine ministry. You may see it and understand it as an intensified form of that same Stream which ever flows unto you from the Divine World in an accommodated form; flows within you in the measure in which you are able to receive its magnetic inrush; ever flows through you as you permit the Ætheric streams to enter your own Life-streams unto the making of you altogether HIS children, in the likeness of HIS fashion from the within to the without.

Such is the Passion of the LORD unto the healing of all things. And as the Earth performs its round, and whilst in that round there is no pausing, yet at each Station in the twelve months of its round, it renders its service and obeys the Divine Command. The Redemption of all things is hastened. As the children respond, the Redemption draweth nigh to them. And in the measure in which the whole House of Israel responds, the Redemption of this world in its life and elements cometh nearer and still nearer.

It is, therefore, the Passion of GOD that calls you. It is the LORD'S Passion in you. Even your Soul-travail is begotten of HIS Passion. And if ye have known the journey from Olivet to Calvary, ye may know in this day the journey from Calvary to Olivet; the journey from the state of crucifixion with its pain, and sorrow, and anguish, to that consciousness of the Blessed Presence, and that realization of the transcendent Light within your Sanctuary, wherein your LORD meets you again upon Mount Olivet to have speech with you, to illumine you, to pour HIS Glory upon you and through you, and to reveal to you the meaning of all things.

Is not this Life worth living? Even this Life of Soul travail from Calvary to Olivet? This return-life from Edom to Bozrah? This glorious resultant of the motion of the Divine Love expressed in you as the Passion of the LORD?

It is the Lord's Passion. If you would only acknowledge that divine fact, and not look at yourself introspectively, and think only of yourself, and relate everything to yourself; but if you would only think of HIM Who is your LORD, and bow before HIM and be one with HIM even in the Passion, and the sorrow and the hour of the anguish, as that Passion moves through you unto the manifestation of HIM, then your Being would be caught up into HIM.

Let your Soul be filled from HIM! Let your Ætheric Body's stream be HIS Own! Let your Mind be balanced in HIM! Let all your Desire-body and all your outer attributes, be HIS Own!

That is the way to make HIS Passion effective. That is the way to reveal that you have verily shared in the Passion of your LORD. That is the way to make manifest that you have stood at the Stations of the Cross and there worshipped, and praised, and blessed, and adored HIM Who gave those Stations for your enrichment, and Whose Passion found expression through them as ye made your way Homeward to the High Altar of HIS Abiding, where HE is beheld in HIS Glory and realized in the splendour of HIS Love.

THE OBEDIENCE OF CHRIST

THE OBEDIENCE OF CHRIST

A DIVINE LAW IN OUR BEING

Obedience is part of the Law of Life. It is a resultant of the Divine magnetic motion within a Soul. It is the exposition of Life's fruition. It is inwoven into the fabric of individuated Being, and its ultimate brings that individual into perfect oneness with the Divine Mystery, whether that individual be as a God in the Celestial Hierarchies, or a Celestial embodiment amid the sphere of the Gods, or an Archangel, or Angel, or Human Soul unit. For all have the same Principle, the same Mystery, the like magnetic motion differing only in degree. This Law of Obedience is thus inwoven into the fabric of Being, because it is of the very nature of the consciousness which obtains in the universal Ætheria. For a Soul to oppose it in its motion is to miss the way into the Great Realization. For the Soul's endeavour to attain unto the realization of the Divine Presence is dependent upon its compliance with and its response to the motion of the Law of Obedience.

That obedience, in the Mystery at the heart of it, is something very different from the variable idea of interpretation which obtains upon the Earth in relation to earthly obedience.

That it is a Divine Inheritance, a glorious gift, a revelation of the share the Soul has in the Divine Motion, what we have to unveil to you, we trust will make manifest unto your vision, and that henceforth the Divine Law of Obedience will be a living factor within your consciousness, vision, and ministry.

We would look at obedience as it obtains in the Divine Worlds. We would there seek to understand it. For, as we apprehend its inner significance there, so shall we understand the real obedience and the meaning of it upon the earth planes.

When thinking of obedience in an earthly way, we associate it with a ready response of the individual to some command given by one in authority, or a response, perhaps, not readily given, yet though not heartily given, nevertheless, a submission because of that authority.

Obedience in the Divine World is not of that order. To obey there is not simply to bow down before a command; it is to understand HIM Who commands, and that which is commanded. It is not simply a response to one who says, "Ye shall go thither!" or " Come hither!" It is the outflow of the Being in its deepest desire to fulfil the Law of the Divine motion within itself, as that Law's motion affects it. It is to realize that unto which the Divine Will calls the Being. If it be in relation to Life, to make it concrete. If it be in relation to service, to make that service manifest through giving, through interpreting, through revealing.

AS OBTAINING IN THE DIVINE WORLD

In the Divine World obedience is the exquisite expression of that Law of the Divine motion within the Being, as the Being recognizes what the Divine Love desires, what It purposes, what It counsels, what It commands in the sense of calling for the expression of its Life in the way of manifestation and service.

In the Divine World there is no such thought as disobedience. Even the term obedience would not obtain in the way in which it does upon the earth-planes, because the natural motion of the Soul is to respond to the Divine motion, and thus to meet the request for consecrated service in absolute giving by the ready response "Here am I: send me!" For sacrifice am I here; take me!

There is no sitting down and calculating what will be the resultant, what powers will be acquired, what enrichment will be poured out as a reward of the obedience. There is no such thought. Those who serve in the Innermost before the Altar, seek for no other reward than to be HIS children, and to reveal HIM in their own individual embodiments, and in the motion of their life in service with intent to interpret HIM. All the ingathering that comes as the result of such obedience is a natural fruitage; and it is an unconscious ingathering. It is the natural corollary of the equation of the Being wherein it fulfils the sum of God's Will. It is beautiful to see obedience in the Divine World. There is no compulsion. There is not constraint in the sense of compulsion. There is only that constraint which is the expression of the effect of the motion of the stream of the Divine Love upon the Being, within the Being, and expressing itself through the Being. It is the Love of Christ. And Christ is GOD's Man whom the Love of GOD constrains.

That is the language of the heavens. In the Inner World, obedience is founded in the consciousness of perfect childhood to the FATHER-MOTHER. There is the consciousness that whatever HIS Law demands is right; that whatever the motion of HIS Will unto us, into us, and through us, commands, that same must be given. There is the ever-ready response, *Lo! I come to do Thy Will, O God, even as Thou has written it in the volume of the Book of my Life, and hidden it within the Mystery of my Being. For such writing is Thy message within me, and its motion fills me with obedience unto Thee. For Thou art all and in all to me. Thy Law is supreme. Thou art my Lord, my Regnant One.*

This Law obtains right through the whole of the Divine World, the whole of the Celestial Hierarchies, the whole of the Angelic Kingdom, in the measure in which each one within the various Realms has entered into the realization of the Mystery of Life in the consciousness of the LORD of Being.

CONCERNING THE FALLEN ANGELS

Even in relation to the tradition concerning those who are said to have fallen from their first estate, and which, in many writings has been graphically described, and almost immortalized in a poetic sense in Milton's *Paradise Lost*, there is a great truth. For the Angels who left their first estate through disobedience failed to fulfil the Law of the Divine motion within them, and had to pass out from the Kingdom. For that Law necessitates obedience to the central Mystery of Life and all that it stands for, all that it purposes, all that it commands.

In that myth story there is great truth. For no one even in the Celestial Hierarchies could remain in exalted state if there was the spirit of disobedience, an attitude of mind that was unwilling to fall in with the perfect motion of the Divine Will, and Purpose, and Love, and the manifestation of these in the glorious creative and fashioning Wisdom of the FATHER-MOTHER.

You will understand this even by analyzing your own will, your own love, your own vision, your own motion, your own desires.

Though such is the Law of Obedience in the Divine World that it obtains wherever the FATHER-MOTHER can be said to reign, wherever the LORD of Being is supreme, yet you should understand that, although that Law must be obeyed, every individuate life exposition of the Mystery—Celestial, and Angelic, and Human Soul—is a free agent, is a living centre of Divine potencies, and that in all service and life there has to be the individual choice.

THE WAY OF PERFECT LIBERTY

For it is the sum of our response to GOD that we choose to be like HIM. If we were mere machines and all the Celestial Heavens were only machinery, and all was of GOD the perfect ONE, then all the machinery would be perfect, and every Soul that was an exposition of HIM would be perfect. But the Soul and the Universe, being only machines, would have such limitations as all machines have, and could not deviate one iota from HIS Law. Therefore, though there would be nothing but what would be perfect, there could be no individuate Soul volition, nor spontaneity, nor responsibility.

But that is not the way of Love. Love does not make its object a mere machine. Love loves its object into becoming a centre of living forces. And that is what GOD has made of us, centres of Divine potencies. These Divine potencies have motion, and in their natural flow return to HIM; for HE is the Central Magnet of all things. But we have the power to intercept, to withhold, to restrain. We even have the power to disobey. And if we should disobey, or even fail to fulfil, there is no happiness, no joy, no comfort; because, to set the stream of our life in a direction contrary in its motion to HIS direction and motion, is to set up tumultuous conditions within ourselves.

So you will understand, that this Law applies right through the whole of the Divine Creation; that it is a Law which affects every individual embodiment and every Soul with its living consciousness, and all the powers within it for expansion, even until the Soul knows the glorious Mystery of the FATHER-MOTHER. But each one has liberty of choice. No Soul is a machine. It is exquisite in fashion, and a wondrous Temple which is the abode of GOD and the home of the potencies of the Gods. It is, therefore, a world tremendous in its possibilities. For it has within itself the Elements of all the Celestial potencies, and the beauty diffused throughout the Angelic World. Because of these things the Human Soul can be, and is meant to be, crowned as a Man-angel, an Archangel, a Son of GOD, one who is in Atonement with the Divine, even unto the knowing of the Great Mystery of the LORD of Being, Whom we name the FATHER-MOTHER.

OBEDIENCE THE LAW OF CHRIST

Now you will understand the meaning of the Law of Christ and the Obedience of Christ. These exquisitely beautiful expressions have come to be associated entirely with the Master. It is represented that He was obedient to the FATHER-MOTHER; that His obedience was revealed in His willinghood to suffer according to the Will of the FATHER-MOTHER; that He bowed Himself unto death, which experience is usually associated with His passing away from the outer vehicle. It is thus that He is supposed to have been "obedient unto death, even the death of the cross."

Oh, it is quite true that He was obedient. It could not have been otherwise with one Who knew the Great Love, the radiance of that Love, the splendour of it, the tenderness of it, the majesty of it, the immeasurableness of it, the wealth of the shedding of its Life-giving potency, its marvellous power for fashioning a Soul into the likeness of the Sacred Mystery of the FATHER-MOTHER. No Soul who knows that Love in a high state of realization could be other than obedient to it. It could not be otherwise.

There was, therefore, nothing extraordinary in His being obedient to that Love. He loved to be obedient. The motion of His Being was one with the motion of the Divine within Him. It never was a question with Him as to whether or not He should be obedient. With Him there was no querying, "Shall I do this or that? What will it bring to me if I go this way or do that thing?" His answers to all such questions would have been, "If it be the Will of the FATHER-MOTHER then HIS Will be done. And whatsoever the motion of that Will be, wheresoever it may carry me, whatsoever HE may Will to accomplish through me, such must be. It could not be otherwise."

His obedience, however, is associated with His earthly pilgrimage and ministries. He is thought to have been obedient, and suffered in His obedience during the days of the Manifestation. It is supposed He was obedient in permitting the Divine Will to outwork in the manner and nature of His betrayal, in the repudiations of Himself and His Mission during the crucifixion; that He was obedient in His willinghood to die as men and women are said to die, and to pass through the darkness.

In the Theological Schools, and the writings which emanate from students, the obedience is associated also with the burden He is supposed to have borne on the Cross of Calvary, wherein He was willing to endure being accounted a "publican and sinner," and even a malefactor; and that, in His sufferings He was obedient unto the bearing of the burdens that the FATHER-MOTHER imposed upon Him in relation to the karmic burden of this world; and that thus He was obedient unto death, even the death of the Roman Cross.

Here it is the personal Master who is thought of as the CHRIST. It is quite true that the Master was in Christhood; that

He was in that high state of consciousness associated in the Soul's attainment with the glorious Christhood manifestation. He was Jesus Christ. But not as a person. In His consciousness and love He was Jesus and Christ. He was one with the LORD; yet He was not the LORD. He was one with the Realm of the Lord Regnancy; and so He contacted that Realm continuously during His ministry in the days of the Manifestation.

THE SUFFERINGS OF THE MASTER The sufferings of the Christ unto which, it is said, He was obedient, were the sufferings that He had to endure through giving up the Christ-consciousness. There was such a change to be effected as would take from Him a conscious operativeness within the Lord Regnant Kingdom. Herein was the laying down of the Christ-consciousness. There had to be the sacrifice of even the wonderful and beautiful Jesus state in which He had been manifesting throughout the days of the Manifestation. He had to take up another burden which necessitated His laying down these glorious privileges which had been gifted unto Him from the FATHER-MOTHER, upon the High Altar of the Divine World; that, being divested of them, He might be fitted to do another work to which He was appointed. It was the result of the Divine motion in Him.

If the Great Love calls a Soul to lay down some great gift it has given to that Soul, there is far more in the motion of the Divine Love than there could possibly be in the motion of the Soul who has to lay down the gift. For Love loves to give, and never to withhold. Love loves to give, and never to take back again that which It has given. It loves to give unto all fulness.

And so, HE Who had given the gifts must have felt it more than the Servant Who had to lay them down, though it is said of the latter that He had to learn to be obedient.

Oh, it is lovely to know the Divine Will, and to love it, even unto the laying down of one's Being; to be willing to be as the Divine unto the giving of all the wealth within the Soul's treasure-house.

Obedience! It is the natural Law of a Soul in its Divine Estate. It is the fruitage of its Celestial inheritance. It is Angelic in the breaths of its motion.

So it is no wonder that the Master was obedient unto the FATHER-MOTHER, even unto the death of the cross.

THE MEANING OF THE DEATH OF THE CROSS

Yet there is a far deeper meaning in the expression that He was obedient unto death, even the death of the cross, than has yet been unveiled to you. And in this hour I would lead you where you might glimpse it, learn the secret of it, behold the Mystery of it, witness the majesty of it, and be assured of the wealth of the Love in the Heavens that could call Him to fulfil the Divine purpose, and enable Him to carry it through.

For the obedience of the Master was the obedience of the Christ in Him, even unto death. Aye, more! It was not simply the death for Him of the Vision He had given to the world through its sad betrayal; it was not only the loss unto Himself of the blessed Jesushood and the beautiful Spiritual Christhood, and the transcendent visions which obtain in the higher degrees of Christhood; but it was also obedience unto that death of the Cross which was the complete surrender of the consciousness of the Luminous Cross within Him. He was obedient unto the death of that Cross. It was not the crucifixion upon the Roman Cross. He had nothing to fear from that. He suffered a greater agony in the betrayals meted out to Him by many of His friends, and in the manifold betrayals by His enemies of the glorious vision of GOD and the Soul unveiled in His Teachings. For the Teachings He gave from the FATHER-MOTHER were betrayed by those who professed to receive them, until the Image of Christ was so greatly changed that none could recognize it, and not even the Jesushood be understood, because there was no true portraitures of Jesus and Christ.

The obedience of the Master unto death was the Obedience of the Christ in Him. It was the obedience of the Divine Will in Him unto the yielding up of the Christ estate, the Christ consciousness, the Christ Presence, even unto the loss of the consciousness of the Luminous Cross. He was obedient unto the death of that Cross in Him, so that He knew it no more throughout the ages of the Oblation-Travail; though He sought for it without knowing what the motion within Him meant, what that urge was which made Him seek unto the finding of the inner Mystery of the Cross, but seemingly without success until the Oblation was fully accomplished.

Now, I would have you understand this sublime Soul-experience, that, to be in a state of Christ-consciousness of a high order is also to be in a state of supreme service to the LORD of Love, and to be full of sweet willinghood to give up all, even unto the loss of such a high gift; yea, even unto the giving of it up absolutely. For, although that is never asked, yet the willinghood must be there. Indeed, such willinghood is of the very nature of obedience.

THE CALL AND THE RESPONSE OF THE SOUL

The Great Love Who fashioned me is my FATHER-MOTHER. I am HIS in the Substance of my Being, in the Spirit of my Life, in all the consciousness that HE has given me. All the potencies whose motion express themselves within me and through me, are HIS; therefore, I am HIS. And likewise is it with you. You can never be out of HIM, if you be true to yourselves, because then ye shall be true to HIM. And whatsoever change HE purposes to effect in you, and make manifest of HIS Holy Purpose through you, it is yours to know that obedience, even unto the death of Christ, even unto the death of HIS Cross in you, in the measure in which you have realized the splendour of that glorious Mystery within your Being.

I would have you also understand the Obedience of Christ in you. Do not for one moment imagine that you can ever reach Christhood without perfect obedience to the Divine. It could not be done. Because Christhood is a resultant. It is a realization. It is, to use the earthly illustration, a flower of the Divine plant in you. And it can be come at only through obedience to the Divine Law that is within you; obedience to the motion of that Law within and through you; obedience to the Divine urge that calls you whilst pressing you forward, which call is upward, ever upward, still upward into the immensities of consciousness. For you have the potencies within yourself for entering into the Eternities in your consciousness, until you even become one with the Eternal.

Now, when ye are called to be obedient unto your Lord Christ Jesus, it is that ye follow the way of the call through Jesushood into HIS Christ Realm; in sweet obedience, willing to be ever for HIM and like HIM; willing to be in manifestation for HIM after the manner in which HE calls for the manifestation; willing to be in service for HIM wheresoever HE appoints the service, and in the service which HE appoints, and not in something ye might care to choose for yourselves.

In the Christ Realm there is perfect obedience to the Will of the FATHER-MOTHER. So when HE says:—

O Son, lay down those marvellous gifts with which the Heavens of My Dwelling have enriched you, so that ye may minister unto some whom, with those gifts ye cannot touch, the Soul at once responds, *Here am I! The gifts are Thine, Lord. Take them, and have care of them for me until Thou dost call me back to re-enter into the inheritance of them, should such a blessed lot be mine. But I am Thine, ever Thine, only Thine, to be for Thee, always for Thee, willing to be nothing if it will bring blessing unto some.*

Oh, it is easier to enter into the great inheritance and receive Divine gifts and attain to that high consciousness whither the great gifts lead, than it is to pass out from the consciousness of the inheritance, and lay down all the precious and much cherished gifts, and to say to the LORD of Love:—

I am Thine alone. Even if I be stripped of everything with which Thou hast enriched me, it is mine to love Thee, worship Thee, and serve Thee. I am Thine alone and always, even unto the outpouring of my Being, if its elements would heal a world's passion, and sorrow, and anguish. Unto that end am I Thine. As Thy servant, take me.

There is no littleness in the obedience of the Soul that knows HIM. There is no littleness in the Servant who fully knows HIS Love. For the whole of his life is his LORD'S, in every part of it; every feeling of it; every power of it; every motion of it; every gift of it; all the attributes of it; all are for HIS service.

There is no littleness in Jesus, Christ, the Lord. For that Divine Estate is the realization in the Soul of the Lord Christ. That realization is shown forth in a manifested Jesus. The Lord Christ in the Soul is the acme of all Spiritual and Divine realization, the apex of a Soul's desire wherein it climbs to that radiant point which, henceforth, is also the magnetic centre of its Being.

Now you will understand what it means to be obedient to the FATHER-MOTHER. And in the light of it you will understand also what it would mean for you to give obedience and command obedience on the earth planes. It cannot be done as an outer command. For, where you force obedience you do not get obedience. You simply get a compulsory response to your command, because you have the power to enforce it on the outer planes. But that which is given you is not obedience.

OBEDIENCE IS FREE AS THE AIR!

OBEDIENCE IS THE SPIRIT OF THE GODS!

IT IS ANGELIC IN ITS FLIGHT!

IT IS OF LOVE ITSELF!

And the truest obedience you could ever have would be the result of constraining the Soul to respond to the exquisitely beautiful motion of the Life that is ever sublime, because it is ever radiant.

Thus, ye yourselves have to learn how to be obedient unto the Great Love, even to the laying down of your imaginary greatness of mind and will-power upon the Earth, and the acquiring of the knowledge of how to rule as HE rules above; to attain to the regnancy of Love, and rule in gentleness and tenderness, in wisdom and majesty, with might that is never more beautiful than in the exquisite revealings of itself in great gentleness.

Oh, it is no mean thing to be a child of GOD, and learn obedience unto HIM, and the secret of how to touch everything as HE commands! *For that is the secret of Life.* It is the secret of Love. It is the secret of HIS Holy Wisdom. It is the secret of HIS Motion from out that Sanctuary wherein HE doth have HIS Abiding, even the Sanctuary of your Being.

To know the Obedience of Christ through the realization of the Christ in you, is to know the willinghood to be just what HE would have you be, and to do what HE would have you do. And if you are not sure what HE would have you be and do, then enquire of HIM and HE will show you. For you wil find out if you seek correctly. HE will reveal the obedience that leads you to the Altar. HE will give you that motion which carries a Soul up to the Golden Altar of HIS Presence, and enables it to lay the whole of itself on that Altar in a sublime, sacrificial act, for HIS service. And that service is not up in the Heavens only. It is easier to think about that perfect service above, than to do that same service upon the Earth. But it is upon the Earth that HE needs that service just now. The Earth needs your ministry. And to lay all your Being on the Altar for HIS service, so that your entire attitude, your full embodiment, and all your motion will express HIM, is to be a child whose obedience makes the FATHER-MOTHER concrete in every attribute, in every motion, and in every ministry of the daily Life.

* * * * *

Come up there with me! It is not in the clouds, though it can bear you into the Eternities. It is in the clear vision of the Divine Atmosphere even upon the earth planes, when the

Soul knows how to yield itself in most blessed obedience for service unto HIM.

Ever Blessed be HIS Glorious Name! Ever Blessed be HIS Wondrous Love and Wisdom!

Ever Blessed be for HIM, HIS CHRIST in you and in me, even unto that service of Love that will contribute to the coming of perfect obedience within all HIS children!

OUR LORD
AND
OUR LADY

OUR LORD AND OUR LADY

Under the Figures of

THE VINE AND THE FIGTREE

Our LORD and our Lady are terms intimately associated with much religious thought. In the western religious beliefs, ritual and liturgy, we find both terms used. The former term especially is in vogue throughout the whole of Christendom; the latter term chiefly within the Church of Rome.

But although that may appear to be the limit or circumference of the terms in their religious ramification, yet it is well to know, that, under other signs and terms, they were known great ages prior to the coming of the Master and the growth of what has come to be known as Christianity.

For the western world's religious outlook, we turn to the religious centres where the LORD is said to be directly approached and worshipped; and to those other centres wherein there is some recognition of the Mystery of Our Lady, though there most obviously is no true and full understanding of the sublime truth lying behind it.

THE MYSTIC MEANING OF OUR LORD

We know that in Christian nomenclature, with rare exceptions, the term "Our LORD" has come to be associated with the Master known to the world as Jesus Christ the Lord. For the Master is thought to have been, and to be so for evermore, the Only Begotten Son of the FATHER-MOTHER, and that ONE Who was crowned LORD of all as the concrete expression and exposition in the Divine World of the Eternal Mystery of the FATHER-MOTHER. And it has been and still is thought, that it was the ADONAI Who came to these realms to make manifest in the days known as those of the Manifestation, to teach where. HIS message could be received, to show the way of true life, and to become the Redeemer by dying for the world. It was thus that even the Cross itself came to be chiefly, and in many, many minds and hearts, altogether, associated with the Master in His burden-bearing.

Herein did the western world development of religious thought go all astray. For you might as well expect the full exposition of the Divine Wisdom in relation to form and beauty, rhythm and motion, to be expressed in a flower, as to imagine and look for the full embodiment of the Eternal Mystery we name the LORD, in any servant sent to these planes, however exalted in estate that one might be. And by estate we mean consciousness; and through that consciousness, realization; the consciousness coming as the result of the growth of the Being in deepening and expanding; and through the expansion, deepening still more and ascending in state, the Soul rising into the fuller apprehension of the Divine Mystery, and into the comprehension in great measure of the Mystery of the Indwelling ONE.

THE LORD AND THE ABSOLUTE

At the same time, and along with this personal aspect, the LORD of Being is thought of as Universal; as the Absolute ONE; the Express Image of the FATHER-MOTHER; equal in Deity; in attributes equal, being a member of what is known as the Divine Trinity; without beginning and without end; not greater, but not less than the Eternal Mystery we name the FATHER-MOTHER.

Now, the Divine Mystery is in all Souls. Therefore, GOD is in all. Yet HE is greater than all. HIS substance is in everyone. HE is in me. I have nothing that is not HIS; nor desire I to have anything that is not from HIM, and of HIM, and for HIM. For life is not worth living except for HIM, however glorious it might be. Indeed, the more glorious, the more one would wish to live for HIM. HE is in you. The substance of your Being is HIS own. It is of the primary Substance of all things. That is how you can turn to seek GOD. For only that which is of GOD, of HIS very nature, of His essence and attributes, could possibly apprehend HIM, and seek unto the comprehension in ever larger measure, of HIS exceeding Glory.

Therefore, no Soul however great, or however glorious in estate, or high in consciousness, or profound in realization of the Transcendent Mystery, could say, "The pleroma of GOD is in me; therefore, HE is not anywhere else." Because GOD is in every Soul; in the Heavens above, and on the Earth beneath. The LORD of all Being could not be confined within the limitations, even for Manifestation, of one child of the Kingdom, or one Son of the FATHER-MOTHER.

The LORD of Being comes to all. HE is potential within all. Therefore, the LORD of Being is to be dissociated as an embodiment from any servant who may come; even from the Master known as Jesus Christ the Lord.

These prefatory words will enable you to understand some things I would say to you. You will see how the western world has thought of the LORD of Being as embodied in the one personal equation, and how it has carried that equation into the Heavens. Had it been as the western world has presented it, with that one under such limitation whilst here, the LORD could not possibly have appeared to any Soul in the Universe; whereas the Heavens are ever adoring in their service and worshipping through the use of their attributes, adoring in embodiment and worshipping through sacrificial action, the LORD of Being Who is ever present.

But HE makes manifest through HIS Servants. The Master was a Servant. He was a vehicle of Divine Revelation. He came for the unveiling of the Mystery of the LORD of Being; and He came to unveil that Mystery in the Divine Passion.

I would have you understand how the whole *passion of the Divine Love* must be associated alone with the LORD; and also how it became circumscribed by the personal equation of the idea of the Master, and thus lost its full Divine significance. For the Passion of the LORD is the motion of the Divine Energy which used one of the FATHER-MOTHER's children for high and holy services. *It was the Passion of the Divine Love.* So, the Cross has ever to be related to the LORD of Being, and through

HIM to the Great Mystery we name the FATHER-MOTHER Who is at the heart of all things, and is the Macrocosmic Cross or Eternal Balance of all things.

THE FEMININE ASPECT OF DEITY Now, "Our Lady" gives the feminine aspect to the Divine idea of the LORD's manifestation. But this manifestation is not simply that given through the Servant in the days of the Manifestation, but rather the Divine embodiment throughout all ages. And you know how in Christian thought where "Our Lady" is worshipped and prayed unto by many, she assumes the part of a high mediator, becoming the intermediary between her son Jesus Christ, the one who was supposed to have borne the burden of the Cross, and the suppliant; and how she is thus exalted to high station in the Heavens as mediator.

It is beautiful to see reverence for women in any church. And if it could only come through reverence for "Our Lady," the supposed mother of the Master, then let there be that reverence, that child-like worship and even adoration. But that is the worship of those who are in spiritual childhood, little ones who are needing help to lift them up by means of embodied ideas. If only it could be made beautiful and pure, and interpreted in the right way, it could be made reverent and other than idolatrous. For though we must worship GOD alone, yet we may revere the good in every man and woman. To love goodness is to revere it, to cherish it. To love goodness in men and women, is to cherish the good. To cherish them for the good that they are in themselves, is to manifest our love for the good.

Now, what takes place in the worship we refer to is the result of failure to understand the Divine Mysteries. It is to misread the Philosophies. It is to fail to discover the treasures which were, at one time, gathered into the Church. And it is to show a strange lack of understanding of the Teachings of the Master Himself, concerning the feminine aspect of Deity as well as concerning the masculine aspect. We use these terms, feminine and masculine, though they are altogether inadequate. They have become associated with form and sex on the outer planes. In the innermost realms they are associated with potencies, motion, direction, and ministries.

That Our LORD and Our Lady have great mystic signification for the Soul, you will presently discern.

SYMBOLS OF SOUL INITIATION We will look for a moment at the place occupied by the Vine and the Figtree, in occult philosophy. Those of you who are artists will remember how both these wonderful symbols have come down through the ages from the times of the high days of Greece. They were known long before the days of Greece; for Greece gathered them in from Egypt. They were symbolically used in the great Egyptian civilisations, centuries before the Greece of Divine Art was born.

The Vine and the Figtree were sacred symbols. They were applied to the progression of religious life, and were used in the various occult Schools and Temples in the path and processes of initiation.

The Figtree came before the Vine in the order of degrees. For the Figtree was associated with the Wisdom of the Gods. The Fig itself was related to the Mystery embodied and hidden in that Wisdom. It was, however, a less Mystery than that associated with the Vine. It was supposed that the neophyte, in taking a Fig from one higher in initiation, symbolized the receiving from that one the Bread of Life as knowledge, knowledge concerning those things which were designated as belonging to "the Lesser Mysteries." The same idea comes out in the Teachings of the Master set forth in that wonderful allegory wherein it is said that He fed the multitude on "a few barley loaves and two small fishes,"—the word "fish," *ichthus*, being a symbol of that which is taken out of the deep, or the Mystery of Being.

Then, as the Soul grew through partaking of the Wisdom,

of which the Figtree was the symbol, it had given to it the cup containing the fruit of the Vine. But at first there were uses made of the Fig-leaves and the Vine-leaves. These represented the teachings symbolized by them; and then came the flesh of the Fig and the Grape, and last, the Cup of the Wine of the Grape.

You will have noticed, you who love to observe nature, how like the form of the human hand the leaf of the Vine is, and also that of the Figtree. When outspread they are both like the outspread human hand. Even such formation and likeness was used as a symbol. The leaves were the outer expression of the Wisdom—*the covering knowledges*. The fruits were the inner expressions of the Wisdom—*the Substance and Life-stream*. The leaves were not partaken of, except in a mystical way; but the fruits were eaten. It is supposed that even in that marvellous house of initiation known as the Pyramid of Ghizeh, the Fig and the Vine are represented in the Queen's Chamber and the King's Chamber. The Queen's Chamber represents the Chamber of "Our Lady"; and the King's Chamber that of "Our LORD."

Now, that marvellous house was built by the real Israel thousands of years ago when there was a dearth, in all the land, of those high spiritual things for which their Being thirsted. They built that Pyramid, not as a tomb or house of death in any sense whatsoever, but as a house of Light and Mystery. For it is known that it was originally covered with a garment of such marvellous stone, that when the sun shone upon it, the reflection was so glorious it could be seen for many miles across the desert. It thus became the symbol of Ra, the Radiant ONE, in the midst of a desert land. The Lesser Mysteries were expressed in the chambers and galleries; and the Greater Mysteries in the inner Chambers. The great symbols which the builders fashioned were put in the Queen's Chamber, which Chamber had first to be reached before an entrance could be effected into the King's Chamber. In this latter was the greatest Mystery of all.

It was because they knew the sacred Mystery of the Soul and how it finds its LORD, that they built the Pyramid. For no one could have built such a house, with such hidden knowledge expressed in its formation, but those who knew the LORD. It has oft-times been thought that the house was built by great occultists for purposes of occult initiations. But that was not the case. It was the handiwork of the Sons of GOD; and they were not occultists. It was a house which, whilst it may have been used by the Egyptian priests for initiatory purposes at certain times and in secret ways in later ages, yet it was built amid a desolate land to hold in stone formation the secrets of the Eternal Mysteries.

No Soul can reach the King's Chamber without first passing through the Queen's Chamber; neither can any Soul drink, mystically, of the Cup of the Vine, until that Soul has understood the meaning of the Fig-leaf and the Fig, and clothed himself with the former and partaken of the latter. All through the various initiations the Soul is nourished from that ONE Who is the Vine; but the *Mystery* of the Vine can be understood by the Soul only as it grows in spiritual and Divine knowledge.

Thus, all true initiations are inward. They are spiritual. They are accomplished by that process known as the clothing of the Soul with the Fig-leaf, and the nourishing of the Life through partaking of the flesh and seeds of the Fig, which represent the *secret substance.* And onward, and still onward, until the Soul is able to clothe itself with the leaves of the Vine. But in this there is no Bacchanalian, sensuous delight. The Soul knows itself clothed from on High with the Mystery. For thus it is prepared to drink of the fruit of the Vine, even until the cup of fulness can be partaken of.

SYMBOLIC USES OF THE FIGTREE AND THE VINE

Now, look for a moment at the place given to the Vine and the Figtree in religious thought, and in the Books that are associated with Revelation. There are other sacred books besides the Bible, where you will find the like teaching. But here the reference is specially to the Old Testament.

The first introduction to the Fig-leaf in the Bible story is where it is written that the first parents of humanity (as Adam and Eve are understood to have been according to the orthodox interpretation), violated some command which had been given them by the Great Love, and then discovered that they were naked; and that they made themselves garments of Fig-leaves to cover their nakedness.

Then we come to stories associated with the Vine, happy and unhappy; the unhappy being the inversion of the things that bring true happiness. For the Vine, all through the Old Testament's story, is a sacred symbol of the Divine Mystery. GOD's vineyard is so frequently spoken of as the place where HIS Vines and Figtrees grow. In the prophetic utterances it is found that the Vine and the Figtree play a considerable part in the outlook and hope of Israel, concerning whom there are spoken many prophetic promises concerning the Divine Love and Wisdom, under the imagery of the Vine and the Figtree. For it is frequently indicated that these shall blossom again. And it is also shown that, unless the Figtree does blossom and bear rich fruit, and the Vine bring forth great clusters of grapes, the LORD of Being shall be unable to come into manifestation; and consequently there can be no restoration of HIS people, nor an entering into the Promised Land by them.

Even in prophetic story it is said that in that day, the day of the Redemption, the day of the healing of the nations, the day of the return of the LORD, the day in which HE would speak again unto HIS people and reveal HIMSELF, every man and every woman should dwell beneath the Vine and the Figtree.

Time does not permit us here to give the numerous references in the Old Scriptures to this marvellous symbolism of the Figleaf and the Fig, the Vine and the Grape. We must rather hasten to unveil that meaning which was given by the Master to the intimate ones in the days of the Manifestation.

Even He had to teach His intimate ones concerning that story with which the Old Scriptures open, *viz.*, the apparent historic beginnings of humanity. He had to unveil to them the meaning of the two who were placed in the Garden of Eden, who discovered their nakedness and then were clothed with the leaves of the Figtree. Where there is perfect beauty and absolute purity; where truth obtains in its divinest revealings and unveilings; where the Being is illumined and clothed from on High, there is no consciousness of shame. Shame is begotten of an inherent consciousness of a fallen state. And it is even the effect of the consciousness of the fallen state upon the mind, that gives the mind certain ideas with regard to shame itself. True, everyone is clothed in the Presence of the King. Every Soul is garmented from on High. It is true that every Soul in its constitution is enriched in itself with the glorious Ætheric Substances. Out of these, as it moves along the path that takes it to GOD, it weaves its garments. It becomes clothed upon as it moves along that path, evoluting from the Divine centre. It weaves all the garments with which it becomes adorned, changing them through the intensive process of the Being's expansion, and the deepening and ascension into higher consciousness; changing them through the more intensified motion of the Eternal, Magnetic Stream, as that Stream flows within and through the substances out of which the Soul has fashioned its garments.

Thus a Soul is adorned according to its status. The glory of the LORD shines within it and through it, even manifesting through its garments in the measure in which it is realizing HIM, the realization producing magnetic motion by which the Being becomes at last clothed in magnetic light. This magnetic auric garmenting is not from man himself, but from the Divine LORD. And it is not only from the without, even though there is great glory in the Heavens; but it is from the within through HIS motion within the Sanctuary of the Being.

INTERPRETATIONS BY THE MASTER

In unveiling that old world story the Master had to interpret to His intimate ones that the clothing of the form with Fig-leaves was a symbol of a conscious state which was applicable to all the materialized world. It is only in the nakedness of matter, as it is called, that there is shame. In the Divine and in the perfect world, there is no matter as science understands it. That is difficult to interpret. We know it is easier to make a statement than to interpret it. But that which we always mean when speaking of the unfallen elements, is Divine Substance. Matter has descended from Divine Substance. But in the process it has been so greatly changed that its true inherent divine properties and magnetic states are affected in their magnetic motion, and are unable to give perfect response to the law of divine gravitation. If there existed no matter on these outer planes to-day, we should not be having earthquakes and all the seismic things which material science is ever trying to explain. Those very earthquake motions which are supposed to be the result of the contraction and expansion of the outer planes of the Earth, are the results of intense interior motion. They are the outcome of great active potencies operating within the Planet unto the healing of its intermediary planes, and, ultimately, the healing of these outer planes. And that such things must needs be for a time is the most obvious evidence of the Planet's estate, and its needs.

These latter are just fragmentary thoughts by the way, as the vision opens to us and tempts us to reveal and interpret it.

But to return to the question of the shame of nakedness. There is nakedness in matter. But the Seer beholds its nakedness become clothed. When you understand the Divine Wisdom in relation to all the elements, then you can take the Fig-leaf of Divine knowledge and spread it over all matter. Matter is now undergoing such a process of healing; and it will be restored to its primary state in which there was nothing impure, nor hurtful, nor derogatory to the Divine idea and ideal, but only sweet response and plasticity in all things, even in the substantial elements, so that they could be used as the Divine purposed.

The nakedness of a Human Soul must first be clothed by the Fig-leaves of spiritual knowledge. No Soul can eat of the Mystery expressed by the hidden flesh of the Fig and its seeds, until it somewhat clothes the shame of its materiality with the Fig-leaves of Heavenly Wisdom. The Soul must find the pure way in life, the beautiful way of Love, the Divine order of Life. Thus the Master taught.

The story of the Figtree is an allegory. It is an allegory concerning spiritual and Divine things. Emblematically it sets forth that which professed to be a house of Divine Wisdom, a tree full of Divine knowledge. It is an allegory portraying many things applicable to those times, and to ages prior to the days of the Manifestation; and also true of all the ages since.

THE FIGTREE AND THE CHURCH The Figtree has been used symbolically in true Art since pre-Grecian days. It has been applied to the feminine aspect of the Love-principle. Through religious nomenclature, and in religious organization and in religious claims, it has stood as the symbol of Wisdom. Have there not been claims put forth through all the ages prior to and since the days of the Manifestation, that certain institutions have held the Divine Wisdom, and that unless Souls associated themselves with such institutions, they could not be partakers of that Wisdom? Does not this underlie the whole of the historical development that has come to be named Christianity? The historical development must never be confounded with the Christianity which was an embodiment of the Christhood as taught by the Master. It is most true to-day as of yore, that there are Fig-leaves on the historical institution. There is the claim to Heavenly Wisdom. But where is the Wisdom? If such fruit be upon the tree, it is held in secret. The story of the barren Figtree could be applied, indeed, to historical

Christianity during "the Three Days" of the Naros. For, during "the Three Days" of the Oblation, the three great cycles of the Travail, fruit was sought for upon that tree; but none was found, though there was a show of leaves. The same can as truly be said of the Church development as was said of the materialistic Jewish development. And this does not mean there were no beautiful Souls in the heart of Jewry and in the Church of the West during more recent ages. Many of the Israelites were in Jewry, though they were not of Jewry. The Sons of God have travailed through the venues of historical Christianity in its development; but without being of it. Truth is true always, and for all ages; and that which does not bear the fruitage must pass away. Even in relation to national life, this is true. Men and women think that nations rise simply in order that there may be certain development through them, and then set as another nation rises. That is how nations have risen and set, it is true; but it is not how it should have been. Does a nation pass away before it has attained to the Divine realization in its national life? Where have the nations gone which have been divine expositions of the Divine Idea? Is it not true that they have passed away because they had had a show of Fig-leaves without the Wisdom of God as a living substance within their Being?

* * * * *

Now we will look at the Vine! The Vine has led to the way of spiritual dissoluteness because of the uses to which men and women have put it. They have used it religiously unto a super-sensuousness which has resulted in the degradation of individuals, and communities, and national life.

Nations rise for a divine purpose. They rise in the evolution of the people and of the races. But great nations like this nation, had they understood the days of their visitation, would have arisen to shake themselves free from the shackles of slavery to materiality in every form, and to clothe the whole national life with the Fig-leaf. For the leaves of the Figtree represent true spiritual knowledge; and the leaves of the Vine, are of the true, the good, the beautiful. And with the possession of such knowledge they would have provided the ways and means by which the children could get the Fig or Divine Wisdom, for nourishment, the real spiritual substance with which to enrich the Being, and find their way to the true wine of GOD.

Oh, when will this materialized world be clothed again with the Fig-leaves? For then the shame of its nakedness will not appear. When will the children have partaken again of the sacred Mystery, even in the limited degree of a portion of a Fig? When they have eaten of the Divine Substance expressed in the lesser Mysteries, they will know how wonderful GOD is, how transcendent, how glorious! They will know that there are no indignities where HE is present; that where HE makes manifest there is only what is beautiful. When HE is revealed the revelation speaks of that which is exquisite in form; fulness of beauty and radiance, expressing in the motion of service, HIS holy purpose. When this world's nakedness is thus clothed with true Soul vision and Divine Wisdom, then will its shame, and all the shameful things in it, pass away.

OUR LADY AS UNVEILED BY THE MASTER

The Master unveiled the Figtree. He unveiled "Our Lady." The idea and saying related to the Soul's feminine mode. Without "Our Lady" the Being cannot grow. Without this Divine Feminine motion, the LORD cannot be brought forth into manifestation. There are glimpses of this great truth of "Our Lady," even in the reverence for womanhood by man. For this means the recognition of the need of the Intuition, of which woman is the symbol. The intuitive faculty is at once perception and treasure house, the perception being the door through which the treasures are mediated, imported, or gathered in to be exported or brought forth for service. And woman even in ancient symbology, is taken to represent the intuition and man the mind. And when man, as representing Divine mind, came to be regarded as the lord of the woman, it was not meant that man should lord it over the woman. For even the LORD HIMSELF never lords it over any one. HE is the revealer within and through all. What was meant was this, that the man became a type of the centrifugal and masculine motion of the Divine Mystery and, therefore, of the Creative Potency. But it was never meant that he should be spoken of as the LORD in any Divine sense. Man was only to be the woman's lord in the sense of protector and provider.

"The Figtree putteth forth her green figs, and the Vine her tender grapes." And note this, that when it is said they make manifest "the time is at hand." What time? The re-manifestation of the LORD. The Soul must partake of certain degrees of the Divine knowledges called "the lesser Mysteries," ere it can enter into the Inner Vineyard of the FATHER-MOTHER, and know the garmenting that is given there. It must eat of the fruit of the Land, the Divine Wisdom, ere it can know the Presence Who walks there, and realize the might, the power, the potency, the inspiration, the exaltation, the Divine majesty, of drinking of the Cup of the Gods, the Wine of GOD, the Wine of the Divine Mystery. For that Cup the Presence gives to the Being to drink of. The Wine that is in that Cup, of which the Being drinks, and by means of which it is elevated into the King's Chamber and at last into the King's Presence, is the Life-stream of the Lamb. Thus is the Being elevated into the Realm wherein the LORD is known.

But Souls cannot get to the LORD, except through the mediation of "Our Lady." You may discern the great truth that is in the heart of the doctrine of the *Ave Maria*. You can never get to any high degree of understanding of the LORD of Being except through the house of the Intuition. You can never find that glorious Presence, but by the royal road of reverence and the purity associated with it. And these are begotten of the motion of Love within the Being.

The LORD is the true Vine; the FATHER-MOTHER is the husbandman. The LORD is the concrete expression in the

Inner Realms to our thought and vision, of the Eternal Mystery. HE is ever nourishing the Vine, ever enriching it.

OUR LADY AS MEDIATOR FOR THE LORD

Now, you see how a Soul can know the LORD, without the LORD being put under limitation. If the LORD were incarnated, HE would be put under the limitation of one vehicle and one life. But the LORD of Being could not be put under such limitation. When HE is to be made manifest in glorious fulness, HE chooses one who knows HIM, who has realized in great measure the glory of HIS Indwelling. And HE sends such an one to represent HIM. That one has to come under limitation in order to become incarnate. Then through the life wherein there is, for a time, limitation, there is the gradual process of expansion. There is a gradual revealing through the consciousness of the persona, through the mind and the heart, and then through the Being, until there is a revelation of the Mystery of the Presence. And then, such an one, having known the LORD, can rise up into the consciousness of that One Life out from which he came for the purpose of entering into these realms for ministry. There are many in that Inner Realm who know the LORD of Being in the same way; thousands and tens of thousands. For the Heavens of the Most High are vast, and HIS Sons are many. And when HE, the LORD of Being, reveals HIMSELF through a Servant, behold how HE mediates within that Servant through "Our Lady," the Intuition in a high state of illumination. Thus as HE reveals HIMSELF, "Our Lady" is the mediator in the Soul, between the LORD and the manifestation.

How beautiful it is! The way of the Divine Love is perfect. Man cannot improve on it. Oh, would that it were revealed to Souls everywhere in so far as could be, and in so far as Souls could receive the unveiled way! Would that it were revealed to all true seekers, and that the nakedness of the materialized Christhood could be covered again with the Fig-leaf of the Divine Wisdom; that those who profess Christ could eat of the Life-giving Figs from the living Figtree of the Divine

Wisdom! Oh, that all the children could find their way to that Vine out from the bosom of Whose Mystery they have all proceeded; and drink again of the vitalizing elements of its Wine, and know the Life-Eternal!

The day is coming when the LORD of Love is again to be made manifest. Behold! The Figtree has clothed itself with full fruitage, and the Fig in its sacred Mystery is being revealed. The LORD is coming. HE is coming as the LORD of the Vineyard. HE is coming as the living Vine. HE is coming to have that real festival of the Vine, to give HIS children that Cup which, if they drink thereof, they shall never thirst any more; for they shall know HIM. They will know that they have found HIM; and they will desire to know HIM more and more, and to drink still more and more deeply of the sacred Mystery expressed in and through the Vine.

Oh, beloved ones of the FATHER-MOTHER, children of HIS Love, dwellers awhile, like Nathanael, beneath the Figtree and the Vine; in whom HIS Mysteries have been in large measure unveiled; unto whom HE hath spoken in many ages—the LORD HIMSELF doth call you! HE doth call you through "Our Lady," your own Intuition, HIS heavenly perceptions in you. That you may reverence and adore HIM, gather in of HIS Wisdom and grow stronger; and, in that strength, adore HIM in increased embodiment; and in adoration, worship HIM in fuller and more beautiful service; and in worship, praise HIM with a richness of motion of Being wherein everything speaks of HIM, every act reveals HIM; and in such praise of HIM have HIS Blessing pouring itself through you, with nought of yourself in it but only that which is of HIM, HIS Love, HIMSELF.

SANTA MARIA

SANTA MARIA!*

The significance of the Santa Maria, can be understood only through a true apprehension of that for which the day stands, and which I would unveil to you.

AT THE PLACE NAMED CALVARY

It is the Day of the Cross. Come with me, therefore, to Calvary. Calvary is reminiscent of other days, and prophetic. The whole story as told in the New Testament Records, bears upon the face of it such a materialization of sacred fact, that the truth is not easily discerned. For the truth is not to be found in the outwardness of that of which the day is the memorial. The truth of the Passover and the Crucifixion lies deeper than any objective presentation of them. The significance of the Passover itself, for which, it is said, the Jews were preparing, lies far beyond any outward, historical interpretation. And the trials following the betrayals, and the condemnation and crucifixion, all lie hidden from observation where the observer is simply looking at them from the objective Realm. For they are of spiritual import. They can be apprehended only mystically. They must be understood soulicly. Indeed, they can be understood only by those who have in some measure given themselves sacrificially, for high and holy service.

The passing away of the Master in the sense of His betrayal and trial, condemnation and crucifixion, has been associated with the Passover. It culminated on the eve of the Passover, according to the Records; that is, it was on our Friday. For the next day, the seventh day, was the Jewish Sabbath.

What was the Passover? Of what does it speak? Is it merely of outward history in relation to the Jewish people as they came out of Egypt? Was the eve of the Passover the memorial of the eve of their deliverance? And if so, why should it have any relationship whatever to the passing away of the Master?

It is true that earnest students of divine things in their

*Spoken to friends in London, on Good Friday, 1928.

endeavour to understand His relationship to the past histories of the world, have interpreted them in the light of His sacrificial ministries, and applied the Passover to His own Burden-bearing and passing away. The subject of the Passover has also had given to it a planetary interpretation in relation to the Sun and the Planet. And it has likewise had an interpretation in relation to the Soul, as it passes out from the land of bondage into the experience of high liberation.

But that wonderful story of old time wherein it is said that a lamb was slain, part of it partaken of as food, and its blood sprinkled upon the uprights, the lintels and doorposts, in order that "the destroying angel" might observe the sign, and know that there had been a passover celebration, and that those within were the people of God, belonged to one of the sacred Soul Mysteries. It is also represented that "the destroying angel" was the Angel of the Lord, which is a most fearful perversion of the truth. How could an illuminated Soul imagine that the Angel of the Lord could destroy the Lord's own children, because they had not some outward sign upon them that they belonged to a distinctive religious profession, or made certain confession, or observed certain ritual, or that they were of distinctive racial descent? The blindness of the children of men through the ages in not discerning the monstrous perversions of divine truth, is as amazing as the perversions themselves.

THE LAMB OF THE PASSOVER

The story of the Passover was an allegorical statement in the sacred Mysteries of Israel, and in a prophetic sense, it came to have relation in the interpretation given to it to the passing away of the Master. The Lamb slain, was the Lamb of God. The Lamb of God is the Divine Love in its sacrificial capacity. That Love is always pierced where the play of forces is opposed to the way of Love, the way of all that Love stands for, the Life unto which Love calls. The Lamb of God that taketh away the sin of the world is the Divine Love. The sin of the world cannot be healed in any other way. Love heals all things, Divine Love is perfect in everything; in desire, in outlook, in attitude, in purpose, in interpretation, in ministry. There is nothing wherein it is lacking in perfection. To heal the world is to fill it with the Love that will give to it a right outlook, a right attitude of mind, a right motion of heart, a right purpose of spirit, a right manifestation in all its ways.

That Love is the Lamb of God. And it has had to make itself manifest in diverse ways in different ages to find the children and bring to such as could receive of it, the Divine Vision, teaching them how to embody it, how to acquire the way and the power of its motion, unto blessed embodiment and service.

The Passover Lamb is ever the way of deliverance from Egypt and the sign of the Soul's motion towards the real land of Canaan. To enter into Canaan is not to dispossess others, nor take from them the land of their inheritance. It is to enter into that estate of spiritual consciousness wherein the Being realizes the Divine Inheritance which is so absolute in its universality, that there is a portion for every child; so that no one individual, or people, or race, even if such were able to, need think of taking from another. Everyone has his and her inheritance in the Great Love.

* * * * *

It was on the eve of the Passover, it is said, that the Crucifixion took place, the eve of the memorial day of a great event in Jewish story.

That Passover, in the ancient times, was known to Israel. Its prophetic significance had relationship to the Divine Love's Passion, and the Divine purpose to accomplish the healing of the world through the motion of that Passion.

THE MYSTERY OF THE DESTROYING ANGEL

Who was "the destroying angel" who passed over the households of Israel because upon the lintels and doorposts of their dwellings, the Blood of the Lamb had made its signature? Why, it is the spirit that is opposed to all the onwardness of life and the upwardness of the Being. And the relationship of that ancient Passover to the Passover said to be accomplished by the Master, is in this respect, that, at that time, there was something done by the Great Love for this world.

What was it that had to be accomplished, and how was it done? What was the nature of that destroying force? Why, it was that spirit of negation, that spirit of the Devil which means negation, that Satanic spirit which embodies the evil influence, which was working against any manifestation of Christhood, and was determined to destroy it, if possible. For that is the inner significance lying behind all betrayals—not simply the betrayal of the Master in a personal way, though He was betrayed; nor his Crucifixion in an outward sense, though it is true He was crucified. That spirit sought to smite the Christhood in relation to the Manifestation that was given through the Master and His intimate ones. He had to tell His friends that they themselves would be smitten and scattered; and they underwent such an experience. But that which was operative against the return of the children, was the state of the Planetary Heavens; and the compass of the Passover had to do with the whole of the Oblation, "the passing over" being the first act. The Passover as a festival, as a sacrifice, as a deliverance, was the whole process of the Travail, from the beginning of it until the consummation of it. And its work has only been completed in these days of our own manifestation.

And just to indicate to you the reality of the Passover story as an allegory hidden amongst the Mysteries which were lost amidst the Jewish story, I might say to you, that, where there is the mark upon the lintels and doorposts, or upon the very Life of the Being, even unto the outer life, "the destroying angel" has no power to hurt that one; the Devil and Satan have no power over that life, for Divine Love is triumphant in and through such an one; for the Blood, or Lifestream of Love—the Lamb of God has written its insignia upon the Being, even unto the outer portico of the life. That same destroying spirit continues to seek wherever it can, to betray, and will do so until it is altogether overthrown. And, of course, the powers named the Devil and Satan, can be overthrown only through all the children having the seal of the Blood of the Lamb upon them, the hallmark of Divine Love, of real childhood to HIM Who is the FATHER-MOTHER. Childhood to HIM must be more than nominal. There must be no perfunctory profession of childhood. A mere acknowledgment of childhood in belief may be no childhood at all. There must be a living childhood that fills the Being with the motion of HIS Own glorious Lifestream, so that the Life is embodiment for HIM in its desires, its feelings, its energies, in all its potencies, in its substance, and in the glorious essences out from which the Breath of HIS Love ascends, and the Sacred Flame of HIS Spirit moves. That is the childhood to HIM, for which end the Passover was borne.

THE REAL PASSOVER AND THE CROSS

Herein is the meaning of the Passover. We stand at the Cross. But it is not on the little mound called Golgotha outside of Jerusalem that we stand looking upon the body of the Master crucified. We look upon the Divine Love as that Love has become crucified for the world. We see that Love wounded in its feet—the ways of its going; wounded in its hands—the ways of its service; wounded in its head, crowned with the thorns of mockery which the opposing forces have placed upon its brow; and wounded in its side, because pierced through and through, yet so Immortal and Eternal, that it could not die. The Divine Love could not die. The hurts of ages could not kill it. The hates of fallen ones have failed to change it. If there has been anything that has been named Love, and it has died, there has been some mistake in the name given to it. Love cannot be killed. It is Eternal and Immortal, of the very nature of HIM Who is Eternal and Immortal Our GOD is unchangeable. HE is Love; and HE is ever sure.

We stand before the Cross. All that the outer Crucifixion

symbolised, we look upon. We see the Passion of our LORD, and the wondrous motion of the Love that could endure all things, bear all things, have such purpose and action towards all things as to ultimately accomplish their healing. And this healing shall be done now, for the Passover is accomplished; the path of the Oblation has been followed, and the world-burden borne, and the Divine Purpose wrought. Though the long shadows of its cross lie athwart the ages, and lighten upon the threshold of the memory, they grow less and less through the shining of HIS Radiant Presence, and soon the shadows will disappear altogether.

Now you will understand that wondrous apocalyptic song concerning the Lamb of God that taketh away the sin of the world. You may recognize that it is the Divine Love in its Passion and its Burden-bearing, in its wondrous testimony of endurance, in its exquisite gentleness, and in its unspeakable lowliness. *There is no other way to take sin away* than by the healing Love gives. It was Love that accomplished the Oblation. It was Love that bore the Passion. It was Love that descended into the Hells, accommodating itself by a process of limitation through a most amazing ministry. It was Love that made it possible for the Servant to be let down into the Hell-states unto the extinguishing of their fires, the bringing of those who were in those states into an ordered life, through changing the whole of the conditions of the Planetary Heavens and effecting their redemption. It was Love in its motion giving the full assurance that all the world would be redeemed, the elder children coming first, redeemed, healed, found, and raised up; and then all the children through the changing of their ways, helping them to see the true and the beautiful; aiding them to seek joy in purity, nobility, and blessed service; teaching them to understand that even true happiness is to be found in living the beautiful life, and in serving nobly. It was the Divine Love that sought the elder children unto the finding of their diviner qualities, and the restoration of their consciousness, to realize that there is no such thing as abiding happiness on the earthplanes until all the world's sorrow is dried up, and that, until that time, they must be in the very Lifestream of the Lamb of God, caught up by its motion to become once more the vehicles through which it may flow and make itself manifest; that they may again become the burden-bearers and the cross-bearers for the Divine Love, the real, heroic Souls who will endure unto the uttermost for God, and account it joy unspeakable and honour high to be HIS servants, HIS Redeemers.

* * * * *

THE DRAMA WITHIN THE JUDGMENT HALL

It is no longer the eve of the Passover. That night is passed. It is the morning of the Return. There has been a passing of the hour that cast the shadows. It is the day; and the shadows are all to have the light thrown upon them until they flee away.

Still are our meditations at the Cross. It is said in the New Testament that, when the Master was taken into the Hall of Judgment, John went with Him, because he was a friend of the High Priest; and that John asked permission to go and fetch Simon Peter, who remained outside of the Hall; that he went to Peter to bring him in also; that Peter essayed to follow, but as he entered the Hall he was challenged, and accused of being a disciple of the Master, which he vehemently denied.

Here there is something I have never unveiled to you as to its inner, mystical significance. And in order to get the real meaning you must dissociate it from the person of two disciples.

The real High Priest is the Divine Presence. John is the one who represents the Love-principle, the Love embodied in the Servant. Simon Peter is the faithful friend recognizing the glory of Christhood, who, nevertheless, in the hour of great testing, wavers. He is asked to go into the Hall of Judgment. He fears to go there. Love does not fear to go into the Judgment Hall. Love fears nothing, for perfect Love casteth out all fear. Love is full of perfect trust. But Simon Peter is the mind; and even in its higher understanding, it often trembles and fears. Simon Peter stood before the fire warming himself, but when challenged denied the Great Love, and then, it is said, went out to weep bitterly.

It is a glimpse of what the heart will do, and what the mind often does. If your love be perfectly equilibrated, in the Divine Heart in you, you need never fear to follow its motion. You must follow it, because it is the vehicle of the Lifestream of the Divine Mystery within. And to follow the heart, is to follow the way of Divine Love. But it is well to bring the mind into harmony, for *it is the mind that betrays. It is the mind that denies. It is the mind that repudiates, even after it has professed and confessed fealty.* It is indeed something to seek after, to have the mind filled with fidelity!

* * * * *

HOW LOVE SUFFERED AND TRIUMPHED

Yet there is something more. Even in the case of Him Who had to bear the Burden of the Passion of the LORD you will note, that it was Love that endured the Judgment Hall; but it was the mind that had to be the vehicle of the life that was, indeed, an exposition of Love betrayed. For in all the Lives of the Oblation, He was betrayed through his Love. But the betrayals were through operations of the mind. The mind was afflicted. The mind was filled with fear. The mind dreaded. The mind at times, when the inner Being was veiled, did even deny. But it was not the denial of the Great Love. It was the denial of all that the Being loved most concerning that ONE, because of the way the Passion took the Soul.

All that is implied in that strange dread which overtook the Master. I have said to you many times that it would have been beneath the dignity of One Who was a Servant of the Most High, let alone One Who was believed to be a Son of the Gods, and still more so, One Who was believed to be the Son of GOD, to shrink from bearing a burden for a few hours, however great the burden was. And if He did shrink from it, then there was something more than the mere crucifixion by the Romans upon the cross raised by them on Golgotha! He shrank not from the burden, but from the awful loss that would be His during the many ages that the Oblation would continue, the loss of the consciousness of HIS Radiant Presence Who was ever HIS LORD. He had dwelt in that consciousness, rejoiced in that consciousness, lived in the Radiance of the Presence. He had spoken with that ONE as with the most intimate of Beings, and He shrank from having such a consciousness obscured, such a vision veiled, such a realization taken away from Him. In the Judgment Hall of the world He bore the Burden; and as John the Beloved He feared lest His Love should fail. Yet LOVE Itself was to triumph, as it had been promised unto Him. But it was difficult to bring the mind in its higher understanding into that Judgment Hall, and keep it there in a state of equipoise. For it was through the mind He had to be smitten by means of His Love, even unto the denial, betrayal, crucifixion, and repudiation.

Nay more than that. It is said, just a little later, that that intimate disciple who is said to have leaned upon the bosom of His Lord, was laid hold of by an enemy, and that that disciple left his garment in the hands of the enemy. You may see how those mystical "Sayings" have come to be related to mere outward events. It was the garment of the Christhood that clothed the Soul, the garment that the FATHER-MOTHER had given unto Him to wear, the garment of His own Love which He had to leave in the hands of the enemy. His Christhood went. They parted His garments amongst them, and cast lots for His vesture—His seamless robe. He had to go out almost naked from the Christhood state. He had to go unrobed. He was disrobed of all that was associated with the ancient Christhood realization, which He knew well, and which realization was His supremest joy.

At the Cross! Ah, what mystery is there! Not a wooden cross on which the frame of the Master hung for a little time where he suffered the crucifixion of His wondrous vehicle; but before that Cross of the Divine Passion that expressed itself throughout the ages. And though it was through the Master in His various vehicles during the Forty Lives that that Passion was expressed, it must ever be remembered that it was the Divine Passion, and that He was but the Servant of His LORD. So that not even He must be worshipped. *Worship God only.*

* * * * *

THE THREE FAITHFUL ONES AT THE CROSS

Here I would lead you to see the yet more inward significance of those hours before the Cross. O Santa Maria!

It is said that all the disciples fled, and only the three Marys remained. The disciples fleeing from Him were His own attributes passing from their Christhood estate. But the three Marys remained. They were sad, sorrowful, lonely. He had to pass away even from them. In His death He had to leave them all, that He might accomplish the Passover. Who were they? It is said they were, Mary His Mother, and that other Mary (of Bethany), and Mary Magdalene. In the Passion, He had to leave *the Maria estate:* (O Santa Maria!) that estate wherein the Lord manifestation had been made. He had to leave the Maria estate wherein He could sit at the Feet of His LORD and learn still more of the Great Love. He had to leave the estate of Maria Magdalene, which, in its first meaning, does not at all relate to the fallen state to which it is applied, but to nobility and exaltation of Being. The Magdalene estate, as generally understood, is that same divine nobility, that exalted Soul-estate, brought down. As Maria, He was the Mother of the LORD manifestation in His Being; and loved the fellowship of the Presence, as Maria of Bethany; and was endowed in His Being with divine nobility gifted unto Him from the FATHER-MOTHER, as Maria Magdalene. For everything He had of Soul possession, was gifted from the FATHER-MOTHER. He had to leave those estates. And if He seemed to retain that of Maria Magdalene, it was because, in its latter form of interpretation, He became the Burden-bearer, the travail-stained Soul whose garments were red-dyed as one who had been treading the wine vat.

Yet it is said of these three Marys, that they remained at the cross unto the last.

Here we have an exquisite presentation of the fidelity of the Great Love Who is the Soul's Maria in all those estates, and Who, even in the Being of the Master, became as Maria Magdalene, the Divine Love in its wondrous descent. And the fidelity of that Love in the three states is expressed in their endurance when all else seemed to pass away. Friends forsook Him. He had to leave and be left by all. Even His attributes, like the stars falling from the Heavens, had to go down into earthliness. Yet those three Maria states are said to have remained with Him. It is recorded that they sought to embalm Him and keep Him. Behold now the inner significance of that! The Divine Marias, the high Christhood estates, sought to embalm Him! They brought their precious unguents to preserve Him. That was true, not only in those days, but throughout the days of the Oblation. They fain would have fully embalmed Him. They preserved Him, however; for without the Love that was represented in those three Marys, He could never have endured throughout the ages. By means of their embalming, they kept His Love pure in the innermost. They held the motion of His Soul Godward. They were the three great ministrants to His Being, the influences always playing within Him, giving the Divine urge onward and upward. So that, whatever He did (and He had to do many things that became abhorrent to him in order to accomplish the blotting out of the graven images), the urge came back to Him always to rise and seek the wondrous vision of His LORD. For though He was not permitted to enter into the consciousness of it until the close of the Oblation, it was there. Although it had to be withdrawn, it was not lost, except to His personal consciousness throughout the Travail.

So, the three Marias were always there. That is why they were early at the Sepulchre when the day came for His Return. And the one to be first at the Sepulchre was Maria Magdalene. For He had to come back into the consciousness of that state, and then into the consciousness of the Maria state wherein He sat at the Feet of His Lord, and then into that Divine Maria estate wherein He became once more, in His vision and consciousness, one with His Lord.

Now you will see my meaning in the title of this Unveiling, O Santa Maria! It is the term applied to the Mother of the Master, and named the Holy Mother. But it originally had not this meaning; and mystically it is of the Divine in the Soul. The Master's Mother was beautiful and holy, consecrate and exquisite in her love in those days, though heavily burdened with sorrow towards the eve of the Passover. But the Divine Maria is the Soul. In you, it is the realizing of the Blessed One within your Being. It was His Being which had been Mother of the manifestation. O Santa Maria! Mother of many sorrows! It is not the human aspect but the Divine Mother in the Soul that was as the Mother of many sorrows during the Travail. O SANTA MARIA!

THE PURPOSE OF THE UNVEILING You will now understand why I have given you this unveiling. I would bring the great realities to you. I would help you to understand anew the Divine Love in its majestic stooping. And by that I do not mean the stooping of the Master. Oh no! If that were so it would be personal in relation to Him, and such must never be. For in the measure in which He, or any Servant, could stoop in the glory of Love, giving unto the uttermost of all the Being, the Being's attributes, the Being's substance, the Being's elements, the Being's essences, even to give of the Spirit unto the travail of the world-burden and the world-healing, the measure would be the measure of the Divine Love. It is of the Divine Love. It is from the Divine Love. It is accomplished by the Divine Love. The Oblation could not have been otherwise borne. It must, therefore, be related to the Divine Love always. It must always be spoken of as the Divine Love's Passion. Yea, even these most sacred terms, terms most sacred to me: O Santa Maria! O Divine Motherhood! O GOD in the Passion of THY Mother-Love! O Divine world-Nourisher; world-Healer; world-Redeemer; the Bearer of the travail through and in the Servant; the Bearer away of the world's sin and the karmic burden that was written so largely upon the Planetary Heavens; and the bearing of it away through the changing of all the conditions! O Divine Heart! O Divine Mother!

To worship HIM in HIS glorious Motherhood-Love, and Eternal Passion of Love, is to worship no woman, no man, no servant, no Angel nor Archangel. To pray to the Holy Mother, is the Soul's upward motion towards the recognition of Divine Motherhood, and the travail of Divine Sorrow.

I am deeply moved towards you, and would that it were possible for me to unveil more clearly and more fully unto you, the sacred Mystery of the Lord's Passion, that ye should drink of the Lifestream of such Love, and witness anew within your consciousness, the motion of such Love; that ye should feel again the influx of the Lifestream of such Love, even unto the renewing of your Being, aye, until the body of your flesh in the outer became one with the body of your flesh in the innermost. I would have you understand what it means to share the Mystery of the Flesh of the Son of God, and the Divine Heart throbbing within you in its systaltic motion, as it propels HIS Glorious Lifestream through all your arterial Being, even to the outermost, until ye know yourselves filled from the Seat of HIS Presence to the outer court of your life, and the measure of the circumference of your Life is that of the Divine Man!

* * * * *

O most Sacred ONE! Our FATHER-MOTHER! Glorious art Thou in Thy Love, full of a Majesty Thy children yet but faintly glimpse! Yet THY children would adore THEE. In this hour of the triumph of THY Love in the great travail we would bless THEE. We would magnify THY Name through having it written upon every part of our Being. We would know THY Signature upon the lintels and the doorposts of our life, even to the outermost. Though conscious of the limitations of our Being, and the imperfections that still make shadows upon our garments, yet in the Majestic stooping of THY Love, THOU dost come to us. We would adore THEE, and in THY Presence give ourselves to THEE, to be for THEE evermore. We would that our blessing be THY Blessing, THYSELF blessing in us and giving THY blessing through us; our praise of THEE THINE own glorious motion within us, unto the making of perfect harmony, and our Life one with the Eternal Symphonies. We would have our worship of THEE be so complete, that it will be a Life-service in every act, THY act in us and through us. And we pray that our adoration of THEE be of such a nature that, with Cherubim and Seraphim, the whole motion of our Being will be one of adoring Love, wherein the glory of THY Love will be revealed within us and through us. Thus would we be within THY Kingdom, THY glorious Regnancy, the conscious inheritors of THY gifted power to make THEE manifest.

* * * * *

Whatever limitation there must have been in the Unveiling of this to you, it has been a wondrous hour; for the very Heavens have been open, and the Angels of God have been here in great companies, outpouring from HIM of HIS Blessing. An hour of triumph, indeed, it has been, with no veiled Cross to look upon, but the Living Cross full of the Radiance of HIS Presence within the Being. For here is HIS own High Altar revealed to us. Here are HIS Cherubim and Seraphim in inward and outward motion. Here are present with us the glorious Angelic Hosts. Here His Shekinah has been and is still over us. The hour has been full of the glory of HIS Radiance.

O SANTA MARIA!

A THREEFOLD MYSTERY

A THREEFOLD MYSTERY

Following the Santa Maria I would speak of this triple subject of The Three Altars, wherein the Divine Mystery is aspected in The High Altar, The Altar to St. Joseph, and The Altar to Mary. In this hour I would unite these aspects of the Divine. And so I ask you to accompany me whither I would fain lead you, even into the Sanctuary of HIS Presence Who is our LORD. The hidden truths are expressed in some outer symbology with which some of you have been familiar. Others of you, not having come by the way of Symbols and Ritual, will be less familiar with the idea; but, surely you will not be less arrested by the secret divine meaning lying behind that which is set forth symbolically.

SYMBOLS OF DIVINE VERITIES

In visiting ancient sanctuaries, and especially those associated with the Roman Catholic Church, you will remember that there are three Altars intimately related to the main Acts of Worship and Adoration. These are the High Altar and the two which are most intimately related to it. There are many altars and shrines in a large Church, such as you find in the Brompton Oratory or Westminster Cathedral, or even in some of the smaller Churches. But there are three Altars which very specially arrest one. There is the High Altar on which the Host should always be represented in symbolism. And there is the Altar of the Crucifixion. Sometimes this latter is quite apart from the High Altar, though often united to it. The High Altar, however, should not have associated with it within the Sanctuary, the Altar of the Crucifixion. They should be apart. And then (if rightly placed) there should be to the worshipper's vision another Altar to the left—that is, to the right of the High Altar. This is dedicated to St. Joseph. Then (if rightly placed) to the right of the worshipper, that is, to the left of the High Altar, there is another Altar, dedicated to the Holy Mother.

These Altars are associated historically and personally with individuals. The High Altar sets forth the Crucifixion, and the Master Who is elevated in thought and belief to the position of the Lord of Being, and is confounded with the Divine Presence; for the Master is thought of as Deity, and actually to be the Eternal and Only Begotten Son of that Holy and Glorious ONE. The Altar to Joseph is the Altar to the one who was the espoused of the Mother of the LORD; he was accounted the foster-father of the Master. And then there is the Altar to the Holy Mother.

Before each of these prayers are offered, and lights are presented and burned. Oft-times have I said to you that all the great symbolism of the ages is true, when you get at that which lies behind it; that all the great doctrines associated with the Divine, with the Mystery of Life, and with the Soul, are true, if you can get their right interpretation. It is the interpretation through misunderstanding that is wrong, with the resultant that there is misrepresentation of most glorious, divine ideas, ideas vital to the Soul's growth, enrichment, expansion, transformation, the transmutation of its elements, and the transfiguration of its whole Being. Of those three Altars I will speak to you for a little while.

THE THREE ALTARS GREAT GIFTS TO THE CHURCH

Though in the great Churches where you find them side by side, and worshippers bowing before them, they are related to the personal Master, and to His earthly Father and Mother in the days of the Manifestation; and though in the thought of the worshippers there is a great elevation of the three, the Master who is named the Lord to be in the Heavens at the Right Hand of the FATHER-MOTHER; the Holy Mother, Mary, as a great mediator, full of the sweet motion of intercession on behalf of suffering ones, having known sorrow herself, is full of sweet sympathy with all who suffer; and Joseph as an under-shepherd, a semi-shepherd of a high order, and one who may be prayed unto for protection and for blessing;

and though it is sad that the great ideas lying behind these three Altars and those they represent, should have been brought low by the materialization, yet the day has surely come when the resplendence of the Truth will once more shine through all the symbols which were meant to be educational and illuminative and uplifting unto the children!

Who could have instituted the idea of the High Altar but one who knew it in the Heavens? Who could have raised an Altar unto Joseph, with the real spiritual significance lying behind it, but one who knew the mystery couched in the Altar dedicated to I-O-SEPH in the Heavens? Who would have conceived the thought of erecting an Altar to the Holy Mother as the Mother of the LORD in manifestation, and as the sweet Mother of compassion, but one who knew the meaning of that Altar, and the inner significance of IOSEPH and of MARIA?

A DIVINE ADVENTURE

Come with me into the Inner realms; for it is there you will find the truth. It is there that the radiance shines. It is there the meaning becomes clear. It is there the origin of all things may be looked upon, and the understanding of them entered into. It is there that the LORD HIMSELF meets us, as we enter HIS great and glorious Sanctuary. The fashion of it is not that of the human concept, although the human mind has endeavoured to express something of it. We pass up its aisles. We approach the inner Sanctuary; for there are departments even in an Angelic Sanctuary, and in a Celestial Sanctuary, and in the Divine Sanctuary. The Angelic custodian opens wide for us the gates which are represented in the rood screen in the Cathedrals; and we walk up to what in a Cathedral would be named the reredos. But no language could describe what we witness. There is an Altar, but it is not of dead stone or wood but living Substance, every part of it vibrating, and the cells of which it is built up, radiating as if they have motion. It is the High Altar of the LORD. It is the Altar of the Holy ONE in the Divine World, and also in our Being. That Altar is overshadowed by a wonderful *canopy*. This latter is indescribable; though in some of the Cathedral Churches there has been an endeavour to express that canopy.

That Canopy represents the Presence ever Overshadowing the Altar; and it is an actual vision and experience. The things of the Inner Worlds are realities. It is well you should know those realities. Unto that end I would have you come to that High Altar. HIS Host is there. It is the sacred Mystery of HIS Presence. You can look upon it; according to your spiritual estate will it become formulated; according to the power of your perception and receptivity will it be revealed to you. If ye are able to endure standing before that Altar receiving of the mediation of Cherubim and Seraphim, then verily the LORD of Love will mediate unto you of HIS own sacred Mystery in such a fashion that you will come to understand it; yea, to understand even the sacred Mystery. It is not easy to conceive in the human mind the possibility of understanding that Sacred Mystery. But when the Soul is able to enter into such a Sanctuary, and approach such an Altar and stand before it and receive mediation, and learn to mediate before that Altar, then the Soul transcends all the realm of the mind, even of the perceptions, and of the understanding, and even of the reason which is one with the understanding and the perceptions. In such an experience the Soul knows. It is illumined. For you must know that we understand GOD in consciousness, and not outside of consciousness. We understand HIM in the measure in which we realize HIM; and only in that measure. Therefore, the Mind cannot apprehend HIM, though it may apprehend HIS approach and HIS manifestations. The Understanding can reason; and the reason within the understanding is the balancing power of the mind through which it may reason as to the reality being present in and through the manifestations. But it is only in the inner Sanctuary of Being, and within the realm of high consciousness, that the Soul knows the Presence.

THE WAY OF THE DIVINE PROCESSIONAL

It was in this way that ye yourselves came to know the LORD in past ages; and though the vision of HIS resplendence has been dimmed owing to the ages of your travail, yet it was something you realized. If you had not done so, you would not have yearned to get back to that Divine Estate. Souls who deeply yearn, cry out for the living God. And those who are conscious of their need for the touch of that ONE, to them is that ONE most intimately related. And this is so not only in the creative sense in which all Souls are the children of GOD, but also in the sense, that such a Soul at one time must have acquired the estate wherein the LORD of Love was realized. It is thus you may again know the FATHER-MOTHER. And I would have you know the FATHER-MOTHER as the most glorious reality. Unto that end are all these Teachings given concerning HIM, that you should know HIM, come to know HIM again intimately, and realize HIS Presence immanently within you; and that ye should enter through the expansion and elevation of your consciousness, the Sanctuaries of the Heavens, HIS Inner Sanctuary through the Sanctuary of your Being, and reach unto the High Altar, and once more know it to be the Altar of Our LORD. It is the Altar of the Host. It is the Altar of the Chalice. It is the Altar of the Mystery. It is the Altar of the FATHER-MOTHER. Here you get such an Overshadowing as reveals to you the Divine Mystery of the FATHER-MOTHER in HIS Love and Wisdom.

O Sacred ONE, our FATHER-MOTHER! O Sacred LORD of our Being Whose Love is revealed in Life! All Life is the result of motion. Individuate Soul Life is the resultant of the motion of HIS holy Love as HIS Breath or Spirit through the glorious Ætheric Elements out of which HE in HIS great and holy purpose fashioned all things. In it is the Altar of Our LORD Who is the Radiant Presence. Through the motion of the Life-principle as it moves through the Love-principle, the Altar reveals itself in the concrete Life. And HE clothes the

Life with HIS Radiance. This radiance is the divine magnetic light resulting from HIS action upon our magnetic pole by means of HIS Overshadowing. This is it which gives to the Soul who stands before the Altar, the Divine Vision. Upon that High Altar, with its Divine Auric radiance, the Fires of the ELOHIM burn. Its Sacred Lamp is ever lit. The glorious ones around HIS Throne are all resplendent embodiments of HIS own sacred Fire and Radiance; and HIS Altar speaks of them all. This is the chief Altar before which we must worship. It is the Altar of Our LORD. That which is couched in it is sublime, complete, and comprehensive. It represents the all-embracing FATHER-MOTHERHOOD of Being. For what could such an Altar as that of Joseph stand? And also that of Mary? In the Divine World things are not as they are on the earthplanes. The Altar of Ioseph has a profound meaning. Ioseph is a Divine Name. Joseph and Mary are said to have been the father and mother of Our LORD, though Joseph is represented as the foster parent. But all Souls are begotten through the Divine Ioseph Maria, for they are both Divine Names.

MARIA IOSEPH DOMINUS

The Altar of Ioseph is the Altar of the Luminous Cross. Now, in the Mystery of the FATHER-MOTHER there is what might be called informulation. He is informulate; and such formulations as take place, are adaptations to the estate of the Soul who approaches that Altar. For the knowledge and realization of the Divine Mystery belongs to the Innermost. But all Souls can approach, in their consciousness, the Altar of Ioseph. They must; for the Cross is in them; the sacred mystery of the Luminous Cross is their inheritance. That is how it comes to pass that you can enter into the inner understanding of the mystery of the Cross, because it is in you. It is the balance of your inner Life when you are equilibrated. It is indeed the dual Principle of your Being. It is GOD'S Mystery in duality. In you there are the FATHER-MOTHER Principles; but the Fatherhood is represented in I-o-seph, and the Motherhood in

Maria. The Altar of Ioseph is the Altar to the Luminous Cross. It is the Cross of the sublime Mystery of ELOHIM. The Altar to the Holy Mother, to Maria, is the Altar to the Divine Motherhood—the Fatherhood and the Motherhood. Herein is the Mystery of the FATHER-MOTHER expressed in the centrifugal and centripetal motion. The Altar of Ioseph is the Altar of Divine Fatherhood and Shepherdhood. The Altar of Maria is the Altar of Divine Motherhood. The Luminous Cross is centrifugal in its ministry. It pours forth the glory of Divine Being. The Divine Motherhood is centripetal in its motion; it gathers up Souls into the bosom of its tenderness for the outpouring of blessing upon them. It bears within its bosom of Love and gentleness and compassion, pity for the needy, for the afflicted who seek unto that most sacred Altar.

Here we have a glorious Divine Trinity. It is the Divine exposition of the sacred Mystery of the FATHER-MOTHER in the High Altar of all Being, where all ministry and all power are revealed. Ioseph is the Divine Shepherd. His motion is GOD'S shepherdhood expressed. And on the other hand the Motherhood of GOD is revealed in the Altar to the Divine Maria. For though these terms relate to the Soul, as I have said at other times, just as the Fatherhood-Motherhood are in Principle in the Soul; so also do they relate to the Divine.

THE DIVINE PROCEDURE FOR THE SOUL

I would take you with me to those Altars. But I would blot out the earthly shadows that have fallen upon their threshold through their materialization and degradation. I would have you transcend the limitation of tradition, and what you may have learnt on the way. I would have you escape from the bondage of fear that may be in you in relation to the earthly altars, which are but endeavours to express something spiritual, soulic, angelic or divine. I would have you come with the freedom of children of the FATHER-MOTHER into the understanding of the great realities in the unseen Universe, but seen in the realm of realization. I would have you know that the

Altar before which the whole Being trembles is the High Altar of the Overshadowing Presence. But the Soul who finds its way there, is supported by the magnetic action of the Altars of Ioseph and Maria, the shepherdhood of the FATHER-MOTHER expressed as I-o-seph, and the Motherhood of the FATHER-MOTHER expressed as Maria. You will see how, if symbols of such Altars were used in an endeavour to represent them on the earth planes, they should be most exquisitely beautiful. Everything should be perfect in symbolism. Nothing tawdry, or derogatory, should be present. There should be no false light, no false tinsel, nor glory represented by tinsel. For all the Altars in the Divine World are realities. You could not get away from them. Woe unto you, dear ones, if you wish to get away from them. When I say woe, I mean it would impose upon yourselves great limitations.

In the approach to the High Altar, a Soul has to learn to receive from the Altar of I-o-seph, HIS benison WHO is the Shepherd of us all. Through HIS Shepherdhood the Soul arrives at that estate wherein it can in advanced degree apprehend the sacred mystery of the High Altar of GOD with that eternal motion of Cherubim and Seraphim. Nor can anyone reach that High Altar unto the realization of the glorious mystery which it represents, by other way than through the realization of the Motherhood of GOD. For through that Motherhood the Soul realizes the Divine Pity that speaks of guardianship in the sense of Divine protection, and the Divine Compassion, the tender influx of which is the Divine Lifestream passing into the Being; for in this way there is administered unto the Soul from out the Eternities, the Ætheric Elements of the Divine Kingdom for the enrichment of the whole spiritual life, and the uprising of the Being into that estate wherein it can move before the Altar of I-o-seph with the radiating forces playing upon it, and the Altar of the Divine Maria, and also stand before the High Altar of HIS Presence, unclothed yet clothed upon; alone yet never alone; seemingly a solitary witnesser of that transcendent glory, and yet but a unit amid the Blessed Hosts; alone in consciousness for the time being, and yet never more alone because *the Soul there enters into the realization of oneness with the Father-Mother*. This is the Altar of the great Atonement—*The At-one-ment*. There are atoning acts along all the way. There are great atonements upon each Plane of consciousness, within each Sphere, within each Atmosphere, and within the Dimensions. Within that Sanctuary there are also degrees, each of which is an atoning act. There is in the consciousness such illumination that the correlation becomes perfect, according to the realm into which the Soul has entered. Thus it moves to the High Altar. And when it stands there, upheld by the Shepherdhood of I-o-seph the great Archbishop of Souls, *the real Divine Papal See;* and, on the other hand, nourished in all the tender attributes, by the gentle emotions and exquisite motions of a Divine order from the Divine Mother, then the Soul can accomplish its perfect Atonement.

THE TRINITY OF WORSHIP AND BLESSING

Now you may glimpse what those Altars stand for in the Churches. And in the vision you will see the almost infinite contrast between the reality and the outer show. Yet there is truth lying behind the earthly symbols. To repudiate the symbols does not mean that the truth has been discerned. No! To discern and hold the truth with an enlightened understanding, is for the truth to become part of the Being; and in such an experience there is an understanding of the endeavours of those who are seeking to get at some hidden meaning, though they know not even what they are seeking after. These are conscious of the spiritual motion within them, an inner urge after something they feel they should have, and know, and understand. But for you who have known so much, heard so much, received so much, there should be discernment that the symbols speak of those Altars which are within you. For you, there should be a coming up into HIS Sanctuary. There should be the Holy

Processional of your Being. That will not be anything ostentatious. The phenomena of the Soul are inward; the observed phenomena are Divine. For you there should be a motion to that High Altar unto the realization of all that it stands for. It is thither I would lead you that you may know the FATHER-MOTHER in the Fatherhood of I-o-seph, the Luminous Cross, The ADONAI; and in the Motherhood of the Divine Maria. In these are the Shepherdhood and the Motherhood of GOD. Through these in you, you should know that Sacred Mystery of the FATHER-MOTHER, and that that Mystery is within you, and is to be made manifest within you and through you.

O most Sacred Maria, Holy Mother! O most Sacred Ioseph, Divine Father! O most Blessed and most Holy LORD of Being, the ADONAI! Thus would we address the Presence at those Altars—at that of the Divine Maria, that our very Being may be full of the Motherhood of GOD unto Souls; that we may love divinely; that we may have the qualities in us of the Divine Mother, those Motherhood qualities of the Eternal, which are inexpressible; so that we can take to the bosom of our Love everyone who needs succour; not only those in lower estate, but those in higher estate who, nevertheless, need nourishing; that we may have the capacity to give unto the uttermost, even unto the bringing forth into manifestation of Our LORD, by living the Life of the LORD upon the earth, in the sweet tenderness of Love, in the outpouring of Love, in the immeasurable giving of Love! We would pray before the Altar of I-o-seph in the Divine World; for He is the radiant Shepherd, the One Who is Shepherd of our Being, Who leads us amidst the green pastures and by the waters of the Great Deeps of Being. For it is HIMSELF Who shepherds our attributes and overshadows our Life when we are consecrated to HIM. It is HIMSELF Who fills us with that energy by which we are able to express HIM through our attributes in active service unto HIS children. With all the resultant of such Shepherdhood and such Motherhood of Souls, we would stand before the High

Altar of our LORD, being for HIM in our degree shepherds and mothers, divine shepherds, divine mothers, Souls full of that divine yearning to constrain, to hold, to uplift, to bless; Souls full of Divine energy, ever seeking to radiate that energy as the glory of Our LORD. Before HIS High Altar would we stand, overshadowed by HIM, conscious of HIS Cherubim and Seraphim ministering unto us, and ministering through us for HIM.

BEFORE THE ALTAR OF HIS PRESENCE

Beloved ones! when will you realize something more of *the great realities of the Inner Sanctuary?* These fragmentary thoughts are broken unto you that they may help you to come into that realization, and that you may be once more the children of the Light, and able to interpret correctly and Divinely the things that are used upon the earth as symbols of the things which are in the Heavens.

Assuredly ye are related to that High Altar; for ye are children of the Luminous Cross, and of the Household of the Divine Maria. And as such, surely, you will understand the significance of such a Trinity in Altars, such a dual motion as the Fatherhood-Motherhood of GOD represented in those Altars! I would lift you into that Sanctuary where HIS Presence fills the whole Heavens with glory. I would have you not only witness the motion of Cherubim and Seraphim, but feel that motion within your Being. I would have you cognize even unto such cognition as would bring you recognition and realization of the glory of the Divine Shepherdhood of the FATHER-MOTHER, and His wondrous Motherhood. I would have you share in the motion of Cherubim and Seraphim, and the ministry of Angels in both high estate and the more lowly estates.

We stand now, in consciousness, within that Sanctuary. There is HIS High Altar, the Altar upon which is made the absolute oblation of the Soul. We stand before HIM canopied by HIS Overshadowing Presence, and receive the Light of HIS

ELOHIM from HIS Luminous Cross. We are crowned in our Love in this hour from the Divine Motherhood, that we may be regnant embodiments upon this earth for HIM Who is Love; for all HIS Children must be like HIM. To-day we stand in consciousness within HIS Sanctuary and enter into the great Reality; tomorrow we shall have to go down into the world to share in its burden of ministry. We would take with us the consciousness of HIS Presence, and express it as we go forth to minister in daily round, in the home, in the venues of business, in the school, and in the broad thoroughfares of the world. We would take with us the consciousness of HIS Overshadowing at that High Altar. We can always be before that Altar, even though serving in lowly estate in the world. If once we go there to stay, we are evermore there in consciousness. Therefore take with you the radiations from the glorious Luminous Cross, and let them pass through your own magnetic centre and be reflected and sent forth in most blessed reflections of HIM in manifestation and ministry; for thus will you testify of the Shepherdhood of our FATHER-MOTHER, and reveal and make manifest the Glory of the Renascent Redemption, and the Radiance shed by GOD's Renaissance.

O most Holy One, our Father-Mother, Lord of our Being, Whose Altars are in the Eternities and also in lowly estate within the Sanctuary of our Being; before Thee we bow! We would ever know Thee as our Shepherd, the glorious, Divine, Eternal I-O-SEPH. We would know Thee in Thy glorious Motherhood, in the Divine Maria estate wherein Thou canst dwell within the chalice of our Being unto making manifest the resplendence of Thy Mystery even through the daily round in our labours and our service. For thus would we Adore Thee in embodying these Altars of Thine; and Worship Thee in making all our activities a service for Thee; and Praise Thee in all the motion of our Life before Thy High Altar in our consciousness, and out through the various gates of the Sanctuary in active ministry unto Thy children. We would bear within ourselves Thy Holy

Motherhood of Souls, and upon ourselves the exquisite beauty of Thy Love. Thus would we be Thy children evermore in all our service, and in all our embodiment.

Ever blessed be Thy most glorious Name unto us, within us, and through us!

Ω ʽΑΓΙΑ ΜΑΡΙΑΜ
(O Holy Mary-Mother)

Ω ʽΑΓΙΕ ΙΩΣΗΦ
(O Holy Joseph-Father)

ʼΩ ΚΥΡΙΕ ʽΑΓΙΩΤΑΤΕ
(O Most Holy Lord)

PART IV

THE REALMS OF THE GODS

A DIVINE ORATORIO

THE MINISTRY OF THE GODS

THE DIVINE GOVERNMENT

THE MYSTERY OF PRAYER IN RELATION TO GOVERNMENT

THE COSMIC CONSCIOUSNESS

THE REGNANCY OF CHRIST

A NOTABLE THEOPHANY

A DIVINE ORATORIO

A DIVINE ORATORIO

(Suggested by the passage in the Book of Job, where it is said:—*The Morning Stars sang together and all the Sons of God shouted for Joy.*)

THE SONG OF THE SONS OF GOD

The title of this address seemed the most apt to express how the Morning Stars sang together, and the Sons of GOD cried aloud for very joy. The Oratorios with which we are familiar are reminiscent of Sacred Story. Usually it is such story as is found in the sacred books. It is easy to understand "The Elijah," because of its historical sketching of Religious Life. And "Judas Maccabeus" for a like reason. "Saul" likewise fascinates us because of the inweaving of apparent history and the outworking in a dramatic presentation of that history. And we can understand "The Messiah" in its outlining of the great pathetic and majestic Drama, with its tragic scenes and action, and its triumphant issue.

But in this Divine Oratorio, it is not so apparent what it was all about. What actually did happen? What was the reason for the Song? And how can we know what the subject-matter of it was? For, surely there is always joy in the Heavens of GOD. There is joy in the consciousness of Being. There is joy in ministry unto and for the Divine Love and Wisdom. There is joy in serving other worlds and individuals in any way for the Great Love.

Yet, as a prelude thought, there is given to us this hint, that they sang for joy because of something that was accomplished.

The Song is, therefore, reminiscent of some great history. That history is gathered up and hidden in the casket, like a most precious jewel. Job is represented as having been asked where was he when the foundations of the world were laid, and the balance given to the spiral of the Earth. And he is reminded that surely he knew of those things, and that the knowledge was the gift of GOD unto him. Also that at that time the Sons of GOD shouted, but not as men and women in their hilarity shout to one another. They cried aloud for Joy. Even the Stars sang.

* * * * *

We will look, first, at the subject-matter of their Song and their Rejoicing.

THE FASHIONING OF THE EARTH It was a great epoch in this world's history that called forth the Song. It was concerned with the fashioning of the Earth. There is Divine Joy in the Celestial Realms in their ministry by which creative acts are accomplished, and when that which has been created becomes manifest.

It was concerning this world that the Stars sang. It was in relation to a Divine Product, the resultant of glorious motion and action, that the Sons of GOD shouted for Joy.

There are great Ages gathered up into the simple phraseology of the saying—"when all the Morning Stars sang together, and all the Sons of GOD shouted for Joy." The sentence expresses a vast period. Yet the period had a culminating point wherein the Song reached its *finale*, and the triumphant notes rang forth in most glorious Alleluiahs and Halleluiahs—the joy of praise expressed unto GOD, and the proclamation of that joy of praise unto and through all the Heavens.

Men and women take it for granted that a world is fashioned. They think lightly of it. They are so accustomed to live on these planes that they receive the ministry of the world unconsciously. They have looked up into the heavens at night, to see the stars shining, without wondering how they all became manifest. They may think a little about the Planets as they behold one or more of them in the Celestial Heavens at the same time; but concerning the creation of a little world like this one, they do not think much.

Yet concealed within this wonderful passage, which is like a gem that has been hidden and is now brought forth to radiate the glory of God upon the world, there is a triumphant note and real joy expressed, wherein we may learn that the world creation meant something high and holy to those who took part in it.

The writers of the Psalms, and especially the writers of Psalms viii, xix, and civ, had a great conception of the Divine Immanence, the Overshadowing Presence, the potent motion revealed in the Handiwork of God; and how the glory of the Eternal Mystery is expressed in the fashioning of a world like this.

THE NEBULAR HYPOTHESIS If I were to speak to you along scientific lines concerning what has been thought possible in relation to the fashioning of a world like this, I would have to speak to you of the various theories which have been propounded. All of these are but endeavours to get at the heart of the great Secret. Sometimes a new theory is proclaimed and accepted, and held for a time as the true explanation. But later it is laid aside as inadequate. The one theory which is outstanding even to this day, and which was propounded by the great Astronomer, LAPLACE, is known as *the Nebular Hypothesis.* But this theory was known long, long before his day, though not expressed in the scientific language of modern usage.

This theory proclaimed that a world system was fashioned out of nebulous incandescent matter of *nebulae* through receiving motion by which at first it became concentrative and concentric; and that through this motion there were gathered into the heart or centre, the greater potencies and elements. And then there was given to the gathered nebula another motion. This gave to the nebula, eccentric and centrifugal motion. By this latter there was a gradual throwing off of parts. Then in the parts there was a repetition of the original motion; and each part became concentric, having a real centripetal motion, in which there was the gathering in of the elements, and a building up by means of them, which, in modern terms, meant a consolidating, followed by centrifugal action by means of which the planetary moons were fashioned.

It is thus the human mind has sought to explain the Sun as the centre of this system, and the various members supposed to have been thrown off from it.

Even the moons of the Planets have been considered as the children of the Planets to which the parent bodies minister, or from whom they derive ministry. The inner significance of this thought, of course, has not obtained in material science. It does not fill the outlook of science that Suns, Planets and Satellites, by a like procession of Elements in motion, came to be embodied expressions of the Eternal Mystery of Divine Ætheria and Spirit; that the Divine Ætheria is revealed in the embodiment; and the Divine Spirit in the motion and form.

THE METEORIC THEORY

It was a great conception of the origin of worlds to be put forth from a materialistic standpoint. But in later days Scientists found it inadequate to explain many things. Then another theory was introduced, equally remarkable. It was concentric, with the chief motion centripetal. It was named the Meteoric Theory. Its chief apostle was Richard Anthony Proctor.

It gathered in all the meteoric bodies, those smaller bodies in our system which had become solidified embodiments of the Divine Ætheria. Thus was the world supposed to have been built up. So, lying behind the thought of the Meteoric Theory, are to be found the vestiges of the history written in the meteoric stones which from time to time alight upon the earth. We pass through the congregations of these fragments of a one-time Planet, at different parts of the year. Especially during November do these meteoric bodies come like shooting stars. They have been named falling stars. Of course, they are not stars at all, but a stream of very small bodies moving round the Sun, and at times coming within the orbit of the earth.

These considerations of the two principal theories are just by the way; for they are wonderful projections of thought, with the endeavour to interpret and explain the mystery of the fashioning of a world like this.

THE VALUE OF BOTH THEORIES

The pronouncement of Laplace concerning the Nebular Hypothesis, seems a remarkable and wonderful discovery, which is true in its principle, although not in the materialistic concept of it. And Proctor's Meteoric Theory was equally marvellous; and it did seem to account for many things which were left unexplained by the Nebular Hypothesis.

GOD works by Law. HE operates through agencies. HE causeth the Breath to pass through the Divine Elements. HE works through that glorious Substance we have spoken of as Divine Ætheria, the most glorious embodiment of which (to the human eye, that is), may be seen in its translucent elemental state in the Milky Way of the Celestial Heavens.

The fashioning of this world was a most glorious ministry. There were no such things as meteoric stones in those days; but there was Divine Ætheria. The meteoric stones are the vestiges of a great Celestial calamity. Their motion through the earth's atmosphere wherein they become luminous, contributes to their passing out. Ultimately they will be dissipated and resolved back into their original Divine Elemental states.

The fashioning of this world was according to Divine Law. There was no chance in it. The Mind would be filled with wonder and awe if it had true vision and understanding. But then, surely, Souls who have been in Christhood do know inwardly the process by which a world like this becomes; how it is generated, fashioned, built up and clothed; how it receives its motion; what the Secret is that is at the heart of it, even the Divine Secret. It is said that the Secret of the LORD is with them that have HIS Holy Fear or Awe. For GOD speaks from the Innermost to a Human Soul. HE speaks out of the centre of the SPIRAL from amid the Sacred Seven. That is true in every world and in every system. It is also true in individual Celestial Beings. It is likewise true concerning the Human Soul. For it is through the Spiral that you can hear God. You cannot hear Him anywhere else, nor in any other way. It is through what is named "the whirlwind," the Spiral Motion. He is at the top of it. For He is the Alpha and the Omega. He is the Arche; and He becomes the Amen. He is the First and the Last, and the Perfecter.

In the World-Spiral also, He is the Arche; and He becomes the Amen, the consummator and consummation.

The fashioning of this world was, therefore, the fashioning of a most exquisite Celestial body; the giving to it of Divine estate because of its substance; and Celestial estate, because of its Status; and Spiritual estate, or the Angelic nature, because of the ministry it was to receive, and the ministry it had to render.

THE ESTATE OF THE EARTH

Thus the Earth was Divine, Celestial, and Angelic. It was an Angelic Sphere at one time. The Angelic Life obtained here. The Earth had two heavenly names, Judah and Ierusalem. The former spoke of her inherent Glory; the latter had relation to her household of Souls. For Judah signifies that which is glorious and full of Praise, and Ierusalem the City of perfect order (*peace*).

The subject-matter of the Song of the glorious Celestial Hosts spoken of as the Stars and the Sons of God, was the creation of the glorious Earth, when her foundations were laid deep in "the Great Deep," and perfect balance given to all the planes of the Spiral. As an individual member of the Celestial Hierarchy, the Earth was able to respond to the Centre in her motion, and could go forth on her mission of Soul-generation. Then the Heavenly Hierarchies sang their Divine Song, and the Sons of God shared in that triumphant Pæan.

The Stars are embodiments of the Divine Mystery for Divine Ministry. This world was fashioned for a beautiful

Hierarchy to minister through by means of its glorious Elements. Thus you may see the meaning of the Song.

All Divine motion makes harmony. The various orders of motion give combination. You have the simple song. You have the multiple song. You have the great Symphony of Divine Motion resulting from manifoldness. The Oratorio is the Soul's motion expressed in the articulate language of Being—of service, of joy, of praise, unto the FATHER-MOTHER.

When the Hierarchies looked upon the Earth, she was beautiful to behold. She was glorious within and without, an embodiment of the glory of the FATHER-MOTHER. So they sang their Song over her.

Why should not the Heavens rejoice over a piece of exquisite handiwork? Men rejoice over their handiwork when it is a small affair. Yet if it expresses that which is intricate, full of genius, expressive of beauty and truth, why should they not rejoice? It need not be in the boastful spirit begotten of pride, but rather in that they are able to execute a beautiful embodiment as a creation of their inspired genius.

Why should not the Heavens have joy over their work? They must have joy. The Heavens are full of joy over glorious creative embodiments and ministries.

DIVINE JOY AND DIVINE GRIEF

That the subject-matter of that Song was this world, it is hard to think. It is difficult to realize, in these days of travail and sorrow, the reality of that Celestial Choiring. The shadowed Earth obscures such Glory; for are not the dark shadows of the age-long night still lying athwart the world's threshold? It is difficult to realize there was ever such a Grand Chorale, when we read in Sacred Story concerning the Sorrow of the Heavens. For have not even the Prophets spoken of the Grief of GOD?

There are many who believe that there is no sorrow in the Heavens. This shows that they do not understand. There is all the difference in the world between having sorrow begotten of one's own mistakes, and a sorrow which is grief over the mistakes of others. We have, oft-times, had to speak to you of the sorrow of the Heavens. There are those who cannot bear to hear of it. Some will not have it that it is possible. Such an attitude of mind reveals that the objectors do not know the Inner Heavens.

If the Heavens can rejoice, they can grieve. Grief is begotten of great Love when a world or individual Soul suffers through wrong states. Do you think the Sons of GOD who shouted for joy, never knew any sorrow? Verily they have known great sorrow. They have been the children of sorrow in this world for many ages, because of the fallen states of Ierusalem.

But they are to be again children of joy. That is the triumphant note of the Angelic Song. Oh, we shall hear again that Grand Oratorio begotten of the motion of the Celestial Hierarchy, that glorious up-built Song of Praise unto the FATHER-MOTHER, sung by Mazzaroth, the whole Zodiac whose chief ministries have to do with the fashioning, and the nourishing, and the upholding, and the enriching of worlds!

Truly that Oratorio was of the Music of HIS Spheres. Oh, that you could hear again this Song of the Sons of GOD, sung over this world! It was a Song of delight, even as is said in the song we sometimes hear sung for us so beautifully, "The Holy City," with Ierusalem a delight, and her children a Joy; Ierusalem beautiful as a Spiritual Household, and all her children clothed with the garments of heavenly childhood.

Their Song was sung over this world, whose deep foundations had been laid, and whose motion was shedding the Divine glory. They were full of the delight of it and the splendour of it. They rejoiced in the dignity expressed in the equipoise of it, and in the garments with which the whole land of Judah in its various planes was clothed. In every degree of the Spiral of its Being there was the revealing of the Majesty of the FATHER-MOTHER, HIS wondrous Love, and HIS glorious Wisdom.

Whatever men and women think of this world to-day, there was a time when the Heavens did rejoice in it with such songs, even unto the laughter of delight. For in the Heavens you may hear the laughter of real delight proceeding from the Sons of God, and even from the Gods!

Such is a passing glimpse of the subject-matter of that wondrous Song. It was resonant of the Divine Mystery. That Divine Mystery was revealed in the substance and motion of the Planet-Soul. The Song proclaimed the Love of the Father-Mother in all things, how His marvellous Wisdom was revealed in all His Creations. It spake of Ierusalem as a world that was a Praise of God.

* * * * *

THE STARS THAT SANG FOR JOY

Now I would lead your thoughts to the consideration of Celestial Hierarchies.

Who sang the Song which the Sons of God shared in? What were those Stars? We know what a Star is in the ordinary nomenclature of the day. There is the physical scientific definition of it. But when you see things from the Inner World, even the Stars take on quite a different aspect in the vision and to the understanding.

Stars are accounted great worlds. They vary in their greatness according to stature. They also vary in their estate and the degree of their ministry. But concerning Life in the Divine, there is no such thing as greatness as understood on the earth planes. The real greatness is in state. And although the Stars vary in the degree of their embodiment, and in their state and their ministries, they are all great. And they are also all lowly. The least is great as the greatest, and the greatest is lowly as the least. It were well that the Children of the Kingdom remembered this great truth.

Who were those Stars? The term is not only stellar in meaning, but is oft-times applied to Divine Christ-Souls, and therefore, in the innermost sense, to what we have to call Solar

Embodiments. Herein is a great Mystery; because the Stars, or Suns, are not at all what they seem to be. They are spheres citizened by great and glorious Beings who minister through them, mediating of the Eternal Mystery unto other worlds. They may thus be known to be centres of ministry unto other members of the Heavenly Hierarchies.

I have indicated to you that the Stars referred to who sang the Song were the systems called Mazzaroth, or the Zodiac. But more than that. They have been shown to be glorious Beings who ministered through those systems unto the Earth over whom they sang their Song.

It is very difficult for some to think of such exalted states of consciousness. Yet a Human Soul, though it does seem so lowly in comparison, so insignificant, has such capacity within itself that it can rise into those exalted heights wherein it can understand all things related to those realms. For it is possible for a Soul to grow Divine in consciousness; to gather into itself the potencies which, when fully unfolded, enable it to be one with all the systems; aye, to rise on to the Divine Kingdom and be one with even that Sacred Mystery behind all systems, that Mystery we name the FATHER-MOTHER. It is easier to think personally of great embodiments, than it is to think impersonally and divinely. It is natural for the mind to think of a great one in human form, as a great person. The great Ones of whom I speak, have glorious forms. They assume them. According to the nature and degree of the ministry, so is the form assumed by them. And the most transcendent of all forms (apart from that of the Sacred Mystery) is that named the Human Form, of which more hereafter.

I would have you understand something of the real nature of the glorious Ones on those systems. When you look up into the Heavens, I would have you remember again what those systems are, and the nature of the ministry which they render; also their Celestial character, and the Divine characteristics of those who minister by means of them. I would have you hold sacred in your memory those who are ministrants upon those systems, for they are glorious Beings. I would have you realize that though we be so lowly in our estate upon this Earth, yet we have the like potencies, the same Divine Ætheria, and are sharers of the same glorious Pneuma. That the same Divine Substance and Breath are within ourselves, I would have you hold as the most sacred doctrine; and that the glorious FATHER-MOTHER hath given to us Divine Power which enables us to apprehend those who are in such exalted estate, and even to understand the world-embodiments through which they have to accomplish their great and glorious Divine, Celestial, and Angelic ministry. I would have you remember that when you look at the Sun you are not looking at a physical body, a mere globe of incandescent elements; and that you should greet him divinely when he shines.

I would have you think of the Sun as a world full of the most glorious Divine Potencies; a world containing the Sacred Mystery of the FATHER-MOTHER; a world which is the Home of most glorious Beings who are in Staral or Divine Christhood estate.

I would have you think of the Sun as a Home of the marvellous Angelic ministries through Celestial motion and magnetic outpourings, and a Home of the Sons of GOD.

And if you are able to so think of it, you can say to yourself, *I am a child of that Sun. I have the like potencies in me.*

The glory that is there is in me. Though it be in lowly estate in me, yet is it the same glory.

The Mystery of the Sun is in me. Though I am a lowly embodiment, apparently, and it is a great embodiment, because it numbers ten thousand times ten thousand, and thousands of thousands of Angelic Beings, yet I am of them. In the Mystery of my Fashion I am like them, having the same Sacred Mystery hidden in the Spiral of my Being. I have within myself the like qualities which I recognize in their ministry, which are also to be called forth into manifestation, and to be freely given in ministry.

O glorious Sun! We do worship thee. But not as a physical embodiment. We worship HIM Whom thou dost reveal and express. O glorious Sun! When we think of thee, it is to HIM the thoughts of our Mind and the Love of our Heart bow in worship. In thee it is HIMSELF we see, in the Mystery of HIS Substance and Spirit and glorious motion, revealing HIMSELF through all the magnetic outpourings in thy ministries, and in all the potencies and the gifts which HE doth give unto this stricken Earth, and unto the Earth's children, through thee!

THE GLORY OF A SON OF GOD

Yea, more than that; surely still more than that. If ye have known aught of the Song of the Sons of GOD, ye will also know that unto those who are of that Sonship, the Sun ministers in a direct way; in a way in which it cannot yet minister unto the children of this world. For it could not give in the same measure unto the children of this world, of those potencies which it is able to impart to the Sons of GOD.

Therein lies the Divine Secret which is theirs, the secret of their capacity to receive and appropriate and grow up into Divine stature. Men and women seem oblivious of the fact that the Soul's possible stature is immeasurable. They forget there is a stature beyond the outer form. The outer form has, of necessity, certain limitations to its growth according to the ministry to be rendered by the individual, although there is a very real sense in which renewal goes on daily and hourly. But the stature to which a Human Soul may grow is of Divine Measure. Even the term Divinity is comparative. And a Soul can learn to acquire the power to function on the Divine World, gaining increase of strength in its potencies for functioning more fully, gathering into itself the potencies for upbuilding, and then from itself pouring forth that which has been ingathered. For this is the end of Life. We receive from the Divine for our upbuilding to Divine Stature. Herein comes the power to receive unto Divine Measure, and unto the measure in which there is to be a giving out in blessed ministry.

Now you will understand how the dwellers in the Sun sang for joy when they saw this glorious world. And you may now know that that Song was reminiscent of other days.

Hark! For the Herald Angels sing. They now sing of the new Creation that is coming. This they have often sung. We have heard their song on many occasions when it has been a song of great hope. The song of the Heavens over this world has for great ages been not only minor, but it has been full of sorrow. For you can have the minor without sorrow. It may be that you are not able to receive this truism. But it is not difficult to receive such when once you know the inner significance of the minor. You naturally wonder whence the minor came, if not out of sorrow. It is not unnatural for the heart so to think.

The trend of this world is back to GOD, and upward again in states. If you could hear the tones begotten of its motion, you would know that though it is yet far from home, it is journeying thitherward. Bye and bye will be heard that Song which the Sons of GOD sang, and in the singing of which they shouted for joy. Now they sing songs of hope prophetic of the Restoration. Their whole Being cries aloud. Even with them, language is quite inadequate to express what they see, and feel, and anticipate.

You must have felt like that many a time, as if all language, even in the most beautiful song, were too utterly inadequate to express what you have seen and felt, and the ministry you have desired to give of Blessing and Praise, Worship and Adoration.

THE SONS OF CELESTIAL ESTATE

But who were these Sons of GOD referred to, who sang their Song? They are oft-times named in Sacred Story; not only the sacred book held in the western world as the Bible, but in other sacred books, and in occult philosophy. There has been an inner consciousness that some such Beings did once minister unto this world, and visit this world to become dwellers upon it. It is believed that at first they were different from the children of this world, like the Immortals of Mythology; and then, in order to exalt the children of this world, they entered into union with them. That means, that they became like the Human Children, who were the Mortals of Greek Myth.

Now, the Sons of GOD were those glorious children of GOD of whom I have frequently spoken to you. They were the Elect People who were sent here to minister. They had accomplished in great degree their own growth and evolution upon another system. They had various terms applied to them.

In Old Testament Story they are called "Sons of God," "Children of Israel," "Children of Zion," "The Elect People," "The Peculiar People of God," "The Communal Priesthood," "A Nation of Mediators."

But in other times they were spoken of as "The Sons of Love," "The Sons of Wisdom," "The Sons of Light." Those of them who were named the Sons of Love, were so called because Love was the special potency revealed through them in their embodiment and ministry. Those of them who were known as the Children of Wisdom, were so named because they all knew the Divine Wisdom, some, of course, in greater degree than others. For the Children of Love were also the Children of Wisdom, but being what they were in their nature, they were called the Children of Love, because Love was the dominating quality in their embodiment and ministry. The Children of Wisdom were those who had specially to interpret the Divine Wisdom. They were the Celestial Children who brought many of the real Arts and Crafts in the most ancient days. They taught the children of this world the Divine way of Art in its spiritual significance. Indeed, there was no other significance present to the thought of the Sons of GOD, nor given, nor implied in any teaching to the children of this world whom they taught. They brought the knowledge of the Sciences. These Sciences were all spiritual, because the knowledge which those Sons of Wisdom held, was an interior knowledge begotten of their consciousness of the Divine Overshadowing and their illumination from the Inner World. They knew because they were Sons of GOD. For Sonship is a state. It represents a high degree of consciousness which the Being has realized, and which all who would be Sons of GOD must attain through ingathering and giving, upbuilding and enriching, embodying and manifesting, and sacrificing, *till the Sacrifice is Divine.*

Others were named Sons of Light, because it was their special province to radiate Light. That Light is Divine auric glory. They were assumed to be the Children of Ra—the God of the Sun. Is it not wonderful how that old mystery-name for GOD,—Ra, is associated with the Divine Radiance, and related to the Sun who is the Radiant Lord in this system, from whom all glory proceedeth, even in a Spiritual, Celestial and Divine Order?

Now those Sons of GOD, some of them Sons of Love, of Wisdom, and of Light, came here as GOD'S "peculiar people." They were HIS "elect people," for they were elected to come. They came as GOD'S ambassadors to minister. They were asked to come. They rejoiced to come. They sang for joy. Who would not sing for joy when they receive a Divine Commission? An artist rejoices when commissioned to execute some exquisite work. Why should not those who are sent on the most wondrous mission, even that of the upbuilding, the illumining, and the enriching of Souls, sing for joy? So they came as Joy-children. They sang a pæan of Praise unto GOD for HIS Goodness in asking them to undertake such a ministry. They came to this world that was beautiful, and they had joy in it; joy in giving to its children; joy in their ministry; joy in giving of all the gifts they had received, and in teaching Souls concerning the Great Love.

THE SONG OF THE HEAVENS

It was a blessed time in those far-away days. And if we have travailed through great centuries and known other songs than those of joy and gladness, yet there are surely memories of those days. It was no vain dream of the poetic Soul when it conceived of the Golden Age, the unfallen days. Nor is it any vain hope begotten within the poetic Soul to-day, who dreams and sings his dream of a living hope wherein he sees the motion of this world to be forward to the time when Eden shall be restored, and the Edenic state be realized. The prophetic promise fills the Soul, that the glory of Ierusalem in the latter days shall be equal to its glory in the former times; when the Sons of GOD shall be again able to sing for very joy.

Why should we not have something of that Song to-day upon the Earth-planes? It is being sung, in part, in the Heavens. The Stars are again singing. The Celestial and Divine motion is full of gladness over the coming Redemption of Ierusalem and the return of Judah. They rejoice that the time has come when it is possible to so minister to this world that the ultimate Redemption of all its children and its elements, is fully assured. Thus the grief of the Heavens passes and Divine Joy cometh. For, by means of the marvellous ministries of the FATHER-MOTHER through HIS Celestial Hierarchies unto HIS Sons in their travail; and because of that last great expression of the Divine Love in its Travail for the whole world wherein it was made possible for all the Sons of GOD who are on these planes, to return into the consciousness of their Ancient Sonship to HIM; their Redemption and Regeneration are assured. For such is the expected and fitting resultant of *the Travail of the Oblation* wherein the Planetary Heavens were purified. And because of all these things, the Heavens rejoice. They call to all the Sons of GOD upon the Earth to rejoice with them, to be full of divine hope, and to let that hope express itself in a yet more beautiful motion and service, till Life becomes expressive and interpretive of the Divine Motion and the Divine Purpose.

The Stars sing their Divine Song. Their motion is

Symphonic. The Sons of God are asked to shout for Joy. And why should we not have that note of joy to-day? True, the world is still full of travail. It is full of the motion of contrary things. It is shadowed by tragedy in its unfinished drama. Yet it is also full of Divine Motion within its potencies, and this is working unto redemption and great healing. Through the Celestial Hierarchies there are the ministries of the Stars. Through the Regeneration there is the ministry of the Sons of God sent unto the Earth. In the Beyond there is ministry through the Angelic World; and now, at last, upon the Earth there is the beginning, through the ministry of the Sons of God upon these planes, of this Angelic ministry; and also through every Soul full of divine nobility, who glimpses the glory of the Divine Life, who knows within himself or herself that there is nought to live for, nothing worth living for, but the revealing of the Divine Mystery in a beautiful embodiment of it in Life. For the call of the Heavens unto the Sons of God upon the Earth is for the exposition of that Mystery, through making use of all Life's potencies, all Life's activities, all Life's attributes, in blessed service unto Him. And through every Soul so thinking, so loving, so feeling, so living, and so embodying and serving, the Heavens are healing and restoring the world.

THE REALIZATION OF THE SONG'S PROPHECY

The Redemption is thus proceeding, and the world is coming back to the beautiful Life. The Sons of God are asked once more to respond to the ministry of the Stars. The ministry of the Stars is a ministry of God unto them. "The Stars in their courses" work for the Sons of God. It is the ministry of all that is Divine, all that is Angelic, all that is of His Love and Wisdom unto the re-embodying of Him.

The Sons of God are called upon to praise the Lord. How? In the motion of their Being. It is the only true way to praise Him. And we may do this in the songs of praise we love to sing concerning Him, but very specially in the rhythmic outflow of Love.

They are asked to recognize that in everything HE lays the foundations that are sure; and that there are no foundations that are sure, if they be not laid by HIM. The foundations are laid after the order of Divine Law, and by means of the Motion of HIS glorious Ministrants. They are asked to recognize HIM in everything that is beautiful and true; and to be equipoised in their thought, and to strive to embody HIM in everything.

Why should I speak of anything that is true and beautiful, as if they were apart from HIM? All truth is in HIM and from HIM; all beauty is but the revealing of that truth. Why should I fail to recognize HIM in what are considered the substantial things of life, in the beauty of the flowers, in the exquisite beauty of Life truly lived? Why should I fail to recognize HIM in the ministries of HIS children, in all their loving and lovely acts, in their noble purpose, in their sweet giving, in their sublime sacrifice?

I see GOD in all these things. HE is inseparable in me from all things that are worthy of me, of my thought and my desire, of the compass of my vision and the purpose of my ministry, of my touch and my blessing.

My friends, would you hasten the world back to the day when the Stars shall sing together again in that grand *finale*, that triumphant Halleluiah Chorus? Would you share in the glorious accomplishment of a world brought Home, a world healed in its state; and all its children once more made beautiful in their desires, in their vision, in their purpose, in their Love, in their ministry; and when this earthly Ierusalem shall be like the heavenly, full of Angelic children, beautiful for situation, that is, beautiful in their radiance, in their auric outflow; beautiful in their fashion, and radiant with the glory of the Life that garments them? Then the world shall again be the Home of Angel-children, Beings Celestial and Divine in nature, reaching up even unto the Divine Estate wherein the most sacred and glorious Mystery of our FATHER-MOTHER becomes known.

Behold, O Sons of Love, and Wisdom, and Light! O Sons of God in whom the Staral Motion is with glorious potencies for ministry! Is there anything else worth attaching value to, or worth considering living for? Is there anything worthy of being held by you, outside of this glorious relationship wherein is oneness with the Heavens even whilst ye are dwellers upon the Earth?

The Song of the Stars and the Sons of God in the Heavens is sung for you. The Celestial Hierarchies send their streams unto you. Children of Love and Wisdom and Light, children of the Sun, Children of the Heavenly Hierarchies, ye are His Children upon the earth-planes for blessed ministry. The Song is sung again to fill you with Divine Hope; to bring back to you the old Joy; to re-awaken in you the Blessed Vision, that, through the re-awakening, His power, as of old, may come back to you, and have motion within you of high Praise and Blessing; and that the service which is the high Worship of Him, and the glorious Adoration of Him expressed in embodiment the most exquisite, shall once more be yours.

THE MINISTRY OF THE GODS

THE MINISTRY OF THE GODS

THE ASSEMBLY OF THE GODS

The LORD GOD is ONE and there is none beside HIM. HE is the Supreme Mystery of Being, the FATHER and the MOTHER WHO filleth all things. But in that filling of all things, HE has not only deeply hidden the Mystery of Being, but HE has purposed that through all things HE should be mediated, expressed, and embodied.

Therefore all the Gods are HIS Mediators in the Realm to which they belong, in the Spheres to which they have been appointed, in the ministries unto which they have been called, and in the order of mediation for which they have been enriched.

"Great is the LORD GOD in the Assembly of the Gods," wrote an Ancient in one of the Psalms. And the greatness of the LORD in the Assembly of the Gods is HIS regnancy in them and through them. For they are embodiments of HIS glory, and of HIS wondrous Mystery. They are all HIS servants, revealers, interpreters and manifestors, and, therefore, HIS messengers in the Realm to which they are appointed for the mediation of HIM.

Mediation obtains throughout the Universe. The Gods mediate unto all Souls. The combination of their ministries is an unification of those potencies which are in motion from out the heart of the Eternities for the generation, the fashioning, the enrichment, the elevation of Souls within all the Realms.

Therefore, the Gods are the LORD's Servants. And they take the term "Gods," not because they are, as individuals, individually a God in the sense in which we apply that term to the Ever Blessed ONE WHO moveth amongst all the Gods. They are such because of the high estate in consciousness and potency which has become theirs, an estate wherein they are one with HIM WHO is the LORD. They are Gods because they are Divine and Celestial embodiments of that which the term "God" means, *viz.*, the Eternal Good. And the embodiment of Eternal Good in each varies in the degree of their realization, even as all Souls do in the degree of their embodiment, manifestation and mediation. But they are all for GOD, wherever appointed. It is thus they are spoken of as "the Gods."

Even of the Children of Israel it was said (in order to recall to their remembrance), "Said I not unto you that ye shall be as Gods?"

This Divine Idea was begotten within the Being through the motion of the Eternal; for the Soul was meant to reach such an exalted Estate in its consciousness and potencies. But the betrayer made use of this latent inherent motion to urge the Soul to seek the attainment of such an inheritance in a way that was contrary to the Divine Law.

Mediation, therefore, goes on through all the Realms. As I have said to you elsewhere, the heavens are built up numerically and geometrically. But the numbers and geometrical arrangements involved are all expressed and manifested through the motion of what we term Mediation. You cannot get away from Divine Motion expressed in ministry. GOD is mediated everywhere. Wherever Good is given, it is mediated.

THE MEDIATION OF THE GODS It is well to have this idea clearly understood. The Gods mediate unto us. But they never take the place of the Eternal Mystery. They mediate unto us to nourish that Mystery within us. We can cognize the Eternal Good as we recognize it in the Gods; but we only *realize* it for ourselves. They reveal to us the embodiment of the FATHER-MOTHER. They sing their song in the motion of their ministry. In that song they reveal the ELOHIM. The ELOHIM reveal the FATHER-MOTHER.

But the Soul, though it comes to know the Gods, to feel their ministry, to be conscious of their motion, and understand it so as to share in it and become one with the heavenly ministrants; yet for itself the Soul has to enter into the cognition of the Divine Mystery. All that the higher mediation can do for the Soul is to mediate unto it, giving it enrichment.

But the individual Being has to *realize* within himself the Divine Mystery.

The Gods are the Celestial embodiments and messengers of the ELOHIM; and there are many. Indeed, the whole Celestial Hierarchy may be spoken of as the Systems of the Gods, the glorious Hierarchy expressing the Divine Mystery, Divine Motion, Divine Purpose. They are the Divine Creative Expositions of the Divine Idea.

There are those who might be spoken of as Archangels and Angels. They are as Gods.

There is Gabriel, the Illuminator of the Being. He is the Divine Annunciator. And he is also Hermes within the Soul's system, bringing light to the Understanding.

But when Gabriel calls the Soul, He calls not only through its understanding, but through the very Being itself. He calls it into the consciousness of the Indwelling Presence. He foreshadows and foretells the Incarnation. He affirms to the Soul that that which shall be begotten within it, though lowly in the first degrees of its manifestation, shall be none other than the Mystery itself—the Mystery of the Blessed Presence.

There is also Michael. Michael is the Might of GOD (as the word means); he reveals the majesty of the FATHER-MOTHER. He is as a God. He is for GOD, embodying HIS all-potency. He interpreteth in his motion the Omnipotence that overcometh all things. Therefore, in a fallen world like this, He has the power to lay hold on the old Dragon and chain him. This is allegorical as well as apocalyptic. It is he who so changes the conditions, that the dragon is cast out; by that is meant the false states. He has the power to send the dragon and the beast, and the beast that spake like a lamb but had the purpose of the dragon, into the bottomless pit, the abyss, where there is found no more the material with which to lay any foundation wherever to build upon. Thus Evil in its triumvirate, goes out. That is the idea presented in the hieroglyph of the Apocalypse.

It is Michael who is the GOD-appointed Archangel; who, in the might of his glorious potency, overthrows the dragon, the oppressive spirit; and the beast—the sensualising powers; and the false prophet—the false interpretations of GOD and Life; and the beast that spake like the Lamb but acted like the dragon—the persecuting religious mind.

THE MINISTRY OF THE GODS TO THE MESSENGERS

The Gods minister to all the Messengers. Whilst it is ever true that the Messenger is the servant of the Lord, and HIS servant alone, yet the LORD of Being ministers unto HIS Messengers in any age and in any world, through the Gods. The Celestial Hierarchies are media for HIM. This will become clearer to you presently.

Therefore a Messenger is not alone. He may be alone on the outer planes. He generally is very much alone, for few understand him. Only those can understand him, in some degree, who apprehend the significance of the Message, and respond to it. Entering into the spirit of the Message, they enter into that for which it stands—the Life, and the Vision, and then the Realization. But the Messenger is so constituted that he could not endure, but for the mediation of the Divine magnetic ministry through the Gods. The ministry is special in such an instance. This you will understand more fully as the unveiling proceeds.

The Soul who would be Messenger of GOD in the innermost sense, the mediator of HIS Mystery through Message and Embodiment, must know the Gods. He must be in touch with them. Indeed, that one must have all the potencies within the Being which will respond to the motion resulting from the mediation of those glorious Hierarchies. He will be in a state to understand the Mystery of the Gods, and, therefore, to receive the Divine Love and Wisdom mediated by them unto the upholding of his Life, the guarding of his Life; though the direction of Life given unto him, and the illumination of his innermost Being, are from the LORD of Being alone, the Indwelling ONE.

The Gods mediate through the Messenger that which they have to communicate from the Ever Blessed ONE. The Message is communicated unto the Messenger. But his realizations are in the Secret Place; for it is there all his Illumination comes from the FATHER-MOTHER.

(These things would be most difficult for the multitude to understand; and, indeed, even for those who do not belong to what is termed the multitude, yet who have no interior illumination.)

It is thus that through the Messengers of GOD, even the powers and ministries of the Gods can be expressed. They can be revealed, and interpreted, and manifested. It is beyond all mere human energy and strength of endurance, to bear the focussing into the Being of the Divine Mystery, in such high estate, and measure so great, that the Sublime Mystery can be unveiled, revealed and interpreted.

Thus, the Gods minister to the Messenger, strengthening and upholding him whilst he is mediating for the Great Love.

There are ministries that could not possibly be rendered upon these fallen planes of this distraught world, but for the Divine mediation given through the Gods unto the servant who is the medium and the mediator of the Message. *It is in this way that a Soul can become a Divine Messenger of the Most High. Through being dynamically raised in state, in consciousness, in potencies, in elements, in substance,* the Soul is so strengthened that the whole Being is able to receive the necessary measure of power, which, if the Messenger were in a less degree of Realization, would overwhelm the Life.

THE GODS AND ANCIENT ISRAEL

Now this is a prelude to other things I would say to you.

In ancient times, in the world of the Ancient of Days, before any shadows fell upon the threshold of this world, or the system of which it is a sorrowing member, the Children of Israel had been chosen to be for GOD in this world. Individually each was to be an embodiment of GOD, and, as a corporate community of the Gods. It was thus they were all, in some degree, of Celestial estate. Had they not attained so high a status of Life, they could not have endured the full ministry of the Gods within the Celestial Realms.

The Gods had ministered unto them for countless ages. There is no time in those Realms, yet we have to speak of things after the manner of time. This is difficult when one is thinking within the world where there is no time. And yet there is a procession of potencies and motions, events and manifestations, acquisitions and embodiments, ascensions and attainments. It is just that the Soul is not under the limitations that it is here, by that which we speak of as time. But everything in the Divine and Celestial Realms is regulated. Therefore, do not imagine for one moment that, because there is no such thing as time through the rotary motion of the world, there is no regulation. There is perfect regulation. There is perfect harmony there. There is Divine Order through all the Hierarchies. The Eternal Mystery is mediated in an orderly fashion through the Celestial Hierarchies; and also through those Divine Embodiments that may be spoken of as High Priests of God. For all mediation is priestly, even to the lowliest degrees of it upon the Earth.

As has so often been said to you, no one can make a priest. You might as well just fashion an image from a block of marble and call that a priest. No man can make a priest. The whole ecclesiastical idea of priesthood is an inversion of the Divine Idea and Office. For priesthood is a state within the Being. And every Soul is called unto it, must know it, understand it, and realize it. But long before it is known as such, and understood as such, and realized even in the lowly degrees, the Soul learns priestly motion and action through its beautiful acts of mediation.

In those far-away days, whither in flight I would bear you, Israel knew the Divine. They were called to be venues for the ministries of the Gods; and, as a corporate body, to be as God in this world. And as such a body they were the Illuminati of the LORD of Love, understanding HIM, knowing HIS Holy Purpose and outcarrying it. Great were their realizations. In intimate ways they knew the LORD. It was the intimacy begotten of the knowing of HIM as the Indwelling ONE. And because of their recognition of HIS Indwelling, and their realization of it in high degree, they were able to receive of the ministries of the Gods.

THE NAMES OF THE HOUSES OF ISRAEL

Now you should understand that the names of the Houses of Israel, were names which embodied the ministry of the Gods. The names not only denoted the qualities which characterized the whole of the Houses of Israel, but they also denoted the ministries of the Gods. Thus, each name of the Tribes of Israel represented one of the Zodiacal Signs.

Now the Zodiac includes twelve great constellations. The constellations are embodiments of the Divine Mystery. They minister of that Mystery in a special way. So intimately related are the Zodiacal Constellations to the whole Planetary evolution, that a Human Soul passes through all the Signs every day, as we have heretofore indicated to you in speaking somewhat of these Mysteries. For, on an average, in each day every Soul passes for some two hours through each one of the Signs. In the rotary motion the twelve Signs are thus rapidly passed through. They are not passed through as in the Planetary revolutary motion, and in a spatial sense; but in a less intense form the Soul receives the play of their magnetic forces, as these fall on the Planet for some two hours.

Then every year the Planet moves, in another sense, amidst those Signs. It receives into its vortex the magnetic currents which those Signs pour forth as God-embodiments. For every part of the Earth is under the direct magnetic influence of a Sign of the Zodiac for one month. And during that period Souls are receiving ministry from the various Gods.

In a yet higher sense it is said that we, as a system, pass through those same Signs owing to a Solar motion, which it is computed covers some twenty-four thousand years in the passage of the circle, so that one of the Signs, specially and magnetically, dominates the system for about two thousand years.

Thus, as illustration, during the whole historical development of Christianity, we are supposed to have been under the Sign of Pisces—that Mystery-term with which the Master known as Jesus Christ, became associated. For He was known as the Fish—the Mystery. And two fishes are the outer form of the Sign of Pisces.

To-day we are said to be in the Sign of Aquarius, the man with the watering pot. And this is taken as the symbol of Divine outpouring. What is being outpoured? If there be any meaning in it at all, what is it? Surely, it is the Divine Energy through the ministry of the Gods. It is the baptism of the ministry of those Gods who comprise the system known as, and related to, Aquarius.

These are fragmentary thoughts only, for we are not able to give more in passing. Elsewhere a fuller explanation is given. But they will help you to understand more fully something of the wonder of the Mystery of the FATHER-MOTHER in HIS sublime creation in glorious manifestations and mediations, even unto HIS ancient people, the Children of Israel. For, as the Gods minister to the Messengers, so do they likewise minister in some degree unto Israel; and also to this world.

Israel had passed through the Zodiac many times. The whole House of Israel had drunk into itself of the majestic potencies which those Systems magnetically sent forth. They were, therefore, prepared to be the vehicles individually, and as a corporate body, of all the qualities represented by the Gods; and especially, to be the vehicles of the outpouring of those Heavens to which we have referred more particularly in relating the Zodiacal Signs to the twelve names of the Houses of Israel.

THE TWELVE SIGNS OF THE ZODIAC

We will name the twelve Signs of the Zodiac lest there be any here unfamiliar with them. As boys and girls, some of you may remember learning this form of naming the Signs:—

The Ram, the Bull, the Heavenly twins,
And next the Crab the Lion shines,
The Virgin and the Scales,
The Scorpion, Archer, and He-goat,
The man who bears the Watering Pot,
And Fish with glistening scales.

Aries, Taurus, Gemini, Cancer, Leo, Virgo, Libra, Scorpio, Sagittarius, Capricorn, Aquarius, Pisces.

Now, Aries is no doubt taken as the first sign for several reasons, one of which may be, because it is generally associated with the time of the vernal equinox. For, astronomically, the Sun enters the sign Aries as the equinox begins. Yet I should say we enter Aries in the very middle of the equinox. For this latter covers three weeks.

Now, all those terms relate to Celestial and Divine things. It is remarkable that, according to the method of expression in the human thought, in the procession of the twelve Signs, we should begin with Aries and end with Pisces.

But this is also remarkable, that in the procession of the Signs relating to the Sun's motion, we begin with Pisces and move through them all to Aries. We were under the Sign of Pisces during the historical development of Christianity, since the days of the Manifestation until the year 1914;[1] in which year we entered, celestially, the Sign Aquarius. It is remarkable that there should seem to be a procession in one direction of a Solar, and a procession in the other direction of a stellar order. Of course, it is only apparent. We all begin in Pisces in the midst of the great Twofold Mystery of the FATHER-MOTHER,

[1] In 1881 the Piscarian Age drew to a close, followed by the interlude of 33 years ere Aquarius was entered into—1914. This is the year in which "The Master: His Life and Teachings" was first published in a volume.

which Pisces represents. And the coming of the Master and the manifestation of the Christhood in that Sign, were celestially significant. It is said that He came in the "fulness of time." That meant celestial arrangement; but also the preparation through the Heavens of manifold conditions which had to be provided. And more than that. It was the time when it became possible to follow the manifestation with the taking up of the Burden of the Oblation.

* * * * *

ARIES, THE MESSENGER

In order that you may understand the significance and the grandeur of this mediation of the Gods unto Israel through Mazzaroth, we would say to you that, taking them in the procession in which the human mind generally arranges them, Aries is the first, and represents the Lamb of GOD. In the interior of the Being, Aries is the Lamb of GOD. It is the Divine Mystery of Love. Coming forth into manifestation it is the Ram. Now, Rama or Ramah is the Messenger. And Rama is the Kingdom of the Divine Love in the Heavens of a Human Soul. This is true of every Soul who is growing, though it does not become within the consciousness of the Soul for great ages.

But unto Israel Rama was well known. He was no man, but the Messenger of the Highest. And in the Divine Principle of the Soul, it is thus that Aries becomes the Mystery of the Love of GOD in its sacrificial capacity. Aries is both Lamb and Ram. In the Majesty of its manifestation in the higher Realms, it is Rama passing through the intermediary realms wherein it gains power for administration. And this is carried through even to the outer planes. The children of Aries are great administrators, speaking of them in a general way. They have the capacity for mediation in a public capacity. Because of this quality, they should be in high-priesthood.

The next sign is Taurus. This sign is looked upon as earthly. It is thought of as having special reference to the body and mind. But the earthly interpretation is an inversion of the Divine Idea.

THE MAJESTY OF TAURUS

In astrology, Taurus is associated with the bull, and most people think they know what the bull stands for. They do not think it is beautiful. It is quite true, that, on the outer planes, and in an unredeemed state, the Taurian is mischievous. That is because the potencies within the Being are of such an order that, uncorrelated, and lacking perfect polarisation, there is inharmonious motion on the outer planes.

But in the Inner Life of the Soul, that which Taurus signifies is the strength of Divine Majesty, the solidarity of the Life as an immovable rock, like the Rock of Ages. A redeemed Taurian is a most faithful friend forever. Of course, everyone redeemed would be true. I am speaking of the special inward quality of the Sign. Because in symbolism, the ox is taken as a symbol of the body, Taurus is generally related to the body, and is accounted earthly.

But all the Zodiacal Signs are of the Gods. The constellation that is named Taurus must be a stellar formation in the Celestial Realms which has all the qualities of God (in certain specific forms) for mediation. And this is so; for the Sign represents media through which the Divine Majesty of the Ram or Aries can be made manifest. And every Soul must have the quality. That is why all Souls pass through all the Signs; for they have to receive within themselves the vibrations of the magnetic forces sent forth by all those glorious Celestial and Divine embodiments.

In this way we could go through all the Signs, for each one is full of wondrous nobility.

THE TWELVE NAMES OF ISRAEL

But here, in passing, a word about their relationship to the names of the Household of Israel. The names of the Twelve Houses of Israel represented the Divine qualities which are in the innermost of the Soul. Thus Israel was able to be the vehicle of the outpouring of all the Celestial magnetic streams, accommodated through mediatorial ministry unto the children of this world.

The Gods loved to have the Elect Children as their vehicles. The Gods love perfect media. They themselves are the embodiments of the Mystery we name the FATHER-MOTHER. And a Human-Christ-Soul, or a Soul-world (which is a combination of Souls), like our Planet, or a system which is a combination of worlds of Souls, like the Solar System—all such are of GOD and for HIM in the measure in which that Mystery of Love finds embodiment in them, and ministry through them.

The Gods love Israel; and they call unto each House. Though, in a stellar sense, we have emerged from the Sign Pisces, and are passing through the Sign Aquarius, all the Tribes and Houses of Israel are called upon to represent, to embody, and to interpret those profound things for which all the Signs stand—namely, the Lamb of GOD, the Majesty of GOD, the Strength of GOD, the abiding, immovable nature of the Love of GOD; the exquisite motion of HIS centrifugal and centripetal ministries represented by and interpreted in Aries, Taurus, and Gemini; Cancer, Leo, and Virgo; Libra, Scorpio, and Sagittarius; Capricorn, Aquarius, and Pisces.

GEMINI AND CANCER

The Heavenly Twins represent the Hermetic Powers whereby the Soul comes into high illumination, acquires great magnetic force, and becomes a centre full of magnetic activity and radiation, giving forth everywhere to heal and bless, and, when meeting the elements that need changing, separating and transmuting them.

Cancer represents the power of mighty Soul-motherhood, wherein the Being becomes a centre or vortex that draws unto itself all the qualities the Gods send, and, appropriating them, builds up the fabric of the Being for yet greater ministry; and, in that greater ministry, not only gathers in to itself yet more of those glorious Mysteries, but, having acquired the capacity through the intense inward motion, has the power to project and unveil them again unto GOD'S Children.

And through this combination of these qualities the Soul

acquires the power of Leo. Now Leo is a term that has come to be associated with the destructive animal that bears the name. The Lion is destructive; yet he is noble in many ways. And although very near that line beyond which nothing is redeemable back into high consciousness, until it descends and is dissipated by the loosening and disintegration of the elements, yet the Lion is redeemable.

THE TRUE CŒUR DE LION

But Leo has no relationship to the animal. The Soul who is a true Leo—is Lion-hearted. He is *Cœur de Lion.* He is mighty in Being. Thus, though the term has come to have unhappy associations of destruction, pride and arrogance, yet it is a regnant term in its inner meaning. It is of the Divine Knighthood and Kingship. It works through, even to the outer planes; for some of the noblest kings and queens have been born under this Sign. And though it may be said that some of the most disastrous reigning ones have come under the Sign, that they have sought their own way to the hurt of those over whom they ruled, that they were dominated by self-will and self-regard, and that they made the people their slaves, yet such evil states are not in the Sign itself, but are the results of the perversion of the mighty potency inherent in Leo.

Leo imparts the powers necessary for regnancy. It is, therefore, associated with the Reigning House. It is the House that takes all the riches that Cancer has gathered in, and which Gemini would administer; and gives them regnancy, so that in the mediation there is also distribution.

After Leo there comes Virgo. Generally its meaning partakes of an outward application and relationship. But this is through a misunderstanding of the term. We are all to be pure and beautiful virgins. We are all to be beautiful in our bodies, as well as in our minds and our hearts. We are all to be beautiful in our love in its outflowing manifestations. We are all to be full of the sweetness and graciousness of the Divine Love, and also of the Wisdom of that Love.

THE VIRGINITY OF THE SOUL Virgo relates to the feminine exposition of the Soul's force. It speaks of the power of the Soul's motherhood to embody the perfect. Its influence is to seek the perfect Divine Ideal. The Virgin does not merely relate to virginity in a woman, or in a man. Its significance is soulic. Its true meaning is expressed in virginal states of the essences, substances and elements of the Soul. Mere earthly virginity does not necessarily imply such realization.

Virgo is followed by Libra. In the innermost, Libra is the balance which represents equilibrium. It signifies the attainment of that power which gives equipoise of mind and heart. And then it indicates the realization by the Soul of the crowning of the Life with the perfect balance, wherein is found Divine Consciousness.

THE MOTION OF SCORPIO And then comes that which is regarded as an unhappy sign. The Sign of Scorpio is supposed to imply the play of human passion, and the stinging and smiting action. And, in an inverted state, it can, doubtless, be these, though it is not alone in this respect. An unredeemed and greatly fallen son of Scorpio is, however, not necessarily a passionate Soul through the body, though the strong inner motion takes that direction oft-times. The passion of Scorpio, speaking generally, is intense. Therefore, when it turns in the direction of the desire-nature and the will it smites mercilessly. But that is the perversion of the Divine Power in the Sign.

Scorpio is the Divine Chemist and Physician. It is full of healing power. It has to do with the play of the Divine Flame through the standard of the Being. It is related sometimes to the serpent. And even on Hermes Staff there appeared the double serpent. But this is a perversion of the Divine Idea. The Caduceus represented the centrifugal and centripetal motion of the Sacred Flame through the arterial system of the Being. To the outer Body through the intermediary Bodies, and to these through the Etheric vehicle from the Innermost of the Being, the Divine Flame gives potency, energy, and illumination, as it moves up and down the Spiral of the Being.

Scorpio is full of the healing power that comes through all the vehicles from the Cup of Life as that Cup is filled from the Divine. For the Heavens fill the Golden Bowl of the Being.

Therefore, instead of being a most fallen Sign, Scorpio is the Divine Physician from Gilead.

And so through the Archer with his Divine Ideas. For Sagittarius ministers unto the projection of those ideas into concrete formulations and mediations in blessed ministry. It is full of the urge to Divine self-expression in Art and Literature.

THE HEIGHTS AND DEPTHS OF LIFE

Then follows Capricorn, the He-Goat, as the Sign has come to be called. Capricorn represents that power of ministry by which the Soul is taught how to climb the great heights. Even on the outer planes, Capricornians are fine climbers, being sure footed. That is an outer reflection of the inner power. For in the innermost it has reference to the power to climb the Heights of God. The influence has special relation to the Will. When the Will is absolutely consecrated to the FATHER-MOTHER, the Soul can climb all heights. There is no summit it may not reach. The Sign is thus appertaining to the Will.

And then there follows the Man with the Watering-pot. He is Aquarius, the Water-carrier. Aquarius is the Sign that bears the waters for the outpouring. Water is the symbol of Truth. But Truth as knowledge belongs to the intellectual planes. For it is through the mind that you acquire knowledge until you know through realization. Then the knowledge is not the same in its source as that which is held by the mind. It is the knowledge of Being through realization. The waters bear the Being up until they become for it the River of Life. And as the Being still ascends, that which is poured out into the Being is the very Wine of the Gods ; that Wine of the Gods which is the Truth of GOD dynamically changed, transmuted into that vital force which is the Mystery of the Lamb of GOD.

At first it flows into the Great Deep—Pisces, the sublime Mystery of Being. As it has been written, "Out of the Deep hast Thou called me." Even in mythological story, this is set forth. King Arthur came out of the Deep. In the Greek story of Aphrodite, the Soul came out of the sea. And this is true in more senses than one—though not to be unveiled now.

Then in the Great Deep, the mighty Sea of Being, the Soul enters into the consciousness of the Divine Mystery, learns to move amidst the Waters of that Mystery, for it is the Mystery of God in the Being.

These things ye once knew. These powers ye once held. They are in you to-day. For such mediation ye were once centres in high combination, and with many others. And ye are all again to be ingathered and upgathered for the ministry of the Gods in high mediation unto the Earth. For, not only in a Planetary sense are the Gods of those systems pouring out the blessing of their marvellous magnetic streams; but Israel, individual and corporate, when upborne in consciousness and life and realization, is again to become the vehicle of the like wondrous outpouring of all the Gods.

This is but a passing glimpse of sacred history in relation to yourselves in the past, and, through glimpsing it, a call for the future.

THE OFFICE OF HIGH MINISTRY It is the sublimest office to be the vehicle of God! But God ministers through the Gods, who are His embodiments. They minister through the Angelic Worlds. In all the Celestial systems they minister. Think, then, of the marvellous nature of the superstructure of the realms to which you belong! Think of the sublimity of it, notwithstanding the apparent littleness of your individual estates. Think of it, that in thought you can climb into the eternities; that you can interiorly visualize the glory of those magnificent systems of which we have, in fragmentary terms, spoken to you! Think of it! that you have the potencies to rise up again and endure the vibrations that are playing upon the world unto the receiving of them, and the qualifying of your attributes once more for ministry in this world! Think of it! that the whole House of Israel is able to receive the magnetic outpouring of the Twelve Zodiacal Systems, and thus not only in the special mediation of the Sign under which the life has come into manifestation in these days, but able to receive from all the Signs! For they are all inward, Celestial and Divine. The merely outward relationships are not to be compared with the inward relationships, and the play of the inward forces.

Thus the Soul is capable, because of its history, because it has acquired the qualities of those Signs, to receive of their magnetic power to-day, and to be the vehicle for their outpouring upon the world.

Look at the tremendous nature of the ministry that has to be accomplished! Look at the splendour of the Life unto which the FATHER-MOTHER calls all HIS children! See how all earthliness is but littleness in comparison with the Life unto which HE calls, that we may be able once more to be HIS vehicles! Look out upon your earthliness in desire, and the association of the things that hold and bind you to the Earth, and you will see they are but as the dust of the ground, things that bring you into humiliation.

THE SACREDNESS OF LOWLY MINISTRY

And by this statement I do not mean that the ministries you have to render are a humiliation. For all ministry is sacred—in the home, in the office, in the workshop, at the counter, buying and selling where it is necessary to purchase or to sell. All ministry is sacred if it be sacredly accounted; if it be made beautiful by the touch of the Divine Hand, the Hand that vibrates with the motions of the Eternities. Every ministry, however lowly, *is* beautiful if it be sacredly rendered. To such high ministry HE calls you upward! The earthly things that bind you are not worthy of you, of your childhood to HIM, of the divinity HE has given you, of the ministry unto which HE has called you.

And so HE asks you to lay aside the garments of humiliation that have been bespattered with the dust of this world, that you may soar into the heights of consciousness and realization where HIS administrators the Gods, Angels and Archangels, can again mediate unto you of HIM, and prepare you to be HIS mediators as HE pours into you, through those glorious ones, the riches of HIS Love and Wisdom.

Think of the work unto the accomplishment of which we are sent—Messenger and messengers! The Messenger is in the Message, and the Servant is one with that Message. The LORD HIMSELF hath given HIS Message; the Servant is but HIS medium, the mediator of HIS Message unto Israel. Israel is honoured by HIM to hear the Message. All the tribes of Israel are called to be HIS mediators, HIS priests in high estate, concrete embodiments of HIM, distributors of HIS gracious gifts; the manifestors of Love, gentleness, tenderness, compassion, pity, lowliness, majesty and power; revealers of the Life from on High which Aries bestows, even Rama the Lamb of GOD who leads the Soul onward and upward, until the individuate Being can float in HIS lustrous Sea and drink into its fountain HIS Piscarian Mystery.

This is the transcendent ministry unto which you are called. Put away, therefore, everything that belittles you, that shadows the Divine Image in you, that prevents you from being clothed with the Immortal Robes.

IMMORTALITY HERE AND NOW

Most people expect their immortal garments when they pass over. That is not the idea of immortality at all. To be clothed in immortality is to be clothed in the raiment that radiates HIM everywhere and at all times. The Immortal Love doth cause the bloom of the Heavens to alight ever upon the eye and the cheek. It doth make itself manifest in the breaths that go forth from us in the activities of our Being—in the traits, the motion, the gait, the posture, our attitude to everyone, and the outflow of our love everywhere.

Behold and see! and you will understand Isaiah where the

prophet says that with their coming, "the wilderness and the solitary place shall be glad for them; and the desert shall rejoice and blossom as the rose." For their coming shall make the wilderness conditions change so greatly that they shall be filled to overflow with the very joy of the Heavens. And no one shall be solitary any more. For they will bring back to the children the consciousness of the Overshadowing Heavens. The world shall be so changed that even the "reeds and the rushes" that shake with the passing breaths, shall make music—the conditions of life, the Souls that are as the bruised reeds, unsteady in the motion of their spiral, moved with the changing wind. For Souls will have acquired the power to bring forth from these conditions the music of the Heavens. And surely it is a sacred ministry so to live and serve as to bring forth from the Soul the praise of God; even though that Soul, in its potencies, may be compared to the reeds and the rushes.

It is a description of the coming of Israel, and of the changed state of this world through the coming of Israel. It is a description of what is to be accomplished through the ministry of the Gods as a realized fact in every life; and of God in the twelvefoldness of His Life in us. It is a description of the ministry of those majestic embodiments called "Elders around the Throne," which, though spoken of as twenty-four, are the Twelve Divine Attributes; for they are all twofold in their mode of ministry. They are crowned in the inward and the outward motion. As given to His children by the Divine Love and Wisdom, those twelve powers are seen from Aries to Pisces; from Pisces round again to Aries. The Lord of Being hath given these powers that His children may be true radiations of Him; that they may ascend the ladder of Life to be even as Gods; that they may become as living stones in the Temple of God, where the Gods minister, and where, in the very innermost Sanctuary, the mediation is from the High Priest Himself, the Adonaic motion; for, glorious things of thee are spoken, O Zion, the City of our God.

Such are some of those things glinted unto you that you may gleam them in your vision, and understand, and rejoice.

It is difficult to pass from the vision; there is so much lying behind it all. But may this concluding unveiling to you throw light on all that you have heard during these wonderful days concerning the majesty of the Love that calls you, and the Life unto which HE calls. And may this fragmentary statement reveal to you the glory of HIS administration unto you through the Gods and HIS stupendous Hierarchies, in the ministry of HIS Angels in this hour. And together may you all be uplifted to be HIS perfect vehicles again, the twelve-fold Tribes of Israel, capable of revealing the qualities expressed in all the Names of Israel; for these are represented by those glorious Celestial and Divine Hierarchies. And may you restore the infinite majesty of it all, with its exceeding greatness and intense radiance.

The vastness of it is beyond fully unveiling to you. It makes me bow before that Sublime ONE in lowliest adoration, and with a consecration absolute, wherein all my Being in every part of it, and power of it, and attribute of it, is laid on the Altar of Service for HIM WHO is my LORD.

THE DIVINE GOVERNMENT OF THE WORLD

THE DIVINE GOVERNMENT

THE DAY OF THE ADVENT

The Christmas season approaches. The Western World's thought, whilst ostensibly emanating from that glorious central Event, concerns itself with an outer festival. In the outer festival there may be many elements of good. These may be found in the love expressed from friend to friend; in any special endeavour for the remembrance of the poor and needy; and also where the children of GOD desire in special ways to express their gratitude to HIM in renewed consecration of their love through its exaltation and intensification and the motion of their Being in praise of HIM.

But the outer festival as a whole, though having a few elements of good, is far removed from the Divine Idea. For the Christ-Mass is the coming of Christ. Now Christ is no person. He represents a state of consciousness, and the realization of the LORD of Love within the Being. For the LORD is also Christ. HE is the ETERNAL CHRIST unto the Heavens; and unto the Soul HE is the radiant ONE in degrees of manifestation; and these degrees are entered into through realization of HIS Presence.

So that the Christ-Mass is the offering up of Christ; the recognition of the conception, the birth into manifestation, and the growth into glorious fulness, of the Christ Idea, the Christ Love, the Christ Devotion, the Christ Giving, the Christ Service, the Christ Sacrifice; thus making the whole Being a sacred embodiment for the FATHER-MOTHER. We would for you that the coming of the Christ-Mass be in sublime fulness. Unto this end we will look at the Divine Government, what it is, how it expresses itself, how it is revealed, how it is to be made manifest and realized.

THE DUAL MOTION IN THE MANIFESTATION

We have, oft-times, spoken unto you of the Manifestation in its twofoldness; of the dual motion of the Divine, first in the revelation of the meaning of Christhood and Jesushood in life, and then in the Redemption. The Master is mostly associated with the idea of the compassionate man who was also healer and teacher of mankind in a general way, and as doing something that accomplished the world Redemption. So He is looked to, and has been looked to through the ages, as the Saviour of mankind.

But the world has not found Him yet, nor the Redemption it believes in. There is an aspect of the Manifestation that is little thought of, although the songs of the Church speak of it, foretell its coming, and proclaim the majesty of it. The hope of the Church is unto its realization; and that is the coming of Christ in regnancy to be King of all the Kings, and Lord of all.

But with the Church the idea is personal. It is associated with a human embodiment, a Divine Messenger in whom is special embodiment. Even the Divine Idea is lost. This we shall see. And it will be emphasized in contrast to the travail of the world to-day to get back to the Divine Idea. For, if you look first at the Manifestation as a revealing of the FATHER-MOTHER through HIS Servant, of those things the FATHER-MOTHER meant HIS children to understand concerning their life, their relationship to HIM, the way of their going, the Life that was to be embodied, the ministries to be mediated through them to the children of men, the service to be rendered by them, then you will understand the true meaning of Jesus Christ the Lord, and you will see at once the significance and grandeur of the Manifestation. You will behold how the FATHER-MOTHER unveiled HIMSELF in a threefold fashion, first, in the Life which was an embodiment; then through the radiance of Christ, the radiance revealed through the Teachings which the Master had to give from the FATHER-MOTHER; and then in that glorious revealing of the intimate union of the Divine Mystery and the Human Soul, so intimate that the Human Soul becomes a partaker of it; and all its potencies are in motion because of that Mystery, so that they gather around its centre. Their motion is formulative for the upbuilding of the Being into the likeness of the FATHER-MOTHER. And through the fashioning of the Being's attributes, the individuate life comes to bear the express likeness of GOD.

That was the first glorious purpose of the Manifestation. The purpose had to be revealed to those who could understand it. All can now understand the beautiful Way of Life, for they can recognize it even if they are not able to follow fully. It is a star in the firmament. It radiates. It need never speak, yet the motion of every part of it makes harmony whose music is heard within Souls. The Breath of the Highest gives this music to the Being, wafts it through the life, and pours it forth in auric atmosphere so that Souls recognize: they feel; they sense; and they come to know the beautiful Way.

FOR WHOM THE ADVENT WAS MADE

Those unto whom the Manifestation came, could recognize that Life. Therefore, they were asked to follow it. The FATHER-MOTHER never asks of HIS children anything that they are unequal to accomplishing. GOD never makes a mistake. HE does not ask a Soul for a ministry the burden of which would be too great for it to bear. HE never asks for a consecration, the Being would not have power to render. HE never commands a sacrifice where the Soul has not the qualities to enable it to make such sacrifice.

Therefore, when the Manifestation came, its coming was for those who could understand it. The Master sought to find them. Its appeal to the world failed. It failed because the world was not ready for it. The world could only receive it in very small measure through those who could embody it.

The Jewish world should have been ready with all its religious ritual and symbol, and its most elaborate, but sadly perverted sacrificial system; yet it rejected it utterly.

The Grecian world professed to love the beautiful, and aimed at embodying it in Art. It should have welcomed the Life that was the highest embodiment of all that was exquisitely beautiful. Yet that world repudiated it.

The Roman world professed to know the will of the Gods. It sought to impose its laws upon the rest of mankind. But the Roman strove to do that, as most nations in their time have sought to accomplish it, by mental domination. In the Roman there was the inversion of the attribute of the will. He made his conquests through the might of will and arms. He was the greatest of conquerors; yet the Roman rejected it.

There is much mirage found in the historical setting of Christianity. There has been no living Christianity since the Manifestation days, except in the few who found power to embody the Life of Jesus Christ.

Yet the Manifestation was to find the heart of the world. That which was revealed was to touch Souls in the very centre of their Being, and to so influence them that Christ would come to reign within them; that they would become regal children under the government of the King Eternal, even the FATHER-MOTHER, and be HIS princes. For one great purpose, indeed the supreme purpose of the Manifestation, was to restore the third great quality in a Christhood, and that was, THE THEOCRACY. Now, a Theocracy is the government that is from and of GOD.

In order to accomplish this, the Oblation had to be borne. It was absolutely necessary in order to make it possible for the Children of the Kingdom to receive the Vision in its fulness, and to rise into the splendour of the Life of Jesus Christ. And it had become the only way to save the world itself. Through the changing of the elemental states of the Planetary Heavens there were laid sure foundations for the Redemption of all the world. This included the Planetary Household, and even the elemental kingdoms of the world.

The Divine Government can be fully restored only through the accomplishment of the Redemption. Look through the history of the nations as they have risen and set, and you will find that, however beautiful in the outset their government and changes of government may have seemed to be; however ameliorative and stimulative and apparently exalting their administrations and activities; bye and bye the reverse conditions have come to prevail, and the peoples have gone down through the loss of the very Ideal that seemed to bring about the change of their government.

THE MANIFESTATION AND THEOCRACY

Therefore, the Manifestation, or the coming of GOD'S Christ unto the world, was to reveal what Life was, how it could be embodied and was to be embodied, what Life's ministry was, how Souls could prepare for it, and what the LORD meant by Souls coming into the consciousness of HIMSELF through HIS Indwelling. And it revealed how the consciousness of HIS Indwelling as an abiding realization could come only through entering into the Life and following the path of Jesus and Christ. The Branch that grows out of the stem of Jesse, is the wonderful life of love and compassion that grows out of Jesushood, and becomes radiant until it glows even with the glory of the LORD. This is a resultant of Christ regnant within a Soul, and manifesting through it. And the Manifestation revealed that all the children should come to know HIM in HIS most beautiful intimate relationship to them. That relationship is called Emmanuel. And this represents GOD, not only with us in an objective sense of manifestation and government, but as the Divine Presence with us in a subjective sense. For, as Emmanuel is GOD'S Immanence; so Emmanuel is the LORD'S Immanence which is within the Soul, and realized by it.

The great purpose, therefore, of the Manifestation was Revelation; then Redemption; and then Regnancy. The children of Israel understood a Theocracy. They knew that GOD alone was King. HE reigned in their midst. HE had regnancy within them. Every Soul of the Ancient Christhood knew this. All must come again under this Theocratic Government and know GOD'S ruling. No one can get away from it and truly live. No one can get to HIM without it. That is impossible. HE alone is the supreme ONE. You yourselves can only apprehend this according to your comprehension of the Mystery of GOD, and in the measure in which HE governs your Being. For, as you must now realize, to know the LORD GOD of Sabaoth, is not simply to believe that HE is, and that HE is glorious in all HIS wonderful manifestation; but that to know HIM is to come at that intimacy in which Emmanuel speaks within you, even HIS Immanent Presence, and expresses HIS government in your Being. There is no such thing as human autocracy in the Heavens. There, government is by a Divine Autocracy; but it is Theocratic. Wherever GOD is, everything is beautiful. Wherever GOD is, Love is supreme. Wherever GOD is, all things are in perfect accord, and harmony is expressed throughout all. Life is a grand Symphony. Life is a dramatic exposition of Divine Joy. It is an embodiment of the highest Art, the real Divine Art. When GOD is supreme within a human Soul, that Soul is related to the Divine Theocracy. GOD is its King. HIS is the regnancy. HE is the Ruler.

That is the meaning of having "the Will of GOD done within us." This is easier to speak of, and affirm, and even pray for, than to let it be accomplished. The Soul functioning in such a world as this, with its contrary motion, its manifold opposing claims, and the motion of life out of harmony with HIM it is not so easy to fulfil the Will of GOD as, at first, it may seem; and yet it was the purpose of the Manifestation that all the children of Israel should come back into the Theocratic state when GOD was all in all to them. The Psalms are full of this. The real Scriptures in the Bible teem with references to GOD's government in the individual Being.

THE THEOCRACY BEGINS WITHIN The Divine Government begins with the individual, though there must necessarily be laws that govern the Universe. And there are such stellar and Divine Laws. That they are all, in varying ways, expositions of the One Law, One Divine Element, and "One great divine event" is quite true. But in the Law of GOD there are many degrees and expositions of its motion, its purpose, and its embodiments.

It is true there is but the One Divine Element, the Eternal Mystery. And yet all the real elements are as various processional activities from that Mystery; and these are manifold. And they are manifoldly expressed in the various Celestial and Divine Worlds, and in the Angelic as well as the Human embodiments.

And there is one great Divine Event, the event of GOD'S government of the Soul through realization. For the more we know HIM, the more we want to be like HIM. The more we know HIM, the more we want HIM to rule us. And here, by the way (though it is intimately associated with all we have said), understand this, that it might seem that if a Soul gave up everything like this, it would have no will of its own. And there is a sense in which this is quite true. It would not wish to have any will of its own. But if this meant that the Being would have no power to will, then your interpretation of such a yielding up of the Will would be mistaken. The Soul's *power to will* would be intensified in the measure in which it had realized the Indwelling. But its will would only wish to do the Will of the FATHER-MOTHER. It would be one with that Will. Hence, in the measure in which we become like HIM, in that measure do we desire to have nothing of our own, but only to be HIS absolutely.

So GOD'S government through HIS Christ must be in the individual, and have its first expression through the individual Soul.

THE MANIFOLDNESS OF DIVINE GOVERNMENT

And here, in order to make clear what we shall say further, we would indicate that the various forms of government in their terms, have meaning, though not after the interpetation which men and women give to them. The Divine Theocracy is also an Oligarchy. The Divine Oligarchy is also a series of regnancies. The manifold regal states also express administration and administrators, and these again are manifoldly deputized. Thus we have:—

Theocracy, Divine Autocracy: God alone is King: God's rule is absolute.

Divine Oligarchy: God administrates through chosen ones.

Divine Conservatism: The Conservation of Divine Potency.

Divine Radicalism: The Root-motion or Arche-Principle, of all action.

Divine Liberalism: The bountiful outpouring of elements and potency.

Divine Socialism: The government is for the perfecting of all.

Divine Communism: Every member shares in the Divine Distribution.

There is no Nihilism; for that is iconoclasm. It is negation. It is a destroying force. But all these others are living forces, when understood. Wherever the Theocracy reigns, it reigns through the Oligarchy of the twelve attributes in the individual system. They administrate for God. God's twelve Attributes speak to ours. God, through His Divine Oligarchy, speaks to the oligarchical representatives within us, making each attribute regal that it may reign in its own realm. None of the attributes enters into conflict with any other attribute. There is no contrariety. There is perfect union between them all when God reigns and administers through His Princes—all the attributes.

The Theocracy reveals itself through an Oligarchy.

THE DIVINE SEVENFOLDNESS

The regnancy of the attributes expresses Divine conservation. Their regal motion preserves within the Being the Divine Image and likeness of the Father-Mother. In that is a true conservatism. There is a recognition and preservation of the good, and the true, and the beautiful. Such conservation does not shut up the potencies and qualities, nor hold these back from manifestations; but gives to them a service wherein there is that exposition which finds its ministry in a distribution which conserves the beautiful. Indeed, a Human Soul must learn how to be conservative. GOD'S government will teach it to conserve its forces; to grow through conservation; to expand and rise, and become stronger and richer still in potency through the ingathering of the divine elements by which Life is built up, and the conservation of all these, and the transmutation of them into Divine Potencies for the FATHER-MOTHER.

But where the Autocracy of GOD is operating through the Oligarchy of Divine Attributes, unto the Princes who are to reign through their Attributes as represented in the attributes in the Human Soul, and to be so conserving in their ministry that they will preserve everything that is true and beautiful, then they are also Radical. They go to the very root of the matter. They get at the Truth. That is the meaning of the word Radical. Let us dismiss from our mind the political inversions put upon conservatism and radicalism. Political uses of these terms are all at sea. Unless GOD turns you in the very depths of your Being, gets to the root or centre of your Being, HE cannot find you unto your knowing of HIM. Always get to the root of things. Find the radical meaning; and when you do you will find the significance of the term that has been so sadly misused.

At the Radical centre you will find a living Liberalism. For a true Liberalism is an exquisite quality begotten of the Great Love. Liberalism had relation to the Lady Bountiful, to the Lord of the Manor, to the real Divine Squire of Being. For the Soul receiving bountifully from the Infinite Love, poured forth bountifully of that Bounty unto Souls. Herein was and is the real balanced distribution of that which was given as sacred possession for ministry.

Nay more. Through such ministry all the attributes come into beautiful harmony. All the elements become harmonized. There is Living Socialism. It is the true, divine solidarity through unification of all the elements, potencies and attributes of the Being. Man is essentially a social Being; but not simply after the manner of society. That is not to be understood by the expression. For Socialism as understood by society is not Divine Socialism at all. A Divine Socialist is an inspired lover of mankind. He loves all Souls and despises none. He is the beloved friend of all. His Socialism gives him the power to accommodate himself to every Soul, so that he passes by none, nor cuts off any from his ministry. He gives himself to all who claim his ministry.

And thus it comes to pass that even Communism has its real significance within the Soul. For the potencies, elements and attributes have all things in common in the one sublime and supreme Life!

DIVINE GOVERNMENT ENCYCLIC To know GOD'S Government is to know a marvellous thing, great in the majesty and the exquisite lowliness of it; transcendent in the height of it, and in its depth profound, and in the expansiveness of it, far-reaching as the Universe. The terms under which its degrees are expressed have been corruptly used and abused, and are so used even in this day. And the latest cry of the Socialist and Communist could never heal the world, even if it were realized, unless it were realized divinely; and that would imply all the rest. It could never heal the open sores of the world. There is no Earthly and Human panacea for the world's evils; for the true healing of them would be the restoration of true righteousness and equity. And herein is just Judgment. For Judgment is not condemnation. It is the separation of things, and the bringing of them into the exquisite Divine balance. And the equity and righteousness of GOD are expressed through the regnancy of Christ. And Christ means the LORD-Principle reigning within us.

All the National Governments have been the falsification by the rulers of the people of GOD'S Theocracy; GOD'S Oligarchy; GOD'S reign through HIS Princes, or Sons of GOD; GOD'S governors through HIS governments expressing themselves in their administration conservatively, radically, liberally, socially, and communally.

You will observe that when you get to the root of things you find that the world beautiful is within your own Being, to be found there by you, because there the LORD of Being HIMSELF is to be found. And when HE is found, HIS regnancy begins and HIS government becomes.

Now look at this in the light of the Manifestation, the celebration of Christmas, the Christ-Mass. Behold how the LORD comes to the Soul, even until HE becomes the Presence within the Being! Realize what it means for Christ to reign! All the world may go after an earthly potentate to do him honour and serve him. One professing to have been sent from the Heavens may arrest and hold multitudes who are fascinated by personality or great claim; for they are many who seek for the recognition of the supposedly great. But you may know, what is common knowledge to all the world, that though men and women may be fascinated for the time being by outward claims and powers named heavenly, yet changing events effect great changes in them, and cause them to lose what there was of good in the vision. It is not by following anyone outwardly that the Soul can come to the Realization. The road to Heaven is narrow, but each has to walk it alone. It is the road to Realization. It is the path that brings the Being into the presence of Emmanuel, the Divine Immanence, the LORD'S Indwelling.

See then what the Christ-Mass means unto the Soul of Whose government it is prophesied that there shall be no end. For thus is it when you have the Christ Love filling the Being. There is no limit to its measure, no circumscription to its ruling, no end to its outflow and its power for service. There is no end to the Good which it brings to the Being. Its government within makes the Being one with the Divine. Its government, through the Being, mediates of the Divine wherever that one is. Christ cannot reign within any Soul and that one fail to mediate of HIM. Thus, if the LORD as Emmanuel reigns within the Being, that one will surely express HIM—HIS Love, HIS compassion, HIS pity, the beauty of holiness, which is the beauty of Life, the glory of HIS Love and its transcendent power to meet every need.

If you could be transported to the threshold of the Divine World in this hour in response to your desire to behold the glory of the LORD, the glory you would behold there would not be simply a great effulgence. There would undoubtedly be effulgence most wonderful. But the glory of the LORD is in the exquisite beauty of fashion, motion, giving and outpouring in blessed ministry.

Thus the glory of the Lord, which is to cover the land from the rivers to the ends of the Earth, is the glory of beautiful Life. It is thus the Divine comes to the Earth in a Human Soul. It gets its fashion from the Eternal. It realizes the Vision within, and then makes manifest on the Earth. It radiates the glory of the Vision. It embodies it. It strives to interpret it. The Soul's love is like the LORD'S Love. HE loves all and forgets none; the Soul is to be like HIM. Its compassion is like the LORD'S; it takes in all living things. Its pity is like the LORD'S pity; it does not say, "I pity you," and leave you in your needy state. Divine pity is like this, if you could see it demonstrated dramatically and dioramically: you would see an Angel or a host of Angels, flying from the Realm of the Presence unto His children to defend them. That is pity. It is to shelter and defend. The pity of the Lord is unto you. It is defence. It is oft-times said that children have their Angels who defend them, and thus out of the most precarious positions the children seem to be delivered by unseen hands. If only the children of the FATHER-MOTHER could carry the idea further, and understand how HIS Angels do minister unto all Souls, expressing HIS pity, HIS Love to care for them, to provide for them, to encompass them, to defend them!

THE THEOCRACY REALIZED BY THE SOUL

With this inner view of the Divine Government, and this Soulic presentation of Christ, you see a Soul made one with HIM. It is of the Theocracy. It receives of GOD'S Oligarchy. It becomes a Prince for HIM. It serves at the seat of HIS Government, and all its attributes are exalted to be Princes under the one regnancy. And the rule is expressed in doing justly, loving mercy, embodying beautifully, interpreting in every act and through every word, and revealing through the thoughts expressed, the Beauty of GOD, the Beauty of HIS Holiness, the Glory of HIS Love, the Majesty of HIS Being in us.

You will here see how, if a Soul comes to understand the true Theocracy and Oligarchy, and the rule of Princes and the Government of the FATHER-MOTHER within, through attributes making of Life an exquisite home of conserving power and radical motion—the power to go into the very depths of the meaning of things; and social power, wherein all the attributes partake of the one life; and communal power, wherein all are parts of the concrete whole, so that if one member be hurt, all the other members suffer, so intimate is the relationship.

And from this inner vision we turn outward and look for the answer to the query: "How is the world ever to be healed?"

It is probable that many of you have engaged in politics. You may have been conservative, as you thought, or liberal, or radical. You may be what is called socialist, or communist. Well, take your ideas back to the vision that has been presented to you. See the real meaning of government and you will understand how all those terms are true, and all the endeavours under them misdirected.

DEMOCRACY AN INVERSION OF THEOCRACY

There is no such thing in the Divine World as that which is understood as a Human Democracy. Think what this world, and all worlds, would become before the Heavens, if the democracy, as it is named, unenlightened and unredeemed, ruled. Theocratic government does not mean that each one has not a part. Your own attributes have each a part in your life. No one attribute rules you; nor do all of them. If one or more should do so, then there would be so much lacking in you of Divine Government. You may see in a human life where the desires are impure and the attributes are awry and out of harmony with the Divine Will, that there is no true government of a social, liberal, radical, or conservative order. The life is in the maelstrom of contrary forces, unable to resist them unto the conquering of them all. And that is just the state of men and women in the world to-day. There is seeking without finding, because the way of the seeking in the exposition of all the terms we have used, is most manifest. And that they will never heal the world may now be understood. If autocracy has failed, so have they all failed. Human autocracy, as it has been interpreted and applied, is the usurpation of the Divine Government. Divine Autocracy is government by Love.

If, in the Divine World, power is attained, it is by means of an accession of Soul consciousness. The attainment is the resultant of the ascension of the Being into the realms of Divine Realization, wherein the Soul knows HIM Who is KING of all the Kings, and LORD of all. And every ministry is, in a sense, a deputized ministry from the Great Love. HE chooses; all share in the blessing:—communal blessing, social blessing, radical blessing, conservative blessing, the blessing of the ministry of the Princes who rule in Righteousness and Equity.

Christ's burden in administration is said to be upon the shoulders. GOD'S Government is upon the shoulders of Him Who is to be King, and He shall rule in righteousness, embodying the upright life. And it is on the shoulders, the transverse section of the Cross, where the balance rests—that Equity from which the Princes shall decree justice. The shoulders will express Righteousness and Equity in their ministries of mediation from GOD.

Now you will understand how one who realizes the LORD of Being cannot in this day be a politician in the world sense at all. But in the Divine sense he may be, because in that sense all that is true in every form of polity, is embraced.

THE COMING OF THE TRUE KINGS We do not mean by this unveiling that the passing away of earthly Royalties is altogether tragic. Far from that; because those who should have reigned were not upon the Thrones. These were the true Aristocrats of the land. Those who reigned as Kings and Queens did mistake both the source of their regnancy and the manner in which it should have been expressed. For a King should embody the regnancy of GOD in himself, through himself as a great Patriarch, an archfather unto GOD'S children. And GOD'S Princes, who should form HIS conclave of administration, should be so balanced in the Divine Equity, that all their ministry unto the children should express, in exquisitely beautiful fashion, the Divine Purpose, embodied and revealed through the Regal One. It was thus that some of the children of Israel became administrators, even regal administrators, in old time. For many of them had this ministry to render. In attaining to be Prophet, and Seer, and Priest, Interpreter and Manifestor, they had to be regnant ones, giving expression to the Divine Government, bringing to those who could understand, the theocratic idea, teaching the elder children concerning the glorious Oligarchy of GOD. But when the Vision passed away, all the positions that were divinely ordained, and the ministries that were meant to be ever divinely rendered, became changed.

You see there is a spiritual meaning in everything, if you find it. And for all the inversions and perversions and subversions that you witness in the world, there is also a cause when you can find its secret.

Bear with me for having stirred up, as I know I have done, so much within you of your own past. But unto this end is the Message. It is the day of the re-promulgation of the Manifestation. It is the day of the re-Manifestation of the Christ. It is the day of the LORD'S Return, when Christ is to find embodiment in all those children of the FATHER-MOTHER who are able to respond to such a high call and realization. It is the day in which Jesus is to come to reign in the life that is pure and true in eating and drinking, desiring and thinking and acting, and in all ministry.

What exquisitely beautiful dramatic situations we shall find bye and bye when the children are found and healed; those ministries that give delight even to filling the Soul with the laughter of the Heavens, and thus lifting it out of its sorrow by giving to it the motion of Divine Joy! Do not imagine there is no laughter in the Heavens, nor real joy there. There is real joy. There, there is no tragedy. But there is Drama there; yet without the perversions you find on the earth at the present time. And there is the real Comedy, the Drama that fills the Heavens with the laughter of the Gods wherein is the joy that knows no pain nor hurt; and in this the children share.

THE DAY OF THE CHRIST-MASS It is the day of the Christ-Mass. In it is the consecration of all the Being. It is the Mass of Life offered on the Altar to HIM. There is Cherubic motion. There is Seraphic ministry in that motion. Cherubim and Seraphim express GOD'S Government. They bring everything of HIMSELF in the Soul to liken HIM in all its fashion, and to express HIM through all the Being, and interpret HIM through all the Being's motion and ministries.

This is the Christ-Mass hour. HE has returned again. HE is becoming again. The LORD of Love in the Christ state of the Soul is becoming for the glorious manifestation of Jesus. Now is coming the regnancy of Jesus throughout all the world, wherein everyone shall bow (not at the mention of His name) in the state of Jesus, to HIM Who is our LORD. For all the world to bow in the name of Jesus, is indeed a glorious thing. It is for all the world to yield itself beautifully to the Jesus state. Bow down with the mind and Being unto the LORD! Let Jesus be regnant! For that is the state which brings the reign of righteousness, the beautiful upright life, the exquisitely balanced life. It brings peace, a real peace. It brings harmony; for the Jesus Life is a harmonious Life.

It is the Christ-Mass. The LORD is coming. HE has come. HE is again becoming within the Soul, and of HIS Kingdom there shall be no end. This vision of HIM will grow from more to more, and still from more to more, until all the world shall hear of it and behold the beauty of it. For the glory of the Lord shall cover the earth as the waters cover the sea. You could not have a sea without waters! The glory of the LORD shall cover the Earth through the outpouring of the waters from HIS Great Deep.

Beloved children of the FATHER-MOTHER, for you it is the hour of the Christ-Mass. Behold it! You will find it associated even with the Creatures; for they will come into the shelter of your love and the ministry of your true pity. You will see it mingling with the sacred magian visitors of the Divine Love, in Life most radiant. You will see it in the Song of the Angel of the LORD, and hear it in the Chorale of the Heavens; for it is the Christ-Mass hour!

Let it be so for you, that this Christmas season be a real festival within you of Christ Jesus, through your own up-yielding and giving, even unto the Divine becoming within you through the holy estates of Jesus, Christ, the LORD.

Oh, Most Regnant One! Most Glorious One! Most Ever Blessed Father-Mother! How shall we yet tell of Thee, express and reveal and interpret Thee?

In the praise of Thee would be the motion of our Being, always one glad song of sublime thanksgiving. In the service of Thee would be our worship; serving wheresoever we find ourselves, serving through all activities always and only from Thee and for Thee.

We would be Thy children in the embodiment of Thee, that Thy Christ may reign within us, and have His regnancy expressed through us, even unto the healing of many, the conquest of the world, the Return of all Thy Children.

Amen and Amen.

THE MYSTERY OF PRAYER

THE MYSTERY OF PRAYER
IN RELATION TO
DIVINE GOVERNMENT.

It is Lenten time. Lenten songs are sung, many of which will be prayers, and the Offices of the Church will be fulfilled through the prayers. It is a time of daily worship, even where daily worship does not always take place; for it is a time of special intercession.

QUESTIONS OF GREAT MOMENT

Though this has gone on for ages, yet the world has seemed to remain much the same. The Church, including in the term all Christian communities, has prayed; but the world remaineth as if it knew not GOD. And the questions naturally arise, *What is prayer? How does it affect God? Does it alter in any way the policy of the Heavens and change the Divine administration? Can prayers be heard in Heaven? If so, How? And if they be heard and answered, how do the answers come, and how are we to know that prayers are answered?*

These are questions that arise in the minds of many. It is well for us to understand those things which belong unto our peace, the things that belong to the fashion of the Soul and of the Heavens, and, consequently, of those things which belong to the Glorious ONE Whose children we are, and which relate to HIS Nature, HIS Motion, HIS Administration, how HE gives to us, and the Purpose of HIS giving.

These things belong to the peace of the world. As in old time, so might it be repeated to-day, "O that thou knewest the day of thy visitation; and the things that belong to thy peace. But as yet they are hid from thine eyes." The world sees not; it hears not; it understands not, though there is a sense in which it is full of a motion which might be expressed as prayer. Certainly, in the religious aspect of the world-life, the whole Church stands upon the very foundations of prayer. In its manifoldness it represents the Temple where prayer is wont to be made.

If we look first of all at what prayer is, we will be able to understand how it affects the Divine Government, and also in what sense it is in itself a process of divine ministry of mediation.

THE NATURE AND MOTION OF PRAYER

What is true prayer? What is its nature?

There is a sense in which it is a request, the request being the articulation of desire.

There is a sense in which it is motion, the motion being the exposition of that which gave the desire.

There is a sense in which it is realization, and therefore the crown of the motion, as the motion is the exposition of the request.

Prayer is desire. There is the child's prayer and the prayer of the grown up, the prayer of the little one and the prayer of the man and woman. There is even the prayer of the little child in the Soulic sense, and the prayer of the Soul who has grown up into the manhood of attainment and realization.

The natural prayer of a child, when offered to the Divine, is for good, for blessing, for outward joy, for the things that make for joy. It does not understand sorrow, but it does understand joy ; though it has its little sorrows too. The prayer is the child's desire expressed as a request.

The beautiful earthly mother is the child's heavenly mother. She is as God unto it. At least she should be. And she will be if she loves divinely. Even in the human, personal estate, perfect Love is Divine.

The father should be the heavenly friend unto the child. He should be as God in its vision. When the child sees and knows him as its father and friend, it will learn something of God and it will come to understand, bye and bye, still greater things of the great Mystery of Him Whom we speak of as the Father-Mother.

The child's prayer to the parents might not be a request that they felt it wise to fulfil. Yet it would be the child's desire. But as the child grew in understanding, it would only desire those things that were beautiful and true. The child's heavens are around it. Although children bring their dream-visions with them, very few children immediately think of the Heavens above and around them. The beautiful world, the world of the Home, the world of the threshold of Love with its daily activities, is Heaven unto the child.

Prayer, therefore, is the Desire of the Being that articulates itself in a request to receive, to hold, to be blest, even to have power and opportunity to give. For a child may ask permission to give of what it does hold, even of its love and its joy. It may make request to share with others all it has. And this Desire is Prayer. In a wise household the child's desires, so far as they are beautiful, are met. In so far as they will enrich it, the requests are granted. If the child asks for bread, bread is given. If the child asks for Love, Love is given. If the child asks for special blessing of Love, that blessing is given, even unto sublimest sacrifice in parenthood. For there is no limitation in Love's giving. You cannot bottle up Love. If you succeed, you have misinterpreted Love, and taken something that is not itself. You have taken for Love that which is not Love at all. You can put restraint on Love in its manifestation. That may be necessary at times; for the object has to be considered.

But that is Wisdom. It is not refusing the Love that is asked for, and that is needed. It is only wise giving of that Love in sweet and gracious ministry.

This childhood and parenthood relationship to prayer will help you to understand things I would say to you presently of more inward states and experiences, and even of Divine administrations.

There is the prayer of the grown up. Every man and woman, every mother and father, has his and her prayer. The heart desires and requests. Those who are seeking success in the world in the outward paths of life, only pray for such success. But those who are seeking the higher and inmost life, pray that all those things that are of the earth-life may be touched from the Divine, so that the Being may become enriched in and through whatsoever is received.

OF WHAT TRUE PRAYER CONSISTS

Prayer is request to the FATHER-MOTHER that HIS Will be accomplished. If we ask for bread HE gives it to us. HIS Bread is Heavenly Wisdom, the Flesh of the Son of GOD, the Divine Substance. HE gives us this through the enriching of our own Being. We grow enriched inwardly by means of such prayer. It is Divine Desire. If in our request we ask for the Mystery of Love, HE gives us Love. HE never gives something else in its place. In regnant judgment HE does not withhold. There are no judgments in the Divine Heart and Mind, such as men and women have dreamt of and associated with HIM in their dark days. There is no such thing as the quality of Ahriman in God. HE is ever Ormuzd, the Glorious ONE, the Transcendent Love. There are no Satanic shadows bordering the threshold where HIS Love shines. All is as beautiful in the circumference as in the centre of Being. GOD's world of motion is perfect in the circumference, even as in the very centre whence that motion proceeds. When we make request, if we cannot receive that which we ask for; if we are not able to receive in fulness, not understanding all that we have asked for, HE gives in the measure in which we can receive, even in the fulness in which we can endure HIS blessing.

Therefore true prayer is to be understood as the motion of desire and request. It is articulation of desire. Desire itself is begotten of a hidden motion within us. It is the motion of Being. Prayer thus expresses itself in motion. It is most natural when praying, to kneel before the Presence in our Being. Who could do other than bow before the Great and Holy ONE! And in high request, it is most natural either to make HIS Sign on the breast, or raise our hands to HIM to receive the blessing which HE puts within them and pours through them into our Being. Prayer is such Divine motion in us. And its articulation does not mean merely the outward genuflection. You may have that in true prayer. Indeed, it is almost impossible to speak to the Divine, to stand before HIM, to commune with the Presence, and the whole Being fail to be in motion from the innermost to the outermost. You may have many genuflections without prayer at all; but in true prayer the Soul is in Motion. The prayer is the Soul's motion, the inner motion, the Being seeking to find that of which it has latent consciousness. It is the endeavour to realize more fully the meaning of the glimmering vision which from time to time it glimpses. It is a Divine yearning for reality, the possession of which can alone give satisfaction to the Soul, chase away its doubts, fill its Sanctuary with radiance, and bring to it that heavenly vision for which the whole Being yearns.

IRREVERENCE IN PRAYER

Prayer is motion; but do not imagine you pray because you utter some form of prayer in a perfunctory way. I have heard the Lord's Prayer, as given in the New Testament and Prayer Book, uttered in such a way that the vibrations were hurtful, instead of being harmonious and of exalting power to the Being. Because of the sacredness of the prayer itself, it should never be hurriedly recited. When we address the FATHER-MOTHER, there should be no rush. Indeed, if you come into HIS Presence in consciousness, there could be no discord. Would there not rather be that deportment which would express profoundest reverence? If it be so in earthly things, how much more so in Heavenly things! Yet men and women address HIM as if it were of no importance whatsoever how they did it. The indignity of it all!

Prayer is motion, and it is a motion full of harmony. It is the harmonious, rhythmic motion of the Being seeking its Source. And so prayer is of the nature of realization. It is the request unto that motion which brings the Soul to the realm of realization. It is therefore the blooming of Life's flower. It is the opening out of the flower. It is the process by which the perfect blossom becomes. It is that motion which not only reveals the flower and gives the perfectionment in the blossom; but it is such a motion as pours forth fragrance. Prayer fills the atmosphere with fragrance. You cannot truly pray without changing the conditions around you. Should the conditions be beautiful, you enter into harmony with them. Prayer, therefore, is a process of unfolding. It is blossoming. It is the outpouring from the Cup of Being of the sweet breaths of the Spirit. It is the resultant, as well as the cause, of the realization of contact with the Holy ONE.

You cannot know GOD without prayer. You can touch the Realms of GOD only by means of prayer. You cannot ascend into the Heavens without its up-carrying motion. For the heart must desire and the desire express itself in motion; and motion leads on to the realization. You cannot pray without blooming. You cannot pray without loving truly. You cannot pray without pouring forth the fragrance of your Spirit so that others may inhale its breaths and be exhilarated. Life's atmosphere for all Souls is sweetened when GOD moves within the Being in prayer.

What is the nature of the motion that comes with prayer?

It is the motion of the Ætheric atmospheres within us, begotten of the action of the Desire-Principle. That Desire-Principle is Divine. It is the ascension of the Being in a spiral motion. In the Spiral there are many degrees. There comes a realization of blooming, then of the full blossoming, then of the outpouring of the fragrance, followed by the realization of the ascension of the Spirit in us as we pass through the several degrees of the Spiral of Being. In the measure of our prayer we realize. In the measure of its purity we ascend into the Heavens. In the degree of its intensity, so is the answer that comes to us. In the degree in which we pray we make atmosphere; we ascend; we realize; we bloom as GOD's flowers; we ascend the Spiral of Consciousness.

DOES PRAYER AFFECT GOD?

Now we will look at the effect of such prayer upon the Divine Government. And you will note this: *prayer fulfils a law.* It is the law of desire. Desire gives motion, and the motion leads on to realization. Therefore, *it is the Law of God in you.*

So many people imagine that the Law of GOD is something written in words. The Law of GOD is written, but it is written within each embodiment of HIMSELF. It is written in your noble desires, for it is in your Divine Essences. It is written in those potencies which enable you to come into high, conscious realization of HIMSELF. The Law of God is within you, written on the fabric of your Being and revealed in your fashion.

"Thy Law have I hid in my heart," wrote the psalmist, "that I offend not against Thee." Ah, what wealth of meaning is couched in these words! And this is specially so when rightly expressed. Thy Law hast Thou written in my heart, that I offend not against Thee.

You may see the beauty of it, for it is obvious to the discerning. THY Law hast THOU written in my heart, so that when its pulsation is correct, then the whole arterial streams of my Being are harmonious in their flow. In THY Law I do not make mistakes. I do not hurt the Life THOU hast given me. I do not make it impossible for the Life within me to grow, to blossom, to pour out its fragrance and reveal THEE.

Real prayer, Soul desire, Divine yearning, is the fulfilment of the Law of GOD. You cannot get away from it. If you have been too proud to pray, as men understand prayer, nevertheless you may have felt a motion within you, a hidden desire to realize something. You cannot get away from prayer. You may get away from praying as men and women understand it outwardly, but you cannot get away from Soul prayer. Your desires are articulations in the hour when you say your prayers. The desires are the prayers. Your efforts to realize your desires express the motion of your life to make your desires concrete, whether as attainment and possession, or distribution in giving. Prayer is the fulfilling of the Law of GOD. His Law is within. For the exquisite Wisdom of the FATHER-MOTHER has given us a nature that can never be at rest away from HIM, that is, away from some degree of the realization of HIM. We are held magnetically by HIM: and no Soul finds equipoise other than in HIM. HE is our rest, our radiant point of perfect balance. HE is the apex of our life. It is in HIM alone our own radiant centre receives its Divine illumination. HE is the fashion of our Being. Without HIS Law in motion within us, HIS fashion cannot become, nor come into manifestation.

HOW PRAYER AND HIS LAW BECOME ONE

Prayer is HIS Law operative within us. It is behind our desire expressed in our motion; and it is hidden in the heart of all our realizations. That is the meaning of, "The prayer of a righteous man availeth much." But it does not avail to change GOD. You cannot change HIM. HE is the Eternal Good. But through prayer you can change yourself. You can change the conditions around you. You can change the conditions over you. You can affect atmospheres. You can enter Spheres. You can ascend into the Heavens to bring blessing down. By prayer you can come to the very Seat of the Almighty ONE, and you expand in consciousness. For it is only in consciousness that we can realize HIM. HE is not known outside of it. It is impossible to know HIM except through consciousness. HE is no man. HE is no individual person. HE is no individual SOUL. HE is all Being, the Absolute ONE WHO filleth all things, of Whom we ourselves are expositions as embodiments.

It is in consciousness we know HIM. So that when we come to HIS Seat, we come to HIS Seat in consciousness. But it is a reality. It is not a dream. It is not a vague realization. It is the most glorious of Realities. The most transcendent experience of the Soul is to know HIM, to come to HIS Seat, to look upon HIS Glory, to behold the beauty of the LORD within the Sanctuary.

Prayer is the Fulfilment of the Law of the LORD.

Prayer, therefore, instead of changing the Divine Government towards the individual Soul, fulfils that Government. The motion of Prayer expressed fulfils the Divine Purpose in the Government. It is God's Governmental way of fashioning and exalting a Human Soul even to the Seat of HIS Presence. It is wonderful in the beauty of it, the sublimity of it. And yet it is characterised by the exceeding child-likeness of it all; so that each one can apprehend and understand in his and her degree, the Eternal Mystery.

THE EFFECTS OF COMMUNAL PRAYER

Having shown to you what prayer is in relation to the individual, you will the better understand what its effects are in its real motion, and what its accomplishments may be in relation to the communal life.

Do you think for a moment that, if the prayers of the Churches throughout the ages had been living prayers full of Divine Motion, the world could have remained as it is quite outside the real knowledge of HIM, and apart from the true contacting of the influences of HIS Presence ? Do you think the world could have remained in darkness even unto this day ?

Do you think the Church itself could have remained in such deep darkness, that it has never understood the meaning of the Master's interpretation of the Divine Love and Wisdom, and the meaning of the holy estates of Jesus, Christ, and the LORD?

Do you think it would have been in a dense cloud that would have prevented it from understanding those things which it professes to believe concerning the manifestation of the Divine Love as a Passion to redeem the world by means of a Redeemer ?

Do you think it would have been as a traveller in a strange land regarding the meaning of what the Redeemer was, and how the Redeemer accomplished His glorious task, and fulfilled the Divine Purpose ?

Do you think the Mystery of the Sin-Offering would have remained unto this day so veiled that no glimmer of light shone out from it, and that a Redemption that is not redemptive could have been accepted?

Do you think that the world so ostentatiously religious, would have lain as the Western World has lain and does lie to-day, in the great darkness of Sheol, not knowing HIM WHO is our LORD?

Yet the Church has prayed morning and afternoon, daily and weekly, from year to year; but the Heavens have seemed to remain as they were, and, consequently, the Earth also.

When we pray, we must pray with the understanding illumined. When we pray, we must ask nothing from GOD that HE cannot accomplish, because it would be in direct opposition to HIS Law and a violation of the motion of HIS Law in us and through us. When you think of the ages in which one race has prayed against another race, and one people against another, wherein they have asked the FATHER-MOTHER common to both to blot each other out and overthrow all their enemies—not simply to redeem themselves, but to overthrow all to whom they were in opposition, in casting them out, as it were, from the very Kingdom of Promise—you can see that such prayers were begotten of Satan the deceiver. They are an exposition of the Devil. They are of the spirit of negation that prevents the children from realizing the sacred Love and Glorious Presence of the FATHER-MOTHER.

Why! when Souls pray truly, they get into an atmosphere where everything that is narrow and mean, little and belittling, falls away and must fall away. You cannot approach GOD holding on to your narrow traditions and to limitations you put upon your vision and love. You must leave those things outside the Door. The Portal is narrow. It will take in yourself, but not the things you have accumulated. Everything that is not of HIS planting must be uprooted. Everything that is a deflection of truth, honour and love, must be put away.

What a world it would have been if the Divine Love had not been perfect, and the Divine Wisdom so Glorious! What would have happened if GOD had responded to the various races in their states and conditions ! What a realm of tartarean tragedy the world would have been ! It has been pandemonium notwithstanding the ministrations of the Heavens ; but it would have been hell itself in every part of it, had the Divine Love and Wisdom been other than HE is. The Great Love knows best. There is nothing equal to that Love, nothing like it. It is impossible to understand unless you have realized that Love, how in its way it likens HIM, and reveals HIM in everything that is perfect. It is the perfect flower. It is the perfect blossom. It is the exquisite fragrance. It is that motion that is ever truly rhythmic, filling the whole universe of HIS Dwelling with harmony and music, sublime, triumphant and glorious.

You may see that while the world prays through its various religious avenues to get its desire fulfilled, and to have some kind of confirmation for its motion, the Divine Government goes on, infinite in patience, awaiting the time when the great outpouring can take place in response to all hearts that are truly yearning, earnestly making request, having true motion, and seeking unto Divine Realization.

Prayer, when it is Soulic, fulfils the Law of God. When it is worthy of the name of prayer, it fulfils the Law ; and, therefore, it accomplishes in the individual and the community, in the race and in the world, HIS Divine Purpose. But when men and women do not pray correctly ; when they do not desire beautifully ; when the motion of their love is not harmonious within and making for harmony everywhere, then they are defeating the Divine Purpose. They are intercepting or diverting the streams that make for the out-carrying of the Law of the Lord.

Prayer is an essaying to find oneness with HIM ; and it is never self-seeking. It is a motion towards union with HIM; never a desire to be apart from HIM. It is a unifying motion wherein the aspirant becomes one with all Souls, and learns to love them all, even without exception. This is something greatly needed to be remembered. Few seem to understand the claims of the Divine Love. If you stood on the threshold of the Divine World, and you could not love everyone, there are those who would say to you,—*You have mistaken the meaning of the Divine Love and its measure unto all Souls; so you must go back to the earth-life till you learn to love everyone. The Divine Love loves all and despises none.*

PRAYER AS A SERVICE OF MEDIATION

Prayer is a mediation by means of which the Heavens minister unto the Soul and the individual life. It is by means of prayer that the Angelic World is in continuous motion. Its blessed activity is one prayer in manifoldness, like the manifold prayers upon the Earth of all true and noble Souls, fulfilling some aspect and in some degree, the Divine Purpose. Prayer is GOD's mediating motion within the Being, throughout the Heavens, and amid the Realms of the Gods.

Here I would say this word to you that ye may understand a great Mystery. Do not imagine for one moment that prayer is confined simply to these realms. Prayer is not begotten in the Soul because of its needs arising out of what is considered its fallen state. Prayer is of its own very nature, whatever modifying influence its fallen states may have upon its motion. Prayer is the Divine desire in it working up and out to the personal life. It is begotten of that magnetic desire seeking to express itself in some degree of realization, and in the realization revealing the Divine qualities of the life, as the Life-flower in its blossoming, in its out-pouring of fragrance, and in the motion of its spirit God-ward.

Let me here take you to the Angelic World that you may witness this Mystery. Of course, you may be in consciousness in the Angelic World now. That is the state you should be in always. If you cannot constantly function within that higher Realm, still you can always be in a state of Angelic Love. The Angelic World is in us. This must be so ere we can enter into any sphere of that world, whether relating to the Angelic World of the Planet, or the Angelic World of the Solar Body, or the

Angelic World of the Divine Centre. If you were in the Angelic World of these realms, you would find that prayer was wont to be made; that it had to be made; that you could not get away from it; that if you ascended into the most Inward Spheres of the Eternal, you would find prayer obtaining and prevailing. Behold the motion of Cherubim and Seraphim! What does that ministry signify? One is the prayer of adoration and overshadowing; the other is the prayer of mediation, transference and distribution—the giving of the Divine Gifts unto the Soul. The Cherubic motion is the prayer of Adoration: it is the centripetal. The Seraphic is the prayer of Blessing: it is centrifugal. All Angels pray. Archangels pray. The Gods pray. All Divine Desire is prayer. All individuals everywhere, however exalted, pray. For the Absolute is in all and over all. HE is the Sum of them all. HE is the Mystery-Centre of all and for all. In all such embodiments, is HIS Own Mystery. But however great that Mystery, it may be realized in the individuation, whether in a Celestial System, known as the Realms of the Gods; or in Archangel; or Angel; or in the Human Soul; HE is ever greater than all. And so that Sublime ONE is adored by all. HE is prayed unto by all. For prayer is the desire of Individuated Being. It is the Law of GOD in the Being. It is the request to be ever more like HIM, and to ever more nobly, ever more fully, and ever more gloriously serve HIM.

THUS PRAYER IS OF THE ETERNAL

Prayer is mediatorial everywhere. You cannot get away from it. And he who prayeth best and learneth best how to pray now, will pray yet more and more as in consciousness the Being ascends. And by this I would have you understand that it is not prayer as mere utterance of formula that is meant. For whilst you may express that which you are desiring in a form of words, yet you may find language and the oral expression far too inadequate. In such a case the motion must express it. We make request in our deepest devotion; the motion has to bear it up and convey it as a stream of magnetic rays. Then it is revealed to the Heavens by the motion. The Watchers say,—"Look at that Soul! Behold how he prayeth! He has expanded. He has opened out his chalice: we will fill it." This is the fulfilling of the Law of God. The flower cannot kiss the sunbeams whilst it is shut up in the calyx, though the calyx can do so. The calyx protects the bud with its bloom. It hides it. But as the hidden flower grows, the calyx opens and the flower expands. It kisses the sunbeams. It revels in the wealth of the sunshine. It responds not only in revealing its beauty, but also in pouring forth its fragrance.

Thus is it with the Being as it grows and expands. It kisses the Divine Sunbeams. Yes, it is wonderful for the calyx to be opened and the bloom set free, and to open out yet more and more to the Divine, kissing His Sunbeams, receiving into the Being's chalice from Him. For the wealth of His Love as sunshine sets in motion that which produces the sweet breaths; and then the fragrance of Love goes out to fill all the room of the Sanctuary of our Being, till our atmosphere becomes sweet as the fragrance of the Heavens.

That is how God answers prayer to the Soul. He answers it in like fashion to the community. A community praying for greater realization of Love and Life and for blessing to come unto the world, surely does not expect to change God! Is He not ever seeking to bless all? He loveth all and forgetteth none. Hath He not made provision for all? He hath given of the Bread and Wine of the most Sacred Mystery. Hath He not so provided that all who obey His Law of Prayer shall even partake of the Divine Substance, and drink of the Divine Life-stream, and that they may thus become in the fashion of God? A community of Souls so praying must know that they do not change Him. But His Law is thus fulfilled. They change the atmosphere. Indeed, they contribute largely in helping the Angelic World to pour out its streams to stimulate the conditions of men and women. The first result of their prayer may be disturbing. By changing the conditions men and women become affected. They wonder what is wrong with them. The effect of true prayer is unto the healing of them. It contributes to the awakening of them. It makes the ascension of their life possible. Its motion effects the crowning of their life with purity. It is a fulcrum by which there is accomplished the filling of their heart with joy. It works for the Joy of Love to be begotten and made manifest. Its whole trend is unto the giving to their minds of the great Peace, the Peace begotten of equipoise in HIM, and the Joy of coming to HIS Seat to know HIM.

THE FERVENT PRAYER EFFECTUAL

Prayer is, therefore, effectual. But its effectiveness is not because it changes GOD, but rather because it fulfils HIS Law. Communal prayer is effectual; it accomplishes the Divine Will. Yet not by changing the policy of the Heavens, nor altering the administration of the Divine Love and Wisdom. Prayer fulfils the Law, and thus provides the conditions by means of which the Heavens can minister; it generates the atmosphere through which the Heavens can pour magnetic streams. The Heavens wait to do it: they are awaiting the prayers of the Saints. If you would help GOD through HIS Heavens to redeem and heal this world, to restore it to true balance, to bring back to the children the degree of equilibrium necessary for an upright walk in life, then pray without ceasing. But to pray without ceasing is to so live and move that your life will articulate itself. Your request will be expressed in action. The motion of your life will affect the atmosphere around you. Your consciousness of the Heavens Overshadowing you and Encompassing you, and the measure of your consciousness of HIS Indwelling Presence, will bring to you high realization of HIS Power, so that you will be contributing to the coming again of the Regnancy of GOD in the world, and the accomplishing of HIS will through the healing of all the woundings of the children.

This is the way the Heavens make use of prayer. This is how GOD answers prayer. This is real mediation at HIS Right Hand.

The children of this poor, afflicted world, distraught in its life and darkened in its vision, have for great ages been taught to believe that the Master Himself went to the Right Hand of the FATHER-MOTHER to make intercession for them, to plead for all Souls and thereby so to affect HIS Love, HIS Compassion, HIS Justice, HIS Righteousness, as to bring blessing to the world through HIS Church. Yet that Church has not observed deeply that there has been no change as the result of all the praying! It is not that the Heavens have been withholding the change. It is that the conditions in the thoughts, and the desires, and the hearts of men and women have remained unchanged and thus they have prevented the blessing.

How could the Master plead with His FATHER-MOTHER, other than in the motion of His Being, wherein He fulfilled the Divine Law? In His prayer He said,—"Send me wheresoever THOU wouldest to minister, THOU Who lovest all and blessest all, that I may be like THEE and more and more reveal THEE."

THE OBLATION ONE LONG PRAYER

Was not even the Oblation one long prayer! Was it not a Lenten supplication, an age-long Soul Litany, a tragic monastic Travail? It was the Travail of the sorrow of the Forty Days. Yet it was a prayer wherein was revealed the Divine Law of motion, the Divine Will of Purpose, even that of sacrificially bearing unto the uttermost, the burden, the sorrows, the travail of the Ancient Christhood, and the sins of the children of this world. Think, in so far as you can, what would happen throughout all the Western World if such a motion of travail were understood. Think what it would mean, even in this country, if in it true illumination took place when all the Sanctuaries are celebrating Lent ; and if it shone even amongst those who reject the idea of Lent, but who sing their Lenten songs nevertheless! If they all came into the understanding of the real meaning of prayer, and their Desire was divine and selfless, and their motion Angelic and Godlike, and in the consecration of their lives they gave themselves unto the healing of all Souls, think what prayer within the Sanctuary would accomplish for this land! Why, the Sanctuaries would be full of the atmosphere of the Inner Heavens, and men and women would drink of that atmosphere as they entered within the gates. And abroad from those generating stations, would go forth magnetic Divine power unto the rectifying of all the human wrongs that obtain and prevail, unto the healing of the cause of all human sorrow and travail, unto the unearthing of every evil state and the abolishing of every false and iniquitous condition. Then the children of this land would find true healing.

And if that glorious power of true prayer prevailed here, surely it would come to prevail throughout the Western World. And if it did so, then the Western World who received Christ into its mansion, as Simon the Pharisee is said to have received the Master, without knowing what it was doing, would fulfil its real destiny in bringing the Christ-Light to all Souls—revealing the Light through embodying the Light, and thus interpreting the Light—that Light which is the Light of Life, and is the Radiance of the Love of our FATHER-MOTHER.

Pray, therefore, unto this end, not only for your own ascension of Being, but for the arising of all Souls. In the measure in which you ascend, so will you have power in prayer to accomplish and give forth. Pray unto this end that the wondrous venues which exist for worship and service may be purified, that the Breaths of the Heavens may fill them unto the exaltation of desire and the clarifying of vision, and the bringing of realization unto the Souls of all who seek their Altars. Unto this end pray ye, and ye will be sharing in the Divine Government, fulfilling the Divine Will, and mediating for God. Thus will ye be HIS beautiful ones once more, HIS noble children who are selfless, lovable, beloved, loving, even unto the giving of all that HE hath bestowed upon you for the enrichment of your Being, giving of it in blessed fulfilment of HIS Love: In such giving is high mediation for HIM.

Oh Wondrous One! The transcendency of Thy Love and Wisdom is so great, we feel its immensity. And yet Thou hast given us to share it. Oh Wondrous One! Supreme in Love and Wisdom, Majesty and Lowliness, we adore Thee! We would ever adore Thee. And in our prayer of request and motion unto realization, and of sacrifice unto service most sacred, we would ever fulfil Thy Holy Law, and accomplish Thy most sacred Purpose.

THE COSMIC CONSCIOUSNESS

THE COSMIC CONSCIOUSNESS.

Concerning this sublime Mystery in its fact and possible realization, I have frequently given indications; so that it should be the more easy for you this morning to come with me whither I would fain lead you.

That there is such a thing as consciousness, we must all recognize. What cosmic consciousness is in itself, and how it becomes, may not be so easily differentiated and apprehended unto complete understanding. For the things that are of the highest and, therefore, of the innermost, can be fully apprehended and understood only when the Soul has attained sufficiently to that Divine Manhood of which its inception is the prophecy and its fashioning the perpetual testimony.

HOW CONSCIOUSNESS BECOMES

What is consciousness, and how does it become? There is in it that sublime Mystery which is found at the heart of all things. Out of that Mystery consciousness becomes. I do not say that it is generated, because the Mystery of consciousness is ever present. That Mystery permeates all Divine Elements, and is related to the Omniscience of God. When it becomes in a Human Soul, it is the result of polarization of those conscious Elements.

When a Human Soul is incepted, generated, and fashioned, there is motion through these Elements caused by the Pneuma, or Divine Breath. We have no terms to express adequately the Mystery. The impoverishment of language is never realized so fully as when one essays to express and interpret Divine Mystery.

That Breath we sometimes name the Spirit. The Spirit is also a living Flame. Such Breath and Flame are aspects of *pure Spirit*. The motion of that Breath brings together the glorious Divine Essences. And, as a result of such a process, the fashion of a Human Soul becomes. As those Elements contain consciousness (*for they are of the very elements through which the Eternal Mystery is expressed as Omniscience*), there becomes a concrete individuated aspect of that Omniscient Mystery in what we term a Human Soul.

Such is the manner in which the consciousness of a Soul-child becomes individuate. And then consciousness as something to be understood has to be apprehended through recognition. Thus, even where such a thing as the mystery of consciousness does not enter the human mind or heart, and where the realm of Being has not yet been touched within consciousness, such a life can cognize and recognize. In this way a child becomes conscious of a world outside of itself, of objects around it, of atmospheres playing upon it, of things of beauty and things otherwise than beautiful.

In self-relationship you become conscious of pain, if hurt; or gladness, if the wave of happiness beats upon the shores of your Being. You are conscious of the pain, of the gladness, or of both; one following the other as oft-times happens.

You become conscious of the desire to acquire, not simply in the sense of acquisitiveness, which, in its real meaning, is the process of acquisition, but acquirement to meet the requirements of your Being. Thus there is gain, and you become conscious of enrichment. It may be at first external to yourself; but it also operates upon certain other realms and becomes subjective, a part of your inner self. And so you have the consciousness of gain.

And because you have the consciousness of gain, and are conscious of the elements which make up the gain, you become conscious of loss when those elements which make the gain seem to pass from you—from your hold, from your vision, from your realization. Then you can become conscious of sorrow. And it is not only that you observe it in the world where men and women sorrow; but you become conscious of it in yourself as a state, some strange quality revealed in your experience. It is indeed really the motion of that quality within you which enables you to sorrow. And having such a quality you can become conscious of joy. As the sorrow passes away through the changing motion of that quality through which the sorrow came, you have joy.

Thus, consciousness is known to you, and to every Soul, through cognition and recognition. You recognize things; the world outside of you; the motion of life within you; the world of motion without, the world of feeling within. How great this motion is should become obvious to you presently.

HOW CONSCIOUSNESS DEEPENS

Through cognition (which is apprehension), and recognition (which is recovered knowledge, a coming back into the memory and into the consciousness of which memory is a faculty), you recognize the things you have known of old time. Knowledge grows. It is in this way that consciousness is expanded, deepened and elevated. It is in this way that consciousness is enriched; for all real enrichment must ever be through the motion of your attributes. But enrichment comes through the deepening of your consciousness. It is the result of acquisitiveness and acquisition; the taking into yourself of those things which you require, having acquired the power to do so and enrich your own Being.

Knowledge is, therefore, the outcome of cognition, consciousness, recognition; and knowledge is a path of the Soul. What was the world fashioned for? (And here we think of the world in its unfallen days.) Surely not merely that you should tread its planes, walk upon them, work upon them, and have pleasure within them? This world was fashioned that the children dwelling upon its planes upon the outermost circle, should move inward, and learn of the Divine Wisdom revealed upon those planes, through the various degrees of the manifestation of form, colour and rhythm. For in these is expressed GOD's own glorious Mystery of Love and Wisdom. From this it will be seen that the path of true knowledge is not to be despised. And we emphasize, *true knowledge*; for it must needs be that this is not confounded with merely intellectual attainments, which may be great without true knowledge.

And so the Soul's consciousness grows from less to more, from the little child to the older child, the greater child; the child of deeper feeling, of stronger motion upward, of more expansive vision. Through knowledge the expansion of Soul consciousness comes. And this is true even in a fallen world. You can have expansion, real expansion of consciousness, through the acquisition of knowledge. Sometimes the knowledge is not correct, and sometimes it is far from correct; yet, the consciousness is so deepened, intensified, made more alert, that the Being begins to feel more and more its own mystery, that there is a greater mystery hidden in life than hitherto was imagined.

What is this strange motion that seems to find no abiding resting-place anywhere, until it finds it in the consciousness of the Blessed ONE?

THROUGH THE OBJECTIVE

In the expansion of consciousness you will readily recognize that there is a dual motion. There is the objective and the subjective. The objective seems the nearest at hand, though it really is not so; at first it is the more obvious. It is easier to apprehend things in the objective world, than to cognize and recognize them in the subjective realms. It is easier to look on things which we pass daily, than to differentiate unto the perfect understanding and placing of those qualities which have their motion within us, and whose true motion gives to us an ever deepening sense of Life's Mystery.

Even through the outer expansion, our attributes gain strength. Knowledge grows from more to more. Life seems to expand, taking in all things; seeing, beholding, touching, appropriating, understanding more and more. That which is gathered in the objective, if rightly used, is turned inward through the process of transmutation; and the knowledge enriches the attributes in their inner motion. Thus the Being grows conscious of other things.

In the objective realm as the consciousness expands, the horizon seems to recede more and more as if the life were rising from one peak of a great range of mountains, to another peak with an ever extending view. The vision looks through the world as a great cathedral with its aisles, its galleries, the triforium and clerestory. For in the great and wonderfully built Sanctuaries, those hidden galleries are marvels of structure whose ancient uses are little known in these days. The conciousness takes in more and still more of the world around, and then turns to the stars to view the magnificent cupola of the Heavens, whose azure dome bespangled with Elohistic Lights, gives the perfect idea of the Divine Overshadowing of a world even such as this is. And such an ascension of consciousness fills the Soul with amazement. It must marvel. If it does not, it is because it is not awake fully. It must marvel at the expressions of the Divine Love and Wisdom in embodiment which it beholds, the exquisite expositions of that Love in the fashion of the embodiment, and the Mystery of the Divine Wisdom also hidden in the embodiment.

Thus the Soul's consciousness grows outwardly, spreading itself over the world to take it in, and then rises to the stars and tries to take them in, but at first only sees them as far off worlds whose Mystery is unknown, radiant points shedding some measure of Light into the great deep of space, and which become visible as the day passes and rolls into the night.

And so the Human Soul, operating through this ever increasing consciousness, seeks to gain the knowledge which the objective world gives by means of the Earth, and through the Celestial Heavens. For with all increase of knowledge there is an expansion of consciousness.

Yet this is but the outer motion. It is the motion which is necessary to the Soul in its growth by means of such knowledges as are to come to it through the objective manifestations.

WITHIN THE SUBJECTIVE REALM

But this knowledge gathered as inheritance, is to be taken into higher degrees of understanding. The cryptic writings of the world looked into, are to be read in the light of a fuller illumination. The meanings of the things beheld are to be learnt even until the Soul can read the Mystery lying at the heart of all it has beheld and ingathered. For it is in this way alone that the Soul finds its path to the heart of the Mystery of Being. That experience comes when its motion turns inward. And when it does so, it finds a world within itself which is not dependent upon objective vision merely, but where all things that are true in the objective find their true exposition. Consciousness in the outward realms grows objective in vision. Consciousness in the inner realms grows as a realization of Angelic, Celestial and Divine Estate.

Here we enter the Inner Sanctuary of which all sanctuaries are human expositions, and are real testimonies of the endeavour of the Soul in its motion to express divine beauty and grace geometrically in design, and numerically in fashion and in structure. For these are symbols of the Mystery of the Sanctuary of Being.

As you go inward you find that, to the consciousness, whilst it is not ceasing to expand in the objective (for that could not be through inward motion, which would bring about the interpretation of the objective), the world of the outer recedes, and the world of the Eternal proceeds. The Divine World comes nearer and still nearer, as the Being passes from court to court of the Inner Realms. Each court represents degrees; and these degrees are entered into through realization of the Divine Love and Wisdom. As it passes inward, which is also upward, and onward to the great Secret, the Soul is looking at those things it looked at objectively; but now sees them in another realm. It sees the Angelic flowering plants with blooms so perfect, that the most perfect outer blooms upon the Earth could not surpass them, nor indeed equal them: the fashion of them is exquisite. It meets with those embodiments of the Sacred Mystery to be found in pillars and their capitals; in the crowns of the arches; in the fashion of them; and in the divine architraves which seem to support an eternity above them.

THE INNERMOST SANCTUARY And then the Soul in its inner motion goes yet further onward and upward, still ascending through all the courts, even till it reaches the innermost Sanctuary. And then upward into that state of which the Lantern in the Cathedral was the Divine expression, the symbol where the Sacred Mystery was found, where the Light dwelt, whence the Glory of the LORD was shed down upon the eastern Altar of the Sanctuary.

Thus does the Soul's Being expand and grow, and deepen more and more, rising up through the perfect Human, bringing all that it can take in of that perfect Human into the status of the Angelic-Human, that glorious state wherein the Soul is one with the Angelic World. And further still it goes till all the glorious things which are to be discovered there become the Soul's inheritance in a state of realization. And then it passes into the Celestial Realms.

These Realms have their representation within you. The Visions read to you this morning were seen by the Soul of the Seer.[1] The Celestial Hierarchies are realities not only as stellar embodiments, but also as magnetic centres whose motion affects the Soul within the corresponding Celestial Realm; till the Soul takes on the formative expressions of their own fashion and their ministry.

Thus the Soul can see those systems and know them. It takes its flight on the wings of the dove or the Blessed Spirit; but not a flight through space merely. For if we took flight through space and reached the glorious constellation of Aries, we would know no more about Aries than we know now as dwellers upon these planes, as students and scientists. But

---

[1] *Vide* HERALD OF THE CROSS, vol. v, pp. 108, 111, 301, 314.

in the inner Sanctuary of Being those realms can be entered, and are entered. It is accomplished through consciousness.

Such is the path of the Soul's motion Godward, until it attains high degree of realization of the glorious Mystery.

Now those of you who are able to enter into the Sanctuary of your own Being, even more, perhaps, than you are able to look out upon this little world and the vastness of the universe; may be assured of this—the power of your entering in and your cognition of the things you meet in the way, and the recognition by you of many things, the strange familiarity of the experiences through which you pass and their obvious relation to you in other days, are testimonies of the Divine Consciousness within you, and speak of your own states in the past ages. And the fact of your forgetting them is the testimony of your travail through great ages, as you have borne the burden of ministry unto the children of this world.

These fragmentary thoughts may help you to understand what consciousness is—its reality, and its inherent, mysterious power to gather all qualities into itself. For it holds even memory within its grasp. It is the chalice wherein are hidden the feelings. It encompasses desire. It holds willinghood. It contains vision. We know nothing outside of consciousness. And the measure of our consciousness is the measure of the Divine equipment within us. It is the sum of the growth of our Being. It testifies of the relationship of ourselves, notwithstanding our apparent littleness, to the Inner Realms.

And now we will look at some of the degrees of Cosmic-consciousness.

THE MEANING OF COSMIC

The word Cosmic relates to the World-consciousness; and in yet higher degrees, to the Solar body and the Universe. Therefore, Cosmic-consciousness is more than individual consciousness. It is the consciousness which ultimates in such a fulness of the Divine Realization as makes the Being one with the Divine. The feeling of oneness with the Divine can be present through the whole process of the unfolding within the Being of what is named Cosmic-consciousness.

Through recognition there is knowledge. Through knowledge there is expansion. Through expansion there is not only an ever widening area of vision and cognition, but an ever deepening sense of upward motion unto attainment. When a Soul reaches a certain degree of this motion, it enters a higher status. In this state, there dawns upon its consciousness its oneness with all living things. It feels that all things are expressions of the Divine Love and Wisdom. It begins to feel sympathy not only for the individual, and attachment to the family through which it has come into manifestation; it not only feels relationship to the tribe to which it belongs, and the nation through which it has come; but it gathers sympathetically the vibrations out of its own home, its communal surroundings and relationships, its tribal relationships and the national karmic burden, until in its consciousness it reaches even the racial idea. Here it may become racially a Patriarch; first of all in the family, then in the community, then in the nation, then in the race. If the vision be still veiled, and the Love-principle not truly polarized, there is so great a tendency to misdirection, that deflections arise—family, tribal, national, and racial. For it is the same thing that happens, whether in the individual, or in the community, or in the nation, or in the race.

But when the Cosmic-consciousness breaks within the Soul, it becomes manifest. Its motion comes through the Soul, and is revealed in love for all. It has learnt on the way to love all and despise none; to love not only its own home, its own tribal relationships, its own community, its own nation, and the race through which it has come,—but all Souls. For, surely, all Souls in their primal qualities, are of the race of the Sons of God. In such a consciousness there is no such thing as the earthly limitations of national and racial motion. There is the one sublime Love for all. For this universal Love can be held by the Being, even whilst recognizing the fact that all cannot receive of the Love in the same measure, nor in the same degree. But the Love is there for all to receive and draw from in the day in which they can receive, and are willing to receive, in blessed ministry.

THE JESUS CONSCIOUSNESS The Cosmic-consciousness, even of a world like this which is infinitely small when compared to the Cosmic-consciousness of the Divine World; nevertheless seems vast in comparison with the Soul unit. For to the human vision, one solitary human Soul is apparently but as a grain of sand upon the shore. Yet the Soul can enter fully into all planetary life, until the Being is one with that life and with all Souls, full of compassion and pity for all. For unto such an one, there are neither bloods, nor descents, with undue value laid upon them; nor rich nor poor; but just the desire so to love all, that the inner Being of those who have been enriched in their estate may give of those riches, and that those who have been impoverished may become enriched, even unto the knowing of their childhood to the FATHER-MOTHER.

Cosmic consciousness of a Planetary order, is the Jesus-consciousness in perfect realization. One in perfect Jesushood is in the first great degree of the realization of the sublime Mystery we name the FATHER-MOTHER. You will understand that it is not to be regarded as personal, though the Master lived as the Manifestor of, and has come to be named and recognized throughout the ages as, JESUS, and CHRIST, and the LORD. But these wonderful terms, which so often have been interpreted to you, represent the great *degrees*, with many sub-degrees or states within them, of the Soul's attainment; its acquisition, its inheritance, its entering into the realization of that inheritance which is potential within it and is the gift of no man, nor of any system, but of GOD alone; and is the gift of GOD to every Soul. All that man can do is to help to give the right opportunities for the expansion of the Being. The Sons of GOD do this. They are the Jesuses of the world.

They must be one with all living things, one with all true life. They are the Souls who dare to love all, and under all circumstances. They are those Souls who, whilst never having even the shadow of scorn within them, would scorn to do the things that are beneath the dignity of a Son of GOD.

Jesus is the perfect Angelic realization of the Love of the FATHER-MOTHER in its embodiment and exposition. It is a state of consciousness. And the Soul cannot enter the next degree, until it has that consciousness which makes it one with all Souls. True, the qualities of the next great degree that is proceeding from the Divine Centre unto the Being and is coming into conscious realization, are operative in the Jesus state. For a Soul in Jesushood is in Spiritual Christhood. But it enters into the higher consciousness of Jesushood in what is named the second great degree—which is the eleventh house. It is the eleventh of the twelve Altars before which the Soul sacrifices. It is the house of Celestial Christhood wherein the Soul becomes, not only one with the motion of this world in sharing its travail and feeling its burden, but also one with all the motion of Being within the System, loving each World and each Soul, and seeing in every high embodiment, a Son of GOD. If you say unto me "How difficult it is!" I reply to you that it is only seemingly so. It is only the mind's concepts, its prejudices, its narrownesses which make it difficult for the Soul to recognize a Son of GOD in every living one. When I look into your face, I recognize your persona. Your outer form conveys this to me. But I see far beyond your persona, even to that which oft-times you fain would veil,—yourself. Your countenance reveals you. It is lit up, sometimes gloriously, when your motion is inward and upward, and even when it is outward in blessed ministry. But there are times when you would sometimes veil yourself in order to hide from casual passers-by who would not understand, or the inquisitive who might wish to know only to your hurt. *Yet to the Inner Worlds your Sanctuary is ever open.*

THE CHRIST CONSCIOUSNESS

In the realm whither CHRIST leads, all things are known. In the Cosmic-consciousness that comes to the Soul through its expansion, the Initiate rises into the consciousness of the Solar world spheres. You will remember that I have oft-times said to you, the Sun is not what he appears to be. The Solar Orb is a glorious Divine World, by whose magnetic motion this world is nourished and sustained. And His magnetic forces render a remarkable ministry. These have their motion upon and through the marvellous photosphere. The Sun which physical science knows, is only the photosphere; and this latter is only a very little part of the Divine Mystery of the Sun. The Orb is a glorious world of Divine estate and ministry. To attain to Solar-consciousness is to have the power to ascend into it. The Soul has the quality within it of passing in consciousness into that World, seeing its Angelic ministry, hearing the glorious Halleluiahs and Alleluiahs of that Realm, touching not only the realm of the Angel of the Planet, but coming into cognition and recognition and sympathetic oneness with the Angel of the Planet, as in the planetary Cosmic-consciousness. This Angel of the Planet is not to be confounded with the occult teachers known as Masters, nor any occult planetary hierarchy; but to be regarded as a Divine Presence. For the Soul becomes one with the Gods, having passed into the degree of that Cosmic-consciousness which makes it one with the consciousness of this world, and also reaches up into the consciousness which gives it true understanding of the meaning of the formulated bodies upon the Celestial Realms—those glorious embodiments of the FATHER-MOTHER'S Love and Wisdom and Radiance which are there for sublime ministries.

We can get there only through going up the great staircase of the spiral motion of the Divine Being within us. Out of the heart of the Great Deep are we begotten; into the heart of the Great Deep are we sent forth; with wondrous motion out of the heart of the Great Deep do we proceed, the while gathering into the inner consciousness of the Being the knowledge of the Sacred Mystery we name our Lord Christ; and thus to the LORD HIMSELF, as the Soul takes the great degree. In this last, HE becomes so real within the Being that all the Universe opens to the Soul; and this, not only as a *belief* of the mind, but very specially as a consciousness in the Being.

THE LORD CONSCIOUSNESS All things that are true and beautiful are HIS embodiments, from the least to the greatest; but the greatest express HIM more fully. And the Being is conscious of the meaning of the fashion of all things; and their purpose, their qualities, and their ministries.

All along the way of the Soul's ascent, there is a gathering up into the Being of those elements which, at the outset I said were related to the Mystery of the Divine Omniscience. The fashion of the Soul becomes more and more like the fashion of the Divine. It is known amongst the Gods. It functions and moves amid the glorious Celestial embodiments of the FATHER-MOTHER. It understands them and their ministries. And thence it can return to the Innermost Sanctuary, and enter into that sacred Lantern where the Lamp of the Mystery of GOD hangs, and the Sacred Flame burns as the Light within that Lamp. That Sacred Flame is produced as the result of the motion of the Divine Breath which has blown for ages through the Divine Essences and Elements of the Being. At first it is but a little Flame. It is as the flame of the candle. From the flame of the candle it grows in volume and intensity, becoming the Flame of the Divine Mystery to light up that great Lamp in the Lantern of Being, until it resolves itself, in its passage through the Being, into a radiance that is even as the Sun in his glory.

It is thus the Divine HIMSELF is beheld by the Soul in the vision of the ADONAI. It is thus the Eternal ONE is realized within the Being. And the Sanctuary of the Being becomes clothed with the glory. The radiance is HIS Radiance, which is produced through the motion of HIS Sacred Flame as it moves through the Spiral of our Being, giving to the whole fashion of our Life the likeness of God.

Such I would have you understand to be the ultimate of a Soul. And yet the ultimate is indescribably more, far further reaching than any words can give in description.

Oh, the wealth of the Mystery of God in us! The splendour of God in the fashion of our Being! What a delight it is to be His child! How great is the joy of knowing, even in a world like this of travail and sorrow, that we are His; that His Fashion is within us; that we are in His Likeness; and that He, through His blessed ministries, will enable us more and more to reveal that Fashion as our consciousness deepens and expands and ascends. And as the effect of that expansion and deepening and ascension becomes manifest in our attitude to Souls, in our ministries unto others, in our giving for Him, even unto the uttermost of our Being, our Joy is increased manifold.

Do you ever have unworthy thoughts of God, or of His Fashion within you, or of His Fashion in another Soul? Put away from this hour every unworthy thought of Him, or of yourself in His Likeness, or of another Soul who is also His child, even of those in whom you may behold garments dyed-red through travail, and countenance of Soul tear-stained because of the travail.

To be a Son of God is no mean thing. There is nothing mean in any one who stands in Sonship to God. Therefore, put everything that is mean away. Are ye not of those who once knew these glorious things we have endeavoured to bring back to your remembrance through this fragmentary unveiling of His Glory? Then be Sons of God again. Be of those who are such in their compassion and pity, because of the divinity of their Love unto all Souls; of their recognition of the Divine ministry through all Celestial Realms; who are one with the Gods, Heaven's helpers, and contributors, and servants of the Gods. Be one with Him Who is your Lord and Who calls you to be absolutely His own; in every quality of your Being;

in every attribute and power; in every part of HIS glorious fashion in your Being.

Unto what end is Life if it be not to know HIM and embody HIM? Could there be anything with a greater dignity, with more transcendent and yet tender appeal, with a greater measure of Immanency? For this touches HIS Indwelling Presence in our life, and HIS call to us to embody HIM.

The perfect embodiment of HIM implies all consciousness lying behind the Mystery of that term "cosmic," one with the Universal Love and Life and Radiance, a dweller in the Radiance, an embodier of the Life, a glorious Divine exposition of the God-Mystery Who is Love.

It is in you all; doubt it not. The power of HIS own Mystery is in you; let it grow, filling you full of sweet reverence and gentleness, majesty and strength. Let the exposition of HIMSELF through you proceed until HE again becomes within you as your LORD, and you take on the glorious fashion of ADONAI.

THE REGNANCY OF CHRIST

THE REGNANCY OF CHRIST

THE RELIGIOUS OUTLOOK

The outlook of the Religious World wherein its hope is expressed for the future, is always such an anticipation as is implied in the coming regnancy of Christ. And this divinely begotten hope holds it, notwithstanding the conditions of the world made manifest in the social fabric and the communal life, in national purpose and racial ambitions, with all the striving, social and communal, national and racial, begotten of misdirected thought and misapplied activity.

For in the Religious World there is such a motion as this even where things are most stereotyped, transcending the ordinary conditions of life, which fills the heart with the hope that a great, much needed change will come soon, and that the transformation will be effected through what is termed the *Regnancy of Christ*.

In anticipation of such, many are looking for the personal appearing of that One who is to have the regnancy. We hear voices calling all over the world concerning this transcendent and Divine Event. All do not think after the same manner. All do not pursue the same path in their thinking. All are not confined within the limitations of the like realm of thought. Yet all who do anticipate this personal form of manifestation, do look for a regnancy through a Great One.

Even within quite recent days, without and within the Church the question is again postulated: Was Jesus the Christ? For however full of assurance the Church with its manifold shades of thought may have appeared to be, you may be assured of this, that, except in the matter of its affirmations and statements, it has never had any real assurance, as anyone familiar with the study of the History of the Church in relation to Beliefs, well knows.

If all those who have been students of theological theories and beliefs concerning the Master, the constitution of His

Nature, the mission on which He came, His going away and His return, could have liberated themselves from the limitations of the traditional venues and statements, what a proclamation there would have been throughout the ages! But there have been few who have found liberation; and there have been only echoes from time to time through those who felt they must have liberty to say something of that which moved within their Being.

QUESTIONS OF GREAT MOMENT It is not to discuss such traditions and statements that the subject has been brought before you this morning; though it is well to understand these things. It is rather that you may have a clear and unmistakable vision, with an ever-deepening consciousness of the great reality; that you may have a deeper understanding of Who CHRIST is; that you may know the nature of His regnancy, even such as He may have in this world. The following questions have again been raised:—Was Jesus the Christ? Was He, as it has been said of Him, CHRIST and LORD? Is it He of whom the scriptures speak saying that His shall be the regnancy; that He shall be KING of all the Kings and LORD of all the Lords?

And if so, who are the Kings, and who are the Lords, over whom His regnancy shall take place, and through whom it shall be revealed?

And even concerning this Earth, we enquire what are the kingdoms which are to know the regnancy of Christ until all power and authority within them be laid at His feet?

These are questions that need understanding. Blessed be the Great Love, salvation is not dependent on the understanding of them, for salvation is to be found of GOD. But if ye would know Him Who is to reign within you and through you, it is well that ye also understand the questions and the answers to them. And in finding the answers to the questions, ye shall see correctly *how Jesus reigns*, what is the nature of *the Christ regnancy*, and *how the Lord is supreme in His Regality* over all the Kings and Lords.

HOW THE MASTER SPOKE OF HIMSELF

Now, the Master in the days of the Manifestation spake of HIM Who was the LORD of Being. He drew aside the veil so that His intimate ones could behold HIM who was the CHRIST, the revealing One. When the Master spake of HIM, it was as of one whom He knew.

But he never spake of that One as Himself! He never referred to Himself in the Teachings as the LORD of Being, or even as CHRIST. The Master was the servant of the LORD of Love, unto the end that, as John in the Manifestation Life, he might be the vehicle of the Revelation of the LORD CHRIST JESUS. He was crowned with the consciousness of Jesus, Christ, the Lord: that is, He was able to move within the realms to which those terms belong, and share in the mystery of the life which those states signify.

But He was only the Servant.

That He knew the beauty of the Jesus state He revealed in His Love, compassion, pity, tenderness, gentleness; and in His understanding of Souls through His Love.

That He knew the realm of the Christhood was made manifest through Him in the radiance that streamed through the Message He had to give. For there was an understanding of all Souls; and within that Message all Souls were comprehended and blest, though the Message was specially for those who could understand the Christhood.

And that He could speak intimately of the FATHER-MOTHER, LORD of all Being, was but the revealing that He knew that ONE with an assurance that was neither self-begotten, nor the result of mere belief of traditional heritage, but which was begotten of most blessed consciousness and realization of HIM.

In that consciousness He could speak of the FATHER-MOTHER as the LORD of Being Whom He knew.

These things are true.

Yet though He realized so much in Himself, He was but the Servant; and He knew this, even as He knew and taught that

Jesus is not Christ, though Jesus is the way to Christ; that Jesus Christ is not the LORD, though Jesus is the way to the Christ Radiance and the LORD Consciousness.

Until men and women understand that whatever may happen upon the Earth and in the Heavens regarding personal and individual embodiments, and world embodiments, none of them can be spoken of as the LORD CHRIST in any absolute sense. *For the Lord is never a man.*

The LORD is Being!

Christ is the Radiance begotten of High Being in motion!

Jesus is the manifestation of that motion of Being expressed in concrete embodiment and service.

Now, it is said that Christ is to reign, King of Kings and Lord of Lords, and that there is to be no end to His regnancy. And the question arises, which involves and anticipates much: Is Jesus the one who is to reign, King of kings and Lord of all lords?

THE COMING AGAIN OF JESUS That is what the religious world in general believes where it is not yet illumined in this matter It is what Christians as a whole believe so they look for a personal appearing. They are prepared to look for personal and individual claims, and to listen to them.

But the LORD is never a man, as we have observed—though, potentially, HE is present in the consciousness of all Souls. And we have seen that Christ is the glorious state potentially in everyone. For Christ in you is the glorious hope of the perfect realization of Christ-consciousness, and the attainment of the realization of Divine power through the Divine Presence, by which even all worlds are transcended. Such realization and attainment lift the Being beyond the limitations of the motion begotten of time, and the confines of space, until the Being becomes one with the Universal, understood in the Divine sense—that Universal BEING from Whom all Souls have proceeded, and of Whom all are individuations, and unto the realization of Whom all must attain.

But if it were the man Jesus, the man of Nazareth, who was to reign King of kings and Lord of lords, it would be merely personal, having all the elements of the merely Human. And where are the kings and the lords? If you look out upon the world, earthly kings and kingdoms are seen to be changing, and even earthly lords are passing out of their heritage.

Men and women sometimes speak and think and write as though the coming of an individual from the Innermost Realms to make manifest, could effect change in the hearts and minds of kings and lords, and command their principalities and powers by his mere appearing! Such transformations are only effected through change wrought in the desire, outlook, purpose, motion and direction. To alter the life of the world means that the transposition of the thought of men and women must be effected; the healing of their wrong feelings by helping them to desire rightly and beautifully; the restoration to true polarity of their inverted vision, and the taking away of all the spiritual astigmatism which is so prevalent.

Men and women must needs learn this living truth, that great inward changes giving outward spiritual transformations, are not accomplished merely by Divine manifestations through personalities. The Divine Regnancy over the kings and the lords is of a wonderful order. And we hope the time will speedily come when there will be kings and lords in this world in a redeemed state; kings and lords who do not claim to be such, but are actually regal ones; who, though not necessarily crowned outwardly, are, in reality, crowned with the dignity of Divine Childhood and enrobed with spiritual administrative capacity. And these will be full of that Love by which Souls can be understood, and sympathized with, and ministered unto for their healing and uplifting and illumining.

But we anticipate; for the question has still to be answered: Who are the Kings and Queens and Lords over whom CHRIST is to hold regnancy?

THE LORDS AND KINGS TO BE SUBJECT TO CHRIST

CHRIST is the Eternal Manifestor of the FATHER-MOTHER. He has this office in all realms; and all the realms (and here we think of unfallen realms) are under His regnancy. Throughout the Universe the LORD CHRIST reigns. Our own Divine World, that is, the Divine World of this system, is under the regnancy of the LORD CHRIST. That means that our own glorious Sun is the embodiment of the Logos, as understood in the sense of our mystical, soulic, divine terms. HE is ADONAI in one of HIS glorious manifestations. So that the Lords of the Divine World ruling within the central body of this system, express the motion and the glory of the LORD CHRIST. For the Sun is not what he appears to be, nor yet what he is thought to be. For He is none other than a most majestic embodiment of ADONAI, and is the centre of this planetary system. He is Sol, the Head of the Solar system. It is thus it is named the System of Sol.

But as Sol, the Sun represents manifold embodiment. It is a world denizened with the most glorious Beings whose ministry is unto this world and all other parts of the system. Yet though so glorious, Sol does not stand alone as Divine embodiment, for every member of the Celestial Hierarchy might be spoken of as King and Lord for GOD. For each has ruling power. As King each one has a regnancy. Each reigns to express the LORD CHRIST—the Divine Mystery, through embodiment and ministry. Each reveals true Divine Government. Each represents the LORD'S government; that is, the right motion, ministry and purpose; but not government as understood historically, nor as this world has known it for great ages. As we have said elsewhere recently, the true government is Theocratic and not democratic. It is GOD'S government through HIS own appointed ones, through those who can embody HIM, and administrate from HIM and for HIM.

It is in this sense that the LORD CHRIST is King of all the Kings and LORD of all the Lords. For in the Celestial Hierarchies, the Will of the FATHER-MOTHER is pre-eminently embodied. It is executed and accomplished. Divine administration prevails there. It once prevailed in this world in the Golden Age; and the return of the regnancy of Christ is to be the return of the glorious Government of GOD within this system, when the resplendent Solar Body shall be able to return unto the high estate from which it had to descend for the accommodation of its photosphere unto this world in order to minister to it under the changed conditions.

This is just a glimpse of the Regnancy of Christ through all the worlds, through all the embodiments in those worlds, where the Divine Kings and Lords reign and rule and administrate, full of Divine responsibility.

It is true that what is macrocosmic is also microcosmic. As it is in the Above so is it to be in the Beneath or Lower Worlds, and also in the Within.

AS IS THE ABOVE SO IS THE WITHIN

This is likewise true: If Christ doth not rule the central principle within any world or Soul, then such can have no Life. If its motion be not the motion of the LORD CHRIST, then there is no true radiance begotten. If the LORD CHRIST doth not reign within all the Being, there can be no true administration from the Heavens of Being to the individual World or Being; it has then all to be accommodated in a way quite different from the Divine accommodation to the Soul in its natural condition of Divine Heritage.

This will lead us to look for a few moments at the kingdoms through which the regnancy of Christ is to prevail within this world, when the kingdoms of this world are to be Christ's and when He shall reign for ever and ever.

All earthly kingdoms have had a Tribal significance.

The Communal life is built up of the family life.

The Home is the little tribal centre for the individual and personal life.

Then there is the larger communal life of the families, and through the combination of them, the tribal life. Tribes had their origin in spiritual and soulic relationships and states; and, through the tribal combinations, peoples and nations were built up and, through nations, the races.

Herein you will understand that all those expressions have spiritual significance. There is the kingdom in the home. It is first within the individual. Through the comity of individuals the home becomes, and the kingdom is expressed through the family unto the tribe; then through the comity of tribes unto peoples, then nations, and through the many nations unto the still more comprehensive community expression we name the racial Life.

The regnancy of Christ must touch every aspect. But that does not imply that it shall, or must needs necessarily, refer to outward rather than to inward regnancy. And this inwardness of regnancy is first in the individual, then in the communal, to expand into the national life, and then to permeate the race.

The regnancy of Christ is the regnancy of radiance that shows the true way. It is thus also the regnancy of Jesus, revealing the beautiful life which is the exquisite embodiment of what the Divine Love of the FATHER-MOTHER stands for. This will be manifested gloriously when Christ reigns within the kingdoms of this world.

THE KINGDOM IS WITHIN You have the Kingdom of Christ in your own Heart. Its realms are your thoughts, your desires, your feelings, your purposes, your heart's motions, your aspirations. The Kingdom of Christ in you is one, though it expresses itself in the manifold departments of your Being. In the regnancy of Christ within the individual, all the individual kingdoms of every part of the Being become obedient unto the Law of Christ. The Law of Christ is that of true motion. Obedience unto the law of true motion is, therefore, obedience unto the LORD CHRIST.

Now, a Manifestation from the Heavens is an intimation and

illustration of the state to be sought after. It relates to embodiment as a resultant of Divine Law operating through the Being's motion. The regnancy of Christ in the Within, is the regnancy of Christ carried through into all the kingdoms of experience. In centrifugal motion it is from the innermost to the outermost; and in the centripetal, from the outermost to the innermost. The reign of Divine Law in the individual makes that individual a partaker of Christ. There is a sense in which such an one is a member of the Body of Christ. Such a Soul is a citizen of the Christ-Kingdom; to become an inheritor of the LORD CHRIST, as it becomes conscious of HIS Divine Presence radiating supremely through the Being.

All these things are to be effected with the coming of Christ.

Yet the question is not fully answered.

The regnancy of Christ is also related to the elemental kingdoms; to all the substances out of which the embodiment named the world, has become manifest. It is the regal, triumphant motion of all the Elements, all the Breaths, all the Powers and their influences, contained within this world as a system.

That Christ shall reign for ever and ever, and all things be laid at His Feet, means that there will be a restoration, a re-upliftment, a re-building of the whole planetary constitution, until every part of the Earth responds to the Law of Christ, and is the beautiful exposition of the Divine Government.

This is a triumphant vision and may seem a long way off. But it is not so far away as men and women wot of! The day is hastening. It is coming; and is at hand. The morning is heralded! The night of the world's travail passeth away. CHRIST is coming! HIS Kingdom is coming! HE has made HIMSELF manifest in the restoration of Jesus. The LORD WHO was, and WHO is, and of WHOM it was said that HE was about to come again, is now coming upon every beautiful Breath, through every noble thought, within all motion of Being begotten of Divine Purpose.

The LORD is coming back to HIS own.

CHRIST is revealing Himself to those who once knew Him!

Jesus is rising from the dead within the heart of those who once knew the blessed state, to find embodiment again in their life, and come forth into manifestation.

The day thus hasteneth when the kingdoms of this world shall become the kingdoms of our LORD and HIS CHRIST, and HE shall reign for ever and ever.

And now for a moment we will look at the inner significance of the terms Jesus, Christ, THE Lord.

THE EXTENT OF THE REIGN OF JESUS

The Life expressed as Jesus is made manifest upon the Celestial Realms. Though it seems to be a lowly estate compared with the greater radiance of the Christhood, yet wherever Life is pure and beautiful, and full of joy and gladness begotten of the consciousness of God, there Jesus reigns. Thus, in the Celestial Hierarchies Jesus has His regnancy. But it is not the regnancy of any man, nor even of a servant of the Highest. It is the regal expression of the Divine Principle; *for Jesus is a state.*

And when this world is restored, Jesus shall reign from the rivers to the ends of the earth—that is, He shall reign through all the Streams of Being as these flow from the Divine Centre to Life's circumference. The Streams of Being are the Ætheric and magnetic elements proceeding from the Divine Heart. He shall reign through these, and be expressed by means of them. The Children of compassion and pity, gentleness and purity shall become manifest once more. It will not be the regnancy of any one man but the regnancy of GOD in all men. In and through all shall the Sublime One reign when the Jesus-life is fully made manifest. Jesus so affects the Being that Love is manifested. And this is true whether it be here in the life of the individual, or in the Celestial Hierarchies. The Jesus manifestation relates to embodiment, and the revealing of the Divine Love through the embodiment. For remember, the beautiful Life is not one simply to be realized and manifested here, but is a Life to be taken with us wherever we go. It is the state of Life realized in the Divine Love. In those days to which we rejoicingly look forward, it may not be required of us to show pity as we have to do to-day. For compassion and pity will prevail, and the lesser children will be shielded. But in the Divine sense there is always pity. Yet, it is not that which is understood by pity in the human presentations of the term.

Compassion is the mediation of Divine Love unto those who require love for their growth.

Pity is the exquisite gentleness that covers them; that takes them into the very bosom of that Love.

There is always pity and compassion where the Divine Love is realized. For Divine Pity and Divine Compassion are the twin great attributes of Love in ministry.

This much will you understand, that, if you would bring the reign of Jesus to the Earth, the best way to help its coming is not to look for the coming of any Messenger in a personal sense, but rather to lift humanity up into noble conditions. All life is a miracle. It is not, according to the laws operating in the lower degrees, but it is according to the Law of GOD operating in the Soul's constitution; which is Divine.

If you would bring Jesus back to the Earth, then embody Him. That is the only way.

Merely to follow any Heaven-sent servant will never bring the LORD CHRIST back to the world. Only the Vision, and the Embodiment of the Vision in the life, will bring back CHRIST to the world. To welcome Jesus back is not simply to welcome back the man who was the Servant through whom the Divine Manifestation was made, although even His return will be welcomed. But to bring Him back is to make that for which He stood a reality in the life. It is to embody the Divine Love.

THE EFFECTS OF THE REGNANCY

Jesus has relation to Life; therefore, He relates to that which we reveal through Life; that which we interpret by means of the motion of Life; that which we unveil of the Divine Love through our ministries. Therefore, Jesus has to do with Divine Feeling; with Divine Desire; with Love Divine.

Christ has to do with Being in high consciousness. His reign is associated with great Divine Potency, for He is Sublime Realization within the Being. His regnancy in the Life of Manifestation is through Jesus.

But Jesus can reign though Christ be not yet regnant (except in the purpose and potency of the Spirit, whose motion doth give the power to embody the Jesus-life). Though in this state the resplendent radiance of Christ is not yet become. For such transcendent experience is the abiding state of Divine Illumination. And such things come only through great degrees of Soul Realization.

Christ has relation to the Light, as Jesus has to the Life. He is the Radiant One cognized and dwelt in through intensified consciousness. The magnetic motion of His Principle, gives the Being perpetual Illumination. And in the degree in which that Principle has motion, so is the Being illumined from GOD. It is thus that Illumination comes. It is not simply seeing visions in the Heavens. Such Visions do come to those who are on their way to Seership. And they are coming more and more to those Souls who are awakened and who have the power of clairvoyancy belonging to the persona, and also that of the Soul. And all Souls have this power of mind and Soul clairvoyancy latent within them.

But such experiences are not to be confounded with Illumination. This latter is from the Within. It is the resultant of the motion of the Christ Principle. There is no other way of Illumination. Even the Divine World cannot inspire a Soul except in the degree in which Christ is realized within it. For the measure of inspiration can only be commensurate with the Soul's capacity to receive, and its power to endure the Divine Magnetic Streams.

It is true that Souls receive heavenly vision for education.

For Souls grow through receiving heavenly visions from the Angelic world, though, at the time, they do not understand their full import; but bye and bye the meaning breaks upon them and light illumines their understanding.

But Divine Illumination and Inspiration are of the innermost realms. They are the fruitage of the flowing of the magnetic streams generated from the motion of the Christ-Principle within the Being. For the Soul becomes uplifted in state and power, till it can stand in the full splendour of the Radiant Indwelling Presence we name the LORD CHRIST.

Therefore, the regnancy of Christ within the Being is the regnancy of the Light. It is the Divine gift to the Soul of its true regal inheritance, the crowning of the exquisite manifestation of Jesus with the splendour of a Son of God—which splendour is the effulgence of God in the measure in which it can be bestowed upon one in the state of Sonship to Him.

HOW TO REALIZE THE INDWELLING CHRIST

And if you should ask, as oft-times your heart doubtless does: How are we to know that the Christ-Principle is in motion within us? I would say to you:—It is always in motion! Christ is your Life, even when ye may appear to be far away from the consciousness of Him.

But it has two streams; and these might be spoken of as *the passive and the active*. Most Souls are confounded for a time by the awakening to consciousness within them of the activity of the Divine magnetic Christ-Principle, and the deep emotion begotten of the passive.

When we use the terms active and passive, the mind naturally thinks of action and inaction. But that is not what is meant. In the Divine Realm there is no such thing as inaction. Even the most passive streams are most active. The most apparently passive potencies are most active. Passivity does not mean inactivity. It has relation to the magnetic state. In the Soul's passive motion, it is ascending GODWARD. This is its inward motion. It is most active, though it is moving in the passive or centripetal direction. In the active mode of the Christ-Principle there is the Divine urge, and the manifestation of the Divine urge to find expression through the Mystery that is within. Through the vision that has come and the ideal that has been built up, there is the endeavour to embody. Bear these two thoughts in mind.

Jesus reigns through Life in feeling, desire, purpose; our love, compassion, pity; our gentleness, tenderness, and our humility; and our selflessness.

GOD reigns through Jesus. GOD gives Jesus a name which is above all human names, and a glorious regnancy that is the heritage of no one man, but is HIS Gift unto all HIS children who are willing to live the Life. And unto all those who are willing to so live there comes, bye and bye, the call from HIM to enter into the consciousness of the Christ motion in the Within, of which there is begotten high Illumination, transcendent Vision, most glorious Power for radiation. And thus the Being is caught up into the Divine motion. And the Christ-Principle through the Divine motion of the Being gives the Radiance. The Being is illumined. And the Light being in the Within, it must shine forth. Even though at times it may have to be veiled, yet it always has the power to reveal itself and come forth into radiant manifestation, and flash upon Souls the Glory of the Divine LORD.

And thus you will understand how Christ reigneth within the Being, giving the Soul Divine Illumination.

Yet there is more; for the Soul is microcosmically what the great macrocosm is. It therefore has the cosmic potencies within itself. And, having such, the Being can rise still higher. Its motion is upward, still upward, and yet still higher in state till it knows in high Realization the LORD of Being. To know HIM thus, is to move within the Kingdom of GOD.

Now, as Jesus has relation to the Life and Christ to the Light, so the LORD has relation to Being. Now, Being is Love in its Absolute State.

GOD is Being: HE is Love.

JESUS, CHRIST, AND THE LORD Jesus is the embodiment of the Love for ministry in Life, Christ is the manifested Divine Radiance of Love; but the LORD is Being. HE is absolute consciousness. HE is, within the system of the Soul, the consciousness of Divine Oneness with all Being. When HE reigns, it is within and through the consciousness of the Being.

And you will note this, that in Christ all Light comes gradually. The Soul is conscious of stages of Illumination. It knows the hours of Inspiration when these come. It grows conscious of passing through the great degrees of Illumination and Inspiration. And when it reaches the Lord Consciousness, it does not leave these things behind, but goes onward and upward, passing through still greater degrees. It leaves nothing behind that it has gathered up into itself as realizations. But then it so transcends the realms beneath, that all its Illumination and Inspiration are begotten of the consciousness of the Presence in the Within, so that its Illumination is not by the hour, nor by the day, nor by the month, nor even by the year. It just lives in the consciousness of HIM. HE is ever the Life of the Being. In HIS regnancy HE fills all things in the Within, so that the Being has but to be tapped for the power of that regnancy to flow out in blessing.

* * * * *

It is reported that the Master said:—

"Hitherto ye have asked nothing in my name; ask that ye may receive."

Of course He never requested them to ask anything in His name, but in the sacred Name of the FATHER-MOTHER. All honoured names are sacred to us, if we love truly. But we make request for Divine Gifts in that Name alone, which is above every other name, even that of the FATHER-MOTHER. There is profound significance in this fact. Whilst His Mediators are manifold, it is HE alone Who must be entreated. And this we shall do if HIS Sacred Name radiates its glory within us and illumines our understanding. And then shall the Blessing of HIS Sacred Name find a true venue through which to make itself manifest.

Did the Master chide those intimate ones who gathered around Him for their lack of inquiry concerning the real Divine things? Verily He often had to lead them away from themselves, and incite them with visions of the glorious world.

For He was as a fountain full to overflow with the waters of living knowledge and consciousness of HIM Who was His LORD. And there was so much in that fountain that could not be poured forth until His intimate ones asked. In the measure in which they asked and could receive, He gave to them. It was not always necessary to ask in words. If the heart truly asks, its desire will be known. The attitude of the Being will be such, that there will be no mistaking its motion. And then shall the asking heart have abundance.

It is through such an æonial process of asking and receiving that the Soul at last enters into the consciousness of Being.

Often has it had to be said to you, that ye have nothing of your own; that all your gifts are GOD given. As ye have asked in your Being, so have ye received from HIM. If you think you have anything of your own apart from HIM and acquired by yourself, it is vanity! And there is no room for vanity in the Kingdom. All true things are from GOD. All great things are HIS Gifts. Love itself is HIS OWN Sublime Mystery within the Being. The Radiance of Christ is HIS Gift. It is HE alone Who sets in true motion HIS OWN Divine Principle within the Being! And when the Being realizes HIM, it knows full well that it has nothing of its own, no worthy power from itself, but from and in HIM only all high and holy gifts. And should shadows steal across the threshold and cast themselves upon the garments, as may happen in this world, these are known not to be of the LORD. And the Being just stands in the conscious regnancy of the LORD of Love. It knows HIM. There is no more any questioning. Whatever the experiences, its trust is perfect. It knows all is well, for HE gives the illumination. There is no Life sought outside that consciousness; nor is Life to be come at in any other form. Outside of that consciousness the Being seeks no life, has no Light, finds no Love. But in the consciousness of HIS Indwelling there is Life, Life in abundance, Life in sublime fulness.

Here then is the full-rounded vision of the regnancy of the LORD CHRIST JESUS. Here is the transcendent meaning of the call of Jesus Christ the LORD.

THE CHRIST REGNANCY IS LOVE, LIFE AND LIGHT

Here is the regnancy of Love, and Life, and Light: Life expressing the Light; Light begotten of the Radiance of the Christ Motion in the Divine Principle of Love; and Life in the sense of Being or Divine Consciousness. It is ZOË—Being; the realization in high consciousness of the Glorious One!

Now, Children of the FATHER-MOTHER, you may apprehend the real significance of Life in Jesus Christ the LORD. And you may see how the children of the world have been taught to believe that which is not the truth concerning their own history and the way of the LORD of Love, and HIS holy purpose; and how they now have to begin anew to find their way back to the Edenic life; to the life of pure feeling, thinking, desiring, eating, drinking, attiring; wherein is beautiful motion, noble purpose, and blessed giving and ministry in all of life's service. For they have again to be shown how the regnancy of Jesus is begun in the life, and how it affects everything.

And you may see also this wondrous event of Christ coming to you as a state of High Illumination begotten of the motion of the Christ-Principle within you?

And you may now realize what all these Teachings are meant to bring back to your vision, even the Divine Glory which once you looked upon within the Sanctuary of Being, and the Transcendent Things which were interior knowledges of Divine Inheritance entered into as an abiding possession through the most blessed Realization.

Therefore, behold and see the full meaning of the regnancy of the LORD CHRIST JESUS, and how HE is to reign in High Consciousness in HIS OWN Realm within the Being!

* * * * *

This is the Day so long looked for, of the Manifestation of the Communal Christhood. It is the return of the Day of the LORD. It is the Day of Divine Illumination and Inspiration, and the opening again of the Tabernacle of Being, in order that the Sacred Mystery itself might again be understood!

Come with me, O come with me into the Most Holy Place! It is only there that the Divine Mystery of the LORD CHRIST is known. Within HIS Holy Tabernacle the Radiance of HIS Glory doth play upon all the walls of the Sanctuary of Being

A NOTABLE THEOPHANY

A NOTABLE THEOPHANY

AN ARRESTING STORY OF ISRAEL

A Theophany is a divine manifestation. Amidst all the stories relating to Theophaneia, and especially those associated with the history of Israel, there is none so remarkable in its way as that of the appearance of GOD unto Israel as a Pillar which by day was a Cloud, and by night a living Fire. For it is said that in the history of Israel, the LORD was with them, sojourning and journeying as they sojourned and journeyed; and that HE was very specially present in the Pillar of Cloud by day and the Pillar of Fire by night.

The story is arresting. Those who love the Old scriptures and believe in their verbal inspiration, or that they contain a wealth of sacred story, might find it difficult to change their belief, putting aside the very idea that the Divine could appear unto a people, dwell with them, have motion in their motion, precede them, be also their rearguard as well as their vanguard in the form of a Pillar of Cloud by day which became a Pillar of Fire by night. If in these days a people, consecrated to great and holy things, affirmed that the Divine Presence was with them in the form of a cloud by day that became a fire by night, who would believe it? Yet this story is essentially Theophanic. It is a wonderful story veiling yet revealing, unveiling for the purpose that the children of the FATHER-MOTHER might gain a larger vision concerning HIM, a truer concept of HIS nature, a deeper realization of HIS Love, an abiding consciousness of the exquisite beauty of that Love in its unfailing Wisdom.

The story is also Messianic. For it was unto Israel the Messiah was to come. The Messiah was to be the revealer of that ONE Who dwelt in the cloud and in the fire, the unveiler of HIS glory, the interpreter of HIS Will, the embodiment of HIS fashion. It is Messianic in that the Pillar of Cloud by day and the Pillar of Fire by night, guided and protected and illumined Israel as a people, and provided that they should all be redeemed from their enemies. And, as you will readily understand, their enemies were not simply related to the outer planes, as has been set forth in Jewish story concerning the peoples who inhabited the land of Palestine before the Jews got there. The enemies of Israel were all those who were opposed to the true way of the life unto which the GOD of Israel called every Soul; those who loved not divinely, except in the clouds of imagination and belief, and who repudiated *divinity* as a living principle within the Being to find exposition in the fashion of the life, and in all the ministry of everyday action. The Theophany was so Messianic that it was meant to bring back Israel as a redeemed people into the consciousness of Theocratic Regnancy, so that GOD once more should be all and in all.

THE VEHICLES OF THE THEOPHANY

The story is wonderful in the outwardness of its setting, and also in the symbolism in which it is expressed; but it is more wonderful in its inner significance. To arrive at a true consciousness of what that Theophany meant, we will look at it under the two great aspects. The first aspect seems to be related specially to the phenomenal world, and the second to the inner realms.

In the outer aspect we will consider the vehicles through which the LORD GOD of Israel, the JEHOVAH of all the Heavens and of the Heavenly Hosts, and the LORD of all Being, is said to have made HIMSELF manifest.

The Presence in the fashion of a cloud. Clouds take form; but they are insubstantial, although composed of substantial elements. They are ever changing; and the elements composing them undergo processes wherein there is change. Yet the primary elements abide; for they are of the Eternal. But the clouds come and go; they are of the evanescent things. The cloud is the symbol of that which can veil even whilst it is containing great elements of blessing. Even the clouds in the atmosphere of the earth containing the moisture which bye and bye must necessarily be condensed, must be changed and showered upon the earth to refresh it; and to refresh not only the outermost of the elemental kingdoms, but also all the life upon the outer planes, and contribute to the spiritual enrichment of everything that grows upon those planes. For even in the elements, there are spiritual forces. They are vital with spiritual power. This would be more so if the Planet were restored again to her original glorious state wherein her elements were all unfallen, as well as her children.

The metaphor of the cloud, therefore, is beautiful. The symbol is characteristic of the Old scripture. Jehovah appeared in a cloud upon Mount Sinai; upon Mount Horeb; upon Mount Tabor as recorded in the New Testament; above the Heights of Galilee; even upon Olivet.

In the transcendent vision of the Seer as presented in the Apocalyptic section of the scripture, the LORD came in a Cloud of glory. In the New Testament it is also said that the Presence appeared in a Cloud at the Baptism, and that the Voice spake from out the Cloud, with a similar message to that given at the Transfiguration. Thus the symbol runs through all the scriptures.

The Pillar of Cloud is the auric splendour of the Divine. It is the Cloud which in its very nature is HIS own aura Radiance which changes as HE purposes from being a Cloud that veils the Being to become a flashing Fire that creates, changes, transmutes, and illumines.

THE LAW OF THE LORD

The Law of GOD comes in the Cloud, as on Sinai. It is veiled; that is, it is of the Mystery of the Presence. But it becomes revealed as the Soul realizes the meaning of the Law of the LORD. There is only one Law of GOD. It is Universal Law. It is the Absolute Law. But it has manifold degrees of manifestation. It is accommodated from the central realm of all things right through all the realms, even to those realms of the lowliest manifestations where the consciousness is still what we might speak of as diffuse, or not sufficiently polarized to give individuation sufficient to enable the embodiment to recognise its Creator, and understand the Mystery of the FATHER-MOTHER. But in a Human Soul there is such an upgathering of this Mystery that man is able to contact that centre, to apprehend the Mystery at the heart of it, to enter into communion with HIM Who is in the Cloud, still unrevealed, except partially in the motion of the Being, and then in the realization. So that man can come up into the consciousness of HIM Who is the Law of the universe. For GOD is Being. HE is Universal Being. That does not mean simply a diffusion of consciousness in an atmosphere. Being is alive. It is Divine Consciousness, Potency, Energy, Motion. It is Love! Wheresoever Being is, there is the Eternal Consciousness we name Omnisciency. GOD is Being. That is why you can contact HIM. For HIS Mystery of Being is in you, and you can only reveal HIM through being like HIM.

The Cloud upon Sinai is HIMSELF in the Presence WHO is within a Soul as Law. GOD is in the Cloud that is Law to you. HE is also in the cloud on Mount Horeb. There HE revealed the train of HIS Presence. The train of HIS Presence is the radiance streaming from HIM. Though the Soul could not look into the heart of the Mystery at that time, yet it could look on the Light the Presence shed. And the Soul heard the Voice from out the cloud thus speaking "*The Adonai! The Adonai! The Lord God of the Heavenly Hosts, is full of compassion and mercy.*" Compassion is the ministry of Love, and mercy is its healing quality. It is something more than mercy as understood by men and women when they think they will be merciful and not exercise judgment upon their fellows. Oh, to be merciful is to let our love heal where there has been wounding: it is compassion's touch.

HOW GOD SPAKE UNTO ISRAEL

GOD thus spake unto Israel through HIS Law. HE spake unto them through HIS compassion and HIS mercy and HIS tenderness. At first it was a Voice from out the Cloud. The children could not understand. They had lost the vision. They had to be recalled. They could not understand HIM, so HE had to speak under the imagery that they could apprehend with their understanding. It is thus it is set forth that HE came as the Cloud and as the Fire. But here where the Cloud comes you have Law, the revelation of Love in its compassion and mercy. And Love is never more majestic than when it stoops. The beauty of it is it never knows it stoops. For Love never knows it stoops. The mind knows when it stoops, and has pride in it, because it is unredeemed. But when the mind is redeemed it does not know it stoops. There is no such thing as stooping in the vocabulary of a Soul who is Divine in Estate. When GOD stoops (we have to speak in such terms) HE comes down to meet HIS children where they are, to lift them up again. HIS Cloud descends that it may envelop them, encompass them, enfold and uphold them and bear them up. That is how you have been borne up. Though you may not have seen the Cloud, you have felt it. Though you may not have realized HE was with you, yet HE has been with you. Oh, that men would think of the Great Love in HIS ministry unto them, and praise HIM, and have the motion of their Being unto HIM! For HE is ever beautiful. When HE would baptise a Soul unto all fulness of Being, HE comes as a Cloud. It is the Cloud of HIS Radiance. Oh, the radiance of GOD felt in the Innermost, is the influx of HIS own glorious stream to the Being. It is magnetic. It drives back everything that is not like itself, and of itself; everything that must not be, HIS Radiance drives back. It makes the Being quiver. It fills the Being with HIS Light. When GOD baptizes the Soul, HE comes in the cloud. Was not that the cloud that it is said Israel was baptized into by Moses? Moses was a divine Manifestation. He was a Theophany, though the story has been made human and earthly, yet when it is gathered from out the midst of its strange setting, it is a gem of the first water, scintillating with the Light which speaks of the Splendour of GOD.

O Israel! O Israel! what a day it was when HE as your LORD spake through the Cloud as Moses! And what a day this is wherein HE speaks again from out the Cloud! It is the day of the baptism into the Cloud, the baptism unto the Redemption and the Regeneration, and thus unto the fulfilment of the Jesus Christ embodiment.

HOW GOD UNVEILS HIS GLORY

GOD comes to-day in the Cloud. If you said that to anyone, and they thought you meant a cloud in the planetary atmosphere, they would repudiate the thought. Yet that is how many people read the Bible. They think GOD appears in that kind of cloud, and as an earthly fire. When HE comes to you HE comes in the Cloud of HIS baptism to cause the waters to condense, and by marvellous transmutory processes, to shower the magnetic streams of HIS own Being upon you, and cause them to flow into you. HE is the Pillar of Cloud. HE descends in the might of HIS majesty, in the strength of HIS Love, to encompass you, to uplift you. For you cannot approach that Cloud, or that cloud may not approach you, without your being drawn to it. It is magnetic. It is Solar, and more than Solar. It is said the Sun draws all the members of His system, and that he holds them; but that he even holds them through their own response. And in like manner, when GOD comes near HE holds the Being. But more! The Cloud, like the photosphere of the sun, opens, and through the great apparent cavities, there is the outpouring of HIS own glorious Mystery-stream into the Being. So even unto this day that story is true. We are in the age of Theophaneia. We are in the day of the Divine Theophany. We have given to us a real Divine Manifestation once more. This is not to be thought of in the human and personal sense as in a man or woman; though no one can realize Christ and not be Jesus. That is impossible. No one can realize Christ and not be Jesus; because Jesus is the vehicle through which the glory of the Christhood is revealed and distributed. But the manifestation is in the Being, and through the Being into all the life.

A Manifestation is given within the Cloud; and the Cloud is the auric Radiance of the Presence.

It is through the Fire, the Theophany takes place. It is the Fire of the Presence, the Glory upon the Sanctuary, the Fire upon the Altar. It is the Divine Canopy overshadowing the Shekinah of the Soul, and the Fire upon the High Altar of the Soul's spiral. It is wonderful imagery. Only the great resplendence of the Eternal Mystery hides HIS Fashion from our vision. He is in the Cloud of HIS glory. The imagery in relation to Fire is also marvellous. How the symbolism follows the reader of the sacred scriptures! The real scriptures arrest the mystic. They open and almost close with the imagery of both Cloud and Fire. The Cherubim appeared with the flaming sword at the eastern gate of Eden; which means that the Cherubim took the form of the Luminous Cross. When Moses is said to have been called to the divine mission of leading Israel, He had a vision, marvellous in its nature and profound in its significance. The imagery is that of a Tree of Fire. But again it was the Luminous Cross. The Cross is the Divine Tree. The Seer beheld a Cloud of Fire. It was an auric revelation of the Eternal, a scintillating Radiance enveloping the Soul, and ensphering the whole Cross of the Being. From out of the midst of it there spake that ONE, Whom to hear is never to forget—"I AM." That means *I AM BEING.* The verb "to be" is like no other verb in our tongue, or any other tongue. It is the verb relating to Being. The I AM. There is no mere existence there. Existence is the outer manifestation of the activities which take place in and through Being. Existence is that which is postulated out from Being; but Being is the great realization. Thus speaks the I AM. *I AM BEING.* But he who would be revealer of that ONE must know Being as Universal Being. You can reveal GOD only as you know HIM. And to know HIM as Universal Being, the Great and Glorious ONE, is to know HIM as Life, the Eternal Life.

GOD IS UNIVERSAL BEING

From out the heart of the Fire of Universal Being HE spake. It is said that HE also called Abraham from out of the Heart of the Fire. For Ur of the Chaldees means The Sacred Fire. The word Ur, when we use it in another form, as Uriel, is the Fire of GOD. The word means Fire. And Abraham, who represented a Divine estate of the whole Planetary life, and also the Divine in certain administrations as well as embodiment, came from Ur of the Chaldees, the Fire that was in the Heart of the sacred Mystery of the glorious Presence. Some of the most precious gems of Truth are often found amid strange settings even as we find these jewels; and when you get them there is no mistake as to their origin and their source, for the light that flashes forth from their facets is of the Eternal, and speaks of the FATHER-MOTHER. Thus do we meet many times with the idea of GOD as a Living Fire, even as a Chariot of Fire, the symbol of HIS motion between the Heavens and the earth. And so through the Old scriptures even to the New scriptures the symbolism of living Truth obtains. And we read that "*He will baptize you with Fire.*" HE Who spake from out the Cloud, was to baptize with the Holy Ghost and with Fire. HIS own glorious potencies were to fill the Being with HIS own glorious magnetic streams which, when directed and polarized, would become not only a Cloud of Radiance, but a consuming, energizing force that is the Divine Fire.

Such is the meaning of the vehicles through which GOD revealed HIMSELF in old times, the Pillar that was a Cloud by day, and a Fire by night.

And now we will look at the aspect which brings us face to face with the Innermost Things.

HOW ISRAEL WAS GUIDED AND DEFENDED

The marvellous cloud is said to have gone before Israel. And when Israel was plagued by enemies, it moved to the rear of Israel and so defended the people. As night stole upon them it became towards them as a fire, but to the enemy still a cloud, veiling and protecting. The Fire illumined the way and revealed the path they were to tread; the Cloud overshadowed and guarded. Through their journeyings for forty years in the wilderness (and here is a great mystery we cannot touch upon this morning in relation to the Forty Years' journeyings in the wilderness), the cloud rested upon the Sanctuary. It was over the Tent. It was also over the Shekinah. But it was movable. *It was an overshadowing Cloud; it was a movable Cloud;* it was an abiding Cloud. It is said it moved from place to place along with them. It sojourned with them. When and whither they journeyed, it journeyed with them. In its ministry it passed from overshadowing the Sanctuary to rest even at the door of the Tent, before which they bowed in recognition of the Presence in the Cloud; and then it moved back again to the Sanctuary. It is also said that God looked out upon their enemies from the Cloud, and confused and confounded them; and that from the Fire He sent forth lightning rays that smote them.

Those who wish to find natural rather than mystical interpretations of the scriptures speak of these wonders as natural phenomena which an imaginative people without scientific enlightenment, attributed to God making Himself manifest in a miraculous way, and believed that God was in the actual clouds of the earth; and that through storms which He was believed to send He overthrew their enemies; that He was in the Fire or the Lightning, amidst the thunder-storms proclaiming against the enemy, and, through the lightning, destroying them. When will the thoughtful children of the Father-Mother understand that language itself is but a vehicle, and that the Innermost Things through speech have to be expressed in language, and that it is almost impossible to express them in any tongue? Indeed they have to be realized; for no language can reveal them. To speak of Theophaneia in the form of a Pillar of Cloud and of Fire, is not only most natural, but it is Divine. When Souls reach the threshold of the Divine World, they will find Clouds there. They are not clouds like those in the atmosphere of the earth, but the unveiling of the glory of the majestic Presence is gradual to a Soul. Even the various Heavens are shut to a Soul. It must pass through the portals gradually and as it is able.

THE MYSTERIES OF THE PILLAR OF FIRE

Every realm could be represented by the Presence in the Cloud gradually unveiling HIMSELF to the children. And so also with the Fire of GOD. You meet that Fire everywhere. It is in all the Realms. It is the Light and Energy of all the Kingdoms. It is the Eternal Mystery lying behind all creation, and may be expressed as the Radio-Active-Principle of the Eternities. It is a Fire full of energy; giving power to the Being; giving light to the Soul; giving to the Divine Principle within power to endure. Yes, it is through the Cloud and the Fire that the marvellous blessing comes from the Great Love. It is the token of HIS goodness, even as it was unto Israel. It was a wonderful Theophany. Through the ministry of the Presence, the raiment of Israel did not wear out during the forty years' sojourning and travail. What a depth of meaning lies hidden in that statement! In a human sense you would say that it was impossible. Yet in a mystical sense it unveils a great truth. And it is likewise true concerning the endurance of the feet. It is said of Israel that their feet were not swollen as the result of the journey.

When we get to the inner significance of these things, how beautiful they are! In the inner realm of the Being of one who loves divinely, the garments of the Soul never wear out. That Soul is always clad from the Most High ONE in immortal raiment. Such a Soul's garments are fashioned out of the inherent properties of the Divine. For spiritual raiment is the resultant of the motion of the Divine Elements and Essences within our Being. According to the degree of the polarization of these, according to the estate into which the Soul has entered, according to the strength, the depth, and the height of the realization which the Soul has of HIM Who is its LORD, so has it power in its journey to appropriate the elements of every realm which it enters; and in the measure in which it is able to appropriate these, so does it become adorned. In unfallen states raiment does not wear out; though it changes in this sense, that, as the Soul rises, it puts on the raiment suited to the realm into which it is entering. It must needs be so. And in all the journeying of a faithful Soul, however the outward way may have seemed shadowed, and the footmarks reveal such treads as tell the story of stumbling in the hour of great burden-bearing, travail and sorrow, yet the feet endure throughout the travail. For the Understanding of a Soul that has been illumined from the Divine, endures through all the travail, because the Cloud is still upon the Sanctuary and the Fire upon the Mercy Seat. The Cloud is HIS Shekinah; the Fire is upon the High Altar of HIS Tabernacle.

HOW GOD BECOMES KNOWN

That Cloud is within you. HE Who is the real Theophany is within. You cannot see GOD in the manifest world. You can see the multitude of stars in the Firmament. You may know many of the names given to them individually and constellarily. You may understand something of the motion of worlds, or, in the lesser degrees of the embodiments as manifestations of the Eternal Mystery, you may see something of HIS Wisdom expressed in the flowers, the trees, and, surely above all in the mystery of a human life—than which there is nothing at once so sorrowful because of the travail of these days, and so majestic because of the constitution, the possiblities, and the prophecy of the very constitution of the Soul itself in finding perfect fulfilment! Yet, though you see all these things, you do not see HIM. No; for you are only in HIS studio where you are beholding the living expositions of HIS handiwork. But to know HIM is to get behind all these. And to get behind them does not mean you can get there through outward vision. You get behind them only by getting to the Theophany. To get there is to realize HIM in HIS Overshadowing, HIS Encompassing, HIS Indwelling. HIS Cloud is upon your Sanctuary.

It is a Pillar of Radiant Fire. Do not be afraid; HE will not smite you by day nor by night. HIS Cloud veils the effulgence of HIS glory; yet even whilst it veils HIS fashion for a time, it also tells you HE is present. Why doubt it? HE is present within you. The Divine Principle of your Being is a miniature of HIMSELF. HE is all Divine magnetic force, all Ætheria, all the Radiance begotten of that force as it plays through the Ætheria. Your Principle is of HIS own Mystery. In it HE abides with you. Because of that you have an eternal relationship to HIM; and however far away you may have gone, you are held by HIM. You cannot ultimately get away from HIM, unless you desire it; you would have to choose to go away from HIM. Thanks be to HIM Who so fashioned us, few ever reach that state in which they would choose to go away. HE holds you by your own magnetic centre; and HE overshadows you from that centre. There is HIS Shekinah. There is the Ark of HIS Testimony and HIS Covenant. HIS Covenant is HIS Presence within you; and the Ark is the Testimony that HE is with you, that you are HIS, that you are of HIM, that in the Divine Principle of your Being you are fashioned like HIM, to express ever more and more fully HIS glorious Fashion, as you are able to embody HIM in Life's service, and equal to realizing HIS Love in sublime fulness, and shedding the Radiance of HIS Wisdom.

THE PURPOSE OF ALL THEOPHANEIA

You must understand that the real meaning of all Theophaneia is the culture of HIS children. GOD does not appear at any time to frighten HIS children; those Ahrimanic thoughts are of the darkness. GOD appears in order to culture in HIS children the likeness of HIMSELF. HE planted the miniature Image of HIMSELF within the Divine Principle of the Being. HE comes that the child may know HIM as the FATHER-MOTHER; learn that HE IS, and that HE is the great Lover; the great Revealer of that Love, the great Interpreter of the Mysteries of Life. Thus come all Theophaneia; for thus doth HE flood the consciousness with the Radiance of His Mystery. And thus the Soul knows. It knows Him; beholds His fashion; realizes Him; eats of His Bread; and shares the motion of the Eternal Mystery expressed in the Pillar of Cloud and of Fire.

Once more it is the day of Theophaneia. It is the day of the coming again of our Father-Mother, Lord of all Being, the Regnant One of the Heavenly Hosts, and of the host of divine qualities within us. It is the day of His coming upon the Clouds of the Heavens. It is the day of His coming in the Fire of Divine Energy. Do you doubt the truth of it that He is with you? For your needs He accommodates Himself in His Cloud, when you are not able to endure dwelling in the Sanctuary all the days of your life. The Psalmist said it was his great longing to dwell in His Sanctuary all the days of his life; but to dwell in His Sanctuary all the days of your life, is to dwell for ever in the consciousness that He is with you and filling you. When you are not able to do that (for it is a very high state), He accommodates Himself. He moves with you. He meets you where you are. He seems to leave the Overshadowing of the Tent, and the Sanctuary, whilst He moves to the door of the Tent, that He may shed His Radiance and draw you in. Thus He strengthens and encourages you by the way. Oh, God is a great encourager. He never discourages Souls. He is the great Lover of His children. He never casts a shadow upon their threshold; but when He sees a shadow, He comes with His Radiance even to the door of the Tent, to chase that shadow away.

Oh come ye up and back to this Theophanic consciousness of Him. Behold His Theophany unto you! He appears in your own Divine Principle, in your own love; for your love, in the measure in which you have realized His Love, is the realization of Him. Come up into the Sanctuary; and do not be afraid to come. Come into the Innermost Sanctuary; and fear not to approach Him. His Cloud is a canopy for you; it is the Altar of His Presence. Come, His Host is there enveloped in that Living

Fire which is the Radiance of HIS Love. Come to HIS High altar; HE calls you that HE may reveal HIMSELF unto you. Your Soul-garments are not worn out; nor are your feet so hurt that ye cannot walk. Come, HE heals all your woundings. He re-adorns your Being. Come before HIS High Altar; for HE is the Glorious ONE, and HIS Glory is here.

Oh, how my very Being cries aloud in sorrow at my incompetency to unveil to you how glorious HE is! O Israel! My People, Israel! who once knew HIM in the Cloud and in the Fire! Know ye HIM again as the Cloud upon your Sanctuary, and the Fire upon your Altar, and make sacrifice of all your Being unto HIM, complete and absolute! How worthy HE is to possess us altogether, in our downsitting and our uprising, in the Innermost Sanctuary of our Being, and through all the realms of our consciousness, and our activity, and our service, even unto the outermost! If our Love be HIS absolutely, then HE will become in us the ONE Who speaks from out the midst of the Pillar of Cloud and of Fire, and from the Radiance which enveloped the tree—the Luminous Cross. Our very Being will become HIS own. When HE says, I AM, our Being will respond and say, "Here am I" to be one with Thee for evermore!

Ever Blessed be HIS most glorious Name!

Unto HIM be all the Blessing and the Praise, the Worship and the Adoration, the Dominion and the Power, and the Glory of all these, evermore!

IT IS THE DAY OF THE DIVINE RENAISSANCE.

INDEX

TO

THE DIVINE RENAISSANCE, VOL. II

SMALL CAPITALS DENOTE TITLES OF MAIN ARTICLES.
ASTERISKS ARE USED TO SHOW DIRECT DEFINITION.

Pages

SYNOPSIS OF MAIN PUBLICATIONS

THE MASTER sets forth the Inner Meanings of the Master's Teachings and gives a true picture of Him as He was in His Life, public and private. The Birth Stories and the Allegories of the Soul are revealed in their true setting; with the Teachings on the profound Mystery of the Sin-offering, and the Allegories of the Soul's Awakening.

THE LOGIA contains the chief utterances of the Master, in the form in which they were spoken by Him. Here they are restored, including the real Mystic Sayings, found in the Synoptic Records, the Gnostic Record, the Pauline Letters, and the Apocalypse, containing remarkable histories of the Soul, the Planet, the Ancient Christhood Order, and the Oblation or Sin-offering.

LIFE'S MYSTERIES UNVEILED gives the Path of Discipleship and Aids to the Path of the Realization. It includes definitions of terms in their relation to these Teachings and many answers to questions asked at Healing and other Meetings. The principal theme of the volume is Initiations of the Soul.

THE DIVINE RENAISSANCE, Vol. I. i. The Message. The Divine Adept. The Superstructure of Man. ii. The Eternal Mystery. A Divine Apologia. The Seat of Authority. iii. The Path of the Recovery. The Redemption. The Divine Purpose of the Oblation. The Mass and the Oblation. Altars and Sacrifices. The Flame before the Altar.

THE DIVINE RENAISSANCE, Vol. II. i. Unto the Great Silence. Science and Religion. The Angelic Realms. Corpus Christi. The Sabbath of the Lord. ii. Beginnings of Historical Christianity. Pentecost. The Advent of Paul. The Stone the Builders Rejected. The Church of the Living Christ. The Seven Sacraments. iii. A Renascent Redemption. The Seven Thunders. The Healer, Manifestor, Redeemer. The Obedience of Christ. Our Lord and Our Lady. The Three Altars. iv. A Divine Oratorio. The Ministry of the Gods. The Divine Government. The Cosmic Consciousness. The Regnancy of Christ.

THE MESSAGE OF EZEKIEL. *A COSMIC DRAMA.* The Office of a Prophet. The Purport of the Book. The Divine World Unveiled. The Distinction given to Israel. The Mystery of Tyre and Zidon. The Pharaoh of Egypt. The Arising of Israel. The *Logia* of the Prophet Ezekiel: with extensive Notes to the *Logia*. *The Logia of Israel.* Vol. I.

THE MYSTERY OF THE LIGHT WITHIN US. *With 17 coloured plates by Amy Wright Todd Ferrier.* i. The Luminous Cross and the Cross of the Elohim. ii. The Spectra of Souls and Stars. The Solar Fashion. iii. Auric Glimpses of the Master. iv. Celestial and Divine Estates. v. A Holy Convocation. Jacob's Ladder. The Adamic Race. The Secrets of God. The Girdle. The Blessing of Israel. A Divine Rhapsody.

ISAIAH. *A COSMIC AND MESSIANIC DRAMA.* i. The Unity of Divine Revelation. ii. The Prophecy. iii. The Word of the Lord. iv. A Divine Drama. v. The Mystery of the Sin-offering. vi. A Momentous Promise. vii. The Triumph of Adonai. viii. The Drama of Israel. ix. The Sign of the Cross. x. The Daysman of Israel. xi. The Appointed Redeemer. xii. The Five Cities of Egypt. xiii. The City of the Sun. xiv. The *Logia* of the Prophet Isaiah: with extensive Notes. *The Logia of Israel.* Vol. II.

PUBLICATIONS

By the REV. J. TODD FERRIER:

THE MASTER: *His Life and Teachings*	Large Crown 8vo	624 pp.
THE LOGIA: *or Sayings of The Master*	,, ,, ,,	436 pp.
LIFE'S MYSTERIES UNVEILED	,, ,, ,,	480 pp.
THE DIVINE RENAISSANCE, Vol. I	,, ,, ,,	402 pp.
THE DIVINE RENAISSANCE, Vol. II	,, ,, ,,	560 pp.
THE MESSAGE OF EZEKIEL: *A Cosmic Drama*	,, ,, ,,	280 pp.
THE MESSAGE OF ISAIAH: *A Cosmic and Messianic Drama*	,, ,, ,,	436 pp.
THE MYSTERY OF THE LIGHT WITHIN US With 17 plates.	Large Crown 4to	240 pp.
THE HERALD OF THE CROSS (Bound volumes) Vols. VIII upwards	Large Crown 8vo	
HANDBOOK OF EXTRACTS of the Teachings of The Order of the Cross, from the Writings of the Rev. J. Todd Ferrier. Vol. I: Extracts A to D; Vol. II: Extracts E to J. Further volumes in preparation.	Demy 8vo	
LETTERS TO THE CHILDREN	,, ,,	238 pp.

SMALLER BOOKS (Paper Bound)

By the REV. J. TODD FERRIER:

THE FESTIVAL OF THE MASS OF ISRAEL	Demy 8vo	72 pp.
THE STORY OF THE SHEPHERDS OF BETHLEHEM	,, ,,	72 pp.
THE EVANGEL OF ST. JOHN	,, ,,	40 pp.
THE GREAT TRIBULATION . THE WORK	,, ,,	40 pp.
THE CHRIST FESTIVAL . THE WAYS OF GOD AND THE WAYS OF MEN	,, ,,	36 pp.
THE CROSS OF A CHRIST . THE RESURRECTION LIFE	,, ,,	36 pp.
THE CONTINUITY OF CONSCIOUSNESS	,, ,,	28 pp.
IF CHRIST CAME BACK?	,, ,,	24 pp.
THE LIFE IMMORTAL	,, ,,	20 pp.
THE ORDER OF THE CROSS	,, ,,	16 pp.
THE MESSAGE AND THE WORK	,, ,,	12 pp.
THE INNER MEANING OF THE FOOD REFORM MOVEMENT	,, ,,	8 pp.
ON BEHALF OF THE CREATURES	Crown 8vo	128 pp.
WHAT IS A CHRISTIAN?	,, ,,	64 pp.
THOUGHTS FOR THE DAY	,, ,,	52 pp.
THE SECOND COMING OF CHRIST	,, ,,	48 pp.
THE ABRAHAMIC STORY	,, ,,	20 pp.

By E. MARY GORDON KEMMIS:

THE "GREATER WORKS" (Cloth bound)	Crown 8vo	64 pp.

FOR USE IN WORSHIP

PSALMS AND CANTICLES FOR WORSHIP (Paper or Cloth bound)	Demy 8vo	96 pp.
HYMNS FOR WORSHIP (Paper or Cloth bound)	,, ,,	96 pp.

Prices on Application

THE HERALD OF THE CROSS

Vols. I to VII (published 1905-11) are now out of print. Vols. VIII (1934) to XXI (six issues a year) and Vols. XXII upwards (four issues a year) are available separately, paper bound, in limited quantities. (Vols. VIII to XVII, No. 4, edited by the Rev. J. Todd Ferrier: subsequent issues edited according to his instructions.)

Please address all communications regarding Literature, and make remittances payable, to THE LITERATURE SECRETARY, THE ORDER OF THE CROSS, 10 DE VERE GARDENS, LONDON, W.8.

Loan copies of any of the publications may be applied for to THE LIBRARIAN.

The Order of the Cross

FOUNDED OCTOBER 1904

AIMS AND IDEALS

(FOUNDATION STATEMENT)

TO ATTAIN, by mutual helpfulness, the realization of the Christ-life, by the path of self-denial, self-sacrifice, and absolute self-abandonment to the Divine will and service:

It is of these things that the Cross as a symbol speaks. It stands for the Sign of the Order of the Cross, because its three steps are those which have to be taken in order to arrive at that Estate which it symbolizes. It speaks of the quest after the humble spirit and the pure heart. It speaks also of that further state of realization when the Soul gives itself in absolute abandonment for the Divine Service. The Three Steps are:—

PURITY OF LIVING
PURITY OF THE MIND
PURITY OF THE SOUL

Thus to endeavour by example and teaching to win all men to the love of Truth, Purity and Right-doing.

To proclaim the Brotherhood of Man, the essential one-ness of all religious aspirations, and the unity of all living creatures in the Divine.

To teach the moral necessity for humaneness towards all men and all creatures.

To protest against, and to work for the abolition of, all national and social customs which violate the teachings of the Christ, especially such as involve bloodshed, the oppression of the weak and defenceless, the perpetuation of the brutal mind, and the infliction of cruelty upon animals, *viz.:* war, vivisection, the slaughter of animals for food, fashion and sport, and kindred evils.

To advocate the universal adoption of a bloodless diet, and the return to simple and natural foods.

To proclaim a message of peace and happiness, health and purity, spirituality and Divine Love.

EXECUTIVE COUNCIL (1904)

J. TODD FERRIER, *Founder*, *Editor*, "The Herald of the Cross."
ROBERT H. PERKS, M.D., F.R.C.S. (Eng.), *Secretary.*

All Offices of the Order are Honorary